A Reader on
Classical Islam

A READER ON CLASSICAL ISLAM

F. E. PETERS

Princeton University Press

Princeton, New Jersey

Library of Congress Cataloging-in-Publication Data
A Reader on classical Islam / F. E. Peters.
p.   cm.
"Selections . . . almost all of them originally in Arabic"—Pref.
Includes bibliographical references (p.) and index.
ISBN 0-691-03394-3 — ISBN 0-691-00040-9 (pbk.)
1. Islam.   I. Peters, F. E. (Francis E.)
BP161.2.R43   1993   93-14595
297—dc20

This book has been composed in Adobe Perpetua

For
Eamon and Carol Brennan,
with great affection

Contents

CHAPTER 3

The Community of Muslims

CHAPTER 4

The Word of God
and Its Understanding

CHAPTER 5

The Quran, the Prophet,
and the Law

CHAPTER 6

The Worship of God

CHAPTER 7

Saints and Mystics

CHAPTER 8

Islamic Theology

Preface

"Islam" is a word we can understand whether we are Muslims or not. It means "submission," and, more specifically in the context where it first and most familiarly appears, "submission to the will of God." That context is the Quran, the Sacred Book of the Muslims, "those who have submitted." We do not use the word so simply, however. It has been built into an abstract cathedral of connotation, on the same scale and grandeur as "Christianity" and "Judaism." This larger significance of the term is of our own making, of course, derived from whatever else we can read out of the rich pages of the Quran or, more broadly, what we can glean from the writings or observe in the deeds of those who acknowledge themselves as "submitters."

This book is designed to enable the reader to shape, or perhaps reshape, the design and dimensions of his or her understanding of that larger "Islam" by presenting a substantial body of literary evidence on what both the Quran and Muslims understood by that term and its context. For all its broadness, the evidence is limited, however. It is constituted of words rather than deeds, and words derived from the highest of high literary traditions. What follows are the thoughts of professors, lawyers, and *littérateurs*, Muslims all, and masters of the pen as well as of the spiritual life. Popular religion or the actual behavior of actual Muslims is not part of the portrait. Indeed, not a great deal is known of such things, not, at any rate, for the period under consideration here, what I have chosen to call "Classical Islam."

"Classic" or "classical period" is likewise a construct, all the more obviously so since it is being borrowed from one phenomenon, Greek and Roman antiquity, and used to somehow periodize another quite different one, Islam. Muslim historians do not much engage in such categorizations, and if one were to look to them for a "Classical Islam," or an "Age of the Fathers," it would likely embrace a far shorter interval than what is understood here, the generation of Muhammad's own contemporaries, those revered "Companions of the Prophet," or, somewhat more generously, the sub-Apostolic age of the first four rulers of the

Muslim community, the so-called Rightly Directed Caliphs (632–750 C.E.). The emphasis on such notions is itself a rather recent phenomenon in Islamic circles. The harking back to a more authentic era of belief and practice is obviously a function of a sense of decline, of moral nostalgia, when agents of renewal or reform search the past for a model for the present troubled times.

That is not the immediate concern here, however. "Classical" is understood in both a broader and a more restricted sense. It refers primarily to religious literature and to Islam as a religious society, but it does not reflect on the political or social or economic rise and decline of that society. It means most simply the era when the classics of Islamic law and spirituality were written, works of such universally acknowledged importance that subsequent generations of Muslims understood themselves as "successors" and assumed scholasticism's unmistakably characteristic posture of casting their own meditations on Islam in the form of commentaries or glosses on the works of the masters. Concretely, the selections presented here, almost all of them originally in Arabic, the "classical" language of Islam, extend from the early seventh-century Quran to about 1400 C.E. After a brief look at the Muslims' own regard for their pagan, pre-Islamic past (chapter 1), and a survey of what the Muslim sources tell us of the life of the Prophet (chapter 2), the selections are arranged topically, and, in the manner of the writers themselves, with only very rapid glances at the political history of the community.

Before entering the somewhat dense body of texts, we begin with a rapid overview of the forms and modalities of "Classical Islam."

A Reader on
Classical Islam

Introduction:
A Primer on Islam

Islam was not founded by Muhammad (ca. 570–632 C.E.); on the Muslim view, it is better understood as part of God's merciful providence, present from all eternity but revealed at various moments in history through the agency of His Chosen Prophets. Muhammad was one of these latter, a mere man singled out by God—the divine name in Arabic, *Allah*, may obscure the fact that this is in truth the same universal God who spoke to Abraham, Moses, and Jesus—to communicate His final message to His creation. These revealed messages, warnings, and signs for all mankind were communicated verbatim and in Arabic to Muhammad over the course of some twenty-two years and are collectively called in Arabic *al-Qur'an* or "The Recitation." The Quran was recognized by Muhammad's scant body of followers as divinely inspired even as it was being delivered, though its codification into a single book divided into 114 chapters (*suras*) may have taken place only after Muhammad's death. And there will be no more: the Book is closed; Muhammad was the Seal of the Prophets.

The essence of the message is simple. It is a warning to submit (*aslama*, whence the noun "submission," *islam*) to the will of God, to recognize the rights of the Creator over His creatures. For him who does submit, the *muslim*, there awaits eternal reward in Paradise; for the disbeliever or infidel (*kafir*), eternal damnation in Hell. The Muslim's outward sign of submission is a formula of "witnessing" (*shahada*) that has become the profession of faith in Islam: "There is no God but The God, and Muhammad is His Messenger." There flow from this declaration of heart and tongue four other primary obligations for all Muslims:

1. prayer (*salat*) said five times daily at the canonically appointed hours, with the noon prayer on Friday to be said in common. This is usually done in a mosque (*masjid, jami*ᶜ), a building that in form and function is little more than the Arabic name implies, an assembly hall, with a niche (*mihrab*) to mark the orientation (*qibla*) toward Mecca, and a minaret or tower from which the faithful are summoned to prayer at the appointed hours;

2. the payment of alms in the form of a tithe (*zakat*);

3. fasting and other abstentions during the lunar month of Ramadan;

4. and, if practical, at least one pilgrimage (*hajj*) to "God's House," a cubelike building (*ka'ba*) set down in a sacred precinct (*haram*) in the heart of Muhammad's native Mecca in Western Arabia.

A Muslim life of course comprises far more than a simple one-line creed and those four other elemental obligations that make up the "Pillars of Islam." During his lifetime, both in the Quran and in the other reports (*hadith*) attributed to him by the Muslim tradition, Muhammad gave a wide range of command and instruction that was intended to shape the lives of the new Muslim community (*umma*). Detailed prescriptions on marriage, divorce, inheritance, criminal procedure, the care of the poor and unfortunate, and many other subjects, mostly matters relating to personal status, were all parts of Muhammad's teachings on God's behalf. And whether they were formally revealed in the Quran or transmitted in the *hadith*, they all bore the cachet of divine authority. It is not surprising, then, that from those same two principal sources, the Quran and the "custom (*sunna*) of the Prophet," there began to be derived the great body of Islamic Law (*shari'a*). Other legal methods might be invoked for its elaboration—the consensus of the community, for example, or a prudent analogical reasoning—but the Quran and the *sunna* of the Prophet remain the two unshakable foundations of the *shari'a*.

There ruled over the *umma*, whose astonishing political and military success within the first century of its existence created an expanding empire, the "Abode of Islam" (*Dar al-Islam*), a series of men, each acknowledged as Muhammad's successor (*khalifa*; Eng. Caliph), and who had executive but no religious powers. Revelation was forever closed, and while the Caliphs could dispose armies, levy taxes, appoint governors or a religious judge (*qadi*), and in general exercise what was called "polity" (*siyasa*), they could not add a sentence to the Quran or a single provision to the *shari'a*.

The Caliphs were chosen in various ways, none very satisfying to many Muslims. And their impotence, and even at times disdain, in the religious sphere was a source of concern to many others, notably the partisans (*shi'a*) of Ali (d. 661 C.E.), the Prophet's cousin, son-in-law, and the fourth Caliph of the Islamic community. His followers, always a minority in Islam, looked toward a religious, even a charismatic leader (*Imam*) to rule and guide the community. God had appointed such, they were convinced, in the person of Ali and his designated descendants. They counted twelve Imams (on another reckoning, seven) down to a time in the late ninth century, the last of whom would return in the End Time. None of the Imams save Ali himself ever held actual political power in the *Dar al-Islam*, and the *Shi'at Ali*, or Shi'ites, as they are generally known, remained an underground, profoundly revolutionary and generally mystical movement in Islam until the beginning of the sixteenth century, when it was adopted as the "established" form of Islam by the ruling dynasty in Iran. The Sunni office of the Caliphate was formally abolished by Kemal Ataturk in 1924; the Shi'ites still await the return of the Hidden Imam.

The Law is a powerful force in Islam, whether administered by qadis in the religious courts, framed as an authoritative pronouncement (*fatwa*) by widely recognized jurists, or simply studied, debated, and explicated in schools, and there soon emerged a class of men learned in the Law (*ulama*), upon whom the responsibility of shaping an Islamic conscience and Muslim orthodoxy finally rested. Almost every intellectual in traditional Islamic society was trained in jurisprudence (*fiqh*) in what became the premier institution of higher learning in Islam, the law school or *madrasa*, which was supported, like mosques and most of the other religious enterprises in the *Dar al-Islam*, by an inalienable bequest (*waqf*) of land or property whose income subsidized building, faculty, and students alike. Sunni Islam in particular has drawn its spiritual resources, its coherence, and its religious and behavioral ideals from the teaching of the *ulama*, who in most times and most places have remained remarkably independent of government control.

It is commonplace to note that there is no sharp distinction between Church and State in Islam. In a sense this is true; Muhammad was his own Constantine. But in fact there is no Church in Islam in the sense of an organized and institutionalized hierarchy of universally recognized religious leaders with spiritual powers "to bind and to loose." The *ulama* are rabbis rather than bishops or priests—even the Muftis, the most widely acknowledged legal authorities in Sunni Islam and even, in the end, the more charismatic and "spiritual" leaders of Shi'ite Islam, the Mullahs and Ayatullahs of Iran. Nor has there ever been, at least since the death of the Prophet himself, a demonstrably "Islamic State" constructed solely on the principles of the *shari'a*. Quran and *hadith* contain no political instruction or blueprints, and rulers in the *Dar al-Islam* have governed on secular, national, or pragmatic rather than Quranic principles, leavened here and there with a sense of piety, but characterized far more often by a tension of aspiration and practice between the princes and the *ulama*.

Shariᶜa means "path," but it is by no means the only way to God in Islam. Another approach is that of the mystic, the Sufi, an alternative born perhaps out of some Muslims' disdain for the success-bred secularism of an ever expanding *Dar al-Islam* and an impatience with the sometimes frigid legalisms of the *ulama*. The Sufi, like his Jewish or Christian counterparts, seeks to approach God directly rather than simply being dutiful in the manner of the theologian. This leap into the bosom of a transcendent God struck many Muslims as either rash or blasphemous, but eventually Sufism found its legitimate place in Islam and has generated a marvelously varied literature of passion and poetry, much of it in Persian. And in the process it too suffered a kind of institutionalization: next to the "path" of the Law was laid out the "way" (*tariqa*) of the Sufi, limned, somewhat like the religious Orders of the Christian West, by an elaborate and binding body of rule and tradition and a profound veneration for its Founder.

Sufism shows in fact some modest assimilation of Christian spirituality. No wonder: from the beginning there were in the *Dar al-Islam* large numbers of Jews and Christians who were not only under no compulsion to convert to the new faith but whose freedom to practice their own was guaranteed by a sacred contract (*dhimma*) with the Muslim community. These "Peoples of the Book," as the Muslims called them, generally thrived under Islam, and Islam too thrived on their commercial energies and intellectual traditions. It was under Islam that Jews first turned in large numbers from agriculture to commerce and banking, and Christians were in the forefront of the movement to translate from Greek into Arabic the masterpieces of Hellenic philosophy, mathematics, astronomy, and medicine. Aristotle arrived in the *Dar al-Islam* long before Napoleon set foot in Egypt and in his new Arabic raiment set in train an intellectual revolution as profound for Islam, and eventually for the West as well, as that later nineteenth-century confrontation with Europe. There were dangers in this meeting with the Hellenic rationalist tradition (and its Christian and Jewish variants), but Islam soon developed its own defensive weapons, notably a kind of "sacred theology" (*kalam*) to protect and strengthen its faith.

"Islam" is not, then, a very manageable term. It is a religion, surely, as we understand that word in the West, a complex of beliefs and practices characterized by the same perceptible unity, and an equally obvious variety, as Judaism and Christianity. It is as well a community sharing that common set of beliefs and practices but crosscut by ethnic, regional, and, more recently, national aspirations. It is, finally and gloriously, a civilization—urban, bookish, assured, and tranquil— with its own body of literature, monument, art, and thought: all still recognizably "Islamic," at times sharply and obviously, at times dimly but nonetheless surely, from Morocco to Indonesia and beyond.

We turn, however, from the present to where the Muslim himself begins, to the time before Islam, even before the Age of Ignorance that preceded the coming of the Guidance, to the very beginning of Creation.

CHAPTER 1

The Past, Sacred
and Profane

1. The Quran on Creation

*The Christians accept Genesis as Scripture—that is, God's true word—
and so their account of Creation is identical with that of the Jews, though
it was originally read, of course, in a Greek or later a Latin translation,
and was often commented upon in a very different way. For the Muslims,
on the other hand, the Scripture called the Quran superseded the Book of
Genesis; and though its source is the same as that in Genesis, God Himself,
there are obvious differences in detail in its view of Creation.*

It was God who raised the skies without support, as you can see,
and assumed His throne, and enthralled the sun and the moon (so that)
each runs to a predetermined course. He disposes all affairs, distinctly
explaining every sign that you may be certain of the meeting with your
Lord.

And it was He who stretched the earth and placed upon it stabilis-
ers and rivers; and made two of a pair of every fruit; (and) he covers up
the day with the night. In these are signs for those who reflect.

On the earth are tracts adjoining one another, and vineyards, fields
of corn and date-palm trees, some forked and some with single trunks,
yet all irrigated with the selfsame water, though We make some more
excellent than others in fruit. There are surely signs in them for those
who understand. (Quran 13:2–4)

*Much of the "biblical" material in the Quran, or perhaps better, the
Torah material in the Quran—the Quran is in its entirety "Bible" to the*

Muslim—is not presented in a continuous narrative line in the manner of Genesis but often simply alluded to, frequently to support or illustrate another point. Hence the subject of Creation comes up in different places, as here again in Quran 32, where the moral consequences of Creation are homiletically drawn at the beginning and the end of the passage.

It is God who created the heavens and the earth and all that lies between them, in six spans, then assumed all authority. You have no protector other than Him, nor any intercessor. Will you not be warned even then? He regulates all affairs from high to low, then they rise to perfection step by step in a (heavenly) day whose measure is a thousand years in your reckoning. Such is He, the knower of the unknown and the known, the mighty and the merciful, who made all things He created excellent; and first fashioned man from clay, then made his offspring from the extract of base fluid, then proportioned and breathed into him His spirit, and gave you the senses of hearing, sight and feeling, and yet how little are the thanks you offer. (Quran 32:4–9)

It is already apparent that, among other differences between Genesis and the Quran, there is the matter of chronology, as the Muslims themselves were well aware.

The people of the Torah [that is, the Jews] say that God began the work of Creation on Sunday and finished on Saturday, when He took His seat upon the Throne, and so they take that as their holy day. The Christians say the beginning (of Creation) fell on a Monday and the ending on Sunday, when He took His seat on the Throne, so they take that as their holy day. Ibn Abbas [a companion of Muhammad and an active transmitter of traditions from the Prophet] said that the beginning was on a Saturday and the ending on a Friday, so that the taking of His seat was also on a Friday, and for that reason we keep it as a holy day. It was said by the Prophet, may God bless him and give him peace, "Friday is the mistress among the days. It is more excellent in God's sight than either the Breaking of the Fast (at the end of Ramadan) or the Feast of Sacrifice (in connection with the Pilgrimage liturgy). On it occurred five special things, to wit: Adam was created, on it his spirit was breathed into him, he was wedded, he died, and on it will come the Final Hour. No human ever asks his Lord for anything on Friday but that God gives him what he asks." Another version of this prophetic tradition reads: ". . . ask, so long as it is not something forbidden." (Al-Kisaʾi, *Stories of the Prophets*) [JEFFERY 1962: 171–172]

2. Adam and the Angels

Christians found the chief moral implications of Genesis in the story of Adam's sin and the original couple's banishment from Eden. The Muslims too read the Creation story in a moral manner, chiefly because the Quran presented it from precisely that perspective. Here, however, the emphasis is not on the fall of Adam but on the sin of the angels.

He made for you all that lies within the earth, then turning to the firmament He proportioned several skies: He has a knowledge of every thing.

And when the work of Creation was completed, there followed this dialogue in heaven.

Remember when the Lord said to the angels: "I have to place a trustee [the Arabic word is *khalifa*, Caliph; see chapter 3 below] on the earth." They said, "Will You place one there who would create disorder and shed blood, while we intone Your litanies and sanctify Your name?" And God said, "I know what you do not know." Then He gave Adam the knowledge of the nature and reality of all things and every thing, and set them before the angels and said, "Tell me the names of these if you are truthful." And they said, "Glory to You, (O Lord), knowledge we have none save what You have given us, for You are all-knowing and all-wise."

Then He said to Adam: "Convey to them their names." And when he had told them, God said, "Did I not tell you that I know the unknown of the heavens and the earth, and I know what you disclose and know what you hide?"

Remember, when We asked the angels to bow in homage to Adam, they all bowed but Iblis, who disdained and turned insolent, and so became a disbeliever.

And We said to Adam: "Both you and your spouse will live in the Garden, eat freely to your fill wherever you like, but approach not this tree or you will become transgressors."

But Satan tempted them and had them banished from the (happy) state they were in. And We said: "Go, one the enemy of the other, and live on the earth the time ordained, and fend for yourselves."

Then his Lord sent commands to Adam and turned toward him: Indeed He is compassionate and kind. (Quran 2:29–37)

3. The Primordial Ka°ba

The Quran says little else about Adam and his unnamed wife, but the later Muslim tradition was quick to fill in additional details. The earthly paradise of their dwelling was identified as, among other places, Sri Lanka, and various sites, notably Eve's at Jidda, were later shown as the final resting place of the original pair. Of particular interest was Adam's connection with Mecca. The Quran says nothing about the remote origins of a holy place in the Prophet's native city; it speaks only of the era of Abraham and of Ishmael there, and of the providential construction of the Ka°ba, this "sacred House" (5:100), this "ancient House" (22:29). The Islamic tradition did not rest on that scriptural testimony alone, however. Somewhat later generations of Muslims, who had access, through Jewish and Christian converts to Islam, to a vast body of stories and legends about the earliest times of God's dispensation, were able to trace the history of the Ka°ba and its sanctuary back to the very beginning of Creation, and even before.

This tradition has been transmitted by various authorities: When Adam was brought down to earth, his feet were on the earth but his head was in Heaven, where he heard the words of those in Heaven. [He heard] their prayers and glorification of God and was on intimate terms with them. But the angels came to fear him, so they complained about that to God, and He diminished his [size] to sixty cubits the length of his forearm. When Adam was deprived of hearing the angelic voices and their glorification [of God], he felt distressed and lonely, and complained about that to God. So God brought down one of the sapphires of the Garden to where the location of the House [that is, the Ka°ba in Mecca] is today. He said: "O Adam, I have brought it down to you as a House, to be circumambulated as my Throne is circumambulated, so pray there as you used to pray at my Throne." So Adam turned toward Mecca, saw the House, and circumambulated it.

Abu Salih related on the authority of Ibn Abbas: God gave a revelation to Adam: "I have a sacred area opposite my Throne. Go and build me a House in it, and then encompass it as you have seen the angels encompass my Throne. There I will answer your prayers and the prayers of your children who will be obedient to Me." Adam said: "How can I do that? I do not have the power nor the guidance for that!" So God sent him the power, and he went to Mecca.

Whenever he passed by a beautiful garden that delighted him, he would say to the angel (that was transporting him): "Bring me down here!" The angel would then say: "Enough," until he arrived in Mecca. Every place at which Adam descended became populated, and every place that he passed over became a desert wasteland. Then, he built the House. When he had finished building it, the angel took him to Arafat and showed him all of the ritual stations that people visit today. Then he went to Mecca and circumambulated the House for a week. He then returned to the land of India and died on a fire.

Abu Yayha Baʾiʿ al-Qat said, Mujahid said to me: Abdullah ibn Abbas related to me that Adam settled somewhere in India and made 40 pilgrimages [to Mecca] by foot. But I said to him: "O Abu Hujjaj, didn't he ride?" He answered: "What kind of thing could he have ridden? By God, one of his strides equaled a distance of three days (of normal travel)."

Wahb ibn Munabbih said: When Adam was brought down to earth and saw its [great] extent, but did not see anyone upon it other than himself, he said: "O Lord, is there any humanity on this earth who will praise Your glory and extol Your sanctity other than me?" God replied: "I will have your children, those who will praise My glory and extol My sanctity. I will make buildings that will be raised in My honor and in which My creations will praise and mention My name. And of these buildings I will make one House that I single out for My honor. I will bequeath My name to it and will elevate it as My House. I will cause it to speak of my greatness, and I will put my splendor upon it. Then I will make that House sacred and secure, and it will make whatever is around it or underneath it or above it inviolable through its sanctity. Whoever is sanctified by its sanctity will have his prayers answered through My generosity. But whoever causes his people to fear, My religion (belief in me?) is lost, My protection is guarded, and My sanctity is revealed."

He made it the first House given to the people to come to, disheveled and dusty "on every kind of camel, coming from every deep vale" (Quran 22:27), shouting "the Greeting" [that is, the pilgrimage formula "At Your service, O Lord"] noisily, rustling with commotion in weeping, and saying "the Glorification" [that is, the prayer formula "God is great!"] in a roar. He who adores it will desire nothing else, but travels to visit Me and stay as My guest. It is incumbent upon the [Most] Noble that He honors His delegation and His guests, and that He be gracious and beneficent and help all who make His pilgrimage. Inhabit it, O Adam, as long as you live. Then, he will make peoples and generations and prophets from your children inhabit it, nation after nation and generation after generation. (Tha°alibi [d. 1035 C.E.], *Tales of the Prophets* 86–87)

Two motifs emerge from these stories. First, that the Ka°ba is a part of cosmogony and not merely of human history. The Meccan Ka°ba is an earthly counterpart to—and stands opposite or under—God's heavenly Throne, or, as appears in some versions, a heavenly "Well-populated House" (al-bayt al-ma°mur) (52:4), and Adam built the Meccan Ka°ba on its model. Second, just as the construction of the original House is pushed back to Adam and the beginning of the world, so too the pilgrimage rituals were first given to Adam by God through the agency of the angel Gabriel, and they too were modeled on heavenly prototypes, the cultus of the angels.

These are not new notions: almost everything that is said of Mecca and of the Ka°ba—that it predated the creation of the world, for example, or that it stands beneath the Throne of God and thus marks the center of both the earth and the universe (cf. Quran 42:7)—can be found in the dense body of Jewish legend surrounding Jerusalem. The Muslim tradition makes no attempt to disguise the fact that many of these stories came from men like Ibn Abbas, Wahb ibn Munabbih, or Ka°b al-Ahbar, who were either well instructed on the traditions of the Jews, the oft-cited isra°iliyyat, or were themselves converts from Judaism to Islam.

4. The Covenant with Abraham

The Muslim was not constrained, like the Christian, to argue the case of his spiritual descent from the biblical Book of Genesis; he had his own account of the Covenant in the Quran. It begins with Abraham in a state of idolatry, of "associating" as the Quran puts it, other gods with the One True God.

Remember when Abraham said to Azar, his father: "Why do you take idols for gods? I certainly find you and your people in error." Thus We showed to Abraham the visible and invisible world of the heavens and the earth, that he could be among those who believe. When the night came with her covering of darkness he saw a star, and (Azar, his father) said, "This is my Lord." But when the star set, (Abraham) said: "I love not those that wane." When (Azar) saw the moon rise all aglow, he said, "This is my Lord." But even as the moon set, (Abraham) said, "If my Lord had not shown me the way, I would surely have gone astray." When (Azar) saw the sun rise all resplendent, he said, "My Lord is surely this, and the greatest of them all." But the sun also set, and (Abraham) said: "O my people, I am through with those you associate with God. I have truly turned my face toward Him who created the heavens and the earth: I have chosen one way and I am not an idolater."

His people argued and he said: "Do you argue with me about God? He has guided me already, and I fear not what you associate with Him, unless my Lord wills, for held within the knowledge of my Lord is every thing. Will you not reflect? And why should I fear those you associate with Him when you fear not associating others with God for which He has sent down no sanction? Tell me, whose way is the way of peace, if you have the knowledge. They alone have peace who believe and do not intermix belief with denial, and are guided on the right path."

The notion of guidance leads to a typical Quranic opening of the historical perspective to include a broad prophetic landscape.

This is the argument We gave to Abraham against his people. We exalt whosoever We please in rank by degrees. Your Lord is wise and all-knowing. And We gave him Isaac and Jacob and guided them, as We had guided Noah before them, and of his descendants, David and Solomon and Job and Joseph and Moses and Aaron. Thus do We reward those who are upright and do good. Zachariah and John We guided, and guided Jesus and Elias who were all among the upright. And we gave guidance to Ishmael, Elisha and Jonah and Lot; and We favored them over all the other people of the world, as We did some of their fathers and progeny and brethren, and chose them, and showed them the right path.

This is God's guidance: He guides among His creatures whom He will. If they had associated others with Him, surely vain would have been all they did. Those are the people to whom we gave the Book and the Law and the Prophethood. But if they reject these things we shall entrust them to a people who will not deny. (Quran 6:74–89)

Abraham plays another role in the Quran's version of Genesis, and an important one in Muhammad's understanding of his own mission: Abraham was the first muslim, *the first to "submit" himself to the will of the One True God.*

Abraham . . . prayed: "Accept this from us, O Lord, for You hear and know every thing; and make us submitters (*muslimin*) to your will and make our progeny a people submissive to You (*umma muslima*). Teach us the way of worship and forgive our trespasses, for You are compassionate and merciful; and send, O Lord, an apostle from among them to impart Your message to them, to teach them the Book and the wisdom, and correct them in every way; for indeed You are mighty and wise.

And who will turn away from the religion of Abraham but one dull of soul? We made him the chosen one here in the world, and one of the best in the world to come, (for) when his Lord said to him, "Submit" (*aslim*), he replied: "I submit (*aslamtu*) to the Lord of all the worlds." And Abraham left this legacy to his sons, and to Jacob, and said, "O my sons, God has chosen this as the faith for you. Do not die except as those who have submitted to God (*muslimuna*)." . . .

"What will you worship after me?" he asked his sons, and they answered, "We shall worship your God and the God of your fathers, of Abraham and Ishmael and Isaac, the one and only God, and to Him we are submitters (*muslimuna*)."

Those were the people, and they have passed away. Theirs the reward for what they did, and yours will be for what you do. You will not be questioned about their deeds.

And they say: "Become Jews or become Christians, and find the right way." Say: "No, we follow the religion of Abraham, the upright, who was not an idolater." (Quran 2:127–135)

As the Quran itself made all aware, there were others who claimed to be heirs to God's Covenant, and according to the Life of the Messenger of God, *this is how Muhammad urged the matter with respect to both the Jewish and Christian claims to be the sons of Abraham, and so of the Covenant.*

The Jewish rabbis and the Christians of Najran (in South Arabia), when they were before the Messenger (in Medina), broke into disputing. The Jews said that Abraham was nothing but a Jew. The Christians said that he was nothing but a Christian. So God revealed concerning them (Quran 3:55–58): "O People of the Scripture, why will you argue about Abraham, when the Torah and the Gospel were not revealed until after him. Have you then no sense? . . ."

The Jews, then, were not constituted as either a community (umma) *or a religion* (milla) *until the revelation of the Torah, nor the Christians until the "sending down" of the Gospel.*

Abraham was not a Jew nor yet a Christian, but he was an upright man who surrendered to God, and he was not of the idolaters. Lo! those of mankind who have the best claim to Abraham are those who followed him, and this Prophet and those who believe (with him); and God is the Protecting Friend of the believers. (*Life* 383–384) [IBN ISHAQ 1955: 260]

5. Abraham and Ishmael in the Holy Land

The Quran passes directly from Abraham's "conversion" to God's command to construct the Ka‘ba. There is no mention there of Hagar or Sarah, nor of the Bible's elaborate story of the births of Ishmael and Isaac. It was left for the later tradition, which had access to a variety of Jewish and Christian information, to spell out the details of how Abraham and Ishmael got from the land of Palestine to Mecca. There was more than one Muslim version of how that occurred, and the historian Tabari (d. 923 C.E.) presents a conflation of a number of them.

According to . . . al-Suddi: Sarah said to Abraham, "You may take pleasure in Hagar, for I have permitted it." So he had intercourse with Hagar and she gave birth to Ishmael. Then he had intercourse with Sarah and she gave birth to Isaac. When Isaac grew up, he and Ishmael fought. Sarah became angry and jealous of Ishmael's mother. . . . She swore to cut something off her, and said to herself, "I shall cut off her nose, I shall cut off her ear—but no, that would deform her. I will circumcise her instead." So she did that, and Hagar took a piece of cloth to wipe the blood away. For that reason women have been circumcised and have taken pieces of cloth (as sanitary napkins) down to today.

Sarah said, "She will not live in the same town with me." God told Abraham to go to Mecca, where there was no House [that is, the Ka‘ba] at that time. He took Hagar and her son to Mecca and put them there. . . .

According to . . . Mujahid and other scholars: When God pointed out to Abraham the place of the House and told him how to build the sanctuary, he set out to do the job and Gabriel went with him. It was said that whenever he passed a town he would ask, "Is this the town which God's command meant, O Gabriel?" And Gabriel would say: "Pass it by." At last they reached Mecca, which at that time was nothing but acacia trees, mimosa, and thorn trees, and there was a people called Amalekites outside Mecca and its surroundings. The House at that time was but a hill of red clay. Abraham said to Gabriel, "Was it here that I was ordered to leave them?" Gabriel said, "Yes." Abraham directed Hagar and Ishmael to go to al-Hijr [a space at the northwest face of the Ka‘ba], and settled them down there. He commanded Hagar, the mother of Ishmael, to find shelter there. Then he said "My Lord, I have settled some of my posterity in an uncultivable valley near Your Holy House . . ." [with the quote continuing until ". . . that they may be thankful"] (Quran 14:37). Then he journeyed back to his family in Syria, leaving the two of them at the House.

At his expulsion from Abraham's household, Ishmael must have been about sixteen years old, certainly old enough to assist his father in the construction of the Ka'ba, as described in the Quran and as is implicit from the last line of the preceding. Tabari's version of what next occurred is derived from Genesis 21:15–16, transferred from a Palestinian setting to a Meccan one. Its object is now clearly to provide an "Abrahamic" explanation for some of the features of the Mecca sanctuary and the pilgrimage. The helpless Ishmael sounds much younger than sixteen in the tale, and some Muslim versions of the story do in fact make him a nursing infant, which means, of course, that Abraham will have to return on a later occasion to build the Ka'ba with Ishmael.

Then Ishmael became very thirsty. His mother looked for water for him, but could not find any. She listened for sounds to help her find water for him. She heard a sound at al-Safa and went there to look around and found nothing. Then she heard a sound from the direction of al-Marwa. She went there and looked around and saw nothing. Some also say that she stood on al-Safa praying to God for water for Ishmael, and then went to al-Marwa to do the same.

Thus the origin of the pilgrimage ritual of the "running" back and forth between the two hills of Safa and Marwa on the eastern side of the Meccan haram *or sanctuary. Tabari continues:*

Then she heard the sounds of beasts in the valley where she had left Ishmael. She ran to him and found him scraping the water from a spring which had burst forth from beneath his hand, and drinking from it. Ishmael's mother came to it and made it swampy. Then she drew water from it into her waterskin to keep it for Ishmael. Had she not done that, the waters of Zamzam would have gone on flowing to the surface forever. (Tabari, *Annals* 1.278–279) [TABARI 1987: 72–74]

6. Abraham the Builder

Adam, it will be recalled, built the first Ka'ba at Mecca on the model of a heavenly prototype. It was no longer standing in Abraham's day, however, as the resumption of Tha'alibi's narrative explains.

That was the beginning of the story of the Ka'ba, may God protect it. It remained in that state until the days of the Flood. During the days of the Flood, God raised it to the fourth heaven and sent Gabriel to conceal the Black Stone on Mount Abu Qubays, preserving it from being submerged. The site of the House remained empty until the days of Abraham. At that time, God commanded Abraham to build Him a House and call His Name after the births of Ishmael and Isaac. But Abraham did not know where to build it so he asked God to make it clear to him [where to begin]. (Tha'alibi, *Tales of the Prophets* 87)

This is mostly from the tradition, not the Quran, but though the Holy Book knows nothing of Adam's connection with Mecca or the Ka'ba there, it is quite explicit on the subject of Abraham as the builder of God's House.

Remember We made the House a place of assembly for the people and a secure place; and take the station of Abraham (*maqam Ibrahim*) as a prayer-place; and We have a made a pact with Abraham and Ishmael that they should sanctify My House for those who circumambulate it, those using it as a retreat, who bow or prostrate themselves there.

And remember Abraham said: My Lord, make this land a secure one, and feed its people with fruits, those of them who believe in God and the Last Day. . . .

And remember Abraham raised the foundations of the House, yes and Ishmael too, (saying) accept (this) from us, for indeed You are All-hearing and All-Knowing. (Quran 2:125–127)

And again:

Behold, We gave to Abraham the site of the House; do not associate anything with Me (in worship)! And sanctify My House for those who circumambulate, or those who take their stand there, who bow or prostrate themselves there. (Quran 22:26)

What the Muslims were told on divine authority about the ancient cult center at Mecca is summed up in those verses, and it was left to later generations of Muslims to seek out additional information. And many of them did; the authority here is Zamakhshari (d. 1144 C.E.), commenting on Quran 2:127 on the basis of earlier information available to him.

Then, God commanded Abraham to build it, and Gabriel showed him its location. It is said that God sent a cloud to shade him, and he was told to build on its shadow, not to exceed or diminish (its dimensions). It is said that he built it from five mountains: Mount Sinai, the Mount of Olives, Lebanon, al-Judi, and its foundation is from Hira. Gabriel brought him the Black Stone [that is, the one embedded in the south-eastern corner of the Ka'ba] from Heaven.

It is said that Abu Qubays [a mountain rising above the valley of Mecca on the east] brought it forth, and it was withdrawn from it, where it had been hidden during the days of the Flood. It was a white sapphire from the Garden, but when menstruating [women] touched it during the pre-Islamic period, it turned black.

It is said that Abraham would build it as Ishmael would hand him the stones.

"Our Lord" (2:127) means that they both said "Our Lord" [i.e., not Abraham alone], and this activity took place in the location where they erected (the House) in (its) position. Abdullah demonstrated that in his reading, the meaning of which is: The two of them raised it up, both of them saying, "Our Lord." (Zamakhshari, *Tafsir*, 1.311)

Zamakhshari's information does not pretend to add historical detail; it simply fleshes out the story at one or another point, as does the commentator Tabarsi (d. 1153 C.E.) on Quran 2:125, who was by then convinced, as were all of his contemporaries, that the Quran's not entirely self-evident reference to a "station of Abraham" referred to a stone venerated in the Mecca Haram.

God made the stone underneath Abraham's feet into something like clay so that his foot sunk into it. That was a miracle. It was transmitted on the authority of Abu Ja'far al-Baqir (may peace be upon him) that he said: Three stones were sent down from the Garden: the Station of Abraham, the rock of the children of Israel [possibly the rock under the Muslims' "Dome of the Rock" on the Temple mount in Jerusalem], and the Black Stone, which God entrusted Abraham with as a white stone. It was whiter than paper, but became black from the sins of the children of Adam.

Abraham raised the foundations of the House (2:127). That is, the base of the House that was [already there] before that, from Ibn Abbas and Ata who said: Adam was the one who built it. Then its traces were wiped out. Abraham ploughed it (in the original place to establish the foundations). That is the tradition from our Imams. But Mujahid said: Abraham raised it up (originally) by the command of God. Al-Hasan used to say: The first to make the pilgrimage to the House was Abraham. But according to the traditions of our comrades, the first to make the pilgrimage to the House was Adam. That shows that he was [the one who built it] before Abraham. It was related on the authority of al-Baqir

that he said: God placed four columns beneath the Throne. . . . He said:
the angels circumambulate it. Then, He sent angels who said, "Build a
House like it and with its measurements on the earth." He commanded
that whoever is on the earth must circumambulate the House. (Tabarsi,
Tafsir, 1.460, 468)

*This, then, is how most later Muslims understood the proximate ori-
gin of the Ka*ᶜ*ba, alluded to in the Quran: to wit, that the patriarch Abraham, on a visit to his son Ishmael in Mecca, put down, on God's command,
the foundation of the House on a site already hallowed by Adam.*

7. The Beginning of the Pilgrimage Ritual

*Once the building of the Ka*ᶜ*ba was completed, God ordered Abraham to
announce the pilgrimage to be performed there.*

Announce to the people the pilgrimage (*hajj*). They will come to
you on foot and on every lean camel, coming from every deep and
distant highway [?] that they may witness the benefits and recollect the
name of God in the well-known days over the sacrificial animals he has
provided for them. Eat thereof and feed the poor in want. Then let them
complete their rituals and perform their vows and circumambulate the
Ancient House.

Such is it [that is, the pilgrimage]. Whoever honors the sacred rites
of God, for him is it good in the sight of God. (Quran 22:27–30)

*It is clear from these and similar Quranic texts that the original
pilgrimage rituals were not so much being described to Abraham as alluded
to for the benefit of a Meccan audience that was already quite familiar with
them. It was once again left for later commentators to fill in the details, not
of the* hajj, *to be sure, but of Abraham and Ishmael's connection with it.
The authority here is al-Azraqi (d. 858 C.E.), who was not a Quranic
commentator but one of the earliest historians of Mecca, and so an expert
whose interests were somewhat different from those of Zamakhshari or
Tabarsi. In this passage he describes how Abraham, at God's urging, performed that original pilgrimage ritual.*

Abu al-Walid related to us . . . from Uthman ibn Saj: Muhammad
ibn Ishaq reported to me: When Abraham the Friend of the Merciful
finished building the sacred House, Gabriel came and said: "Circle it
seven times!" and he circumambulated it seven times with Ishmael,
touching all the corners during each circumambulation. When they had
completed seven, he and Ishmael prayed two prostrations behind the
stone [= *maqam*].

He said: Gabriel got up with them and showed him all the ritual stations: al-Safa, al-Marwa, Mina, Muzdalifa, and Arafat.

Al-Safa and al-Marwa are, as has been noted, two small hills adjoining the Meccan haram on its eastern side; the other three sites lie some miles eastward of Mecca.

He said: When he left Mina and was brought down to (the defile called) al-Aqaba, the Devil appeared to him at Stone-Heap of the Defile. Gabriel said to him: "Pelt him!" so Abraham threw seven stones at him so that he disappeared from him. Then he appeared to him at the Middle Stone-Heap. Gabriel said to him: "Pelt him!" so he pelted him with seven stones so that he disappeared from him. Then he appeared to him at the Little Stone-Heap. Gabriel said to him: "Pelt him!" so he pelted him with seven stones like the little stones for throwing in a sling. So the Devil withdrew from him.

Then, Abraham finished the pilgrimage and Gabriel waited for him at the ritual stops and taught him the ritual stations up through Arafat. When they arrived there, Gabriel said to him: "Do you know your ritual stations?" Abraham answered: "Yes." He said: It is called "Arafat" because of that statement: "Do you *know* your ritual stations?"

"Arafat" and the verb "to know" are etymologically linked in Arabic, and so some plausible, and Abrahamic, explanation of the name of this important pilgrimage site is being offered.

He said: Then Abraham was commanded to call the people to the pilgrimage. He said: Abraham said: "O Lord, my voice will not reach (them)." God answered: "You call! The reaching is my responsibility."

He said: So Abraham climbed onto the stone [= *maqam*] and looked out from it. He became (as high as) the highest mountain. The entire earth was gathered for him on that day: the mountains and plains, the land and the sea, the humans and the *jinns* so that everything heard him.

He said: He stuck a finger in each ear and turned to face the south, the north, the east, and the west, and he began with the southern side. He said: "O you people! The pilgrimage to the ancient House is written as an obligation for you, so answer your Lord!" So they answered from the seven regions, and from the east and the west to the broken soil: "At Your service, O God, at Your service!"

He said: The stones were as they were today except that God desired to make the stone [= *maqam*] a sign, so his footprint remained on that stone to this day.

The point is then underlined for the benefit of later Muslim readers.

He said: Everyone who has made the pilgrimage to this day was one of those who answered Abraham. Their pilgrimage [today] is a result of their response on that day. Whoever makes the pilgrimage twice had answered positively twice, three pilgrimages answered thrice.

He said: Abraham's footprint on the stone [= *maqam*] is a sign, which is demonstrated by the verse: "In it are clear signs [such as] the *maqam Ibrahim*. Whoever enters it is secure" (3:97). [AZRAQI 1858: 33–34]

As these accounts attempt to demonstrate, the complex ritual the Muslims call the hajj *or Pilgrimage can be traced back, in general and in each specific detail, to Adam, and, more proximately, to Abraham, whose intent and practices Muhammad was to restore so many centuries later. For the outsider, however, the non-Muslim, the Meccan rituals are striking remnants of a pagan, albeit Semitic, past in Arabia, which the Prophet of Islam permitted to survive by incorporating them into his own prescriptions. For the Muslim it is the figure of Abraham who transforms those same rites into an authentic* muslim *cultus. Abraham, the first of the submitters (*muslimum: *Quran 2:131, etc.) was also the first of the generation after the Flood to perform them, and later Muslims are simply commemorating what the patriarch himself had done under God's guidance.*

8. The Prophet Moses

The story of Moses' confrontation with Pharaoh in Egypt is one of the most often repeated biblical tales in the Quran. It was a marvelous story, surely, filled with wonders, but it also emphasized a point on which Muhammad had strong convictions: the punishment reserved for those who disbelieve and mistreat God's Prophets. This is one of the later Quranic versions of the story.

(After these Messengers) . . . We sent Moses with Our miracles to Pharaoh and his nobles, who acted unjustly in their regard. See then the end of the authors of evil. And Moses said, "O Pharaoh, I have been sent by the Lord of all the worlds; I am duty bound to speak nothing of God but the truth. I have brought from your Lord a clear sign; so let the people of Israel depart with me." He said, "If you brought a sign, then display it, if what you say is true."

At this Moses threw down his staff and lo, it became a live serpent. And he drew forth his hand, and behold, it looked white to those who beheld it. The nobles of the Pharaoh said: "He surely is a clever magician. He wishes to drive you away from your land." "So what do you advise?" They said: "Put him and his brother off awhile, and send out heralds to the cities to bring all the wise magicians to you."

The magicians came to Pharaoh. They said, "Is there a reward for us if we succeed?" "Yes," he said, "you will be among the honored." So they said. "O Moses, you may cast your spell first, or we shall cast ours." "You cast it first," answered Moses. When they cast their spell, they bewitched the eyes of the people and petrified them by conjuring up a great charm.

We said to Moses, "Throw down your staff," and it swallowed up their conjurations in no time. Thus the truth was upheld and the falsehood that they practiced was exposed. Thus there and then they were vanquished and overthrown, humiliated. The sorcerers fell to the ground in homage and said, "We have come to believe in the Lord of the worlds, the Lord of Moses and Aaron. . . ."

Then the leaders of Pharaoh's people said to him: "Will you allow Moses and his people to create disorder in the land and discard you and your gods?" He said, "We shall now slay their sons and spare their women, and subdue them." Moses said to his people: "Invoke the help of god and be firm. The earth belongs to God, He can make whom He wills among His creatures inherit it. The future is theirs who take heed for themselves." "We were oppressed," they said, "before you came to us and since you have come to us." He answered: "It may be well that God will soon destroy your enemy and make you inherit the land, and then see how you behave."

Already We afflicted the people of Pharaoh with famine and the dearth of everything that they might take heed. Yet, when good came their way, they said: "It is our due," but when misfortune befell them, they put the omen down to Moses and those who were with him. But surely the omen was with God, yet most of them did not understand. They said: "Whatsoever the sign you have brought us, we shall not believe in you."

So We let loose on them floods and locusts, and vermin and frogs and blood—how many different signs. But they still remained arrogant, for they were a people full of sin.

Yet when punishment overtook them, they said, "O Moses, invoke your God for us as you have been enjoined. If the torment is removed, we shall certainly believe in you and let the People of Israel go with you." But no sooner was the punishment withdrawn for a time to enable

them to make good their promise than they broke it. So We took vengeance on them and drowned them in the sea for rejecting Our signs and
not heeding them. (Quran 7:103–136)

*As we have already seen, the Quran pays particular attention to the
sojourn of the Israelites in Egypt. One of the longer versions of those events
occurs in Sura 7, which resumes its narrative after the escape of Moses and
his people across the Red Sea.*

When We brought the children of Israel across the sea, and they
came to a people who were devoted to their idols, they [that is, the
Israelites] said, "Moses, make us a god like theirs." "You are ignorant,"
he replied. "These people and their ways will surely be destroyed, for
false is what they practice. Do you want me to seek for you," he said,
"a god other than the God, when He has exalted you over all the nations
of the world? Remember the day when he saved you from the people of
the Pharaoh who oppressed and afflicted you, and slew your sons and
spared your women. In this was a great trial from your Lord."

We made an appointment of thirty nights with Moses (on Mount
Sinai), to which we added ten more; so the term set by the Lord was
completed in forty nights. Moses said to Aaron, his brother, "Deputize
for me among my people. Dispose rightly, and do not follow the way
of the authors of evil."

When Moses arrived at the appointed time and his Lord spoke to
him, he said, "My Lord, reveal Yourself to me, that I may behold You."
"You cannot behold me," He said, "but look at the mountain. If it remains firm in its place, you may then behold Me." But when the Lord
appeared on the mountain in His effulgence, it crumbled to a heap of
dust, and Moses fell unconscious. When he came to, he said, "All glory
be to You! I turn to You in repentance, and I am the first to believe."
He said, "O Moses, I raised you above all men by sending my messages
and speaking to you."

And We wrote down on tablets admonitions and clear explanations of all things for Moses, and ordered him, "Hold fast to them and
command the people to observe the best in them." (Quran 7:138–145)

9. The Wisdom of Solomon

*Solomon is mentioned more than once in the Quran, including a long pas-
sage (Quran 27:15–44) describing an encounter between the Israelite king
and the queen of Saba, or Sheba, in the Yemen. Invariably in the Muslim
sources, as in the Jewish ones, Solomon is depicted as possessing extraordi-*

nary power, though with a somewhat different implication regarding its source, since for the Muslims his power included control over the jinn, *those preternaturally gifted spirits who stand just below the angels in God's creation and are often associated with the magical arts, as was Solomon himself. It was the* jinn, *for example, who assisted Solomon in building the Temple in Jerusalem, as these verses of the Quran appear to reflect.*

We (subjugated) the wind to Solomon. Its morning journey took one month, and its evening one month. We made a spring of molten brass to flow for him; and many *jinns* labored for him by the will of his Lord. Any one of them who turned from Our command was made to taste the torment of blazing fire. They made for him whatever he wished, synagogues and statues, dishes large as water-troughs, and cauldrons firmly fixed (on ovens); and We said: "O house of David, act and give thanks." But few among My creatures are thankful. (Quran 34: 12–13)

With this provocative Quranic portrait before them, the later Muslim commentators supplied a great many additional details, like these on the seal and ring of Solomon.

Ibn Ishaq related that when Solomon died the satans wrote different kinds of magic in a book, which they sealed with a seal similar to that of Solomon. On the cover they inscribed "Here is what Asif ibn Barkhiya the prophet wrote for King Solomon." The book was buried under Solomon's throne until the Jews later discovered it; hence they claimed that Solomon was a magician. Another tradition related on the authority of Ibn Ishaq asserts that God took kingship away from Solomon, at which time groups of men and *jinn* apostatized. When, however, God returned kingship to him, they returned to the true faith. Then he gathered the books of magic and buried them under his throne. Satan later brought them out, and people claimed that these books were sent down by God to Solomon. Thus they followed these books, claiming them to be Scriptures. (Tabari, *Commentary* on Quran 2:102) [AYOUB 1984: 129]

Regarding the (following) stories about the signet ring, the satans, and the worship of idols in Solomon's house, God knows best whether they are true.

The first story has to do with the king of Sidon, whom Solomon killed and took his daughter, named Jarada, to wife. Jarada professed her belief in the One True God "and Solomon loved her." His new wife declined, however, into inconsolable grief for her dead father.

So Solomon ordered the satans to fashion an image of her father and dress it in his clothes. Jarada and her servants went and worshiped this image every morning and evening, as was customary in her father's kingdom. When (his vizier) Asaf reported this to Solomon, the king ordered the idol destroyed and he punished the woman. Then he went out to a deserted place to be alone. Ashes were scattered before him and he sat himself down on them, humiliating himself in penance before God.

On another occasion Solomon had a slave girl named Amina who became a mother by him. Once, when he went out to purify himself or to sleep with one of his wives, he entrusted Amina with the signet ring in which his power lay. She had it for a whole day and then the satan who lives in the sea came to her. This *jinn*, whose name was Sakhr, and who had proved useful to Solomon in the building of the Temple, came to her in the form of Solomon himself and said to her, "Amina, give me my signet ring!" Then he put the ring on his finger and sat down on Solomon's throne. This ring placed under his command the birds, the *jinn*, and men. Also he changed the outward appearance of (the genuine) Solomon so that when the latter came to Amina to get back his ring, she mistook him for a stranger and drove him off.

Solomon . . . wandered among the houses as a beggar. Whenever he said, "I am Solomon," people responded by throwing dirt at him and reviling him. Then he went to the fishermen, who employed him to assist them in the hauling in of fish; for this he was paid two fish a day. Solomon remained in this condition for forty days, that is, for as long as idolatry continued to be practiced in his house.

Asaf and the notables of Israel did not acknowledge the sovereignty of the *jinn* (who had usurped Solomon's throne), but when Asaf questioned the wives of Solomon about (the impostor), they answered: "He excuses none of us from sex when she is menstruating, nor does he purify himself afterwards."

The impostor is thus unmasked by his violation of the code of ritual purity. He throws the signet ring of Solomon into the sea where it is swallowed by a fish. The fish comes into the hands of Solomon, the fishmongers' apprentice, who discovers the ring and so regains his powers. The commentator concludes:

Religious scholars reject such interpretations and claim that they belong to the lying stories of the Jews. The *jinns* are incapable of such acts: it is a thoroughly detestable notion that God should give the *jinn* such power over His servants so that they could change the laws (for the community), or that He should give them such power over the wives of the Prophets so that they would commit adultery with them. It is true that there might have been a different law for statues, since God did say in the Quran, "The *jinn* made for Solomon whatever he wished— palaces, statues . . ." (Quran 34:13), but it is impossible to believe that God would permit his prophet to bow down before an idol. Should something take place (in Solomon's kingdom of which he is) unaware, then certainly he was not held responsible. (Zamakhshari, *Commentary on Quran* 38:34)

10. The Muslims' Jesus

The Quran does not much dwell on Jewish history or personalities after Solomon, though in one place (Quran 9:30) it is suggested that at least some Jews regarded Ezra as the son of God in the same fashion as the Christians did Christ. The Quranic account of Jesus begins with the birth of Mary, here identified as "the daughter of Imran." In Numbers 26:58–59 Imran is the name of the father of Moses, Aaron, and their sister Mary, and so there may be some confusion here between the mother of Jesus and the sister of Moses. This, in any event, is the Quran's retelling of the story of Mary's own "immaculate conception," closely linked with that of John the Baptist.

Remember when the wife of Imran said: "O Lord, I offer You what I carry in my womb in dedication to your service, accept it for You hear all and know every thing."

And when she had given birth to the child, she said, "O Lord, I have delivered but a girl"—but God knew better what she had delivered; the boy could not be as that girl was—"I have named her Mary, (she said) and I give her into Your keeping. Preserve her and her children from Satan the ostracized."

Her Lord accepted her graciously and she grew up with excellence, and was given into the care of Zachariah. Whenever Zachariah came to see her in the chamber, he found her provided with food, and he asked: "Where did this come from, O Mary?" And she said, "From God who gives food in abundance to whomsoever He will."

Then Zachariah prayed to his Lord: "O Lord, bestow on me offspring, virtuous and good, for You answer all prayers." Then the angels said to him as he stood in the chamber in prayer: "God sends you good tidings of John, who will confirm a thing from God and be noble, continent, and a prophet, and one of those who are upright and do good."

He said: "O Lord, how can I have a son when I am old and my wife is barren?" The angel answered: "Thus," came the answer, "God does as He wills." And Zachariah said: "Give me a token, O Lord, My Lord." "The token will be," was the reply, "that you will speak to no man for three days except by signs; and remember your Lord much, and pray at evening and sunrise."

The Quran then passes immediately to the scene called by the Christians "the Annunciation."

The angels said: "O Mary, indeed God has favored you and made you immaculate, and has chosen you from all the women of the world. So adore your Lord, O Mary, and pay homage and bow with those who bow in prayer."

This is news of the Unknown that We send you, for you were not there when they cast lots with quills to determine who would take care of Mary, nor when they disputed it. When the angels said: "O Mary, God gives you news of a thing from Him, for rejoicing, (news of one) whose name will be Messiah, Jesus son of Mary, illustrious in this world and the next, and one among the honored, who will speak to the people when in the cradle and in the prime of life, and will be among the upright and the doers of good."

She said: "How can I have a son, O Lord, when no man has touched me?" He said: "That is how God creates what He wills. When He decrees a thing, He says 'Be!' and it is. And He will teach him the Law and the judgment, and the Torah and the Gospel." (Quran 3: 35–48)

And again, in a somewhat different version:

Commemorate Mary in the Book. When she withdrew from her family to a place in the east, and took cover from them. We sent a spirit of Ours to her who appeared before her in the concrete form of a man.

"I seek refuge in the Merciful from you, if you fear Him," she said. He replied: "I am only a messenger from your Lord (sent) to bestow a good son on you." "How can I have a son," she said, "when no man has touched me, nor am I sinful?" He said: "Thus will it be. Your Lord said: 'It will be easy for Me,' that 'We shall make him a sign for men and a blessing from Us.' This is a thing already decreed."

When she conceived him she went away to a distant place. (Quran 19:16–22)

In the Gospel, the doubters of Jesus' role and mission ask for a heavenly sign and cite Moses' reception of the manna in the desert as just such a sign. In the Quran too a sign is demanded of Jesus.

Said Jesus son of Mary: "O God our Lord, send down a table well laid out with food from the skies so that this day may be a day of feast for the earlier among us and the later, and a token from You. Give us our (daily) bread, for you are the best of all givers of food."

And God said: "I shall send it down to you; but if any of you disbelieve after this, I shall inflict such punishment on him as I never shall inflict on any other creature." (Quran 5:114–115)

The Muslim commentators on the Quran were uncertain of the exact meaning of this passage, as indeed are we. What, for example, is the meaning of "may be a day of feast"? Tabari (d. 923 C.E.) explains the disagreement and offers his solutions.

The commentators are in disagreement concerning the interpretation of God's words "which may be a day of feast." Some think that the meaning is: Send down upon us a table and we will henceforth take the day on which it comes down as a feast day which we and our descendants will hold in esteem. . . . Others think the meaning is: Send down upon us a table from which we will all eat together. . . . Still others say that when God here speaks of a feast day, it is meant not in the sense of a festival but in the sense of a benefit which God is vouchsafing us, and an argument and a proof as well. Among these interpretations, that which comes nearest to being correct is the one which includes the following meaning: Send down upon us a table which will be a feast day for us, in that we will pray and worship our Lord on the day that it comes down, just as the people used to do on their feast days. Thus the meaning which we affirm corresponds to the normal usage that people associate with the word "feast day" in their speech and not with the interpretation that reads it "a benefit from God," since the meaning of God's speech is always to be interpreted as lying closer to the ordinary manner of speaking of the one who makes the request than to some significance inaccessible or unknown to the speaker. . . ."

The commentators likewise disagree on whether or not the table was (actually) sent down (from heaven) and concerning what was on it. Some say that it was sent down with fish and other food and that the people ate from it. Then, after its descent, the table was taken up again because of (certain) innovations they (that is, the Christians) introduced in their relationship to God. . . . Others say that it came down with fruit from Paradise. . . . Still others say that on it lay every kind of food except meat. . . . Still others hold that God did not send down a table to the Children of Israel. Those who maintain this view have another disagreement among themselves. Many say that this may be nothing more than a figure that God has offered to His creatures to inhibit their demanding (divine) signs from the prophets of God. . . .

In our view, however, the correct interpretation is as follows: God (actually) sent down the table to those who asked Jesus to request it from his Lord. We hold this because of the information we have received on this point from the Messenger of God, his companions, and after them the exegetes. . . . Furthermore, God breaks no promise, and there will not be any contradiction in what He announces. Thus God announced in His Book that He will fulfill the request of His prophet Jesus when He says: "In truth I do send it down on you." . . . As to what was on the table, it is correct to say that there was (some kind of) food on it. It could have been fish and bread, or it could have been fruit from Paradise. There is no advantage in knowing exactly what it was, nor is there any harm in not knowing, as long as the conclusions drawn from the verse correspond with the external wording of the revelation. (Tabari, *Commentary, ad. loc.*)

One fairly consistent Muslim interpretation of the miracle of the Table was to associate it with the multiplication of the loaves and fishes, here told in Matthew's version.

When he heard what had happened Jesus withdrew quietly by boat to a deserted place; but the people heard of it and came after him in crowds by land from the towns. When he went ashore, he saw a great crowd; he felt compassion for them, and he cured those of them who were sick. When it grew late the disciples came to him and said: "This is a deserted place and it is already late; send the crowd off to the villages to buy themselves food." He answered: "There is no need for them to go; give them something to eat yourselves." "All we have here," they said, "is five loaves of bread and two fishes." "Bring them here," he replied. So he told the people to sit down on the grass; then, taking the five loaves and the two fishes, he looked up to heaven, said the blessing, broke the loaves and gave them to the disciples; and the disciples gave them to the people. They all ate to their hearts' content; and the scraps left over, which they picked up, were enough to fill twelve great baskets. Some five thousand men shared in this meal, not counting women and children. (Matthew 14:13–21)

Some early Muslim authorities on the miracle of the Table:

Muqatil and al-Kalbi say that God answered Jesus, on whom be peace, saying: "Behold, I am sending it down to you as you requested, but whosoever eats of that food and does not believe, I will make him an example and a curse and a warning to those who will come after." They said: "We agree," so Jesus summoned Simon, the brass-worker, who was the most worthy of the Apostles, and asked: "Have you any food?" He answered: "I have two small fishes and six loaves." Jesus said: "Give them to me." Then Jesus broke them into little bits and said: "Sit down in the meadow in rows of ten persons a row." Then Jesus stood up and prayed to God Most High, and God answered him, sending down blessing on them, so that they became excellent bread and excellent fish. Then Jesus arose and went and began to distribute to each row what his fingers could carry. Then he said: "Eat in the name of God," whereat the food became so plentiful that it was up to their knees. So they ate what God willed, and there still remained, though the people numbered five thousand and more. Then all the people said: "We bear witness that you are the servant of God and His Messenger." (Tha'alibi, *Stories of the Prophets*) [JEFFERY 1962: 587–588]

For Muslims, who regard Jesus as one of the greatest of the prophets, the alleged crucifixion did not occur, not at any rate with Jesus as the victim.

And (the Jews were punished) because they said: "We killed the Christ, Jesus son of Mary, who was a Messenger of God"; but they neither killed him nor crucified him, though it so appeared to them. Those who disagree in the matter are only lost in doubt. They have no knowledge of it other than conjecture, for surely they did not kill him. (Quran 4:157–158)

The classical Muslim exegetical tradition on the Quran's account of the alleged crucifixion of Jesus is represented by al-Baydawi (d. 1286 C.E.), and it illustrates the somewhat uncertain attempts to explain what actually occurred in Jerusalem during that Passover in 30 C.E.

There is a story that a group of Jews insulted Jesus and his mother, whereupon he appealed to God against them. When God transformed those (who had insulted them) into monkeys and swine, the Jews took counsel to kill Jesus. Then God told Jesus that He would raise him up to heaven, and so Jesus said to his disciples: "Who among you will agree to take a form similar to mine and die (in my place) and be crucified and

then go (straight) to Paradise?" A man among them offered himself, so
God changed him into a form resembling Jesus', and he was killed and
crucified.

Others say that a man pretended (to be a believer) in Jesus' presence but then went off and denounced him, whereupon God changed
the man into a form similar to that of Jesus, and then he was seized and
crucified. (Baydawi, *Commentary, ad loc.*)

*Some Christian apologists had attempted to confirm Jesus' Messiah-
ship using indications of the date of his arrival provided by the book of
Daniel. One who had trouble with the Christians' calculations was Islam's
foremost authority on ancient chronologies, al-Biruni (d. 1048 C.E.).*

These are the doubts and difficulties which beset the assertions of
the Jews. Those, however, which attach to the schemes of the Christians
are even more numerous and conspicuous. For even if the Jews granted
to them that the coming of the Messiah would take place seventy "weeks
of years" (Dan. 9:24) after the vision of Daniel, we must remark that the
appearance of Jesus the son of Mary did not take place at that time. The
reason is this: The Jews agree to fix the interval between the exodus of
the Israelites from Egypt and the era of Alexander at 1,000 complete
years. From passages in the books of the Prophets they have inferred
that the interval between the exodus from Egypt and the building of
Jerusalem is 480 years; and the interval between the building and the
destruction by Nebuchadnezzar 410 years, and that it remained in a
ruined state for 70 years. Now this gives the sum of 960 years (after the
exodus) as the date for the vision of Daniel, and as a remainder of the
above-mentioned millennium, 40 years. Further, Jews and Christians
unanimously suppose that the birth of Jesus son of Mary took place in
the year 304 of the era of Alexander. Therefore, if we use their own
chronology, the birth of Jesus the son of Mary took place 344 years after
the vision of Daniel and the rebuilding of Jerusalem, that is, about 49
"weeks of years." From his birth till the time when he began preaching
are four and a half more. Hence it is evident that the birth of Jesus
precedes the date which they have assumed (as the time of the birth of
the Messiah). (Al-Biruni, *Traces of the Past*) [BIRUNI 1879: 21]

*While still in Mecca—that is, before his migration to Medina in 622
C.E.—Muhammad was often engaged by his opponents in polemical disputations. One such, reported in his Life, had to do with Jesus.*

Ask him (a certain Abdullah suggested), "Is everything which is
worshipped besides God in Gehenna along with those who worship it?

We (Quraysh) worship angels; the Jews worship Uzayr [that is, Ezra]; and the Christians worship Jesus Son of Mary." Al-Walid and others with him in the assembly marvelled at Abdullah's words and thought that he had argued convincingly. When the Apostle (Muhammad) was told of this he said, "Everyone who wishes to be worshipped to the exclusion of God will indeed be with those who worship him. But they worship only satans and those whom they (the satans) have ordered to be worshipped." So God revealed (the verses) "Those who have received kindness from Us in the past will be removed far from it (the pains of damnation) and will not hear its sound and they abide eternally in their heart's desire" (Quran 21:101). This refers to Jesus Son of Mary and Uzayr and those rabbis and monks who have lived in obedience to God, whom the erring people worship as lords beside God. . . .

Then He [that is, God] mentions Jesus Son of Mary (in the Quran) and says, "He was nothing but a slave to whom We showed favor and made him an example to the Children of Israel. If We had wished We could have made (even) for you angels to act as vice-regents in the earth. Verily, there is knowledge of the Final Hour, so doubt not about it but follow Me. This is an upright path" (Quran 43:59–61), that is, the signs which I gave him (Jesus) in raising the dead and healing the sick, therein is sufficient proof of (his) knowledge of the Final Hour. God is saying, "Doubt not about it but follow Me. This is an upright path." (*Life* 236–237) [IBN ISHAQ 1955: 163–164]

Apart from the Quran, Jesus appears in a variety of contexts in the teachings of Muhammad. Here, for example, is a tradition reported of the Prophet, one that provides a kind of doctrinal summary of the beliefs of the Muslim, with considerable emphasis on Jesus.

It is narrated on the authority of Ubadah ibn Samit that the Messenger of God, may peace be upon him, observed: He who has said: "There is no god but the God, that He is One and there is no associate with Him, that Muhammad is His servant and His Messenger, that the Anointed One [that is, Christ] is His servant and the son of His slave girl, and he [Christ] is His Word, which He communicated to Mary, and is His Spirit, that Paradise is a fact and Hell is a fact," him God will cause to enter Paradise through which of its eight doors he would like. (Muslim, *Sahih* 1.11.43)

But before he could enter Paradise, Jesus would have to return, like Enoch and Elijah, and suffer a mortal's death, as the Muslims were well aware (see chapter 8 below).

11. A Muslim Account of Pentecost

*As with the case of the later history of the Jews, the Quran displays no
interest in the Jesus movement or generally what happened to the Christians
after the disappearance of Jesus. But just as happened with the Jews, there
were converts to Islam to instruct the Muslims, as here, for example, on the
subject of Pentecost.*

Wahb [an early convert to Islam] and others among the People of
the Book say that when God raised Jesus, on whom be peace, to Himself, he remained in heaven seven days. Then God said to him: "Behold,
your enemies the Jews have precluded you from (keeping) your promise
to your companions, so descend to them and give them your testament.
Go down also to Mary Magdalen for there is no one who has wept for
you or grieved for you as she has. Go down, therefore, to her and
announce yourself to her, that she may be the first one to find you. Then
bid her gather the Apostles to you so that you may send them out into
the world as preachers summoning to God Most High. . . ."

When God bade Jesus descend to her seven days after his ascension, he went down to her and the mountain blazed with light as he
came down. Then she gathered to him the Apostles, whom he sent out
into the world as summoners to God. After this God took him up
(again), clothed him with feathers, dressed him in light, and removed
from him his desire for food and drink. So he flew about with the angels
around the Throne, being of human and angelic kind, earthly and heavenly. Then the Apostles dispersed to where he had bidden each one of
them to go. The night in which he descended is the night which the
Christians celebrate. They say that he sent Peter to Rome, Andrew and
Matthew to the land where the inhabitants eat men, Thomas and Levi
to the Orient, Philip and Judas to Qayrawan and Africa, John to Ephe-
sus, the place of the Companions of the Cave (Quran 18), the two James
to Jerusalem, which is Aelia, the land of the Holy House, Bartholomew
to Arabia, that is, to the Hejaz, Simon to the land of the Berbers. Each
one of the Apostles who was thus sent out was made able to speak the
language of those to whom Jesus sent him. (Thaᶜalibi, *Stories of the
Prophets*) [JEFFERY 1962: 594–595]

1 2. Mecca in the Era of Ignorance

According to the traditional accounts preserved by the historian Tabari and the Meccan chronicler Azraqi, Abraham and Ishmael were the first to govern the district of the Ka'ba, then apparently an isolated building in an uninhabited area.

It [that is, the Ka'ba] had not had any custodians since its destruction in the time of Noah. Then God commanded Abraham to settle his son by the Ka'ba, wishing thereby to show a mark of esteem to one whom he later ennobled by means of His Prophet Muhammad. Abraham, the Friend of the Compassionate, and his son Ishmael were custodians of the Ka'ba after the time of Noah. At that time Mecca was uninhabited, and the surrounding country was inhabited by the Jurhum and the Amaliqa. (Tabari, *Annals* 1.1131) [TABARI 1988: 52]

Ishmael, the biblical scion, had, then, two orders of neighbors. The Amaliqa are transparently the Amalekites, another biblical people, while with the Jurhum, the Arab accounts have passed over into an entirely different tradition, a native Arabian one. The Quranic commentators, who generally worked verse by verse, had no obligation to produce a continuous historical line between Abraham and Muhammad, but the Muslim historians attempted just that, and, as we shall see, the standard Life of Muhammad *opens in fact with just such a genealogical line. The material at hand did not easily lend itself to this end. Neither the Quran nor the Muslim tradition had much sense of what went on among the Israelites after Ishmael, while the Arabs' own long tribal genealogies led back into the past in a direction that had no apparent connection with the Bible. There was a further complication. Their own history told the early Muslims that Muhammad's immediate ancestors at Mecca, the people called Quraysh, were in the first place relative newcomers to Mecca, that they replaced another Arab people; and second, that they were pagans. Thus the appearance in the story of the Jurhum, an Arab people who replaced the sons of Ishmael at Mecca and who introduced paganism into Abraham's sanctuary.*

So, we are told, in order to coexist peacefully with his powerful neighbors, the Jurhum and the Amaliqa, Ishmael had eventually to marry a woman of the Jurhum, Sayyida bint Mudad, who bore him twelve sons. It is not entirely certain who the "Amaliqa" were, except that in Arabs' eyes both they and the Jurhum were "genuine Arabs" in that Arabic was their native tongue—as contrasted, for example, to the Banu Ishmael, "made Arabs," because "they only spoke these (Arab) peoples' languages after they

*had settled among them" (Tabari, Annals 1.215). There are Amalekites in
the Bible, of course, where they are Israel's sworn enemies (Exodus 17:8–
16; 1 Samuel 15), but whoever their Arab counterparts actually were,
whether the same historical people or another, their presence in the traditional accounts provides yet another opportunity to connect the Mecca-
Medina tradition to the earliest biblical narratives.*

*At Abraham's death Ishmael became the sole master of the Ka'ba, and
when he too died aged 130, his son Nabat succeeded him, apparently
without difficulty. The difficulty arose in the next generation: at the death
of Nabat, whose mother was a Jurhumite, as we have seen, his sons and
grandsons were too few to compete with the powerful Jurhum, who took
over the sanctuary. Mudad, the father-in-law of Ishmael, was the first
Jurhumite to govern the district of the Ka'ba. Ishmael the son of Abraham
begat twelve sons: Nabat (the eldest), Qaydhar, Adhbul, Mabsha, Misma',
Mashi, Dimma, Adhr, Tayma, Yatur, Nabish, and Qaydhuma. Their
mother was Ra'la daughter of Mudad, son of Amr, of the Jurhum. (Gen.
25:13–14: Nabaioth, Kedar, Adbeel, Mibsam, Mishma, Dumah, Massa,
Hadad, Teman, Jetur, Naphish, and Kedemah.) According to report, Ishmael lived 130 years and when he died he was buried in the sacred precinct
(hijr) of the Ka'ba next to his mother Hagar.*

When Ishmael the son of Abraham died his son Nabat was in
charge of the temple (at Mecca) as long as God willed, then it was in
charge of (Ishmael's father-in-law) Mudad son of Amr, the Jurhumite.
The sons of Ishmael and the sons of Nabat were with their (maternal)
grandfather Mudad ibn Amr and their maternal uncles of the Jurhum—
Jurhum and Qatura, who were cousins, being at that time the people of
Mecca. They had come forth from the Yemen and travelled together
and Mudad was over Jurhum and Sumayda', one of their men, over
Qatura. . . .

When they came to Mecca they saw a town blessed with water
and trees and, delighted with it, they settled there. Mudad ibn Amr with
the men of Jurhum settled in the upper part of Mecca in Qu'ayqi'an and
went no farther. Sumayda' with Qatura settled in the lower part of
Mecca in Ajyad the lower part of Mecca and went no farther.

Mudad used to take a tithe from those who entered Mecca from
above, while Sumayda' did the same to those who entered from below.
Each kept to his own people, neither entering the other's territory. . . .

Then God multiplied the offspring of Ishmael in Mecca and their
uncles from the Jurhum were rulers of the temple and judges in Mecca.
The sons of Ishmael did not dispute their authority because of their ties

of kindred and their respect for the sanctuary lest there should be quarreling or fighting therein. When Mecca became too confined for the sons of Ishmael they spread abroad in the land, and whenever they had to fight a people, God gave them the victory through their religion and they subdued them. (*Life* 71–72) [IBN ISHAQ 1955: 45–46]

The generations that succeeded to Mudad deviated from the path of virtue, we are told; they committed every kind of crime and finally brought the divine wrath upon themselves. They allowed the sanctuary to become dilapidated, appropriated the treasure in it, and subjected to rapine and injustice all who came to visit it. The Ka'ba became a center for the most corrupt people and all kinds of wickedness were committed there, like the illicit love of Asaf and Na'ila, and, as we shall see, the beginning of an idolatrous worship of stones.

13. The Religion of Mecca

The Muslims of the first and second Islamic centuries looked back upon the time of their ancestors before the revelation of Islam and labeled it the "Era of Ignorance." They laid upon it their own version of a "sacred history" that is merely hinted at in the Quran; the religious traditions of Mecca were to a large extent rewritten, or misrepresented, or simply forgotten in the light of new revelation that had annulled the beliefs and practices of an earlier age. It is difficult to find traces of that near-obliterated past, but when Muhammad's biographer Ibn Ishaq comes to speak of how and where the Prophet received his first revelations, he lifts one corner of the veil that covers most of what might be called "religion" in pre-Islamic Mecca.

The Prophet used to sojourn on Mount Hira for a month every year. That was the *tahannuth* which the Quraysh used to practice in the period of the Era of Barbarism. The Prophet used to sojourn during that month every year, feeding the poor who called upon him. After the conclusion of that month of sojourn, before entering his house, he would go to the Ka'ba and circumambulate it seven times or as many times as it pleased God. When the month came when God wished to grant him His grace, in the year when God sent him and it was the month of Ramadan, the Prophet went out to al-Hira as was his custom for his sojourn. With him was his family. (*Life* 152) [IBN ISHAQ 1955: 105]

There is another, somewhat different version of this tradition in Bukhari, reported on the authority of Aisha, Muhammad's later wife, who was

not yet born when these events occurred but presumably received the infor-
mation from the Prophet himself. It reads:

Then he came to love solitude and he sojourned alone in the cave
of Mount Hira and practiced *tahannuth* for several nights before returning to his family; and he used to take provisions for it [i.e., the sojourn],
(and when they were used up) he would go back to Khadija and take
provisions for a similar (period of sojourn). So things went till the Truth
came upon him when he was in the cave of Hira. (Bukhari, *The Sound*
1.5)

There was, then, no great agreement among the early authorities on
either tahannuth *or the Prophet's own practice, whether it was a shared*
annual custom or Muhammad's private devotion, whether solitary or ac-
companied by his family, whether or not it was in a cave, or whether the
devotions included feeding the poor. The word tahannuth *itself was not*
perfectly understood since later generations glossed it in a variety of ways:
to do deeds of kindness, to perform acts of worship, or simply, as Ibn Ishaq's
editor Ibn Hisham preferred, "to act like a hanif" *(see below). Modern*
opinion, which early on noted these obviously important traditions about
Muhammad's religious background, has no greater conviction than its
medieval antecedents. Tahannuth *is described as "leading a solitary life" or*
"acts of devotion," or more specifically as "an ascetic practice that the
Meccans observed in Ramadan on Hira: fasting and sexual abstinence."
Finally, the parallel to the Hebrew tehinnoth, *"prayers"—that is,* volun-
tary *devotions—has also been noted.*

Other texts, not generally noted in this connection, have, however,
come to light, and they somewhat enlarge our understanding of the pre-
Islamic tahannuth *that characterized Muhammad's pre-Quranic piety. One*
describes Abd al-Muttalib as the man who initiated the practice.

He was the first one to practice *tahannuth* at Mount Hira. . . .
When the moon of Ramadan appeared, he used to go to Hira and did
not depart until the end of the month. He fed the poor, he was distressed by the evil of the people of Mecca, and he performed circumambulation of the Ka'ba many times. (Baladhuri, *Ansab al-Ashraf* 1.84)

Another tradition from the same source speaks more generally of the
Quraysh.

When the month of Ramadan began, the people of the Quraysh—
those intending *tahannuth*—used to leave for Hira. They remained there
for a month and they fed the poor who called on them. When they saw
the moon of (the month of) Shawwal they (descended and) did not enter

their homes until they had performed the circumambulation of the Ka°ba for a week. The Prophet also used to follow (this custom). (Baladhuri, *Ansab al-Ashraf* 1.105)

Tahannuth, *then, was a Quraysh practice in the month of Ramadan somehow connected with Mount Hira—how or why we do not know—and included both deeds of charity like feeding the poor or freeing slaves and ritual acts like the circumambulation of the Ka°ba. It was, in a sense, a novelty, an innovation, or, at least, a complex of practices restricted to a few of the Quraysh. Long before tahannuth appeared at Mecca, the Quraysh, like all their neighbors, were devoted to other ritual practices that constituted their "religion." Sacrifices there certainly were, as well as the ritual called the* hajj *or pilgrimage; and, on the part of some, an attraction to monotheism.*

14. Pre-Islamic Monotheism

Allah, we can be sure, was neither an unknown nor an unimportant deity to the Quraysh when Muhammad began preaching his exclusive worship at Mecca. What is equally certain is that Allah had what the Quran disdainfully calls "associates," other gods and goddesses who shared both his cult and his shrine. The processional chant of the pagans of the "Era of Ignorance" was, we are told, "Here I am, O Allah, here I am; you have no partner except such a partner as you have; you possess him and all that is his." The last clause may reflect what was an emerging tendency toward henotheism, the recognition of Allah as the "High God" of Mecca, but it was not sufficient for the stricter Muslims who put in its place their own manifestly monotheistic hymn: "Here I am, O Allah, here I am; You have no partner; the praise and the grace are Yours, and the empire; You have no partner."

On the prima facie witness of the Quran, it was Muhammad's preaching that introduced this new monotheistic urgency into the Meccan cult: the Quraysh are relentlessly chastised for "partnering God," and from what we otherwise know of Muhammad's Mecca, the charge is not an unjust one. But a closer look reveals that the matter was by no means so simple. While he was still at Mecca, Muhammad had begun to invoke what is later called in the Quran the "religion of Abraham."

Strive truly in His cause. He has chosen you and imposed no difficulties on you in religion: it is the religion of Abraham, and it is He who named you *muslims*, both earlier and in this (revelation). (Quran 22:78)

Another verse establishes the continuity of the "religion of Abraham" through the line of the prophets to his own preaching.

He has established for you the same religion that He enjoined on Noah—and which We revealed to you—and that He enjoined on Abraham, Moses and Jesus—namely, that you remain steadfast in the religion and make no divisions in it. (Quran 42:13)

Reports about the religious practices of Abraham, which for Muhammad at least included a strong adherence to monotheism, were not entirely unknown at Mecca. There were traditions that others in that city had connections with Abraham, connections that centered, as Muhammad's own did, on the Meccan Ka'ba, the House that Abraham built. The statue of Hubal was inside the building during the "Era of Ignorance," but the ritual performed there was the Abrahamic one of circumcision (IBN ISHAQ 1955: 67), and a great many Abrahamic associations, all of them pre-Islamic, clustered around the Ka'ba.

15. The Hanifs

In emphasizing the Abrahamic strain in Islam, the Quran calls Abraham a hanif, a somewhat mysterious term, but one that the Quran contextually identifies with muslim *when it speaks of Abraham; and, like Abraham himself, the* muslim *is explicitly distinguished from Jew or Christian on the one hand and from the idolators or "associators" on the other. The sentiment is neatly summed up in a single verse of the Quran.*

Abraham was not a Jew, nor yet a Christian, but was a *hanif*, a *muslim*, and was not one of the "associators." (Quran 3:67)

And it is precisely in Abraham's footsteps as a hanif *that Muhammad and his followers are commanded to worship God.*

They say: "Become Jews or Christians if you want the guidance." You say: "No, I prefer the religion of Abraham the *hanif*, who was not one of the "associators." (Quran 2:135)

God speaks the truth: follow the religion of Abraham, the *hanif*, who was not one of the "associators." (Quran 3:95)

Who can be better in religion than one who submits (*aslama*) his self to God, does good and follows the religion of Abraham the *hanif*, for God took Abraham as a friend. (Quran 4:125)

Muslim scholars took the word hanif, *and its abstract noun,* hanifiyya, *in two senses: first, as a synonym for historical Islam, the religion revealed to Muhammad and now practiced in these latter days by the Meccan Muslims; and second, in the sense that the Quran meant it, as a form of "natural" monotheism of which Abraham was the chief, though not the sole, practitioner. And it was in this latter sense that the Muslim tradition recalled that there were in Mecca and its environs just such monotheists-without-benefit-of-revelation before Islam. Ibn Ishaq presents them to his readers in what is obviously a schematized setting.*

One day when the Quraysh had assembled on a feast day to venerate and circumambulate the idol to which they offered sacrifices, this being a feast which they held annually, four men drew apart secretly and agreed to keep their counsel in the bonds of friendship. They were Waraqa ibn Nawfal . . . ibn Jahsh . . . Uthman ibn Huwarith . . . Huwarith . . . and Zayd ibn Amr. . . . They were of the opinion that their people had corrupted the religion of their father Abraham, and that the stone they went around was of no account; it could neither see, nor hear, nor hurt, nor help. "Find yourselves a religion," they said; "for by God you have none." So they went their several ways in the lands, seeking the *Hanifiyya*, the religion of Abraham.

Waraqa attached himself to Christianity and studied its Scriptures until he had thoroughly mastered them. Ubaydallah went on searching until Islam came; then he migrated with the Muslims to Abyssinia, taking with him his wife who was a Muslim, Umm Habiba, the daughter of Abu Sufyan. When he arrived there he adopted Christianity, parted from Islam and died a Christian in Abyssinia. . . . After his death the Prophet married his widow Umm Habiba. Muhammad ibn Ali ibn Husayn told me that the Apostle sent Amr ibn Umayya to the Negus to ask for her and he married him to her. He gave her as a dowry, on the Apostle's behalf, 400 dinars. . . .

Uthman ibn Huwarith went to the Byzantine emperor and became a Christian. He was given high office there.

Zayd ibn Amr stayed as he was: he accepted neither Judaism nor Christianity. He abandoned the religion of his people and abstained from idols, animals that had died, blood and things offered to idols. He forbade the killing of infant daughters, saying that he worshipped the God of Abraham and he publicly rebuked the people for their practices. (*Life* 143–144) [IBN ISHAQ 1955: 98–99]

This and similar accounts of "natural" monotheists have not been universally accepted by modern scholars as reflecting a historical reality. Some are doubtless the result of special pleading—the stories surrounding

Waraqa ibn Nawfal, for example, Khadija's cousin who serves as a kind of John the Baptist in the accounts of Muhammad's early revelations—but others ring quite true, particularly when they have to do with men known to have opposed Muhammad to the end. And if they are true, we have another important clue to the existence of an Arabian inclination toward monotheism, how broad or how deep we do not know, that was part of the religious milieu from which Islam soon afterwards emerged.

CHAPTER 2

The Life and Work
of the Prophet

*The Islamic document of salvation is not, as in Christianity, a "biography"
but the Quran, a divine proclamation delivered through a frail human
instrument, Muhammad, the son of Abdullah. Muhammad, blessed by God
and raised to the rank of Prophet, was, for all his high calling, merely a
man. The Muslims' subsequent insistence on that fact may have owed
something to what was to them the Christians' scandalous claim that Jesus
was the Son of God, but despite the enormous veneration given to the
Prophet of Islam, the Muslims' conviction about Muhammad's mortality
has remained unshaken. As a consequence, Islam has no Gospel, no divinely
authenticated record of the salvific deeds of the Founder. It has merely historical recollections, the memories of his converts and companions from
Mecca and Medina.*

    *How soon these remembrances began to be assembled into a formal
biography we cannot tell for certain, but our earliest preserved example of
such is the* Sirat Rasul Allah *or* Life of the Messenger of God *composed
in Baghdad by Ibn Ishaq (d. 767 C.E.) and extant in an edition prepared
by Ibn Hisham (d. 833 C.E.). Our version is, to all appearances, a highly
redacted document. Ibn Hisham considerably economized Ibn Ishaq's original document, which, as far as we can tell, had placed Muhammad in a
far broader historical context. Ibn Ishaq himself seems to have introduced
into his biographical narrative a number of biblical and Gospel parallels—
eighth-century Baghdad was a cosmopolitan city with an important Christian and Jewish population—and in addition attempted to explain in
terms of the events of Muhammad's life the settings of various verses of the
Quran.*

The editorial activity visible in and on Ibn Ishaq's Life *has raised doubts about the material collected in its pages, but the* Sira *remains, nonetheless, together with the Quran, the primary document for reconstructing the life of Muhammad.*

1. Muhammad's Descent from Adam

Ibn Ishaq's Life *presents itself as a formal biography. There is a look at events in Arabia in the remote past, a sketch of some more recent political developments, particularly in South Arabia, and then the narrative turns to the birth of the Prophet of Islam. Like the Synoptic Gospels' presentation of Jesus, the* Life of the Messenger of God *begins with a genealogy, here, as in Luke 3:23–38, stretching back to the father of all mankind.*

This is the book of the life of the Messenger of God:

Muhammad was the son of Abdullah, son of Abd al-Muttalib (whose name was Shayba), son of Hashim (whose name was Amr), son of Abd al-Manaf (whose name was al-Mughira), son of Qusayy (whose name was Zayd), son of Kilab, son of Murra, son of Kaʿb, son of Luʾayy, son of Ghalib, son of Fihr, son of Malik, son of al-Nadr, son of Kinana, son of Khuzayma, son of Mudrika (whose name was Amir), son of Ilyas, son of Mudar, son of Nizar, son of Maʿadd, son of Adnan, son of Udd or Udad, son of Muqawwam, son of Nahur, son of Tayrah, son of Yaʿrub, son of Yashjub, son of Nabit, son of Ishmael, son of Abraham, the Friend of the Compassionate One, son of Tarih (who is Azar), son of Nahur, son of Sarugh, son of Raʿu, son of Falikh, son of Aybar, son of Shalikh, son of Arfakhshad, son of Shem, son of Noah, son of Lamk, son of Matthuselah, son of Enoch, who is the prophet Idris, according to what is alleged, though God knows best (he was the first of the sons of Adam to whom prophecy and writing with a pen were given), son of Yard, son of Mahlil, son of Cain, son of Yanish, son of Seth, son of Adam. (*Life* 3) [IBN ISHAQ 1955: 3]

2. The Birth of the Prophet

After this prelude on the remote past, the standard Life of the Prophet *sets the historical scene by laying out various traditions about early Mecca that we have already seen, how Abraham and Ishmael came to build the House of the Lord there and how Ishmael's descendants were forced to leave the place and lapsed back into paganism. After some additional material on South Arabia, the narrative turns directly to the birth of the Prophet.*

It is alleged in popular stories, and only God knows the truth, that Amina, daughter of Wahb, mother of God's Messenger, used to say when she was pregnant with God's Messenger, that a voice said to her, "You are pregnant with the lord of this people, and when he is born say 'I put him in the care of the One away from the evil of every envyer'; then call him Muhammad." As she was pregnant with him she saw a light come forth from her by which she could see the castles of Busra in Syria. Shortly afterwards Abdullah, the Messenger's father, died while his mother was still pregnant. (*Life* 102) [IBN ISHAQ 1955: 69]

The Messenger was born on Monday, the 12th of First Rabiᶜ in the Year of the Elephant. . . . Salih b. Ibrahim . . . said that his tribesmen said that Hassan ibn Thabit said: "I was a well-grown boy of seven or eight, understanding all that I heard, when I heard a Jew calling out at the top of his voice from the top of a fort in Yathrib [Medina] 'O company of Jews!' until they all came together and called out 'Confound you! What is the matter?' He answered, 'Tonight has a star risen under which Ahmad is to be born.'"

We are not sure when the "Year of the Elephant" was—the traditional dating puts it at 570 C.E.—nor is there any reason to think that the early Muslims were any more certain as to when Muhammad was born or, to put it another way, exactly how old he was when he received his first revelations.

After his birth his mother (Amina) sent to tell his grandfather Abd al-Muttalib that she had given birth to a boy and asked him to come and look at him. When he came she told him what she had seen when she conceived him and what was said to her and what she was ordered to call him. It is alleged that Abd al-Muttalib took him before (the idol) Hubal in the middle of the Kaᶜba, where he stood and prayed to God, thanking him for this gift. Then he brought him out and delivered him to his mother, and he tried to find foster-mothers (or wet-nurses) for him. (*Life* 103) [IBN ISHAQ 1955: 70]

Finally the boy Muhammad undergoes a purification at the hands of more than human agents, then is weighed and found worthy of his future role.

Thawr ibn Yazid . . . told me that some of the Messenger's companions asked him to tell them about himself. He said: "I am what Abraham my father prayed for and the good news of my brother Jesus. When my mother was carrying me she saw a light proceeding from her which showed her the castles of Syria. I was suckled among the Banu

Sa'd ibn Bakr, and while I was with a (foster) brother of mine behind
our tents shepherding the lambs, two men in white raiment came to me
with a gold basin full of snow. Then they seized me and opened my
belly, extracted my heart and split it; then they extracted a black drop
from it and threw it away; then they washed my heart and my belly with
the snow until they had thoroughly cleaned them. Then one said to the
other, weigh him against ten of his people; they did and I outweighed
them. Then they weighed me against a hundred and then a thousand and
I outweighed them. He said, 'Leave him alone, for by God, if you weigh
him against all his people he would outweigh them.'" (*Life* 106) [IBN
ISHAQ 1955: 72]

3. The Scriptural Prediction of the Coming of the Prophet of Islam

*When Muhammad was six his mother Amina died, whereupon he was sent
to live with his grandfather Abd al-Muttalib. Two years later this latter
died as well, and Muhammad was then put into the care of his paternal
uncle, Abu Talib. In the passage just cited the Prophet's birth was acknowledged by a Jew, who saw his sign in the stars; later a Christian monk named
Bahira recognized the adolescent Muhammad—he was accompanying his
relatives on a commercial trip to Syria—as the very one of whom Scripture
had spoken as a prophet.*

*The boy Muhammad's identification and acknowledgment by the
Christian monk Bahira was a popular story in Islam, and the motif of the
future holy man identified in the child can be paralleled from the infancy
and boyhood accounts of Moses and Jesus, among others. While such stories
may be no more than the stuff of legend, there is a similar but theologically
quite different question that is proposed for meditation by the Quran itself,
namely, God's own foreshadowing of the coming of His prophet Muhammad in Scripture. It is God who speaks here.*

Those who follow the Messenger, the unlettered Prophet, *described
in the Torah and the Gospel*, who bids things noble and forbids things vile,
makes lawful what is clean, and prohibits what is foul, who relieves
them of their burdens, and the yoke that lies upon them, those who
believe and honor and help him, and follow the light sent with him, are
those who will attain their goal. (Quran 7:157; emphasis added)

*In this first passage God in the Quran makes explicit, though unspec-
ified, reference to the Bible and the Gospels as announcing the coming of*

a future prophet, "whose name shall be Ahmad." We are told this in another passage of the Quran where similar sentiments are expressed from the mouth of Jesus.

And when Jesus son of Mary said: "O Children of Israel, I am sent to you by God to confirm the Torah (sent) before me, and to give you good tidings of an apostle who will come after me, whose name is Ahmad [that is, the praised one]." Yet, when he has come to them with clear proofs, they say: "This is only magic." (Quran 61:6)

On the second of these two passages, the classical Quranic commentaries have this to say.

According to Ka'b al-Ahbar [a rabbi who was an early convert to Islam and the attributed source of much of the material on Judaism in the early Islamic tradition], it is related that the disciples of Jesus asked: "O Spirit of God, will there be another religious community after us?" and that Jesus then said: "Yes, the community of Ahmad. It will comprise people who are wise, knowing, devout and pious, as if they were all prophets in religious knowledge. They will be content with modest sustenance from God, and He will be pleased with a modest conduct on their part." (Zamakhshari *ad loc.*)

". . . whose name is Ahmad . . .": That is, Muhammad. The meaning is: My [that is, Jesus'] religion exists by reason of holding on firmly to the books of God and His prophets. And so Jesus mentions (only) the very first of the well-known books, concerning which the earlier prophets rendered judgment, and only that prophet who (as the last) constitutes the seal of those who are sent by God. (Baydawi *ad loc.*)

The Muslim scientist and chronologer Biruni (d. 1048 C.E.) argues the case somewhat more rigorously in his Traces of the Past. *His point of departure is the chief biblical proof-text for the Muslims' contention that Muhammad had been foretold in earlier Scripture, namely, this passage in Isaiah.*

These are the words of my Lord: Go and post a watchman to report what he sees. He will see horsemen in pairs, riders on asses, riders on camels. . . . And there they come, mounted men, horsemen in pairs. . . . And then he spoke: "Fallen, fallen is Babylon." (Isaiah 21:6–9)

Biruni begins, obviously using a somewhat different text of Isaiah:

This is a prophecy regarding the Messiah, the "man riding on an ass," and regarding Muhammad, the "man riding on a camel," because in consequence of the latter's appearance, Babylon has fallen, its idols have been broken, its castles have been shattered, and its empire has perished. There are many passages in this book of Isaiah predicting Muhammad, being rather hints (than explicit texts), but easily admitting of a clear interpretation. And despite all this, the Jews' obstinacy in clinging to their error induces them to devise and maintain things which are not acknowledged by men in general, to wit, that the "man riding on a camel" is Moses and not Muhammad. But what connection have Moses and his people with Babylon? And did that happen to Moses and to his people after him which happened to Muhammad and his companions in Babylon? By no means! If the Jews had escaped one by one from the Babylonians, they would have considered it a sufficient prize to return (to their country), even though in a desperate condition.

This testimony (of Isaiah) is confirmed in the fifth book of Moses, which is called Deuteronomy, "I will raise them up a prophet like yourself from among their brethren, and will put My word in his mouth. And he shall speak to them all that I command him. And whoever will not heed the word of him who speaks in My name, I shall take revenge on him" (Deut. 21:6–9). Now I should like to know whether there are other brethren of the sons of Isaac except the sons of Ishmael? If they say that the brethren of the sons of Israel are the children of Esau, we ask only: Has there been raised among *them* a man like Moses—in the times after Moses—of the same description and resembling him?

Does not also the following passage from the same book, of which this is a translation, bear testimony to Muhammad: "The Lord came from Mount Sinai, and rose up to us from Seir, and He shone from Mount Paran, accompanied by ten thousand saints at His right hand" (Deut. 33:2)? The terms of this passage are hints for the establishing of the proof that the (anthropomorphic) descriptions inherent in them cannot be referred to the essence of the Creator, nor to His qualities, He being high above such things. His coming from Mount Sinai means His secret conversation with Moses there; His riding up from Seir means the appearance of the Messiah, and His shining forth from Paran, where Ishmael grew up and married, means the coming of Muhammad from there as the last of the founders of religions, accompanied by legions of saints, who were sent down from heaven to help, being marked with certain badges. He who refuses to accept this interpretation, for which all evidence has borne testimony, is required to prove what kinds of mistakes there are in it. "But he whose companion is Satan, woe to him for such a companion" (Quran 4:42). (al-Biruni, *Traces of the Past*) [BIRUNI 1879: 22–23]

4. Marriage with Khadija

We know as little of Muhammad's early life as we do of Jesus', but like his predecessor, he was thought to have grown "in wisdom and age and grace."

The Messenger of God grew up, God protecting and keeping him from the vileness of heathenism because He wished to honor him with Apostleship, until he grew up to be the finest of his people in manliness, the best in character, most noble in lineage, the best neighbor, the most kind, truthful, reliable, the furthest removed from filthiness and corrupt morals, through loftiness and nobility, so that he was known among his people as "the trustworthy" because of the good qualities which God had implanted in him. (*Life* 117) [IBN ISHAQ 1955: 81]

Next we are introduced to Khadija, Muhammad's longtime and, for as long as she lived, his only wife. The motifs of Muhammad the successful and the acknowledged future holy man continue to be entwined in the narrative.

Khadija was a merchant woman of dignity and wealth. She used to hire men to carry merchandise outside the country on a profit-sharing basis, for the Quraysh were a people given to commerce. Now when she heard about the Prophet's truthfulness, trustworthiness and honorable character, she sent for him and proposed that he should take her goods to Syria and trade with them, while she would pay him more than she paid others. He was to take a lad called Maysara. The Messenger of God accepted the proposal and the two set forth until they came to Syria.

The Messenger stopped in the shade of a tree near a monk's cell, when the monk came up to Maysara and asked him who the man was resting under the tree. He told him he was of the Quraysh, the people who held the sanctuary (in Mecca), and the monk exclaimed: "None but a prophet ever sat beneath this tree."

Then the Prophet sold the goods he had brought and bought what he wanted to buy and began the return journey to Mecca. The story goes that at the height of noon, when the heat was intense as he rode his beast, Maysara saw two angels shading the Messenger from the sun's rays. When he brought Khadija her property she sold it and it amounted to double or thereabouts. Maysara for his part told her about the two angels who had shaded him and of the monk's words.

Now Khadija was a determined, noble and intelligent woman possessing the properties with which God willed to honor her. So when

Maysara told her those things she sent to the Messenger of God and—so
the story goes—said, "O son of my uncle, I like you because of our
relationship and your high reputation among your people, your trustworthiness and good character and truthfulness." Then she proposed
marriage. Now Khadija at that time was the best-born woman in the
Quraysh, of the greatest dignity, and also the richest. All the people
were eager to get possession of her wealth if it were possible. . . .

The Messenger of God told his uncles of Khadija's proposal, and
his uncle Hamza ibn Abd al-Muttalib went with him to Khuwaylid ibn
Asad and asked for her hand and he married her. She was the mother of
all the Messenger's children except Ibrahim, namely, al-Qasim [whence
the Prophet was sometimes known as "Abu al-Qasim"], al-Tahir, al-
Tayyib, Zaynab, Ruqayya, Umm Kulthum and Fatima. Al-Qasim, al-
Tayyib and al-Tahir all died in the Era of Ignorance. All his daughters
lived into Islam and embraced it, and migrated with him to Medina. (*Life*
119–121) [IBN ISHAQ 1955: 82–83]

5. Muhammad's Call and First Revelation

*Muslim authorities were as uncertain as we are about which revelation
recorded in the Quran was the earliest received by the Prophet, and which,
if any, of the early* suras *describe the experience of revelation. Ibn Ishaq has
preserved a number of traditions on the subject.*

Al-Zuhri related from Urwa ibn Zubayr that Aisha told him that
when God desired to honor Muhammad and have mercy on His servants
by means of him, the first sign of prophethood vouchsafed to the Apostle
was true visions, resembling the brightness of daybreak, which were
shown to him in his sleep. And God, she said, made him love solitude
so that he liked nothing better than to be alone. . . .

Wahb ibn Kaysan, a client of the family of al-Zubayr, told me: I
heard Abdullah ibn al-Zubayr say to Ubayd ibn Umayr . . . "O Ubayd,
tell us how began the prophethood which was first bestowed on the
Apostle when Gabriel came to him."

Ubayd's remarks on tahannuth, *already cited in chapter 1 above, are
then quoted, after which Ibn Ishaq turns to another authority.*

Wahb ibn Kaysan told me that Ubayd said to him: Every year
during that month the Apostle would pray in seclusion and give food to
the poor that came to him. And when he completed the month and
returned from his seclusion, first of all before entering his house he

would go to the Ka'ba and walk around it seven times or as often as it pleased God; then he would go back to his house until in the year when God sent him, in the month of Ramadan in which God willed concerning him what He willed of His grace, the Apostle set forth for Hira as was his wont, and his family with him.

When it was the night on which God honored him with his mission and showed mercy on His servants thereby, Gabriel brought him the command of God. "He came to me," said the Apostle of God, "while I was asleep, with a coverlet of brocade on which there was some writing, and said, 'Recite!' I said, 'What shall I recite?' He pressed me with it so tightly that I thought it was death; then he let me go said, 'Recite!' I said, 'What shall I recite?' He pressed me with it again so that I thought it was death; then he let me go and said, 'Recite!' I said, 'What shall I recite?' He pressed me with it a third time so that I thought it was death and said, 'Recite' I said, 'What then shall I recite'—and this I said only to deliver myself from him, lest he should do the same again. He said:

> 'Recite in the name of thy Lord who created,
> Who created man of blood coagulated.
> Read! Thy Lord is most beneficent,
> Who taught by the pen,
> Taught that which they knew not to men' (Quran 96:1–5)."
> (*Life* 151–153) [IBN ISHAQ 1955: 105–106]

These are, as a matter of fact, the opening lines of what was later numbered as the 96th Sura of the Quran, and here it is being plausibly put forward as the earliest of Muhammad's revelations. Ibn Ishaq continues with Muhammad's own account, still on the authority of Ubayd ibn Umayr.

So I read it and he departed from me. And I awoke from my sleep, and it was as though these words were written in my heart. . . . When I was midway on the mountain, I heard a voice saying, "O Muhammad, you are the Apostle of God and I am Gabriel." I raised my head toward heaven to see and lo, there was Gabriel in the form of a man with his feet astride the horizon saying, "O Muhammad, you are the Apostle of God and I am Gabriel." I stood gazing at him, moving neither forward nor backward; then I began to turn my face away from him, but towards whatever region of the sky I looked, I saw him as before. I continued standing there, neither advancing nor turning back, until Khadija sent her messengers in search of me and they gained the high ground above Mecca and returned to her while I was standing in the same place. Then he parted from me and I from him, returning to my family.

Ibn Ishaq's account attaches no Quranic passage to the vision of Gabriel, but there are what seem to be two such visions described in an early sura *or chapter of the Quran.*

By the star when it goes down, your companion is neither astray nor misled, nor does he say anything of his own desire. It was nothing less than inspiration that inspired him. He was taught by one mighty in power, one possessed of wisdom, and he appeared while in the highest part of the horizon. Then he approached and came closer, and he was at a distance of two bow lengths or closer. And He inspired His servant with what he inspired him. He [that is, Muhammad] did not falsify what he saw. Will you then dispute with him over what he saw? (Quran 53:1–12)

The same sura *immediately continues:*

Indeed he saw him descending a second time, near the Lotus Tree that marks the boundary. Near it is the Garden of the Abode, and behold, the Lotus Tree was shrouded in the deepest shrouding. His sight never swerved, nor did it go wrong. Indeed, he saw the signs of his Lord, the Greatest. (Quran 53:13–18)

Though none of the pronouns is identified in these verses, there is little doubt that the recipient of the vision was Muhammad. Who it was who was seen is less clear, and if Muhammad's being referred to as his "servant" in verse 10 suggests that it is God Himself, the Muslim tradition preferred to understand, as Ibn Ishaq does, that it was Gabriel in all the other verses, probably because later in his own career Muhammad had unmistakably come to the same conclusion.

Whoever is an enemy to Gabriel—for it is he who brings down to your heart by the will of God a confirmation of what went before and guidance and good news for those who believe—whoever is an enemy of God and His angels and His messengers, to Gabriel and Michael. . . . (Quran 2:97–98)

We return to Ibn Ishaq's account and to the events that followed Muhammad's first experience of revelation. It is still the Prophet who is speaking.

And I came to Khadija and sat by her thigh and drew close to her. She said, "O Abu al-Qasim [that is, Muhammad, here called "Father of Qasim," his first son, who did not survive], where have you been? By God, I sent my messengers in search of you and they reached the high ground above Mecca and returned to me." Then I told her what I had seen; and she said, "Rejoice, O son of my uncle, and be of good heart. Verily, by Him in whose hand is Khadija's soul, I have hope that you will be the prophet of this people."

Then she rose and gathered her garments about her and set forth to her cousin Waraqa ibn Nawfal . . . who had become a Christian and read the Scriptures and learned from those that follow the Torah and the Gospel. And when she related to him what the Apostle of God had told her he had seen and heard, Waraqa cried, "Holy! Holy! Holy! Verily by Him in whose hand is Waraqa's soul, if you have spoken to me the truth, Khadija, there has come unto him the greatest *Namus*, who came to Moses aforetime, and lo, he is the prophet of this people. Bid him be of good heart." (*Life* 153) [IBN ISHAQ 1955: 106–107]

A later generation of Muslims also understood "Namus," the Greek nomos or law, as the angel Gabriel. It is not clear in this passage whether either Muhammad or Waraqa so understood it; it might well have meant, via a previous (Jewish?) personification of the Law / Torah, something akin to "God's Holy Spirit."

Revelation came fully to the Apostle while he was believing in Him and in the truth of His message. He received it willingly, and took upon himself what it entailed, whether of men's goodwill or anger. Prophecy is a troublesome burden—only strong, resolute messengers can bear it by God's help and grace, because of the opposition which they meet from men in conveying God's message. The Apostle carried out God's orders in spite of the opposition and ill-treatment which he met. . . .

Then the revelations stopped for a time so that the Apostle was distressed and grieved. Then Gabriel brought him the Sura of the Morning (Sura 93), in which his Lord, who had so honored him, swore that He had not forsaken him and did not hate him. (*Life* 155–156) [IBN ISHAQ 1955: 111–112]

These momentous events were dated by the tradition to the month of Ramadan in the Prophet's fortieth year, thus, in the standard chronology, A.D. 610.

6. Sadness, Doubt, Consolation

Muhammad for his part was not so certain of what had befallen him. The traditional Life leaves little doubt that it was Khadija who supported him through this difficult period of doubt and hesitation.

Khadija believed in him and accepted as true what he had brought from God, and helped him in his work. She was the first to believe in God and His Messenger and in the truth of his message. By her God lightened the burden of His Prophet. He had never met with contradiction and charges of falsehood (before), which saddened him, but God comforted him by her when he went home. She strengthened him, lightened his burden, proclaimed his truth, and belittled men's opposition. May God Almighty have mercy on her!

. . . Then the revelations stopped for a time so that the Messenger of God was distressed and grieved. Then Gabriel brought him the *Sura* of the Morning (Sura 93), in which his Lord, who had so honored him, swore that He had not forsaken him and did not hate him. God said, "By the morning and the night, when it is still, thy Lord has not forsaken nor hated thee," meaning that He has not left you, forsaken you nor hated you after having loved you. "And verily, the latter end is better for you than the beginning," that is, what I have for you when you return to Me is better than the honor which I have given you in the world. "And the Lord will give you and satisfy you," that is, of victory in this world and reward in the next. "Did he not find you an orphan and give you refuge, going astray and guided you, found you poor and made you rich?" God thus told him how He had begun to honor him in his earthly life, and His kindness to him as an orphan and wandering astray, and His delivering him from all that by His compassion.

"Do not oppress the orphan and do not repel the beggar," that is, do not be a tyrant or proud or harsh or mean towards the weakest of God's creatures. "Speak of the kindness of thy Lord," that is, tell about the kindness of God in giving you prophecy, mention it and call men to it.

So the Messenger began to mention secretly God's kindness to him and to his servants in the matter of prophecy to everyone among his people whom he could trust. (*Life* 155–156) [IBN ISHAQ 1955: 111–112]

7. The Conversion of Ali

This was not yet public preaching, but Muhammad's own firm conviction and the urgency of his message began to have their effect, although at first in a limited circle. Ali, the cousin of the Prophet and later one of the great heroes of Islam, embraced the new faith, but the reaction of his father illustrates the enormous social difficulty of a Meccan rejecting the "tradition of the fathers" for the new "tradition of the Prophet."

Ali [the son of Abu Talib] was the first male to believe in the Messenger, to pray with him and to believe in his divine message, when he was a boy of ten. God favored him in that he was brought up in the care of the Messenger before Islam began. . . .

A traditionist mentioned that when the time of prayer came the Messenger used to go out to the glens of Mecca accompanied by Ali, who went unbeknown to his father, and his uncles and the rest of the people. There they used to pray the ritual prayers and return at nightfall. This went on as long as God intended that it should, until one day Abu Talib came upon them while they were praying and said to the Messenger, "O nephew, what is this religion which I see you practicing?" He replied, "O uncle, this is the religion of God, His angels, His Messengers, and the religion of our father Abraham." Or, as he said, "God sent me as a Messenger to mankind, and you, my uncle, most deserve that I should teach you the truth and call you to guidance, and you are the most worthy to respond and help me," or words to that effect. His uncle replied, "I cannot give up the religion of my fathers which they followed, but by God, you shall never meet anything to distress you so long as I live." They (also) mention that he said to Ali, "My boy, what is this religion of yours?" He answered, "I believe in God and the Messenger of God, and I declare that what he has brought is true, and I pray to God with him and follow him." (*Life* 158–160) [IBN ISHAQ 1955: 114]

8. The Earliest Public Preaching of Islam

People began to accept Islam, both men and women, in large numbers until the fame of it was spread throughout Mecca, and it began to be talked about. Then God commanded His Messenger to declare the truth of what he had received and to make known his commands to men and to call them to Him. Three years had elapsed from the time that the Messenger concealed his state until God commanded him to publish His religion, according to information which has reached me. Then God said, "Proclaim what you have been ordered and turn aside the polytheists" (Quran 15:94). And again, "Warn your family, your nearest relations, and lower your wing to the followers who follow you" (Quran 26:214–215). And "Say, I am the one who warns plainly" (Quran 15:9). (*Life* 166) [IBN ISHAQ 1955: 117]

The 114 suras or chapters of the Quran were eventually arranged pretty much in reverse order of their length, and so it is difficult to be cer-

tain of the precise sequence or chronology of the revelations to Muhammad.
There is, however, general agreement among both Muslim and non-Muslim
scholars on some of the earliest of them, and they offer an insight into the
tenor and tone of the Prophet's preaching to his contemporaries in Mecca.

> You, enfolded in your mantle!
> Arise and warn!
> Glorify your Lord,
> Purify your inner self,
> And banish all trepidation.
> Do not bestow favors in expectation of return,
> And persevere in the way of your Lord.
> For when the trumpet blows
> It will be a day of distress,
> Dolorous for the unbelievers.
> Leave him to Me alone whom I created,
> And gave him abundant wealth
> And sons always present by his side,
> And made things easy for them.
> Yet he wants that I should give him more.
> Never! He is refractory of our signs.
> I shall inflict on him hardship,
> For he had thought and calculated.
> May he be accursed, how he planned!
> May he be accursed, how he plotted!
> Then he looked around,
> And frowned and puckered his brow,
> Then turned his back and waxed proud,
> And said: "This is nothing but the magic of old,
> Nothing more than the speech of a man!"
> I will cast him into the fire of Hell.
> What do you think Hell-fire is?
> It leaves nothing, nor does it spare;
> It glows and burns the skin.
> (Quran 74:1–29)

> I call to witness the early hours of the morning,
> And the night when dark and still,
> Your Lord has neither left you, nor despises you.
> What is to come is better for you than what has
>   gone before;

For your Lord will certainly give you, and you will
        be content.
Did He not find you an orphan, and take care of you?
Did He not find you perplexed and show you the way?
Did He not find you poor and enrich you?
So do not oppress the orphan,
And do not drive the begger away,
And keep recounting the favors of your Lord.
(Quran 93)

Say: O you unbelievers,
I do not worship what you worship,
Nor do you worship Who I worship;
Nor will I worship what you worship,
Nor will you worship Who I worship.
To you your way; to me my way.
(Quran 109)

Say: He is God, the one the most unique,
God the immanently indispensable.
He has begotten no one, and is begotten of none.
There is no one comparable to Him.
(Quran 112)

Have you seen him who denies the Day of Judgment?
It is he who pushes the orphan away,
And does not induce others to feed the needy.
Woe to those who pray,
But who are oblivious in their moral duties,
Who dissimulate,
And withhold the necessities (from others).
(Quran 107)

I call to witness the heavens and the night star.
How will you comprehend what the night star is?
It is the star that shines with a piercing brightness—
That over each soul there is a guardian.
Let man consider what he was made of:
He was created of spurting water
Issuing from between the backbone and the ribs.
God has certainly the power to bring him back (from
        the dead).
The day all secrets are examined

He will have no strength or helper.
So I call to witness the rain-producing sky,
And the earth which opens up,
That this Quran is a distinctive word
And no trifle.
They are hatching up a plot, (Muhammad,)
But I too am devising a plan.
So bear with unbelievers with patience and give them a
    respite for a while.
(Quran 86)

Recite, in the name of your Lord who created,
Created man from an embryo;
Recite! For your Lord is most beneficent,
Who taught by the pen,
Taught man what he did not know.
And yet, but yet man is rebellious,
For he thinks he is sufficient in himself.
Surely your returning is to your Lord.
Have you seen him who restrains
A votary when he turns to his devotions?
Have you thought that if he denies and turns away,
Does he not know that God sees?
And yet indeed if he does not desist We shall drag him by
    the forelock,
By the lying, the sinful forelock!
So let him summon his associates,
And we shall call the guards of Hell!
Beware! Do not obey him, but bow in adoration and
    draw near (to your Lord).
(Quran 96)

The Message of these early suras *of the Quran is clear and direct:
God, who created the world and mankind, will require an accounting from
His creation on the Last Day. The insolent, the worldly, the greedy will be
cast into Hell; the generous and obedient will be rewarded with Paradise.
The appropriate human response, then, is submission—in Arabic* islam—
to the will of God and the directions of His Prophet.

9. The Opposition of the Quraysh

Since the Quraysh have been united,
United to fit out caravans winter and summer.
Let them worship the Lord of this House,
Who provided them against destitution, and gave them
    security from fear.
(Quran 106)

*The earliest Meccan Muslims—literally, "those who have submitted,"
the same term used, as we have seen, of Abraham and his descendants—did
not include many of the powerful first families of Mecca, those same
Quraysh who sent forth their summer and winter caravans to trade in Syria
and the Yemen. The Meccan merchant aristocracy continued to be what it
had always been in living memory: the worshipers of idols, a great many
of which were collected in the* haram *or sacred enclosure that surrounded
the Ka*°*ba in the midst of Mecca.*

When the Messenger openly displayed Islam as God ordered him,
his people did not withdraw or turn against him, so far as I have heard,
until he spoke disparagingly of their gods. When he did that they took
great offense and resolved unanimously to treat him as an enemy, except those whom God had protected by Islam from such evil, but they
were a despised minority. Abu Talib his uncle treated the Messenger
kindly and protected him, the latter continuing to obey God's commands, nothing turning him back. (*Life* 166–168) [IBN ISHAQ 1955:
118–119]

*In the beginning at least there was some attempt, if not to come to
terms with Muhammad, then at least to attempt to bargain with him.*

Islam began to spread in Mecca among men and women of the
tribes of the Quraysh, though the Quraysh were imprisoning and seducing as many of the Muslims as they could. A traditionist told me from
Sa°id ibn Jubayr and from Ikrima, freedman of Abdullah ibn Abbas, that
the leading men of every clan of the Quraysh . . . decided to send for
Muhammad and to negotiate and argue with him so that they could not
be held to blame on his account in the future. When they sent for him
the Messenger of God came quickly because he thought that what he had
(earlier) said to them had made an impression, for he was most zealous
for their welfare and their wicked ways pained him. When he came and
sat down with them, they explained that they had sent for him in order
that they could talk together. No Arab had ever treated his tribe as he

had treated them, and they repeated the charges which have been mentioned on several occasions. If it was money he wanted, they would make him richest of them all; if it was honor, he should be their prince; if it was sovereignty, they would make him king; if it was a spirit that had got possession of him, then they would exhaust their means in finding medicine to cure him.

These broad promises were likely neither sincere nor altogether practical, but they do attest to the magnitude of the threat that Muhammad was thought to pose to the social and commercial equilibrium of Mecca, a city that had combined trade and pilgrimage to its shrine into a profitable enterprise.

The Messenger replied that he had no such intention. He sought not money nor honor nor sovereignty, but God had sent him as a Messenger, and revealed a book to him, and commanded him to become an announcer and a warner. He had brought the message of his Lord and given them good advice. If they took it, then they would have a portion of this world and the next; if they rejected it, he could only patiently await the outcome until God decided between them, or words to that effect.

"Well, Muhammad," they said, "if you won't accept any of our propositions, you know that no people are more short of land and water and live a harder life than we, so ask your Lord, who sent you, to remove us from these mountains which shut us in, and to straighten out our country for us, and to open up in it rivers like those of Syria and Iraq, and to resurrect for us our forefathers—and let there be among those who are resurrected Qusayy ibn Kilab, for he was a true shaykh—so that we may ask them whether what you say is true or false." . . . He replied that he had not been sent to them with such an object. He had conveyed to them God's message and they could either accept it with advantage or reject it and await God's judgment. They said that if he could not do that for them, let him do something for himself. Ask God to send an angel with him to confirm what he said and to contradict them; to make him gardens and castles and treasures of gold and silver to satisfy his obvious wants, since he stood in the street as they did and he sought a livelihood as they did. . . . He replied that he would not do it, and would not ask for such things, for he was not sent to do so, and he repeated what he had said before. . . . They said, "did not your Lord know that we would sit with you and ask you these questions, so that He might come to you and instruct you how to answer, and tell you what He was going to do with us, if we did not accept your message? Information has reached us that you are taught by this fellow in al-Yamama called al-Rahman ["The Compassionate"], and by God we will never believe in the Rahman. Our conscience is clear, by God, we will not leave you and our treatment of you until either we destroy you or you destroy us." (*Life* 187–189) [IBN ISHAQ 1955: 133–134]

10. Persecution and Migration to Abyssinia

Ibn Ishaq traces the deteriorating state of affairs between Muhammad and the notables among the Quraysh.

When the Quraysh saw that he would not yield to them and insulted their gods and that his uncle treated him kindly and stood up in his defense and would not give him up to them, some of their leading men went to Abu Talib. . . . They said, "O Abu Talib, your nephew has cursed our gods, insulted our religion, mocked our way of life and accused our forefathers of error. Either you must stop him or you must let us get at him, for you yourself are in the same position as we are in opposition to him and we will rid you of him." He gave them a conciliatory reply and a soft answer and they went away.

The Messenger continued on his way, making public God's religion and calling men to it. In consequence his relations with the Quraysh deteriorated and men withdrew from him in enmity. They were always talking about him and inciting one another against him. Then they went to Abu Talib a second time and said, "You have a high and lofty position among us, and we have asked you to put a stop to your nephew's activities but you have not done so. By God, we cannot endure that our fathers should be reviled, our customs mocked and our gods insulted. Until you rid us of him we will fight the pair of you until one side perishes," or words to that effect. Thus saying, they went off. Abu Talib was deeply distressed at the breach with his people and their enmity, but he could not desert the Messenger and give him up to them. (*Life* 169–170) [IBN ISHAQ 1955: 119–120]

Mecca was still very much a tribal society, and the message of Muhammad inevitably raised the specter of tribal schisms running across the complex lines of patronage and clientage in the city.

Then the Quraysh incited people against the companions of the Messenger who had become Muslims. Every tribe fell upon the Muslims among them, beating them and seducing them from their religion. God protected His Messenger from them through his uncle, who, when he saw what the Quraysh were doing, called upon the Banu Hashim and the Banu al-Muttalib to stand with him in protecting the Messenger. This they agreed to do, with the exception of Abu Lahab, the accursed enemy of God.

Then the Quraysh showed their enmity to all those who followed the Messenger; every clan which included Muslims attacked them, imprisoning and beating them, allowing them no food or drink, and exposing them to the burning heat of Mecca so as to seduce them from their religion. Some gave way under pressure of persecution and others resisted them, being protected by God. . . . It was that evil man Abu Jahl who stirred up the Meccans against them. When he heard that a man had become a Muslim, if he was a man of social importance and had relations to defend him, he (merely) reprimanded him and poured scorn on him, saying, "You have forsaken the religion of your father who is better than you. We will declare you a blockhead and brand you a fool and destroy your reputation." If he was a merchant he said, "We will boycott your goods and reduce you to beggary." If he was a person of no social importance, he beat him and incited the people against him. (*Life* 205–207) [IBN ISHAQ 1955: 143–145]

There then occurs what is to us a quite unexpected event: a number of the believers are sent across the Red Sea to Abyssinia.

When the Messenger saw the affliction of his companions and, though he (himself) escaped it because of his standing with God and his uncle Abu Talib, he could not protect them, he said to them: "If you were to go to Abyssinia it would be better for you, for the king (there) will not tolerate injustice and it is a friendly country, until such time as God shall relieve you from your distress." Thereupon his companions went to Abyssinia, being afraid of apostasy and fleeing to God with their religion. This was the first *hijra* [that is, emigration] in Islam.

The choice of Abyssinia across the Red Sea as a place of refuge for the beleaguered Muslims is somewhat surprising, but only because we are so scantily instructed by our sources on the larger commercial connections of Mecca. Abyssinia had long since embraced Christianity, a religion to which Muhammad may have felt an affinity. But Abyssinia was also a rising commercial exporter in the shifting international trade of the sixth and seventh centuries, and the tiny band of Muslim expatriates may well have been sent there to explore commercial possibilities.

Whatever the case, the Quraysh sent their own deputation to convince the Christian king of Abyssinia, called the Negus, to send the Muslims

back. The Negus held a public hearing on the matter and requested an ex-
planation of Islam.

When they (the Muslims) came into the royal presence, they
found the king had summoned his bishops with their sacred books exposed around him. He asked them what was the religion for which they
had forsaken their people, without entering into his religion or any
other. Abu Jaᶜfar ibn Abi Talib answered, "O King, we were an unciv-
ilized people, worshiping idols, eating corpses, committing abominations, breaking natural ties, treating guests badly, and our strong de-
voured our weak. Thus we were until God sent us a Messenger whose
lineage, truth, trustworthiness and clemency we know. He summoned
us to acknowledge God's unity and to worship Him and renounce the
stones and images which our fathers formerly worshiped. He commanded us to speak the truth, be faithful to our engagements, mindful
of the ties of kinship and kindly hospitality, and to refrain from crimes
and bloodshed. He forbade us to commit abominations and to speak lies,
and to devour the property of orphans, to vilify chaste women. He commanded us to worship God alone and not to associate anything with
Him, and he gave us orders about prayer, almsgiving and fasting. We
confessed his truth and believed in him, and we followed him in what
he had brought from God, and we worshiped God alone without associating aught with Him. We treated as forbidden what he forbade and as
lawful what he declared lawful. . . ."

The Negus asked if they had with them anything which had come
from God. When Jaᶜfar said he had, the Negus commanded him to read
it to him, so he read him a passage from the *sura* called "Mary" (19). The
Negus wept until his beard was wet and the bishops wept until their
scrolls were wet, when they heard what was read to them. Then the
Negus said, "Of a truth, this and what Jesus brought have come from the
same niche. You two (Quraysh) may go, for by God, I will never give
them (the Muslims) up and they shall not be betrayed." (*Life* 208–220)
[IBN ISHAQ 1955: 146–148]

11. The Boycott

When the Quraysh perceived that the Messenger's companions
had settled in a land in peace and safety and that the Negus had protected those who had sought refuge with him, and that Umar had become a Muslim and that he and Hamza were on the side of the Messenger and his companions, and that Islam had begun to spread among the

tribes, they came together and decided among themselves to write a
document in which they would put a boycott on the Banu Hashim and
the Banu Muttalib that no one should marry their women nor give
women for them to marry; and that no one should either buy from them
or sell to them, and when they agreed on that they wrote it in a deed.
Then they solemnly agreed on the points and hung the deed up in the
middle of the Ka'ba to remind them of their obligations.

*The point does not appear to have been so much to starve Muhammad
and his followers into submission as to exclude them from the commercial
life of that very commercial city.*

. . . Meanwhile the Messenger was exhorting his people night and
day, secretly and publicly, openly proclaiming God's command without
fear of anyone. His uncle and the rest of the Banu Hashim gathered
round him and protected him from the attacks of the Quraysh, who
when they saw they could not get at him, mocked and laughed and
disputed with him. The Quran began to come down concerning the
wickedness of the Quraysh and those who showed enmity to him, some
by name and some only referred to in general. (*Life* 230–233) [IBN
ISHAQ 1955: 159–161]

12. Muhammad's Night Journey

*Deceived by false reports of the conversion of the Quraysh, some of the emi-
grants returned from Abyssinia—others remained until there was a Muslim
community in Medina, and some never returned at all. Though the Quraysh showed no signs of relenting on religious grounds, their boycott
against the Banu Hashim and the Banu Muttalib did in effect collapse. And
it is at this point that the* Life *inserts the account of the famous "Night
Journey" of the Prophet referred to in Sura 17:1 of the Quran.*

Glory be to Him who took His votary by night from the Sacred
Mosque to the distant Mosque, whose precincts We have blessed, that
We may show him some of Our signs. Verily, He is the all-hearing and
all-seeing.

The Life *continues:*

The following account reached me from Abdullah b. Mas'ud and
Abu Sa'id al-Khudri and Aisha the Prophet's wife and Mu'awiya b. Abi
Sufyan and al-Hasan al-Basri and Ibn Shihab al-Zuhri and Qatada and
other traditionists as well as Umm Hani, daughter of Abu Talib. It is

pieced together in the story that follows, each one contributing something of what he was told about what had happened when the Prophet was taken on the Night Journey. The matter of the place of the journey and what is said about it is a searching test and a matter of God's power and authority wherein is a lesson for the intelligent; and guidance and mercy and strengthening to those who believe. It was certainly an act of God by which He took him by night in whatever way He pleased to show him signs which He willed him to see so that he witnessed His mighty sovereignty and power by which He does what He wills to do.

Though there may have been, as this text hints, some hesitations about the destination of this journey by night, there soon developed a consensus that the "distant shrine" of Quran 17:1 was in fact the site of the former Temple in Jerusalem.

According to what I have heard, Abdullah ibn Mas'ud used to say: Buraq [that is, the steed that carried Muhammad; see below], whose every stride carried it as far as its eye could reach and on which earlier prophets had ridden, was brought to the Messenger and he was mounted on it. His companion (Gabriel) went with him to see the wonders between heaven and earth, until he came to Jerusalem's Temple. There he found Abraham the Friend of God, Moses and Jesus assembled with a company of prophets and prayed with them. Then he was brought three vessels containing milk, wine and water respectively. The Messenger said: "I heard a voice saying when these were offered to me, 'If he takes the water he will be drowned and his people also; if he takes the wine he will go astray and his people also; and if he tastes the milk, he will be rightly guided and his people also.' So I took the vessel containing the milk and drank it. Gabriel said to me, 'You have been rightly guided, and so will your people be, Muhammad.'"

In the manner of the Arab historians, Ibn Ishaq provides another version of the same event, this one from Hasan al-Basri, a purported eyewitness to some of the circumstances, though he must have been a very small child at the time.

I was told that al-Hasan al-Basri [642–728 C.E.] said that the Messenger of God said: "While I was sleeping in the Hijr [a kind of semicircular stone porch close by the Ka'ba], Gabriel came and stirred me with his foot. I sat up but saw nothing and lay down again. He came a second time and stirred me with his foot. I sat up but saw nothing and lay down again. He came to me the third time and stirred me with his foot. I sat up and he took hold of my arm and I stood beside him and he brought me out to the door of the shrine and there was a white animal, half mule and half donkey with wings on its side with which it propelled its feet, putting down each forefoot at the limit of its sight, and he mounted me on it. Then he went out with me, keeping close by my side."

In his story al-Hasan continued: "The Messenger and Gabriel went their way until they arrived at the shrine at Jerusalem. There he found Abraham, Moses and Jesus among a company of the prophets. The Messenger acted as their leader in prayer. . . . Then the Messenger returned to Mecca and in the morning he told the Quraysh what had happened. Most of them said: 'By God, this is a plain absurdity! A caravan takes a month to go to Syria and a month to return and can Muhammad do the return journey in one night?' At this many Muslims gave up their faith; some went to Abu Bakr and said: 'What do you think of your friend now, Abu Bakr? He alleges he went to Jerusalem last night and prayed there and came back to Mecca.' Abu Bakr replied that they were lying about the Messenger. But they replied that he was at that very moment in the shrine telling the people about it. Abu Bakr said: 'If he says so, then it must be true. And what is so surprising in that? He tells me that communications from God from heaven to earth come to him in an hour of a day or night and I believe him, and that is more extraordinary than that at which you boggle!'

"Abu Bakr then went to the Messenger and asked him if these reports were true, and when he said they were, he asked him to describe Jerusalem to him." Al-Hasan said that [as a small child] he was lifted up so that he could see the Messenger speaking as he told Abu Bakr what Jerusalem was like. Whenever Muhammad described a part of it, Abu Bakr said: "That's true. I testify that you are the Messenger of God!" until he had completed the description, and then the Messenger said: "And you, Abu Bakr, are the Witness to Truth."

But the entire incident of the Night Journey was, as Ibn Ishaq had warned at the outset, a grave trial of faith for some of the early Muslims.

Al-Hasan continued: "God sent down the verse (Quran 13:62) concerning those who had left Islam on this account: 'We made you a vision which we showed you only for a test to men and the accursed tree in the Quran. We put them in fear, but it only adds to their heinous error.'" Such is al-Hasan's story. (*Life* 263–265) [IBN ISHAQ 1955: 181–182]

This celebrated Night Journey, a frequent subject of Islamic art and legend, was the cornerstone of the Muslim attachment to Jerusalem. How-

ever, there was soon connected to it another event in the life of Muhammad,
which had to do with a heavenly rather than an earthly voyage, his mi-
raculous Ascension into heaven, and we shall see it in that celestial context
in chapter 4 below.

13. Losses, Personal and Political

Muhammad's position was precarious, and it became even more so when,
during the single year 619 C.E., he was deprived of two strong supports,
his uncle Abu Talib, his chief shield against the malevolent Quraysh, and
his wife Khadija, the first to believe in his mission. Muhammad had mar-
ried Khadija in 595 C.E., when he was twenty-five and she, reputedly, but
certainly mistakenly, was forty. She bore him in any event a number of
sons, all of whom died in infancy, as well as four daughters—Zaynab, Ru-
qayya, Umm Kulthum, and Fatima. In the years that followed Khadija's
death, and when he was in his fifties, Muhammad married Sawda, then
Abu Bakr's daughter Aisha, Umar's daughter Hafsa, Hind, Zaynab
daughter of Jahsh, Umm Salama, Juwayriyya, Ramla or Umm Habiba,
Safiyya, and Maymuna. None of them bore him children, however, though
he had a son, Ibrahim, by his Coptic concubine Mary. Ibrahim too died an
infant.

If the loss of Khadija was a strong personal blow, the implications of
the death of his chief protector, Abu Talib, soon became apparent.

His people opposed him more bitterly than ever, apart from the
few lower-class people who believed in him. . . . The Apostle offered
himself to the tribes of Arabs at the fairs whenever the opportunity
came, summoning them to God and telling them that he was a prophet
who had been sent. He used to ask them to believe in him and protect
him until God should make clear to them the message with which He
had charged His prophet.

Muhammad's own growing desperation was matched by the implaca-
ble opposition of Abu Lahab. The conflict between the two men had by now
descended to a deep personal animosity.

I heard my father telling Rabiᶜa ibn Abbad that when he was a
youngster with his father in Mina the Apostle used to stop by the Arab
encampments and tell them that he was the Apostle of God who ordered
them to worship Him and not associate anything with Him and to renounce the rival gods which they worshiped, and believe in His Apostle
and protect him until God made plain His purpose in sending him.
There followed him an artful spruce fellow with two sidelocks of hair

and wearing an Aden cloak. When the Apostle finished his appeal, he used to say: "This fellow wishes only to get you to strip off al-Lat and al-Uzza from your necks. . . . Don't obey him and take no notice of him." I asked my father who the man was who followed the Apostle and contradicted what he said, and he answered that it was his uncle Abd al-Uzza ibn Abd al-Muttalib known as Abu Lahab. (*Life* 281–282) [IBN ISHAQ 1955: 194–195]

14. An Invitation from Yathrib

As his situation in Medina progressively deteriorated Muhammad turned to other places and other people, if not for help, then at least for asylum. An appeal to the Thaqif of nearby Ta'if, longtime rivals of the Quraysh, proved unavailing, as did visits to the bedouin collected at the local fairs.

The Apostle offered himself to the tribes of the Arabs at the fairs whenever opportunity came, summoning them and telling them that he was a prophet who had been sent. He used to ask them to believe in him and protect him until God should make it clear to them the message with which he had charged his prophet. (*Life* 281–282) [IBN ISHAQ 1955: 195]

The petitioning finally paid off, however. Among those who heard the Prophet's pleas were visitors from the oasis of Yathrib, some 275 miles to the north of Mecca. Yathrib, later named "The City (medina) of the Prophet," or simply Medina, was an agricultural settlement of mixed Arab and Jewish population. Ibn Ishaq regarded both the encounter and the presence of Jews at Yathrib as providential.

When God wished to display His religion openly and to glorify His Prophet and to fulfill His promise to him, the time came when he met a number of "Helpers" [that is, future converts to Islam at Medina] at one of the (Meccan) fairs. . . . They said that when the Messenger met them he learned by inquiry that they were of the (tribe of the) Khazraj and were allies of the Jews (there). He invited them to sit with him and he expounded to them Islam and recited the Quran to them. Now God had prepared the way for Islam in that they (the Khazraj) lived side by side with the Jews (of Medina), who were people of the Scriptures and knowledge, while they themselves were polytheists and idolaters. They had often raided them in their district and whenever bad feelings arose the Jews used to say to them, "A Prophet will be sent soon. His day is at hand. We shall follow him and kill you by his aid just as Ad and Iram perished." So when they (the Khazraj) heard the Messenger's message they said to one another, "This is the very Prophet of whom the Jews warned us. Don't let them get to him before us!" Thereupon they accepted his teaching and became Muslims, saying, "We have left our people, for no tribe is so divided by hatred and rancor as they. Perhaps God will unite them through you. So let us go to them and invite them to this religion of yours; and if God unites them in it, then no man will be mightier than you." Thus saying they returned to Medina as believers.

In the following year twelve "Helpers" attended the fair and met at al-Aqaba (a place near Mecca)—this was the first Aqaba—where they gave the Messenger the "pledge of women" (cf. Quran 60:12). . . . "I was present at Aqaba [one of the participants reported]. There were twelve of us and we pledged ourselves to the Prophet after the manner of women and that was before (the obligation of) war was enjoined, the undertaking being that we should associate nothing with God; we should not steal; we should not commit fornication; nor kill our offspring; we should not slander our neighbors; we should not disobey him (Muhammad) in what was right. If we fulfilled this paradise would be ours; if we committed any of these sins it was for God to punish or forgive us as He pleased. . . ."

(The next year) the Muslim "Helpers" came to the fair with the pilgrims of their people who were polytheists. They met the Messenger at Aqaba during the days following upon the day of the (Hajj) sacrifice, when God intended to honor them and to help His Messenger and strengthen Islam and to humiliate heathenism and its devotees. . . . Maʿbad ibn Kaʿb told me that his brother Abdullah had told him that his father Kaʿb ibn Malik said: . . . "We slept that night among our people in the caravan until, when a third of the night had passed, we went stealing softly like sandgrouse to our appointment with the Messenger as far as the gully by al-Aqaba. There were seventy-three men with two of our women. . . . We gathered together in the gully, waiting until the Messenger came with his uncle al-Abbas, who was at that time a polytheist, though he wanted to be present at his nephew's business and make certain that he received a firm guarantee.

"When we sat down al-Abbas was the first to speak and said: 'O people of Khazraj [the Arabs used that term to cover the tribes of both the Khazraj and the Aws]. You know Muhammad's situation among us. We have protected him from his own people who think as we do about him. He lives in honor and safety among his people, but he will turn to you and join you. If you think you can be faithful to what you promised him and protect him from his opponents, then assume the burden you have undertaken. But if you think you will betray and abandon him after he has gone out with you, then leave him now, for he is safe where he is.' We replied, 'We have heard what you say. You speak, O Messenger, and choose for yourself and for your Lord what you wish.'

"The Messenger spoke and recited the Quran and invited me to God and recommended Islam, and then said: 'I invite your allegiance on the basis that you protect me as you would your women and children.' Al-Bara took his hand and said: 'By Him who sent you with the truth, we will protect you as we protect our women. We give our alliance and we are men of war possessing arms which have been passed on from father to son.' While al-Bara was speaking, Abu al-Haytham ibn al-Tayyihan interrupted him and said: 'O Messenger, we have ties with other men—he meant the Jews—and if we sever them, perhaps when we have done that and God will have given us victory, will you return to your people and leave us?' The Messenger smiled and said, 'No, blood is blood and blood not to be paid for is blood not to be paid for. I am of you and you are of me. I will war against those who war against you and be at peace with those at peace with you.'" (*Life* 288–297) [IBN ISHAQ 1955: 198–204]

15. A Turn to Armed Resistance

In the period of time that elapsed between the two meetings at Aqaba near Mecca, another event commemorated in the Quran had occurred, one with enormous political consequences for the nascent Islamic community: a formal rejection of passive resistance to persecution and a turn to the use of force.

The Messenger had not been given permission to fight or allowed to shed blood before the second (pledge of) Aqaba. He had simply been ordered to call men to God and to endure insult and forgive the innocent. The Quraysh had persecuted his followers, seducing some from their religion and exiling others from their country. They had to choose whether to give up their religion, be mistreated at home, or to flee the country, some to Abyssinia, others to Medina.

When the Quraysh became insolent toward God and rejected His gracious purpose, accused His Prophet of lying, and ill treated and exiled those who served Him and proclaimed His unity, believed in His Prophet and held fast to His religion, He gave permission for His Messenger to fight and protect himself against those who wronged them and treated them badly.

The first verse which was sent down on this subject from what I have heard from Urwa ibn al-Zubayr and other learned persons was:

"Permission is granted those (to take up arms) who fight because they were oppressed. God is certainly able to give help to those who were driven away from their homes for no other reason than that they said "Our Lord is God." And if God had not restrained some men through some others, monasteries, churches, synagogues and mosques, where the name of God is honored most, would have been razed. God will surely help those who help Him.—Verily, God is all-powerful and all-mighty—Those who would be firm in devotion, pay the tithe, and enjoin what is good and forbid what is wrong, if we give them authority in the land. But the result of things rests with God." (Quran 22:39–41)

The meaning is: "I have allowed them to fight only because they were unjustly treated, while their sole offense against men is that they worship God. When they are in the ascendent they will establish prayer, pay the poor tax, enjoin kindness and forbid iniquity, that is, the Prophet and his companions, all of them." Then God sent down to him (the verse): "Fight so there is no more persecution," that is, until no believer is seduced from his religion, "and the religion is God's," that is, until God alone is worshiped (Quran 2:193).

This permission to fight, to turn from passive to active resistance to the Quraysh, was no trifling matter, as its divine sanction shows. The Quraysh's commercial enterprises were protected by their own religiously sanctioned prohibitions against violence and bloodshed during the months of pilgrimage and the annual fairs that were connected to it.

16. The Hijra or Migration to Medina
(622 C.E.)

When God had given permission to fight, and this clan of the "Helpers" had pledged their support to him in Islam and to help him and his followers, and the Muslims had taken refuge with them, the Messenger commanded his companions to emigrate to Medina and to link up with their brethren the "Helpers." "God will make for you brethren and houses in which you may be safe." So they went out in companies, and the Messenger stayed in Mecca waiting for the Lord's permission to leave Mecca and migrate to Medina. (*Life* 314) [IBN ISHAQ 1955: 204]

Thus the arrangements were now complete and the hijra, *the migration of Muslims to Mecca began, though gradually and with great caution.*

After his companions had left, the Messenger stayed at Mecca waiting for permission to migrate. Except for Abu Bakr and Ali, none of his supporters were left but those who were under restraint and those who had been forced to apostatize. The former kept asking the Messenger for permission to migrate and he would answer, "Don't be in a hurry; it may be that God will give you a companion." Abu Bakr hoped that it would be Muhammad himself.

When the Quraysh saw that the Messenger (now) had a party and companions not of their tribe and outside their territory, and that his companions had migrated to join them, and knew that they had settled in a new home and had gained protectors, they feared that the Messenger might join them, since they knew that he had decided to fight them. So they assembled in their council chamber, the house of Qusayy ibn Kilab, where all their important business was conducted, to take counsel what they should do in regard to the Messenger, for they were now in fear of him.

After a discussion of various possibilities, it was Muhammad's archrival Abu Jahl who took the floor. He knew well how to play upon at least the religious anxieties of his fellow Quraysh.

"Muhammad alleges that if you follow him you will be kings of the Arabs and the Persians. Then after death you will be raised to gardens like those of the Jordan. But if you do not follow him you will be slaughtered, and when you are raised from the dead you will be burned in the fire of hell."

Abu Jahl had a plan, however.

. . . Each clan should provide a young, powerful, well-born aristocratic warrior; that each of them should be equipped with a sharp sword; and that each of them should strike a blow at him and kill him. Thus they would be relieved of him, and the responsibility for his blood would lie on all the clans. The Banu Abd Manaf could not fight them all and would accept the blood-money to which they would all contribute. . . . Having come to a decision, the people dispersed.

Then Gabriel came to the Messenger and said, "Do not sleep tonight on the bed on which you usually sleep." Before much of the night had passed they [the deputized assassins] assembled at his door waiting for him to go to sleep so they might fall upon him. When the Messenger saw what they were doing, he told Ali to lie on his bed and wrap himself in his green Hadrami mantle; for no harm would befall him. He himself used to sleep in that mantle. . . .

When the Messenger decided to go, he came to Abu Bakr and the two of them left by a window in the back of the latter's house and made for a cave on Thawr, a mountain below Mecca. Having entered, Abu Bakr ordered his son Abdullah to listen to what people were saying and to come to them by night with the day's news. . . . The two of them stayed in the cave for three days. When the Quraysh missed the Messenger they offered a hundred she-camels to anyone who would bring them back. During the day Abdullah was listening to the plans and conversations and would come at night with the news. (Abu Bakr's freedman) Amir used to pasture his flocks with the shepherds of Mecca and when night fell would bring them to the cave where they milked them and slaughtered some.

At Medina meanwhile Muhammad's arrival was eagerly awaited.

Muhammad ibn Ja‘far ibn al-Zubayr from Urwa ibn al-Zubayr from Abd al-Rahman ibn Uwaymir ibn Sa‘ told me, saying, men of my tribe who were the Messenger's companions told me: "When we heard that the Messenger had left Mecca and we were eagerly expecting his arrival, we used to go out after morning prayers to the lava tract beyond our land to await him. This we did until there was no more shade left, then we went indoors in the hot season. On the day the Messenger arrived we had sat as we always had until there being no more shade we went inside, and it was then that the Prophet arrived. The first to see him was a Jew. He had seen what we were in the habit of doing and that we were expecting the arrival of the Messenger, and he called out at the top of his voice, 'O Banu Qayla, your luck has come!' So we went out to greet the Messenger, who was in the shadow of a palm tree with Abu Bakr, who was of like age. Now most of us had never seen the Messenger and as the people crowded around him they did not know him from Abu Bakr until the shade left him and Abu Bakr got up with his mantle and shielded him from the sun, and then we knew."

Ali stayed in Mecca for three days and nights until . . . he joined the Messenger and (also) lodged at Kulthum's house. . . . The Messenger ordered that a mosque be built and he stayed with Abu Ayyub until the mosque and his houses were completed. The Messenger joined in the activity to encourage the Muslims to work and both the (Meccan) "Migrants" and the (Medinese) "Helpers" labored hard. . . . The Mes-

senger stayed in Medina from the month of First Rabi‘ to Safar of the
following year until his mosque and his quarters were built. This tribe
of the "Helpers" all accepted Islam, and every house of the "Helpers"
accepted Islam except Khatma, Waqif, Wa’il and Umayya who were
Aws Allah, a clan of the Aws who clung to their paganism. (*Life* 323–
340) [IBN ISHAQ 1955: 221–230]

17. The Constitution of Medina

*Included in Ibn Ishaq's Life of the Prophet is a document that purports to
record the political arrangements contracted between Muhammad and his
partisans and the citizens of Medina. There is little reason to doubt its
authenticity since it constitutes Medina the same kind of "protected" enclave
found elsewhere in Arabia, though here not around a shrine, as at Mecca,
for example, but on the authority of a recognized "holy man." By it the
contracting parties agreed to recognize Muhammad as their leader and to
accept his judgments. In so doing they were acknowledging, as was the
Prophet himself, that they were one community or umma, not yet uniquely
composed of Muslims, but committed to defend its own joint interests, or
what was now newly defined to be the common good.*

The Messenger wrote a document concerning the "Migrants" and
the "Helpers" in which he made a friendly agreement with the Jews and
established them in their religion and their property, and stated the
reciprocal obligations as follows: In the Name of God, the Compassionate, the Merciful. This is a document from Muhammad the Prophet
[concerning the relations] between the believers and Muslims of the
Quraysh and Yathrib [Medina], and those who followed them and joined
them and labored with them. They are one community to the exclusion of all men. The Quraysh emigrants according to their present custom shall pay all the blood-money within their number and shall re-
deem their prisoners with the kindness and justice common among
believers. . . .

A believer shall not take as an ally the freedman of another Muslim
against him. The God-fearing believers shall be against the rebellious or
him who spreads injustice, or sin or enmity or corruption between
believers. A believer shall not slay a believer for the sake of an unbeliever, nor shall he aid an unbeliever against a believer. God's protection is one, the least of them may give protection to a stranger on their
behalf. Believers are friends one to the other to the exclusion of out-
siders. To the Jew who follows us belongs help and equality. He shall

not be wronged nor his enemies aided. The peace of believers is indivisible and no separate peace shall be made when believers are fighting in the way of God. Conditions must be fair and equitable to all. . . .

The Jews must bear their expenses and the Muslims their expenses. Each must help the other against anyone who attacks the people of this document. They must seek mutual advice and consultation, and loyalty is a protection against treachery. A man is not liable for his ally's misdeeds. The wronged must be helped. The Jews must pay with the believers so long as war lasts. Yathrib [Medina] shall be sanctuary for the people of this document. . . . If any dispute or controversy should arise it must be referred to God and to Muhammad the Messenger of God. (*Life* 341–343) [IBN ISHAQ 1955: 231–233]

18. Jewish Opposition

Almost as soon as the Prophet and his followers had settled down in Medina, or Yathrib, as it was still called at that time, his relations with the Jews of the place began to deteriorate. Soon after his first great victory over his Meccan rivals at Badr Wells, the conflict with the Jews turned to open warfare, as we shall see, but commercial, religious, and psychological differences may have surfaced even before. Muhammad was, after all, claiming to be a prophet in the tradition of Moses and the Torah. In the Jewish community of Medina he encountered, perhaps contrary to his own expectations, a rebuff from the contemporary partisans of that same tradition.

About this time the Jewish rabbis showed hostility to the Messenger in envy, hatred and malice, because God had chosen His Messenger from the Arabs. They were joined by men from (the Arab tribes of) al-Aws and al-Khazraj who had obstinately clung to their heathen religion. They were hypocrites, clinging to the polytheism of their fathers, denying the resurrection; yet when Islam appeared and their people flocked to it they were compelled to accept it to save their lives. But in secret they were hypocrites whose inclination was towards the Jews because these latter considered the Messenger a liar and strove against Islam.

It was the Jewish rabbis who used to annoy the Prophet with questions and introduce confusion, so as to confound the truth with falsity. The (verses of the) Quran used to come down in reference to questions of theirs, though some of the questions about what was allowed and forbidden came from the Muslims themselves. . . . The first hundred verses of the Sura of the Cow (2:1–100) came down in reference to these Jewish rabbis and the hypocrites of the Aws and Khazraj, according to what I have been told, and God knows best. *(Life* 351*)* [IBN ISHAQ 1955: 239–240]

19. Fighting in the Sacred Month

The first real fighting between the Emigrants and the Quraysh took place in December of 623 C.E. and provoked a moral crisis. Muhammad had sent out a raiding party of only eight Muslims with sealed orders. The orders commanded them to spy out the Quraysh at Nakhla on the road between Mecca and Ta᾽if and "find out for us what they are doing." What the Quraysh were doing was transporting, under very light escort, camel-loads of raisins and leather from Ta᾽if to Mecca. Ibn Ishaq continues the story.

When the caravan saw them [that is, the Muslims] they were afraid because they had camped nearby. Ukkasha [that is, one of the Emigrants], who had shaved his head (like a pilgrim), looked down on the Quraysh, and when they saw him they felt safe and said: "They are pilgrims; we have nothing to fear from them."

The raiders took counsel among themselves, for this was the last day of Rajab, and they said: "If we leave them alone tonight they will get into the *haram* and will be safe from us; and if we kill them, we will kill them in a sacred month." So they were hesitant and feared to attack them.

Finally the Muslims decided to attack, holy month or not. Some of the Quraysh were killed and the caravan was taken back to Medina together with two captives. They had set aside a fifth of the booty for the Prophet— this was reportedly the first time this practice, which later became customary, was followed—and divided the rest among themselves, but on their entry into Medina they found a cold reception.

When they came to the Apostle, he said: "I did not order you to fight in the sacred month," and he held the caravan and the two prisoners in suspense and refused to take anything from them. When the Apostle said that, the men were in despair and thought they were doomed. Their Muslim brethren reproached them for what they had done, and the Quraysh said, "Muhammad and his companions have violated the sacred month, shed blood therein, taken booty and captured men." . . . The Jews of Medina turned this raid into an ill omen against the Apostle. . . . And when there was much talk about it, God sent down to His Apostle:

They ask you concerning fighting in the prohibited month. Say: "Fighting therein is a grave offense; but graver it is in the sight of God to prevent access to the path of God, to deny Him, to prevent access to the sacred shrine and drive out its members. Tumult and oppression are worse than slaughter." (Quran 2:217)

. . . And when the Quran came down about that and God relieved the Muslims of their anxiety in the matter, the Apostle took the caravan and the prisoners. (*Life* 424–426) [IBN ISHAQ 1955: 287–288]

20. The Battle at the Badr Wells

This is the background against which a major military operation unfolded in March of 624 C.E. News came to Muhammad that a very large caravan was on its way southward from Palestine to Mecca. Muhammad summoned the Muslims of Medina and said, " 'This is the Quraysh caravan containing their property. Go out and attack it; perhaps God will give it as prey.' The people answered his summons, some eagerly, others reluctantly because they had not thought that the Messenger would go to war." The Quraysh heard of the intended attack and mobilized their own forces, thus setting up a major confrontation between the Muslims and their opponents at Mecca. During the preliminaries, when Muhammad was positioning his forces, the following interesting incident is reported.

Al-Hubab ibn al-Mundhir ibn al-Jamuh said to the Messenger: "Is this the place which God has ordered you to occupy, so that we can neither advance nor withdraw from it, or is it a matter of opinion and military tactics?" When Muhammad replied that it was the latter al-Hubab pointed out to him that this was not the place to stop but that they should go on to the water-hole nearest the enemy and halt there, stop up the wells beyond it and construct a cistern for themselves so that they would have plenty of water. . . . The Messenger agreed that it was an excellent plan and it was immediately carried out. (*Life* 439) [IBN ISHAQ 1955: 296–297]

The fighting began and at first it went badly for the outnumbered Muslims. The Prophet rallied his troops, however, with this promise.

Then the Messenger went forth to the people and incited them saying, "By God in whose hand is the soul of Muhammad, no man will be slain this day fighting against them (the Quraysh) with steadfast courage, advancing and not retreating, but God will cause him to enter Paradise." (*Life* 445) [IBN ISHAQ 1955: 300]

The Muslims were in the end victorious, with a great effect on their own and the Quraysh's morale for the rest of the struggle between them. The jubilation that followed was tempered only by a quarrel about the distribution of the rich spoils.

They ask you (O Muhammad), about the spoils of war. Say: the spoils of war belong to God and the Messenger, so keep your duty to God and adjust the matter of your difference and obey God and his Messenger, if you are true believers. (Quran 8:1)

Thus the event is referred to in the opening verse of Sura 8, called "The Spoils." Most of the sura is in fact devoted to the events surrounding the battle of Badr and is interpreted at length in Ibn Ishaq's Life of the Messenger of God (IBN ISHAQ 1955: 321–327).

21. The Fate of the Banu Qaynuqaᶜ

After the success at Badr, the issue of the Jews of Medina surfaced once again, or at least as it concerned one tribe of them, the Banu Qaynuqaᶜ.

Meanwhile there was the affair of the Banu Qaynuqaᶜ. The Messenger assembled them in their market and addressed them as follows: "O Jews, beware lest God bring upon you the vengeance He brought upon the Quraysh and become Muslims. You know I am the Prophet who has been sent—you will find that in your Scriptures and God's covenant with you." They replied, "O Muhammad, you seem to think that we are your people. Do not deceive yourself because you encountered a people with no knowledge of war and got the better of them; for by God, if we fight you, you will find that we are real men!"

A freedman of the family of Zayd ibn Thabit from Saᶜid ibn Jubayr from Iqrima from Ibn Abbas told me that the latter said that the following verses came down about them: "Say to those who disbelieve: you will be vanquished and gathered to Hell, an evil resting place. You have already had a sign in the two forces which met," that is, the Messenger's companions at Badr and the Quraysh. "One force fought in the way of God; the other, disbelievers, thought they saw double their own force with their very eyes. God strengthens with His help whomever He wills. Verily in that is an example for the discerning" (Quran 3:12–13).

Asim ibn Umar ibn Qatada said that the Banu Qaynuqaᶜ were the first of the Jews to break their agreement with the Messenger and to go to war (with him), between Badr and (the battle of) Uhud, and the Messenger besieged them until they surrendered unconditionally. Abdullah ibn Ubayy went to him when God put them in his power and said, "O Muhammad, deal kindly with my clients"—the Banu Qaynuqaʿ were allies of Khazraj—but the Messenger put him off. He repeated the words and the Messenger turned away from him, whereupon Abdullah thrust his hand into the collar of the Messenger's robe; the Messenger was so angry that his face became almost black. He said, "Confound you, let me go." Abdullah answered, "No, by God, I will not let you go until you deal kindly with my clients. Four hundred men without mail and three hundred mailed protected me from all my enemies; would you cut them down in one morning? By God, I am a man who fears that circumstances may change." The Messenger said, "You can have them."

. . . (Thus) when the Banu Qaynuqaʿ fought against the Messenger Abdullah ibn Ubayy espoused their cause and defended them, but Ubada ibn al-Samit, who had the same alliance with them as had Abdullah, went to the Messenger and renounced all responsibility for them in favor of God and His Messenger, saying, "O Messenger of God, I take God and His Messenger as my friends, and I renounce my agreement and friendship with these unbelievers." It was concerning him and Abdullah ibn Ubayy that this passage from the Sura of the Table came down: "O you who believe, take not Jews and Christians as friends. They are friends one of another. Who of you takes them as friends is one of them. God will not guide the unjust people. You can see those in whose heart there is sickness," that is, Abdullah ibn Ubayy when he said "I fear a change of circumstances." Acting hastily in regard to them they say we fear a change of circumstances may overtake us. Perhaps God will bring victory or an act from Him so that they will be sorry for their secret thoughts, and those who believe will say, Are these those who swore by God their most binding oath that they were surely with you? As for God's words "Verily God and His Messenger are your friends, and those who believe, who perform prayer, give alms and bow down in homage," they refer to Ubada taking God and His Messenger and the believers as his friends and renouncing his agreement and friendship with the Banu Qaynuqaʿ: "Those who take God and His Messenger and the believers as friends, they are God's party, they are victorious" (Quran 3:51–56). (*Life* 545–547) [IBN ISHAQ 1955: 363–364]

22. From Badr to the Battle of the Trench

The triumph of Badr was followed in the next year by a full-scale attack of three thousand foot soldiers and two hundred cavalry mustered by the Quraysh for an assault on Medina, an event commemorated in Muslim history as the Battle of Uhud. It ended in a severe setback for the Muslims.

The Muslims were put to flight and the enemy slew many of them. It was a day of trial and testing in which God honored several with martyrdom, until the enemy got at the Messenger who was struck with a stone so that he fell on his side and one of his teeth was smashed, his face gashed and his lip injured. The man who wounded him was Utba ibn Abi Waqqas. (*Life* 571) [IBN ISHAQ 1955: 380]

The Arabs were not accustomed to hostilities that pitched son against father or brother against brother, and feelings ran intensely high on both sides. The Arab tradition particularly recalled the behavior of one Quraysh woman.

According to what Salih ibn Kaysan told me, Hind, the daughter of Utba and the women with her stopped to mutilate the Messenger's dead companions. They cut off their ears and noses and Hind made them into anklets and collars. . . . She cut out Hamza's liver and chewed it, but she was not able to swallow it and threw it away. Then she mounted a high rock and shrieked at the top of her voice:

> We have paid you back for Badr
> And a war that follows a war is always violent.
> I could not bear the loss of Utba
> Nor my brother and his uncle and my first-born.
> I have slaked my vengeance and fulfilled my vow. . . .

When (the Quraysh leader) Abu Sufyan wanted to leave, he went to the top of the mountain and shouted loudly, saying, "You have done a fine work. Victory in war goes by turns: today is in exchange for the day of Badr. Show your superiority, Hubal," that is, vindicate your religion. The Messenger told Umar to go up and answer him and say, "God is most high and most glorious. We are not equal: our dead are in paradise, yours are in hell." At this answer Abu Sufyan said to Umar, "Come up here to me." The Messenger told him to go and see what Abu Sufyan was up to. When he came Abu Sufyan said, "I adjure you by God, Umar, have we killed Muhammad?" "By God, you have not, he is listening to what you are saying right now," Umar replied. Abu Sufyan said, "I regard you as more truthful and reliable than Ibn Qami'a, referring to the latter's claim that he had killed Muhammad. (*Life* 581–583) [IBN ISHAQ 1955: 385–386]

Just as in the sequel of Badr Muhammad turned to the Jewish tribe of the Qaynuqa, *so the direct or indirect consequence of Uhud was the expulsion of a second Jewish tribe from the Medina association, the Banu al-Nadir. In this case the provocation was the report of a threat by members*

*of the Banu al-Nadir against the Prophet's life. The response was prompt
and direct, an assault on their redoubts in the Medina oasis.*

The Jews took refuge in their forts and the Messenger ordered the
palm-trees should be cut down and burnt. And they (the Banu al-Nadir)
called out to him, "O Muhammad, you have prohibited wanton destruction and blamed those guilty of it. Why then are you cutting down
and burning our palm-trees?" Now there were a number of the (Arab
tribe of the) Banu Awf ibn al-Khazraj . . . who had sent to the Banu
al-Nadir saying, "Stand firm and protect yourselves, for we will not
betray you. If you are attacked we will fight with you and if you are
turned out we will go with you." Accordingly they waited for the help
they had promised, but they (the Banu Awf) did nothing and God cast
terror into their hearts. The Banu al-Nadir then asked the Messenger to
deport them and to spare their lives on condition that they could retain
all their property which they could carry on camels, armor excepted,
and he agreed. So they loaded their camels with what they could carry.
Men were destroying their houses down to the lintel of the door, which
they put on the back of their camels and went off with it. Some went
to Khaybar and others went to Syria.

If this was the end of the Banu al-Nadir in Medina, it went bravely.

Abdullah ibn Abi Bakr told me that he was told that the Banu
al-Nadir carried off their women and children and property with tam-
bourines and pipes and singing girls playing behind them. . . . They
went with such pomp and splendor as had never been seen in any tribe
in their days. They left their property to the Messenger and it became
his personal possession to dispose of as he wished. He divided it among
the first emigrants (from Mecca to Medina), to the exclusion of the
"Helpers." . . .

Concerning the Banu al-Nadir, the Sura of the Exile (59) came
down in which is recorded how God wreaked his vengeance on them
and gave His Messenger power over them and how He dealt with them.
(*Life* 652–654) [IBN ISHAQ 1955: 437–438]

*It was at this point in Muhammad's career that occurred the first of
the raids against Dumat al-Jandal, the present-day oasis of al-Jawf. The
Muslim geographers measured Duma at ten marches from Kufa, ten from
Damascus, and thirteen from Medina. Though distant from the Muslim
base, the oasis was well known to the Arabs since tradition recorded that it
too was the site of an annual fair and was protected by the same guarantees
of security as the other marts. Ibn Ishaq passes over the Duma expedition*

of 626 with the briefest of mentions, but others supply additional details. The raid, if such it was, took place in the month of First Rabi` *of the fifth year of the Hijra, and the Prophet remained there for about a month. Indeed, the entire affair has about it the air of a reconnaissance in force— there were a thousand Muslims, a considerable force, but hardly enough to take a fortified oasis—or of an opportunistic foray that had found no opportunity along the caravan routes and had simply came to rest at Dumat al-Jandal.*

The abortive expedition to Dumat al-Jandal, which produced neither booty nor even a sense of success, was Muhammad's only political act during a stretch of nearly eighteen months in 625–627 C.E. The long period of quietude, and the absence of any tangible profits from what had at first appeared an enormously successful enterprise, may have emboldened the opposition once again to attempt to unseat the Prophet. The lead was taken in March 627 by some of the Banu al-Nadir who had gone into exile at Khaybar.

A number of Jews who had formed a party against the Messenger . . . went to the Quraysh at Mecca and invited them to join them in an attack upon the Messenger so they could get rid of him together. The Quraysh said, "You, O Jews, are the first people of Scripture and know the nature of our dispute with Muhammad. Is our religion the best or is his?" They replied that certainly the Quraysh's religion was better than Muhammad's and had a better claim to be in the right. And it was in this connection that God sent down (the verses of the Quran): "Have you not considered those to whom a part of Scripture was given and yet believe in idols and false deities and say to those who disbelieve, these are more rightly guided than those who believe? . . . We gave the family of Abraham the Scripture and the wisdom and we gave them a great kingdom and some of them believed in it and some of them turned from it, and hell is sufficient for (their) burning" (Quran 4:51–54).

These words (of the Jews) rejoiced the Quraysh and they responded gladly to their invitation to fight the Messenger, and they assembled and made their preparations. Then that company of Jews went off to Ghatafan of Qays Aylan and invited them to fight the Messenger and told them that they would act in concert with them and that the Quraysh had followed their lead in the matter; so they too joined in with them. . . .

When the Messenger heard of their intention he drew a trench around Medina and worked at it himself, encouraging the Muslims with hope of reward in heaven. The Muslims worked very hard with him, but the disaffected held back and began to hide their real object by working slackly and stealing away to their families without the Messenger's permission or knowledge.

When the Messenger had finished the trench, the Quraysh came and encamped where the torrent beds of Ruma meet between al-Juruf and Zughaba with ten thousand of their black mercenaries and their followers from the Banu Kinana and the people of Tihama. Ghatafan too came with their followers from Najd and halted at Dhanab Naqma towards the direction of Uhud. The Messenger and the Muslims came out with three thousand men having Sal at their backs. He pitched his camp there with the trench between him and his foes, and he gave orders for the women and children to be taken up to the forts (of the oasis). . . .

The situation became serious and fear was everywhere. The enemy came at them from above and below until the believers imagined vain things and disaffection was rife among the disaffected, to the point that Mu attib ibn Qushayr said, "Muhammad used to promise that we would eat the treasures of Khusraw and Caesar and today not one of us can feel safe going to the privy!" It reached such a point that Aws ibn al-Qayzi, one of the Banu Haritha ibn al-Harith, said to the people, "Our houses are exposed to the enemy"—this he said before a large gathering of his people—"so let us go out and return to our home, for it is outside Medina." The Messenger and the polytheists remained (facing each other) twenty days and more, nearly a month, without fighting except for some shooting with arrows, and the siege. (*Life* 669–676) [IBN ISHAQ 1955: 450–454]

Muhammad and his followers were dispirited, but the morale in the camp of the Quraysh was at an even lower pitch. Soon the alliance began to disintegrate, and in the end the siege was broken off and the attackers returned to their homes.

23. The Banu Qurayza

According to the Muslim tradition, the Banu Qurayza, the last major surviving Jewish presence in Medina, had bound themselves by treaty not to assist the enemies of the Prophet. This is precisely what the Qurayza had done, it was alleged, at the instigation of Huyayy ibn Akhtab, the leader of the banished Banu al-Nadir. But there was little need for political reasons for what followed: the motivation is said to have come from on high.

According to what al-Zuhri told me, at the time of the noon prayers Gabriel came to the Messenger wearing an embroidered turban and riding on a mule with a saddle covered with a piece of brocade. He asked the Messenger if he had abandoned fighting, and when he said he had, Gabriel said that the angels had not yet laid aside their arms and that he had just come from pursuing the enemy. "God commands you, Muhammad, to go to the Banu Qurayza. I am about to go to them and shake their stronghold. . . ."

The Messenger besieged them for twenty-five nights until they were sore pressed and God cast terror into their hearts. . . . And when they felt sure that the Messenger would not leave them until he had made an end to them, (their leader) Ka'b ibn Asad said to them: "O Jews, you can see what has happened to you. I offer you three alternatives. Take which you please. We will follow this man and accept him as true, for by God it is plain to you that he is a prophet who has been sent and that it is he that you find mentioned in your Scripture; and then your lives, your property, your women and children will be saved." They said, "We will never abandon the laws of the Torah and never change it for another." He said, "Then if you will not accept this suggestion, let us kill our wives and children and send men with their swords drawn against Muhammad and his companions, leaving no encumbrances behind us, and let God decide between us and Muhammad. If we perish, we perish, and we shall not leave children behind us to cause anxiety. If we conquer, we can acquire other wives and children." They said, "Should we kill those poor creatures? What would be the good of life when they were dead?" He said, "Then if you will not accept this suggestion, tonight is the eve of the sabbath and it may well be that Muhammad and his companions will feel secure from us, so come down and perhaps we can take Muhammad and his companions by surprise." They said, "Are we to profane our sabbath and do on the sabbath what those before us of whom you well know did and were turned into apes?" He answered, "Not a single man among you from the day of your birth has ever passed a night resolved to do what he knows ought to be done."

Then the Banu Qurayza sent to the Messenger saying, "Send us Abu Lubaba (of the Banu Aws) . . . for they were allies of the Aws, that we may consult him." So the Messenger sent him to them, and when they saw him they got up to meet him. The women and children went up to him weeping in his face, and he felt pity for them. They said, "O Abu Lubaba, do you think we should submit to Muhammad's judgment?" He said "Yes," but pointed his hand to his throat, signifying slaughter. Abu Lubaba (later) said, "My feet had not moved from the spot before I knew that I had been false to God and His Messenger." Then he left them and did not go to the Messenger but bound himself to one of the pillars in the mosque saying, "I will not leave this place until God forgives me for what I have done," and he promised that he would never go to the Banu Qurayza and would never be seen in a town in which he had betrayed God and His Messenger.

When the Aws, the former patrons of the Banu Qurayza somewhat hesitantly asked for leniency—they recalled what had happened in the case of the other Jewish clients at Medina—Muhammad asked them if they would be content if one of their own number passed judgment on the Banu Qurayza. They said they would. A certain Sa‘d ibn Mu‘adh was chosen.

Sa‘d said: "I give judgment that the men should be killed, the property divided, and the women and children taken as captives. . . ."

Then the Banu Qurayza surrendered themselves and the Messenger confined them in the quarter of Bint al-Harith, a woman of the Banu al-Najjar. Then the Messenger went out to the market of Medina—which is still the market today—and dug trenches in it. Then he sent for them and struck off their heads in those trenches as they were brought out to him in batches. Among them was the enemy of God Huyayy ibn Aktab and Ka‘b ibn Asas their chief. There were 600 or 700 in all, though some put the figure as high as 800 or 900. As they were being taken out in batches to the Messenger, they asked Ka‘b what he thought would be done to them. He replied, "Will you never understand? Don't you see that the summoner never stops and those who are taken away never return? By God, it is death!" This went on until the Messenger made an end to them. (*Life* 684–690) [IBN ISHAQ 1955: 461–464]

24. The Arrangement at Hudaybiyya

Muhammad's political career seems to follow no predictable course of action. The violent purge of the Banu Qurayza was followed by a surprising announcement: the Prophet intended to return to Mecca, not as an attacker but as a pacific pilgrim intending only to make the Umra.

The Messenger stayed in Medina during the months of Ramadan and Shawwal (in 628 C.E.) and then went out on the ‘umra (or lesser pilgrimage) in Dhu al-Qa‘da with no intention of making war. He called together the Arabs and the neighboring bedouin to march with him, fearing that the Quraysh (in Mecca) would oppose him with arms or prevent his visiting the shrine, as they actually did. Many of the Arabs held back from him, and he went out with the Emigrants and the Helpers and such of the Arabs as stuck to him. He took the sacrificial victims with him and donned the pilgrim garb so that all would know that he did not intend war and that his purpose was to visit the shrine and venerate it. . . .

In his tradition al-Zuhri said: When the Messenger had rested (at Hudaybiyya near Mecca), Budayl ibn Warqa al-Khuza'i came to him with some men of the Khuza'a and asked him what he had come for. He told them he had not come for war but to go on pilgrimage and visit the sacred precincts. . . . Then they returned to the Quraysh and told them what they had heard; but the Quraysh suspected them and spoke roughly to them, "He may not come out wanting war, but by God, he will never come in here against our will nor will the Arabs ever see that we allowed it." The Khaza'a were in fact the Messenger's confidants, both the Muslims and the non-Muslims among them, and they kept him informed of everything that went on in Mecca. . . .

. . . Then they (the Quraysh of Mecca) sent Urwa ibn Mas'ud al-Thaqafi to the Messenger. . . . He came to the Messenger and sat before him and said: "Muhammad, you have collected a mixed people together and then brought them against your own people to destroy them? By God, I think I see you deserted by these people here tomorrow." Now Abu Bakr was sitting behind the Messenger and he said, "Go suck al-Lat's tits! Should we desert him?" . . . Then Urwa began to take hold of the Messenger's beard as he talked to him. Al-Mughira ibn Shu'ba was standing by the Messenger's head clad in mail and he began to hit Urwa's hand as he held the Messenger's beard saying, "Take your hand away from the Messenger's face before you lose it!" Urwa said, "Confound you, how rough and rude you are!" The Messenger smiled and when Urwa asked who the man was he told him that it was his brother's son Urwa ibn Shu'ba, and Urwa said, "You wretch, it was only yesterday that I was wiping your behind!"

The Messenger told him what he told the others, namely that he had not come out for war. Urwa then got up from the Messenger's presence, having noted how his companions treated him. Whenever he performed his ablutions, they ran to get the water he used; if he spat, they ran to it; if a hair of his head fell out, they ran to pick it up. So he returned to the Quraysh and said, "I have seen Khusraw in his kingdom and Caesar in his kingdom and the Negus in his kingdom, but never have I seen a king among a people like Muhammad is among his companions."

At some point in the negotiations the Quraysh decided that their best course of action was to come to some kind of face-saving terms.

. . . Then the Quraysh sent Suhayl ibn Amr to the Messenger with instructions to make peace with him on condition that he should return (to Medina) this year so that none of the Arabs could say that he had made a forcible entry. . . . After a long discussion peace was made and nothing remained but to write the document. Umar leaped up and went to Abu Bakr saying, "Is he not God's Messenger and are we not Muslims, and are not they polytheists?" to which Abu Bakr agreed, and he went on, "Then why should we agree to what is demeaning to our religion?" Abu Bakr replied, "Follow what he says, for I bear witness that he is God's Messenger." Umar said, "And so do I." Then he went to the Messenger and put the same questions, to which the Messenger answered, "I am God's slave and His Messenger. I will not go against His commandment and He will not make me a loser." Umar used to say (afterwards), "I have not ceased giving alms and fasting and praying and freeing slaves because of what I did that day and for fear of what I had said, when I hoped that (my plan) would be better."

Then the Messenger summoned Ali and told him to write, "In the name of God, the Compassionate, the Merciful." Suhayl said, "I do not recognize this; write rather, In thy name, O God." The Messenger told Ali to write the latter and he did so. Then he said, "Write, This is what Muhammad, Messenger of God, has agreed with Suhayl ibn Amr." Suhayl said, "If I confessed that you were God's Messenger I would not have fought you. Write your own name and the name of your father." The Messenger said, "Write, this is what Muhammad ibn Abdullah has agreed with Suhayl ibn Amr: they have agreed to lay aside war for ten years during which men can be safe and refrain from hostilities on condition that if anyone comes to Muhammad without the permission of his guardian he will return him to them; and if anyone of those with Muhammad returns to the Quraysh they will not return him to him. We will not show enmity one to another and there shall be no secret reservation or bad faith. He who wishes to enter into a bond or agreement with Muhammad may do so and whoever wishes to enter into a bond or agreement with the Quraysh may do so." . . .

The Messenger then went on his way back (to Medina), and when he was half-way the Sura of the Victory came down: "We have given you a signal victory that God may forgive you your past sin and the sin which is to come and may complete His favor upon you and guide you on an upright path" (Quran 48:1–2). . . .

No previous victory in Islam was greater than this. There was nothing but battle when men met; but when there was an armistice and war was abolished and men met in safety and held discussion, none talked about Islam intelligently without entering it. In those two years double or more than double as many entered Islam as ever before. (*Life* 746–751) [IBN ISHAQ 1955: 504–507]

25. The Pilgrimage Fulfilled

Muhammad turned from the negotiations, and since the Quraysh had effectively tied their own hands, he sent his troopers in a successful foray against the Jewish oasis of Khaybar to the north of Medina. The point of the Hudaybiyya arrangement was not, however, forgotten in the successful flush of Khaybar.

When the Messenger returned from Khaybar to Medina he stayed there from the first Rabi꜄ until Shawwal, sending out raiding parties and expeditions. Then in Dhu al-Qaꜥda—the month in which the polytheists had prevented him from making the pilgrimage (in the preceding year)—he went out to make the "fulfilled pilgrimage" in place of the ꜥumra [or "lesser pilgrimage"; see chapter 6 below] from which they had excluded him. Those Muslims who had been excluded with him went out in A.H. 7 [February 629 C.E.] and when the Meccans heard it, they got out of his way. . . .

. . . The Messenger married Maymuna daughter of al-Harith on that journey when he was on pilgrimage. (His uncle) al-Abbas gave her to him in marriage [and probably became a Muslim at the same time]. The Messenger remained three days in Mecca. Huwaytib ibn Abd al-Uzza with a few Quraysh came to him on the third day because the Quraysh had entrusted him with the duty of sending the Messenger out of Mecca. They said, "Your time is up, so get out from among us." The Messenger answered, "How would it harm you if you were to let me stay and I gave a wedding feast among you and prepared food and you came too?" They replied, "We don't need your food, so get out." So the Messenger went out and left Abu Rafiꜥ his client in charge of Maymuna until he brought her to him in Sarif. (*Life* 788–790) [IBN ISHAQ 1955: 530–531]

26. "The Truth Has Come and Falsehood Has Passed Away"

The breaking of the armistice concluded between Muhammad and the Qur-aysh of Mecca at Hudaybiyya in 628 C.E. came about not through the principals themselves but by an altercation between two of their bedouin allies. The violation might have been settled in other ways perhaps—the Quraysh appeared willing to negotiate—but in 630 Muhammad judged the occasion fit and the time appropriate for settling accounts with the polytheists of Mecca once and for all.

The Messenger ordered preparations to be made for a foray and Abu Bakr came in to see his daughter (and Muhammad's wife) Aisha as she was moving some of the Messenger's gear. He asked her if the Messenger had ordered her to get things ready and she said he had and that her father had better get ready too. She told him that she did not know where the troops were going, however. Later the Messenger informed the men that he was going to Mecca and ordered them to make preparations. He said, "O God, take their eyes and ears from the Quraysh that we may take them by surprise in their land," and the men got themselves ready. (*Life* 808) [IBN ISHAQ 1955: 544]

The surprise prayed for by Muhammad was granted him, along with other good fortune—Abu Sufyan, the Quraysh leader, was captured by chance before the Muslims reached Mecca and persuaded, despite continuing doubts, to save himself and embrace Islam—and the Meccans' will to resist was at a low ebb.

The Messenger had instructed his commanders when they entered Mecca only to fight those who resisted them, except for a small number [perhaps only four] who were to be killed even if they were found beneath the curtains of the Ka'ba itself. . . . The Messenger after arriving in Mecca, once the populace had settled down, went to the shrine and went round it seven times on his camel, touching the black stone with a stick which he had in his hand. This done, he summoned Uthman ibn Talha and took the keys of the Ka'ba from him, and when the door was opened for him, he went in. There he found a dove made of wood. He broke it in his hands and threw it away. . . . (According to another account) the Messenger entered Mecca on the day of the conquest and it contained 360 idols which Iblis (or Satan) had strengthened with lead. The Messenger was standing by them with a stick in his hand saying, "The truth has come and falsehood has passed away" (Quran 17:81).

Then he pointed at them with his stick and they collapsed on their backs one after another.

When the Messenger had prayed the noon prayer on the day of the conquest (of Mecca), he ordered that all the idols which were around the Kaʿba should be collected and burned with fire and broken up. . . . The Quraysh had put pictures in the Kaʿba including two of Jesus son of Mary and of Mary, on both of whom be peace. Ibn Shihab said: Asma the daughter of Shaqr said that a woman of the Banu Ghassan had joined in the pilgrimage of the Arabs and when she saw a picture of Mary in the Kaʿba she said: "My father and my mother be your ransom! (Mary), you are surely an Arab woman!" The Messenger ordered that the pictures be erased, except those of Jesus and Mary.

A traditionist told me that the Messenger stood at the door of the Kaʿba and said: "There is no god but God alone; He has no associates. He has made good His promise and helped His servant. He alone has put to flight the confederates. Every claim of privilege or blood or property are abolished by me except the custody of the shrine and the watering of the pilgrims. . . . O Quraysh, God has taken from you the haughtiness of paganism and its veneration of ancestors. Man springs from Adam and Adam from dust." Then he recited them this verse: "O men, we created you male and female and made you into peoples and tribes that you may know one another; in truth, the most noble of you in God's sight is the most pious . . ." to the end of the passage (Quran 49:13). Then he added, "O Quraysh, what do you think I am about to do to you?" They replied, "Good, for you are a noble brother, son of a noble brother." He said, "Go your way; you are freed." (*Life* 818–821) [IBN ISHAQ 1955: 550–553]

27. Consolidation of Gains

Troops were dispatched to the neighborhood of Mecca to smash the other idols revered in the holy places around that holy city. Then suddenly there came the last real challenge to Muhammad's political supremacy: a bedouin confederation mustered its forces and marched against the Prophet. The encounter occurred at a place called Hunayn, and though at first there was panic in the Muslim ranks, their numerical superiority finally prevailed and the bedouin were routed.

God has given you victory on many fields, and on the day of Hunayn, when you exulted in your numbers, though they availed you nothing, and the earth, vast as it was, was straitened for you. Then you turned back in flight. Then God sent down His peace of reassurance on His Messenger and upon the believers, and sent down hosts you could not see, and punished those who did not believe. Such is the reward of disbelievers. (Quran 9:25–26)

Even before the occupation of Mecca Muhammad had been casting his net of raids and expeditions in an ever wider arc. After the battle of Hunayn, toward the end of that same eventful year of 630 C.E.—his last surviving son, the infant Ibrahim, born of the Egyptian Christian concubine named Mary, also died in that year—he prepared his troops for an expedition northward and deep across the frontiers of the Byzantine Empire to the town of Tabuk. Though it may have revealed to Muhammad the weakness of his international rivals, the raid was not an entirely successful enterprise, either in its organization or in its fulfillment, as many passages in Sura 9 of the Quran testify.

28. The Submission of the Idolators

Upon his return from another far-reaching raid to the north, the bedouin continued to make their peace, political and religious, with Muhammad, though with some caution.

In deciding their attitude to Islam the Arabs were only waiting to see what happened to this clan of the Quraysh and the Messenger. For the Quraysh were the leaders and guides of men, the people of the sacred shrine (of Mecca), and the pure stock of Ishmael son of Abraham; and the leading Arabs did not contest this. It was the Quraysh who had declared war on the Messenger and opposed him; and when Mecca was occupied and the Quraysh became subject to him and he subdued them to Islam, and the Arabs knew they could not fight the Messenger or display enmity towards him, they entered into God's religion "in batches" as God said, coming to him from all directions. (*Life* 933) [IBN ISHAQ 1955: 628]

Submission to the Prophet of Islam and his God was not always simple or easy, since the social, political, and psychological price of disavowing the customs of their own past was a large one. The Thaqif, for example, were willing to "make their submission and accept Islam on the Messenger's conditions provided they could get a document guaranteeing their land and their people and their animals." They got their document but that was by no means the end of the matter. The text from the Life *continues:*

Among the things they asked the Messenger was that they should
be allowed to retain their idol al-Lat undestroyed for three years. The
Messenger refused and they continued to ask him for a year or two
(grace), and he refused. Finally they asked for a month (dispensation)
after their return home, but he refused to agree to any set time. All that
they wanted, as they were trying to show, was to be safe from their
fanatics and women and children by leaving al-Lat, and they did not
want to frighten their people by destroying her until they had (all)
accepted Islam. The Messenger refused this, but he sent Abu Sufyan
and al-Mughira to destroy her (for them). They also asked him that he
would excuse them from prayer and that they would not have to break
the idol with their own hands. The Messenger said: "We excuse you
from breaking your idols with your own hands, but as for prayer, there
is no good in a religion which has no prayers." They said that they would
perform them, though they were demeaning. (*Life* 916) [IBN ISHAQ
1955: 613–614]

29. A Primer on Islam

*As each new tribe embraced Islam, their duties and responsibilities as Mus-
lims had to be spelled out for them, and one case in particular gives us an
opportunity to observe what was understood as "Islam" in those days.*

Now the Messenger had sent to them (the Banu al-Harith, Christians of the city of Najran in the Yemen) . . . Amr ibn Hazm to instruct
them in religion and to teach them the customary practice (*sunna*) and
the institutions of Islam and to collect their alms. And he wrote Amr a
letter in which he gave him his orders and injunctions as follows:

In the Name of God, the Compassionate, the Merciful. This is a
clear announcement from God and His Messenger. O you who believe,
be faithful to your agreements. The instructions of Muhammad the
Prophet, the Messenger of God, to Amr ibn Hazm when he sent him to
the Yemen. He orders him to observe piety toward God in all his doings
for God is with those who are pious and who do well; and he commanded him to behave with truth as God commanded him; and that
he should give people the good news and command them to follow it
and to teach men the Quran and instruct them in it and to forbid men
to do wrong so that none but the pure should touch the Quran, and he
should instruct men in their privileges and obligations and be lenient
with them when they behave aright and severe on injustice, since God

hates injustice and has forbidden it. "The curse of God is on the evildo-
ers" (Quran 5:1).

Give men the good news of paradise and the way to earn it, and
warn them of hell and the way to earn it, and make friends with men so
that they may be instructed in religion. Teach men the rites of the pilgrimage (hajj), its customs and its obligation and what God has ordered
about it: the greater pilgrimage is the hajj and the lesser pilgrimage is
the umra. Prohibit men from praying in one small garment, unless it be
a garment whose ends are doubled over their shoulders, and forbid men
from squatting in one garment which exposes their person to the air,
and forbid them to twist the head of the hair on the back of the neck (in
a pigtail).

If there is a quarrel between man, forbid them to appeal to tribes
and families, and let their appeal be to God. And those who do not
appeal to God but to tribes and families, let them be smitten with the
sword until their appeal is to God. Command men to perform the ablutions, their faces, their hands to the elbows and their feet to the
ankles, and let them wipe their heads as God ordered. And command
prayer at the proper time with bowing, prostration and humble reverence: prayer at daybreak; at noon when the sun declines; in the afternoon when the sun is descending; at evening when the night approaches,
not delaying it until the stars appear in the sky; later at the beginning of
the night. Order them to hasten to the mosques when they are summoned, and to wash when they go to them.

Order them to subtract from the booty God's fifth and whatever
alms are enjoined on the Muslims from land: a tenth of what the foun-
tains water and the sky waters and a twentieth of what the bucket
waters; and for every ten camels (they own), two sheep; and for every
twenty camels, four sheep; for every forty cows, one cow; for every
thirty cows, a bull or a cow calf; for every forty sheep at grass, one
sheep. This is what God enjoined on the believers in the matters of alms
(zakat). He who adds thereto, it is a merit to him.

A Jew or a Christian who becomes a sincere Muslim of his own
accord and obeys the religion of Islam is a believer with the same rights
and the same obligations. If one of them holds fast to his own religion,
he is not to be turned from it. Every adult (non-Muslim), male or
female, bond or free, must pay a gold dinar or its equivalent in clothes.
He who does this has the guarantee of God and His Messenger; he who
withholds it is the enemy of God and His Messenger and all believers.
(Life 961–962) [IBN ISHAQ 1955: 646–648]

30. The Farewell Pilgrimage

At the beginning of the year 632 c.e., the year of his death, Muhammad
went on his final pilgrimage. The details were lovingly cherished, since they
served as the foundation of all future performances of this ritual, which is
a solemn obligation upon all Muslims (see chapter 6 below). Ibn Ishaq
passes over these in his Life; he reproduces instead what turned out to be
the Prophet's final discourse.

In the beginning of Dhu al-Qaᶜda the Messenger prepared to make
the pilgrimage and ordered his men to get ready. Abd al-Rahman ibn
al-Qasim from his father, from Aisha, the Prophet's wife, told me that
the Messenger went on pilgrimage on the 25th of Dhu al-Qaᶜda (20
February 632 c.e.).

(In its course) the Messenger showed the men the rites and taught
them the customs of the Pilgrimage. He made a speech in which he
made things clear. He praised and glorified God, then he said: "O men,
listen to my words. I do not know whether I shall ever meet you in this
place again after this year. Your blood and your property are sacrosanct
until you meet your Lord, as this day and this month are holy. You will
surely meet your Lord and He will ask you of your works. I have told
you so. He who has a pledge, let him return it to him who entrusted it
to him; all usury is abolished, but you have your capital. Wrong not and
you shall not be wronged. . . . All blood shed in the period of paganism
is to be left unavenged. . . . Satan despairs of ever being worshipped in
your land, but if he can be obeyed in anything short of worship, he will
be pleased in matters you may be disposed to think of little account, so
beware of him in your religion. . . .

"You have rights over your wives and they have rights over you.
You have the right that they should not defile your bed and that they
should not behave with open unseemliness. If they do, God allows you
to put them in separate rooms and to beat them, though not with severity. If they refrain from these things, they have the right to their food
and clothing with kindness. Lay injunctions on women kindly, for they
are your prisoners, having no control of their persons. You have taken
them only in trust from God, and you have the enjoyment of their persons by the words of God. So understand my words, O men, for I have
told you. I have left you with something which, if you hold fast to it, you
will never fall into error, a plain indication, the Book of God and the
practices of His Prophet, so give good heed to what I say.

"Know that every Muslim is a Muslim's brother, and that (all) the Muslims are brethren. It is only lawful to take from a brother what he gives you willingly, so wrong not each other. O God, have I not told you?" (*Life* 968–969) [IBN ISHAQ 1955: 650–651]

31. Muhammad's Illness and Death
(June 632 C.E.)

Abdullah ibn Umar from Ubayd al-Jubayr, from Abdullah ibn Amr ibn al-As, from Abu Muwayhiba, a freedman of the Messenger, said: In the middle of the night the Messenger sent for me and told me that he was ordered to pray for the dead in this cemetery and that I was to go with him. I went, and when he stood among them he said: "Peace upon you, O people of the graves! Happy are you that you are so much better off than men here. Dissensions have come like waves of darkness one after the other, the last being worse than the first." Then he turned to me and said, "I have been given the choice between keys of the treasuries of this world and a long life here followed by Paradise, or meeting my Lord and Paradise (at once)." I urged him to choose the former, but he said he had chosen the latter. Then he prayed for the dead and went away. Then it was the illness through which God took him began. . . .

Al-Zuhri said that Abdullah ibn Ka'b ibn Malik told him on the day that he asked God's forgiveness for the men of the battle of Uhud: "O Emigrants, behave kindly to the Helpers, for other men increase but they in the nature of things cannot grow more numerous. They were my constant comfort and support. So treat their good men well and forgive those of them who were remiss." Then he came down and entered his house and his pain increased until he was exhausted. Then some of his wives gathered to him, Umm Salama and Maymuna, and some of the wives of the Muslims, among them Asma daughter of Umays, and his uncle Abbas was with him, and they agreed to force him to take some of the medicine. Abbas said, "Let me force him," but it was they who did it. When he recovered he asked . . . why they had done that. His uncle said, "We were afraid that you would get pleurisy." He replied, "That is a disease God would not afflict me with.". . .

Al-Zuhri said, Hamza ibn Abdullah ibn Umar told me that Aisha said that when the Prophet became seriously ill, he ordered the people to tell Abu Bakr to superintend the prayers. Aisha told him that Abu Bakr was a delicate man with a weak voice who wept much when he read the Quran. He (Muhammad) repeated his order nonetheless and I repeated my objections. He said, "You are like Joseph's companions; tell him to preside at prayers." "My only reason for saying what I did [Aisha said] was that I wanted (my father) Abu Bakr to be spared this task, because I knew the people would never like a man who occupied the Messenger's place and would blame him for every misfortune that occurred, and I wanted Abu Bakr spared that."

Al-Zuhri said that Anas ibn Malik told him that on the Monday on which God took His Messenger he went out to the people as they were praying the morning prayer. The curtain was lifted and the door opened and out came the Messenger and stood at the door of Aisha's room. The Muslims were almost seduced from their prayers at seeing him, and he motioned to them that they should continue their prayers. The Messenger smiled with joy when he marked their demeanor at prayer, and I never saw him with a nobler expression than he had on that day. Then he went back and the people went away thinking that the Messenger had recovered from his illness. . . .

Ya'qub ibn Utba from al-Zuhri from Urwa from (Muhammad's wife) Aisha said: The Messenger came back to me from the mosque that day and lay on my lap. A man of Abu Bakr's family came in to me with a toothpick in his hand. The Messenger looked at it in such a way that I knew he wanted it, and when I asked him if he wanted me to give it to him, he said yes. So I took it and chewed it to soften it for him and gave it to him. He rubbed his teeth with it more energetically than I had ever seen him rub them before. Then he laid it down. I found him heavy on my breast, and as I looked into his face, lo, his eyes were fixed and he was saying, "No, the most Exalted Companion is of Paradise." I said, "You were given the choice and you have chosen, by Him who sent you with the truth!" And so the Messenger was taken. . . .

Al-Zuhri said, and Sa'id ibn al-Musayyib from Abu Hurayra told me: When the Messenger was dead Umar got up (in the mosque) and said: "Some of the disaffected will allege that the Messenger is dead, but by God, he is not dead: he has gone to his Lord as Moses son of Imran went and was hidden [on Sinai] from his people for forty days. By God, the Messenger will return as Moses returned and will cut off the hands and feet of men who allege that the Messenger is dead." When Abu Bakr heard what had happened he came to the door of the mosque as Umar was speaking to the people. He paid no attention but went into Aisha's room to the Messenger, who was lying covered by a mantle of Yemeni cloth. He went and uncovered his face and kissed him saying, "You are dearer than my father and mother. You have tasted the death that God had decreed; a second death will never overtake you."

Then he replaced the mantle over the Messenger's face and went out. Umar was still speaking and Abu Bakr said, "Gently, Umar, be quiet." But Umar refused and went on talking, and when Abu Bakr saw that he would not be silent, he went forward himself to the people who, when they heard his words, came to him and left Umar. Giving thanks and praise to God, he said: "O men, if anyone worships Muhammad, Muhammad is dead; if anyone worships God, God is alive, immortal." Then he recited this verse "Muhammad is nothing but a Messenger. Messengers have passed away before him. Can it be that if he were to die or be killed you would turn back on your heels? 'He who turns back does no harm to God and God will reward the grateful'" (Quran 3:144). By God, it was as if the people did not know that this verse had not come down until Abu Bakr recited it that day. The people took it from him and it was constantly on their tongues. Umar said, "By God, when I heard Abu Bakr recite those words I was dumbfounded so that my legs would not bear me and I fell to the ground realizing that the Messenger was indeed dead." (*Life* 1000—1013) [IBN ISHAQ 1955: 678—683]

32. The Beginning of the Muslim Era

The central event in the Christian view of history is the death and resurrection of Jesus. The Muslims, on the other hand, though they cheerfully celebrate the birth of Muhammad, pay little attention to the anniversary of his death. For them, the crucial event of Islam, the great divide between the Era of Ignorance and the Muslim era, is the Prophet's migration (hijra) *from Mecca to Medina in 622 C.E. In his* Traces of the Past *the Muslim chronographer Biruni (d. 1048 C.E.) reports the traditions concerning the beginning of the reckoning of a special era for Muslims, and the choice of this event to mark it.*

The era of the Hijra [or Migration] of the Prophet Muhammad from Mecca to Medina is based upon lunar years, in which the commencements of months are determined by the (actual) appearance of the new moon and not by calculation. It is used by the whole Muslim world. The circumstances under which this point was adopted as an epoch and not the time when the Prophet was either born, or was entrusted with his divine mission, or died, were the following. Maymun ibn Mihran relates that Umar ibn al-Khattab [Caliph, 634–644 C.E.], when people one day handed him a check payable in the month of Sha'ban, said: "Which Sha'ban is meant? The one in which we are or the next Sha'ban?" Thereupon he assembled the Companions of the Prophet and asked their advice regarding the matter of chronology, which troubled his mind. . . . Then Umar spoke to the Companions of the Prophet: "Establish a mode of dating for the intercourse of people." Now some said, "Date according to the era of the Greeks, for they date according to the era of Alexander." Others objected that this mode was too lengthy, and said, "Date according to the era of the Persians." But then it was objected that as soon as a new king arises among the Persians he abolishes the era of his predecessor. So they could not come to an agreement.

Aisha relates that Abu Musa al-Ash'ari wrote to Umar ibn al-Khattab: "You send us letters without a date." Umar had already organized the (government) registers, had established the taxes and regulations, and was in want of an era, not liking the old ones. On this occasion he assembled the Companions and took their advice. Now the most authentic date, which involves no obscurities or possible mishaps, seemed to be the date of the Hijra of the Prophet, and of his arrival at Medina on Monday, the eighth day of the month First Rabi', while the beginning of the year was a Thursday. Now he adopted this epoch and fixed thereby the dates in all his affairs. This happened in 17 of the Era of the Hijra [that is, 638 C.E.].

The reason why Umar selected this event as an epoch, and not the time of the birth of the Prophet, or the time when he was entrusted with his divine mission, is this, that regarding those two dates there was such a divergency of opinion as did not allow it to be made the basis of something which must be agreed upon universally. . . . Considering further that after the Hijra the affairs of Islam were thoroughly established, while heathenism decreased, that the Prophet was saved from the calamities prepared for him by the infidels of Mecca, and that after the Hijra his conquests followed each other in rapid succession, we come to the conclusion that the Hijra was to the Prophet what to kings is their accession and their taking possession of the whole sovereign power. (al-Biruni, *Traces of the Past*) [BIRUNI 1879: 34–35]

CHAPTER 3

The Community of Muslims

To this point Islam has been spoken of in somewhat general terms and
without inquiry into what it was that gave it its unique identity during the
classical period, an identity that persists to this day. To speak of a "religion" is to speak of many things—a system of beliefs or an accepted complex of ritual, for example. But when one looks at how a Jew, a Christian,
or a Muslim regards himself and his coreligionists, it is the sense of community that asserts itself at every turn: Bene Yisrael, ekklesia, and umma all
speak, each in its own context, of a powerful sense of group solidarity.

The effect of God's earlier revelations was, as Muhammad understood
very well, the creation of communities, most notably the "Peoples of the
Book," the Jews and Christians. The Arabs, now in possession of a "clear
Arabic Quran" (Quran 16:103), had become just such a community
(umma). But even during Muhammad's lifetime, his community achieved
such a remarkable degree of political success that it had become in effect a
state—a responsibility faced by Judaism and Christianity only at a considerably more advanced stage of their development. Thus Muhammad was not
simply God's envoy; he was also, for much of his later life, judge, spiritual
guide, and military and political leader, first of a community, then of a
city-state, and finally of a burgeoning empire.

1. The Peoples of the Book

Islam is, on the testimony of the Quran itself, a successor community to
those other peoples who had gone before it. They had had their Messengers
and they too had been given the benefit of God's Book.

Remember We gave to Moses the Book and sent after him many
an apostle; and to Jesus son of Mary We gave clear evidence of the
truth, reinforcing him with divine grace. Even so, when a messenger

brought to you what did not suit your mood, you turned haughty, and called some impostors and some others you slew.

And they say: "Our hearts are enfolded in covers." In fact, God has cursed them in their unbelief; and only a little do they believe. (Quran 2:87–88)

How many of the followers of the Books having once known the truth desire in their heart to turn you into infidels again, even after the truth has become clear to them! But you forbear and overlook till God fulfill His plan; and God has power over all things.

Fulfill your devotional obligations and pay the alms-tithe. And what you send ahead of good you will find with God, for He sees all that you do.

And they say: "None will go to Paradise but the Jews and the Christians," but this is only wishful thinking. Say: "Bring the proof, if you are truthful."

Only he who surrenders to God with all his heart and also does good, will find reward with his Lord and have no regret and fear.

The Jews say, "The Christians are not right," and the Christians say, "The Jews are in the wrong," yet both recite the Scriptures. And this is what the unread had said too. God alone will judge between them in their differences on the Day of Reckoning. (Quran 2:109–113)

2. The Errors of the Jews

The first of those people to have been given Scripture were the Jews.

Men belonged to a single community; and God sent them Messengers to give them happy tidings and warnings and sent the Book with them containing the truth to judge between them in matters of dispute; but only those who received it differed after receiving clear proofs, on account of waywardness among them. Then God by His dispensation showed those who believed the way to the truth about which they were differing; for God shows whom He pleases the path that is straight. (Quran 2:213)

The Muslim commentators on the Quran were not sure about the duration of the period when "the people were one community." But the Book that was sent down and to whom it was given and why was the matter of no dispute.

. . . God means that the Book, that is, the Torah, should decide between the people on matters on which they disagreed. God has assigned the decision to the Book and established it and not the Prophets and the Apostles as the decisive criterion between the people, since whenever one of the Prophets or Apostles had to bring down a judgment, he did it on the basis of the indications which are contained in the Book which is sent down by God. . . .

God's words "they disagreed concerning it" mean that they disagreed concerning the Book that God had sent down, that is, the Torah. His word "those to whom it had been given" refers to the Jews of the Children of Israel. They are the ones who had been given the Torah and its knowledge. . . . Thus God proclaims that the Jews of the Children of Israel disobeyed the Book, the Torah, and they disagreed concerning it in spite of the knowledge which it contains. In so doing they deliberately disobeyed God since they violated His command and the decision of His Book.

"Then God showed those who believed the way to the truth . . ." means that God granted success to those who are believing, that is, those who support belief in (the one) God and His Apostle, Muhammad, and who put their trust in him and are convinced that his message, about which the previous recipients of the Book had earlier disagreed, comes from God. The disunity in which God left these people alone, while rightly guiding and helping to the truth those who believe in Muhammad, refers to (Friday as) the "day of gathering" (for worship). Although this day had been enjoined on them [that is, the Jews] as an obligation just as it had been enjoined on us, they deviated from it and changed (their day of worship) to the Sabbath. The Prophet has said: Although we are the last, we surpass (the others in obedience to God's commands), even though the Book was given to them before it was given to us, and so we possessed it after they did. God has rightly guided us even to this day, on matters on which they disagreed. The Jews have taken (as their day of worship) the day following (Friday) and the Christians have taken the day after that.

Concerning the matters about which the people disagreed, Ibn Zayd is reported to have said, according to Yunus ibn Abd A'la, that God's words "then God showed those who believed the way to the truth" mean that (He led the believers) to Islam. The people disagreed concerning prayer. Some prayed facing toward the East while others faced toward Jerusalem. Then God led us to the right direction of prayer toward Mecca. Also the people disagreed concerning fasting. Some fasted at certain times of the day while others fasted at certain times of the night. Then God led us to the right times for fasting. Also the people disagreed concerning the day of congregational worship. While the Jews chose the Sabbath, the Christians took Sunday; then God led us to the right day (on Friday). Also the people disagreed about Abraham. The Jews considered him a Jew and the Christians considered him a Christian. Then God freed him from such suspicions and demonstrated that he was a *hanif* who was surrendered to God, and that he also was not to be classed among the heathen, as some maintained, who claimed that he had been one of the unbelievers. Finally, the people also disagreed about Jesus. The Jews considered him to be the victim of a lie, while the Christians considered him to be a god. Thereupon God led us to the truth concerning him. (Tabari, *Commentary, ad loc.*)

3. The Jews Warned by Their Own Prophets

We sent down the Torah which contains guidance and light; in accordance with which the prophets, who had surrendered themselves [or became *muslims*], gave instructions to the Jews, as did the rabbis and the priests, for they were the custodians and witnesses of God's writ. (Quran 5:44)

This is one of the central Quranic texts explaining the position of the Jews with respect to God's revelation, and as such it receives full treatment at the hands of the commentators.

". . . the prophets who had surrendered themselves": Submission [that is, *islam*] is an attribute which is used in praise of the prophets generally and not as a distinguishing characteristic (of the Jewish prophets), just as is the case with attributes one uses in reference to the Eternal One. The use of this attribute (with reference to the biblical prophets) shows that the Jews are far from acknowledging Islam, which is the (true) religion of the prophets in both ancient and modern times, and that Judaism is remote from acknowledging this. God's words, "the prophets, who had surrendered themselves, gave judgment against those who were Jewish" emphasizes this in a forceful manner.

"As did the masters (of the Law) and the rabbis": This refers to the ascetics and the learned men among the descendants of Aaron, who remained faithful to the ways of the prophets and have remained aloof from the religion of the Jews.

"Following the portion of God's Book that had been entrusted to them": The portion of God's Book that the prophets had instructed the rabbis and masters (of the Law) to preserve was the Torah. That is, the prophets had ordered them to preserve the Torah from change and distortion. (Zamakhshari *ad loc.*)

4. The Error of the Christians

The Christians too had been in Muslims' eyes unfaithful to God's word.

O People of the Book, do not be fanatical in your faith, and say nothing but the truth about God. The Messiah who is Jesus, son of Mary, was only an Apostle of God, and a command of His which He sent to Mary, as a mercy from Him. So believe in God and His apostles, and do not call him "Three." Refrain from this for your own good; for God is only one God, and far from His glory is it to beget a son. (Quran 4:171)

Once again Zamakhshari provides the proper exegetical perspective.

"Do not be fanatical in your faith": The Jews went too far in that they degraded the position of Christ in regarding him as an illegitimate child (of Mary). And the Christians went too far in that they unduly elevated him in considering him a god.

"His word": Jesus is designated as "the word of God" and as "a word from Him" (Sura 3:39) because he alone originated through the word and command of God rather than through a father and a sperm. For this reason he is also designated as "the spirit of God" (Sura 66:12) and "a spirit from Him," since Jesus was a spirit-endowed man who originated without any element from a spirit-endowed man, such as the sperm that is discharged from an earthly father. He was created by a new act of creation by God whose power is unlimited.

The word "Three" (in this verse) is the predicate of an understood subject. If one accepts the Christian view that God exists in one substance with three divine persons, namely, the Father, the Son and the Holy Spirit, and if one accepts the opinion that the person of the Father represents God's being, the person of the Son represents His knowledge, and the person of the Holy Spirit represents His life, then one must supply the subject (of the clause) as follows: "God is three(fold)." Otherwise, one must supply the subject thus: "The gods are three." According to the evidence of the Quran, the Christians maintain that God, Christ and Mary are three gods, and that Christ is the child of God by Mary, as God says (in the Quran): "O Jesus son of Mary, did you say to men: 'Take me and my mother as gods, apart from God'?" (Sura

5:116) or "The Christians say: 'The Messiah is the Son of God'" (Sura 9:30). Moreover, it is well known that the Christians maintain that in Jesus are (combined) a divine nature derived from his Father and a human nature derived from his mother. God's words (in this verse) "The Messiah, Jesus son of Mary, was only a Messenger of God," are also explained on the basis of such an interpretation (of the Christians). These words confirm (the Christian view) that Jesus was a child of Mary, that he had with her the usual relationship between children and their mothers, and that his relationship to God was that he was His Messenger and that he became a living being through God's command and a new act of creation without a father. At the same time these words exclude (the Christian view) that Jesus had with God the usual relationship between sons and their fathers. (Zamakhshari *ad loc.*)

5. The Muslim Community

Christianity had three centuries to brace for the shock of finding itself the part proprietor of a Christian Roman Empire. Islam was from its inception both a religious and a political association. As we have seen in chapter 2 above, in 622 C.E. he accepted an invitation to leave his native Mecca, where he was the charismatic leader of a small conventicle of believers, and to emigrate to Medina as the ruler of a faction-ridden community of Arabs and Jews. This was a crucial period in Muhammad's life, and the years following his "migration" (hijra; Eng., Hegira) were spent in trying to forge some kind of community (umma) in accordance with his religious principles and the political realities of the situation. The first umma at Medina was not yet a fully Islamic association—both Jews and pagan Arabs were included—but as Muhammad's political fortunes began to prosper, religious considerations came to the fore. The Jewish tribes of Medina were purged from the coalition, and the pagans were dragged willy-nilly into it; the umma became a community of believers who accepted the dominion of Allah and both the Prophethood and the leadership of Muhammad.

These were not artificial associations. Muhammad's role as a Prophet (nabi) within a community that he himself had summoned into being necessarily included the functions of legislator, executive, and military commander of the umma. God's revelations continued to spill from his lips. Now, however, they were not only threats and warnings to nonbelievers, but more often legislative enactments regulating community life, and particularly the relations of one Muslim with another.

For its community model, the Quran cites, but does not use, the example of the Jews and Christians, both of whom constituted defined and already existing religious communities, corporate bodies of believers in possession of an authentic revelation. But how these communities were governed or what political or social institutions they possessed, the Quran does not explain. Indeed, the Book offers no systematic or extended discussion of the new community of Muslims whose birth it was chartering. But the notion of community nonetheless occurs often there, sometimes in the context of the Muslims' treatment of each other, sometimes in their distancing themselves from those other older communities of the "Peoples of the Book."

O believers, if you follow what some of the People of the Book say, it will turn you into unbelievers even after you have come to belief.

And how can you disbelieve? To you are being recited the messages of God, and His Prophet is among you. And whosoever holds fast to God shall verily be guided to the path that is straight.

O believers, fear God as He should be feared, and do not die except as those submitting to him. Hold on firmly together to the rope of God, and be not divided among yourselves, and remember the favors God bestowed on you when you were one another's foe and He reconciled your hearts, and you turned into brethren through His grace. You had stood on the edge of the pit of fire and He saved you from it, thus revealing to you His clear signs, that you might perchance find the right way.

So let there be one community among you who may call to the good, enjoin what is esteemed and forbid what is odious. They are those who will be successful.

So be not like those who became disunited and differed among themselves after clear proofs had come to them. For them is great suffering. . . .

These are the commandments of God We recite to you verily; God does not wish injustice to the creatures of the world. For to God belongs all that is in the heavens and the earth, and to God do all things return. Of all the communities raised among men, you are the best, enjoining the good, forbidding the wrong, and believing in God. If the people of the Book had come to believe, it would have been better for them; but only some believe, and transgressors are many. (Quran 3: 100–110)

The foolish will now ask and say: "What has made the faithful turn away from the direction toward which they used to pray?" Say, "To God belongs the East and the West. He guides who so wills to the path that is straight." We have made you a middle community that you act as witness over man, and the Prophet as witness over you. (Quran 2:142–143)

The Quranic notion of Islam as a "central" or "middle" community elicited considerable reflection from the medieval commentators.

I regard the word "middle" in this context as signifying the mean between two extremes. God described the Muslims as a people of the middle path because of their middle position in religion. They are neither people of excess like the Christians who went to extremes in their monastic practices as well as in what they said concerning Jesus, nor are they people of deficiency like the Jews, who altered the Book of God, killed their prophets, gave the lie to their Lord, and rejected faith in Him. Rather they are people of the middle path and of balance in their religion. God characterized them as people of the middle path because the things which God loves most are those of the middle position. (Tabari, *Commentary, ad loc.*)

The word "middle" or "in the middle" was originally a designation for a position with equal distances on each side. Then it came to refer to certain praiseworthy attributes of character because these lie (in the middle) between extremes of excess and exaggeration on both sides. Thus, generosity lies between wastefulness and stinginess and boldness between foolhardy recklessness and cowardice. The word is now also applied to a person who possesses such characteristics. . . . From the words of God in this verse one can (also) draw the conclusion that consensus is a valid authority (in questions of faith), since if that on which Muslims are agreed were delusion, then a gap would be created in their integrity (and thus they would not stand in the middle). (Baydawi *ad loc.*)

6. An Arabic Quran

Islam is a universal community, it is clear from the Quran and Muhammad's own preaching, but it is also true that Muhammad was an Arab sent to preach God's message in the first instance to Arabs. The Arabs were not a "chosen people" the way the Israelites understood themselves to be, but Arabic was in some sense God's "chosen language." A number of verses in the Muslim Scripture lay emphasis on the fact that this is an Arabic Quran. The language is in fact such an important element in interpreting the Book, and particularly in understanding its legal prescriptions, that the jurist al-Shafiʿi (d. 820 C.E.) devoted considerable space to it in his Treatise on the Roots of Jurisprudence, *and his reflections cast an interesting light on the tension between cultural Arabism and religious Islam.*

Someone said: There are in the Quran Arabic and foreign words.

Shafiʿi replied: The Quran indicates that there is no portion of the Book of God that is not in the Arab tongue. He who expressed such an opinion [namely, that there are foreign words in the Quran] . . . perhaps meant that there are certain particular words which are not understood by some Arabs.

Of all tongues that of the Arabs is the richest and most extensive in vocabulary. Do we know any man except a Prophet who apprehended all of it? However, no portion of it escapes everyone, so that there is always someone who knows it. Knowledge of this tongue is to the Arabs what knowledge of the tradition of the Prophet is to the jurists: We know of no one who possesses a knowledge of all the tradition of the Prophet without missing a portion of it. So if the knowledge of all the scholars is gathered together, the entire tradition of the Prophet would be known. However, if the knowledge of each scholar is taken separately, each might be found lacking in some portion of it, yet what each may lack can be found among the others. . . .

In like manner is the (knowledge of the) tongue of the Arabs by the scholars and the public. No part of it will be missed by all of them, nor should it be sought from other people; for no one can learn this tongue save that he has learned it from the Arabs, nor can anyone be as fluent in it as they unless he has followed them in the way they learned it. He who has learned it from them should be regarded as one of the people of that tongue. . . .

Someone may ask: What is the proof that the Book of God was communicated in a pure Arabic tongue, unmixed with others?

Shafiʿi replied: The proof is to be found in the Book of God itself, for God said:

"We never sent a Messenger save in the tongue of his people." (Quran 14: 4)

But if someone says: Each of the Messengers before Muhammad was sent to his own people, while Muhammad was sent to all mankind. This may mean either that Muhammad was sent with the tongue of his people and that all others must learn his tongue—or whatever they can learn of it—or that Muhammad was sent with the tongues of all mankind. Is there any evidence that he was sent with the tongue of his own people rather than with foreign tongues?

Shafiʿi replied: Since tongues vary so much that different people cannot understand one another, some must adopt the language of others. And preference must be given to the tongues that others adopt. The people who are fit to receive such a preference are those whose tongue is their Prophet's tongue. It is not permissible—but God knows best—for the people of the Prophet's tongue to become the followers of peoples whose tongues are other than that of the Prophet even in a single letter; but rather all other people should follow his tongue, and all people of earlier religions should follow his religion. For God has declared this in more than one communication of His Book:

> "Truly, it is the revelation of the Lord of the worlds, brought down by the Faithful Spirit, upon your heart, that you may be one of those who warn, in a clear Arabic tongue." (Quran 26:192–195)

And He also said:

> "Thus have We sent it down as an Arabic Law." (Quran 13:37)

And He said:

> "And so we have revealed to you an Arabic Quran in order that you may warn the Mother of the Towns and the people of its vicinity." (Quran 42:5)

The "Mother of the Towns" is Mecca, the city of the Prophet and of his people. Thus God mentioned them in His Book as a special people and included them among those who were warned as a whole, and decreed that they were to be warned in their native tongue, the tongue of the Prophet's people in particular.

It is obligatory upon every Muslim to learn the Arab tongue to the utmost of his power in order to be able to profess through it that "there is no god but the God and Muhammad is His servant and Apostle," and to recite in it the Book of God.

Shafiʿi finally returns to his lawyer's point.

The reason I began to explain why the Quran was communicated in the Arab tongue rather than in another, is that no one who understands clearly the total meanings of the (legal) knowledge of the Book of God would be ignorant of the extent of that tongue and of the various meanings of its words. . . . Doubts that appear to one who is ignorant (of the Arab tongue) will disappear from him who knows it. . . . Calling the attention of the public to the fact that the Quran was communicated in the Arab tongue in particular is advice to all Muslims. This advice is a duty imposed on them which must not be put aside and is the attainment of a supererogatory act of goodness which no one will neglect. (Shafiᶜi, *Treatise*) [SHAFIᶜI 1961: 88–94]

7. "Catholic" Islam: Staying Close to the Tradition

In Muhammad's own day membership in the community of Muslims might be understood simply as including anyone who acknowledged the unity of God and the Quran as the Word of God, and who performed the ritual acts prescribed in the so-called Five Pillars described below. Those grounds had soon to be extended to a detailed affirmation of the teachings of the Quran, as broadened and explained by the various "sayings" or "Prophetic traditions" attributed to Muhammad himself. But the process of enlargement did not end there; it soon came to embrace the notion of "consensus," the agreement of Muslims on certain points of belief and practice, even without the authority of a Quranic text or a "Prophetic tradition" to support it (see chapter 5 below).

The validity of "consensus" as an operative element in Islam was argued in what became the classic statement of the position, Shafiᶜi's already cited Treatise on the Roots of Jurisprudence. *In the following passage an anonymous questioner is willing to concede the binding nature of the Quran and the "Prophetic traditions," but requests further proof on the matter of "consensus."*

What is your proof for following what people have agreed upon, where there is no command in a text from God [that is, in the Quran], or related from the Prophet? Would you assert what others have held, that consensus can never occur except on a firm "tradition," even though it may not have been related [that is, even if it has not reached us in the form of a "Prophetic tradition"]?

I told him (said Shafiᶜi): As to what they agreed upon and say that it has (also) been related from the Prophet, let us hope that it is (accepted) as they say. However, as for what is not related [that is, there is no specific Prophetic tradition on the matter], it may be that it was actually said by the Messenger of God, or it may be otherwise. It is not, however, permissible to attribute sayings to him (without grounds), for one is only permitted to relate what one has heard, and it is not permitted to relate anything one fancies, in which there may be things (the Prophet) did not say.

Therefore we hold to what they held to, following them. We know that if these were practices of the Messenger, they would not be remote to the generality of Muslims, even though they are remote to the few; and we know that the generality of Muslims will not agree on what is contradictory to the customary practice of the Messenger of God, or on an error, please God.

If it is asked, is there anything to indicate or prove that? we reply: Sufyan informs us on the authority of Abd al-Malik ibn Umayr from Abd al-Rahman the son of Abdullah ibn Mas‘ud, from his father, that the Messenger of God said, "God prospers a servant who listens to what I say, remembers it, pays attention to it, and passes it on. Often one may transmit insight who himself is not perspicacious, and often he transmits it to one with more insight than he. There are three things which cannot be resented by the heart of a Muslim: sincerity of action for God, good advice to the Muslims, and keeping close to the community of the Muslims. . . ."

It was asked, what is the meaning of the Prophet's command to keep close to the community?

I said: There is but one meaning to it. . . . Since the community of the Muslims is scattered in different countries, one could not keep close to the physical community whose members were scattered, and besides, they were found together with Muslims and unbelievers, with pious men and sinners. Thus it could not mean a physical "closeness" since that was not possible, and because physical nearness would in itself effect nothing, so that there is no meaning in "keeping close to the community" except in agreeing with them in what they make lawful and forbidden, and obedience in both these matters. He who maintains what the community of the Muslims maintains is keeping close to the community, and he who deviates from what the community of the Muslims maintains deviates from that community to which he is commanded to remain close. Error arises in separation. In the community there can be no total error concerning the meaning of the Book, of the Prophetic tradition, or of analogical reasoning, please God. (Shafi‘i, *Treatise*) [SHAFI‘I 1961: 285–287]

Much the same point is made in this ninth-century statement of belief from Ahmad ibn Hanbal (d. 855 C.E.), whose views on the nature of orthodoxy and heresy we shall see again below. Ibn Hanbal may have differed from the somewhat older Shafi‘i on important points of the law, but *he was as convinced as Shafi*c*i that the essential truth of the community lay in its adherence to the "tradition."*

*This "creed" begins, then, with what is, in effect, a conservative's plea for unity, for adherence to that same "tradition and the collectivity" (sunna wa al-jama*c*a) from which the so-called Sunnis took their name.*

Ahmad ibn Hanbal said: The principles of "the tradition" for us are holding fast to the practice of the Companions of the Messenger of God and seeking guidance from that; and abandoning innovation, for every innovation is an error. Also, abandoning quarrels and not consorting with people who do as they please and leaving off strife and contentiousness in religion. "The tradition" to us means the footsteps of the Messenger of God, may God bless him and give him peace, and "the tradition" explains the meaning of the Quran and is the indication of the Quran. There is no use of logical analogies in "the tradition," or coining of similitudes or perception by use of reason or inclination. It is only following, and giving up one's own inclinations.

The statement then grows more specific, and we have before us a ninth-century theological agenda: points of belief that had already been debated to the point of orthodoxy and heresy.

A part of the essential "tradition," such that if one leaves aside any part of it, not accepting and believing it, he cannot be considered as being of the "People of Tradition," is belief in the predestination of good and bad, and the affirmation of the Prophetic traditions about it and belief in them, not saying "Why?" or "How?" but simply affirming them and believing them. If anyone does not know the explanation of these Prophetic traditions or his intelligence does not apprehend them, it is still sufficient, and his sentence is that he shall believe in them and submit to their authority, such as the Prophetic traditions (affirming predestination), and those that the beatific vision is possible, all in their entirety. And even if he turns away from hearing about this, or feels dislike at hearing about it, still he must believe in it, and must not contradict a single letter of it, or any other Prophetic tradition transmitted by dependable narrators. No one should dispute, or speculate about it, or recognize any contention about it, for speaking about predestination and the beatific vision and the (nature of the) Quran and other matters established by the Prophetic traditions is disapproved of and to be avoided. Whoever speaks of them, if he criticizes "the tradition," is not one of the "People of the Tradition" until he abandons contention and submits and believes in "the tradition."

*A number of specifics follow in turn: the Quran as the uncreated Word
of God, the vision of God on the "Day of Resurrection," the reality of the
details of the Final Judgment, the coming of the False Messiah and then the
return of Jesus, who will "slay him at the Lydda Gate" of Jerusalem. And
finally there is an article on the nature of faith.*

Faith is word and act, and increases and decreases, as is stated in
the Prophetic traditions. "The most perfect of believers in faith is the
best of them in morality." Also, "He who leaves off the ritual prayers has
rejected God," and there is no act which, when neglected, occasions
infidelity except the ritual prayers. Whoever quits them is an infidel,
and God makes killing him lawful. (Ahmad ibn Hanbal, *Creed*) [WIL-
LIAMS 1971: 28–30]

8. A Shi°ite View of the Community

*Shafi°i's view soon became the orthodox one in Islam, particularly among
those Muslims like Ahmad ibn Hanbal who identified themselves as "People
of the Tradition (sunna) and the Collectivity," and whom we call simply
"Sunnis." But as Ibn Hanbal stated, "The principles of 'the tradition'
(sunna) for us are holding fast to the practice of the Companions of the
Messenger of God and seeking guidance from that. . . ." There were those
among the Muslims, notably the "Partisans (shi°a) of Ali," generically
called "Shi°ites," who preferred not to go the way of the "Companions of the
Messenger of God," particularly since these latter had elected first Abu Bakr
and then Umar and Uthman to lead the community instead of the one on
whom the divine and prophetic choice had obviously fallen, the Prophet's
cousin and son-in-law, Ali ibn Abi Talib, about whom more will be said
below. This is the way the case is argued by the Shi°ite scholar Ibn Babuya
(d. 991 C.E.), beginning with the Quran itself.*

Every verse in the Quran which begins with the expression, "O
you who believe" refers necessarily to Ali ibn Abi Talib as their leader
and prince and the most noble among them. And every verse which
directs the way to Paradise applies to the Prophet or to the Imams [that
is, Ali and his designated successors], the blessings of God be upon them
and all their partisans and followers. . . . These (Imams) are immune
from sin and error. . . . They may be likened in this community to the
Ark of Noah; he who boards it attains salvation or reaches the Gate of
Repentance. (Ibn Babuya) [WILLIAMS 1971: 39–40]

The Shi°ite was not, then, willing to grant infallibility to the "collectivity" in the manner of al-Shafi°i. The community had, in fact, already

erred, or at least part of it allowed itself to be carried into error on the issue of the Imamate (see below). The issue is stated clearly in a Shi'ite creed of the thirteenth century.

The Imam [that is, the head of the community; the officer called "Caliph" by the Sunni Muslims] cannot be elected by the community. He is the absolute ruler, who imposes his final judgment upon his followers. The principle of "consensus" in accepting certain religious laws and practices is completely false. If one were to accept this principle, he should regard Muhammad as not a real Prophet, because all of the people to whom he first addressed himself, or at least the majority of them, did not at first recognize him as such. . . . Only the Imam, appointed by God, is infallible, but the community obviously cannot be considered as infallible. . . .

The community became split and fell into disagreements after the death of the Prophet, thus taking the way of error. This was chiefly due to their reluctance to follow "the Household" [that is, Ali and his descendants]. Only a small group among the Muslims remained faithful to the commandments and the will of the Prophet, suffering for this reason at the hand of different oppressors. . . .

One who follows the religion of his ancestors by "the tradition," without having ascertained for himself whether it is correct or wrong, is not right. He should know and act in accordance with the Quran and "the tradition" as taught by the Imams of the family of the Apostle. . . .

Religion and faith are to be found only in Shi'ism (along with true) following of the tradition of the Prophet. . . . The Prophet predicted the splitting up of the Islamic community into seventy-three sects after his death; and of these only one brings salvation. It is the one which follows the Prophet and his descendants (through the house of Ali), who are the Ark of Noah, giving religious salvation. (*A Shi'ite Creed*) [WILLIAMS 1971: 40–41]

9. Wrong Belief and Unbelief

The split between Sunni and Shi'ite was only one of a number of fissures that opened within the Muslim community even in the first century of its existence. Some were, like Shi'ism, the result of differing views on such fundamental political questions as "Who is a Muslim?" or "Who shall rule the community?" Others were more theological in their orientation, though not without political implication, like the questions of free will and predetermination that troubled the early community.

*Opinions might differ, but there were differences of substance and importance even among those varying opinions. Muslims came to recognize in practice and in theory a juridical distinction between "unbelief" (kufr), the rejection of one of the basic teachings of Islam, and so disqualification as a Muslim, and "heretical innovation" (bida*ᶜ*), the introduction of some belief or practice unsupported by Islamic teaching or custom as described in the Prophetic traditions. In matters of doubt an authoritative judicial opinion could be solicited, as the Caliph Mustazhir (1094–1118 c.e.) did of the jurist-theologian Ghazali on the subject of certain radical Shiᶜite groups. Ghazali carefully builds a legal case for their exclusion from the Muslim community, with all the political consequences of such a judgment.*

Their declarations fall into two categories, one of which makes it necessary to declare they are in error, are astray and are guilty of innovation, the other of which makes it necessary to declare that they are unbelievers and (the community) must be cleansed of them.

What constitutes for Ghazali the heretical innovation of the group in question is a set of standard Shiᶜite beliefs on the legitimacy and nature of leadership in the Islamic community, questions that will be reviewed below. Ghazali proceeds with the matter of innovation.

With regard to the first category (of beliefs) which makes it necessary to declare that they are in error, are astray and are guilty of innovation, it is where we encounter those unlearned folk who believe that the leadership (of the community) belongs by right to the immediate family of the Prophet, and that he who should rightly have it in our day is their Pretender [that is, the contemporary descendant of Ali who laid claim to the office]. Their claim is that in the first (Muslim) century the one who should have rightfully had it was Ali [the cousin and son-in-law of Muhammad], may God be pleased with him, but that he was wrongly deprived of it. . . . Nevertheless, they do not believe that it is lawful to shed our blood [that is, the Sunni Muslims who have a different view of the leadership question], nor do they believe that we are in unbelief. What they do believe about us [and, Ghazali might have added, we about them] is that we are iniquitous folk whose minds have erroneously slipped from comprehension of the truth, or that we have turned aside from their leader out of obstinacy and a spirit of contention. It is not permissible to shed the blood of a person in this category nor to give judgment that he is in unbelief because he says such things. . . . Judgment should be confined to the declaration that such a one has (merely) gone astray, for he does not express belief in any of the erroneous teachings of their sect . . . concerning certain theological beliefs and matters of resurrection and the Judgment. With regard to all such matters they express no beliefs other than those we express ourselves.

For the Sunnis, the "people of tradition and the collectivity," the notion of a consensus of the Muslim community was an important one. Does not, then, the Shi⁽ites' violation of the universal consensus on the question of the early leaders of Islam qualify them as unbelievers?

But someone might ask: But do you not declare them in unbelief because of what they say about the office of community leader in the first years (of Islam), how it belonged by right to Ali and not to Abu Bakr and those who succeeded him, but he was wrongly deprived of it, for in this they go contrary to the consensus of Muslims? Our answer is that we do not deny the dangerous nature of this opposition to the consensus, and for that reason we go beyond charging them with being in undisguised error . . . and charge them with leading others astray, causing heresy and introducing innovation, but we do not go so far as declaring them in unbelief. This is because it is not clear to us that one who goes contrary to the consensus is an unbeliever. Indeed, there is a difference of opinion among Muslims as to whether the proof of a doctrine can rest on consensus alone.

The objection is pushed a step farther by Ghazali. Some Shi⁽ites were not content to say merely that Ali had been wrongfully passed over for the leadership on four successive occasions; they went on to denigrate those first four "Successors of the Prophet," men who in the Sunni tradition were called "the Rightly Guided Caliphs."

If someone should ask: Then if someone were to say plainly that Abu Bakr and Umar were in unbelief, ought he to be considered the same as one who calls any other of the Muslim chiefs or judges or leaders who came after them an unbeliever? Yes, we do so teach. To charge Abu Bakr or Umar with unbelief is not different from charging unbelief to any of the leaders or judges of the community, nor, indeed, to any individual who professes Islam, save in two regards. First, it would also be going against and contradicting consensus, though, indeed, one who charges them with unbelief because of some perplexity might not even be contradicting reliable consensus. The second is that there are many traditions from the Prophet passed down concerning the two of them, according to which they were promised Paradise, are eulogized, have judgments expressed as to the soundness of their religion and the steadfastness of their convictions and declaring that they have precedence over the rest of humanity. If these traditions from the Prophet have reached the ears of those who make the charge (of unbelief against Abu Bakr and Umar), and in spite of it he expresses his belief they they are in unbelief, then he himself is an unbeliever, not because he accused them of unbelief, but because he is giving the lie to the Apostle of God, upon whom be God's blessing and peace, and by general consent anyone who treats any word of his sayings as a lie is an unbeliever.

Ghazali now comes to the rock-bottom issue: Who is a Muslim and who is not? What must one believe to be reckoned a member of the community, secure against all attempts to read such a one out of the community?

Let us suppose someone asks: What is your teaching with regard to someone who declares a fellow Muslim to be in unbelief, is such a one an unbeliever or not? Our answer is: If such a one is aware that this (fellow Muslim whom he has accused of unbelief) believes in the divine Oneness, had confident trust in the Apostle, upon whom be God's blessing and peace, and held other proper doctrines, then whensoever he declares him an unbeliever with respect to these doctrines, he is himself an unbeliever, since he is expressing an opinion that the true religion is unbelief and is untrue. On the other hand, if he thinks (erroneously) that a fellow Muslim believes that the Apostle was false, or that he denies the Creator, or is a dualist, or some such other that necessarily involves one in unbelief, and so, relying on this opinion, declares him to be in unbelief, then he is in error with respect to his opinion of this person but right in declaring that anyone who so believes is in unbelief.

Ignorance, Ghazali explains, of anything beyond the two propositions in the simple profession of faith does not affect one's position as a Muslim.

It is not a condition of a man's religion that he knows the state of belief of every Muslim or the unbelief of every unbeliever. Indeed, there is no one person who can be imagined who, if we did not know about him, would affect our religious standing. More, if a person believes in God and His Apostle, diligently performs his acts of worship, and yet had not heard of the names of Abu Bakr and Umar, in fact dies before ever hearing of them, he would nevertheless die a Muslim, for belief in what is told about them is not among the pillars of religion, such that any mistake with respect to what must or must not be attributed to them would necessarily strip one of his religion.

What makes this group of Shi͑*ites infidels, then, is that they have read the Sunni Muslims out of the religion of Islam, and this despite ob-*

*vious evidence to the contrary. Ghazali constructs that "obvious evidence"
into a small Muslim creed.*

They believe that we (Sunnis) are in disbelief, so that it is lawful
to plunder our property and shed our blood. This necessarily leads to
their being declared to be unbelievers. This is unavoidable since they
know that we believe that the world has a Maker, Who is One, Powerful, Knowing, Willing, Speaking, Hearing and Seeing; Who has no one
like Him; that His Apostle is Muhammad ibn Abdullah, upon whom be
God's blessing and peace, who spoke the truth in all that he told about
the resurrection and the Judgment, and about Paradise and Hell. These
are the doctrines which are pivotal for sound religion. (Ghazali, *On the
Disgraceful Doctrines of the Esoteric Sects* 8.1) [JEFFERY 1962: 255–260]

10. The Caliphate

*Muhammad had no more appointed a successor to himself than Jesus had.
In the case of Christianity, immediate eschatological expectations made
that seem a natural course of events, but there is no trace of such expectations in Islam, and the umma undertook to guarantee its own political
survival by choosing someone to lead its members. They reverted to a type
of tribal selection, and the choice of the senior Muslims was designated as
"Successor (khalifa; Eng., Caliph) of the Messenger of God." The word first
appears in the Quran in a passage describing the fall of the angels.*

Remember, when the Lord said to the angels: "I have to place a
deputy on the earth." They said: "Will you place one there who would
create disorder and shed blood, while we intone Your litanies and sanctify Your name?" And God said: "I know what you do not know."
(Quran 2:30; emphasis added)

*This dialogue reported between God and the angels refers to God's
creation of Adam, but the Arabic word used in 2:30, and here translated
as "deputy" or "viceroy" is khalifa, the same word employed by the early
Muslims to designate Muhammad's successor as the head of the Islamic
community. The same word appears again in the Quran, here in connection
with the king and prophet David, where it presents an even more apposite
context for the later Islamic office.*

And We said to him: O David, we have made you a trustee (*khalifa*) on the earth, so judge between men equitably and do not follow
your lust lest it should lead you astray from the way of God. (Quran
38:26)

There was no question of there being another prophet after Muhammad, and neither in his Life nor in the other traditions attributed to him is there anything to suggest that Muhammad appointed a member of the community as his political "viceroy." But a "successor" or Caliph there was, though the question of who should hold this office was a matter of controversy. The historian Tabari (d. 923 C.E.) gives an account of what occurred in Medina immediately after the Prophet's death.

Hisham ibn Muhammad told me on the authority of Abu Mikhnaf, who said: Abdullah ibn Abd al-Rahman ibn Abu Umra, the Helper [that is, a Medinese convert] told me:

When the Prophet of God, may God bless him and save him, died, the (Medinese) Helpers assembled on the porch of the Banu Sa'ida and said, "Let us give this authority, after Muhammad, upon him be peace, to Sa'd ibn Ubada." Sa'd, who was ill, was brought before them, and after they had assembled, Sa'd said to his son (or one of his nephews), "Because of my illness I cannot speak in a manner that all the people will be able to hear my words. Therefore, listen to what I will tell you and then repeat it to them so that they may hear it." Then he spoke, and the man memorized his words and spoke in a loud voice so that the others could hear.

He said . . . "O company of Helpers! You have precedence in religion and merit in Islam possessed by no other Arab tribe. Muhammad remained for more than ten years (here in Medina) among his people, summoning them to worship the Merciful One and to abandon false gods and idols. But among his own people (in Mecca) only a few men believed in him, and they were not able to protect the Prophet of God or glorify his religion nor to defend themselves against the injustice which beset them. It is for that reason that God conferred merit on you and brought honor to you and marked you for His grace. . . . And when God caused him to die, he was content and pleased with you. Therefore keep this authority for yourselves alone, for it is yours against all others."

They all responded, "Your judgment is sound and your words are true. We shall adhere to what you say and we shall confer this authority on you. You satisfy us and you will satisfy the true believer." Then they discussed it among themselves, and some of their number said: "What if the (Meccan) Migrants from among the Quraysh refuse and say, "We are the Migrants and the first Companions of the Prophet of God; we are his own clan and his friends. Why then do you argue with us over the succession of his authority?" Some of them said, "If that turns out to be the case, we should reply to them, 'Then let there be a commander from us and a commander from you. And know that we shall never be content with less than that.'" Sa'd ibn Ubada, when he heard this, said, "This is the beginning of weakness."

News of this meeting reached Umar, and he went to the house of the Prophet, may God bless and save him. He sent for Abu Bakr, who was in the Prophet's house with Ali ibn Abi Talib preparing the body of the Prophet for burial. He sent asking Abu Bakr to come to him, and Abu Bakr sent a message replying that he was busy. Then Umar sent saying that something had happened which made his presence necessary, and he went to him and said, "Have you not heard that the Helpers have gathered in the porch of the Banu Sa'ida? They wish to confer the leadership on Sa'd ibn Ubada. . . ."

They [that is, Umar and Abu Bakr] hurried to the Helpers, and on their way they met Abu Ubayda ibn Jarrah. The three of them went on together and they met Asim ibn Adi and Uwaym ibn Sa'ida, who both said to them: "Go back, for what you want will not take place." They replied, "We will not go back," and they came to the meeting.

Umar ibn al-Khattab said: We came to the meeting, and I had prepared a speech which I wished to make to them. We reached them, and I was about to begin my speech when Abu Bakr said to me, "Gently! Let me speak first, and then afterwards you say whatever it is you wish." Abu Bakr then spoke and Umar said, "He said everything I wanted to say and more."

Abdullah ibn Abd al-Rahman said: Abu Bakr began. He praised God and then he said, "God sent Muhammad as a Prophet to His creation and as a witness to His community that they might worship God and God alone. . . . It was an enormous act for the Arabs to abandon the religion of their fathers. God singled out the first Migrants of his people by allowing them to recognize the truth and believe in him. They consoled him and shared in his suffering at the cruel hands of his people when the Quraysh rejected them and all were against them and reviled them. . . . They were the first in the land to worship God and to believe in God and the Prophet. They were his friends and his clan and the best entitled of all men to this authority after him. Only a wrongdoer would dispute this with them.

"And as for you, O company of Helpers, no one can deny your merit in the faith or your great preeminence in Islam. . . . (But) we are the rulers and you the viziers. We shall not act against your counsel, nor shall we decide things without you." . . .

Abu Bakr said, "Here is Umar and here is Abu Ubayda. Swear allegiance to whomever of them you choose." The two of them then objected, "No, by God, we will not accept this authority above you, for you are the most deserving among the Migrants and the second of the two who were in the cave (Quran 19:40) and the deputy (khalifa) of the Prophet of God in prayer, and prayer is the best part of the religion of the Muslims. Who would then be fit to take precedence of you or to accept this authority before you? Give us your hand so that we may swear allegiance to you."

And when they went forward to swear allegiance to him [that is, Abu Bakr], Bashir ibn Saʿd went ahead of them and swore allegiance to him . . . and when the (Medinese) tribe of Aws saw what Bashir ibn Saʿd had done . . . they came to Abu Bakr and they too swore allegiance to him. (Tabari, *Annals* 1.1837–1844)

11. Caliph and Imam

Thus the Muslim community seems to have taken its initial successful steps in the direction of establishing a first non-Prophetic ruler of the community, the "Caliph" or "Successor of the Prophet." If the Quran itself gave little or no guidance on this new office in Islam, there were soon circulating Prophetic traditions on the nature and qualifications for the office of Caliph, or the Imam, "he who stands before," as he is more frequently called in theoretical discussions. The philosopher-historian Ibn Khaldun (d. 1406 C.E.) explains the difference between the two terms.

The Caliphate substitutes for the Lawgiver (Muhammad) in as much as it serves, like him, to preserve the religion and to exercise political leadership of the world. The institution is called "the Caliphate" or "the Imamate." The person in charge is called "Caliph" or "Imam." . . .

The name "Imam" is derived from the comparison with the leader of prayer [also called an *imam*] since he is followed and taken as a model like the prayer-leader. Therefore the institution is called "the Great Imamate." The name "Caliph" is given to the leader because he "represents" the Prophet in Islam. One uses "Caliph" alone or "Caliph of the Messenger of God." There is some difference of opinion on the use of "Caliph of God." Some consider the expression permissible as derived from the general "Caliphate" of all the descendants of Adam . . . [based on the Quranic verses cited above]. But in general it is not considered permissible to use the expression since the Quranic verses quoted have no (specific) reference to it.

Ibn Khaldun then reflects briefly on the circumstances under which the office arose.

The position of Imam is a necessary one. The consensus of the men around Muhammad and the men of the second generation shows that the Imamate is necessary according to the religious law. At the death of the Prophet the men around him proceeded to render the oath of allegiance to Abu Bakr and to entrust him with the supervision of their affairs. And so it was with all subsequent periods. In no period were the people left in a state of anarchy. This was so by general consensus, which proves that the position of Imam is a necessary one. (Ibn Khaldun, *Muqaddima* 3.24) [IBN KHALDUN 1967: 1:388–389]

The Caliphate had thus come into existence by "the consensus of the men around Muhammad," and the Caliph was, in fact, the chief executive of the umma. *He appointed and removed political subordinates. He decided military strategy and was commander (amir) of the armies of Islam. He was the chief justice and principal fiscal officer of the new regime. Most of the Caliph's military, judicial, and fiscal responsibilities were soon delegated to others, however; the community was actually a number of armies on the march far from the centers of power, and though decisions might be made in the name of the Caliph, they were increasingly made by others.*

The Caliph and his delegates might decide, but they could not or did not legislate. They now had the closed and completed Quran, and they could not add to that text, which, like Jewish law, addressed itself in great detail to matters of personal status but was mute on the political governance of what was rapidly becoming an immense empire. The Caliph and his delegates resorted instead to a great many devices to shape their purpose: tribal practices, local customs, pragmatic necessities, and, to some extent, whatever precedents the practice of the Prophet suggested to them. There is no suggestion, on the other hand, that the Caliph regarded himself or was regarded by others as the possessor of special spiritual powers. He was the head of the umma, *and though the* umma *was based entirely on a shared acceptance of Islam, the Caliph was not a religious leader but the leader of a religious community.*

12. The Ruler, Chosen by the People
or Designated by God?

With the rise of the Shi˓ite movement—never quite politically powerful enough to seize the rulership in Islam but sufficiently potent in its propaganda and ideology to constantly threaten it—the rest of the "Sunni" community, so called because they supported "tradition (sunna) and the commonality." were forced to reexamine and defend their own positions on the nature of sovereignty in Islam. The issue raised by the Shi˓at Ali was who should rule the community. The Sunnis were willing to accept the verdict of history as reflected in the choices of that "whole first generation" of Muhammad's contemporaries and their immediate successors. The Shi˓ites argued against history in asserting the preeminence of Ali, but in so doing they were forced, to one degree or another, to attack the consensual wisdom of the "Companions of the Prophet" from whom all the Prophetic sunna ultimately derived.

The polemic of the Shi˓ite movement forced the Sunni Muslim community to reexamine its own, highly pragmatic premises, and here one of them, the essayist al-Jahiz (d. 886 C.E.), easily converts necessity into a virtue.

. . . If we were to be asked, which is better for the community, to choose its own leader or guide, or for the Prophet to have chosen him for us? Had the Prophet chosen him, that would of course have been preferable to the community's own choice, but since he did not, it is well for it that he left the choice in its own hands. . . . Had God laid down the procedure for the nomination of the Imam in a detailed formula with its own precise directions and clear signs, that would indeed have been a blessing, for we know that everything done by God is better. But since He did not make specific provision (for the office), it is preferable for us to have been left in our present situation. How can anyone oblige or constrain God to establish an Imam according to a formula simply because in your view such a solution would be more advantageous and less troublesome, and better calculated to avoid error and problems? (Jahiz, *The Uthmanis* 278–279)

This was the view of most historians, the Shi˓ites of course excepted, but at least one Prophetic tradition took no chances and put the choice of a successor directly in the Prophet's mouth.

Aisha reported that during his illness God's Messenger said to her: "Call me Abu Bakr your father, as well as your brother, so that I may write a document, for I fear that someone may desire to succeed me and that one may say 'It is I,' whereas God and the believers will have no one but Abu Bakr." Muslim transmitted this tradition. (Baghawi, *Mishkat al-Masabih* 26.30.1)

And again, with even more extended foresight:

Jabir reported God's Messenger as saying, "Last night a good man had a vision in which Abu Bakr seemed to be joined to God's Messenger, Umar to Abu Bakr, and Uthman to Umar." Jabir said: When we got up and left God's Messenger we said that the good man was God's Messenger and that their being joined together meant that they were the rulers over the matter with which God had sent His Prophet. (Baghawi, *Mishkat al-Masabih* 26.34.3)

We return to Jahiz:

The Imam may be established in three different ways: first, as we have described [that is, following the overthrow of a usurper], or in the circumstances in which the Muslims put Uthman ibn Affan [Caliph 644–656 C.E.] in power, after Umar [Caliph 634–644 C.E.] had designated (a council of) six person of comparable worth and they in turn had elected one of their number. . . . A third possibility is the situation that prevailed when the community made Abu Bakr Caliph [Caliph 632–634 C.E.]; the circumstances were different from those of Uthman's election, since the Prophet had not appointed a council as Umar did. . . . In Abu Bakr's case the community did not compare the respective merits of the Emigrants or announce the reasons for the superiority of the person elected; for they were Muslims who had known each other intimately for 23 years . . . , so that Abu Bakr's merits were immediately obvious to them; on the Prophet's death they had no need to form an opinion, since they already knew. (Jahiz, *The Uthmanis* 270–271)

*The developed Shi*ᶜ*ite view on this obviously crucial matter of the selection of the Imam or Caliph of the Muslim community is presented in the theological handbook called* The Eleventh Chapter *written by the Shi*ᶜ*ite scholar al-Hilli (d. 1326 C.E.), with a commentary by another later author with the same name. The thesis is set out in the section devoted generally to the Imamate. In the passage immediately preceding, Hilli had demonstrated that the Imam had of necessity to be immune to sin. He then continues:*

The Third Proposition: It is necessary that the Imam should be designated for the Imamate since immunity to sin is a matter of the heart which is discerned by no one save God Most High. Thus the designation must be made by one who knows that the Imam has the immunity to sin necessary for the office, or else some miracle must be worked through him to prove his truthfulness.

[Commentary] This refers to the method of appointing the Imam. Agreement had been reached that in appointing the Imam the designation can be made by God and His Prophet, or by a previous Imam in an independent way [that is, without the consent of the people]. The disagreement concerns only whether or not the Imam's appointment can be effected in any way other than by designation. Our fellow Imamites (Shiʿites) deny that absolutely, and hold that there is no way except by designation. For, as we have explained, immunity to sin is a necessary condition of the Imamate, and immunity to sin is a hidden matter, and no one is informed of it except God. In such circumstances, then, no one knows in whom it might be found unless He who knows the unseen makes it known. And that occurs in two ways: first, by making it known to someone else immune to sin, such as the Prophet, and then this latter tells us of the Imam's immunity to sin, and of his appointment; and second, by the appearance of miracles worked through his [the Imam presumptive's] power to prove his truthfulness in claiming the Imamate.

The Sunnis, on the other hand, say that whenever the community acknowledges anyone as its chief, and is convinced of his ability for the Imamate, and his power increases in the regions of Islam, he becomes the Imam. . . . But the truth is contrary to this for two reasons: first, the Imamate is a "Caliphate" [or "succession"] from God and His Messenger and so it cannot be acquired except by the word of them both; and second, the establishment of the Imamate by acknowledging someone as chief and by the latter's claim to the office would result in conflict because of the probability that each faction would acknowledge a different Imam. (Hilli, *The Eleventh Chapter* 186–188)

13. Ali, the First Imam

If, on the Shiʿite view, the Imam must be "designated" rather than simply "acknowledged," that must have occurred in the case of the very first of them, Ali ibn Abi Talib. The Fifth Proposition of that same section of Hilli's work takes up that much-disputed question.

The Fifth Proposition: The Imam after the Messenger of God is Ali ibn Abi Talib: First, because of his designation, which has been handed down in a number of distinct lines of Prophetic traditions; and second, because he is the best of his generation, by the word of the Most High

. . . ; and third, because it is necessary for the Imam to be immune from sin, and there is no one among those who claim the office who is so immune except Ali, as all agree; and fourth, because he was the most knowledgeable (about Islam), since the Companions consulted him about their problems . . . ; and fifth, because he is more ascetic than any one else, so that he divorced the world three times.

The first point is critical here, since the Shiᶜite proposition of the Prophet's designation of Ali was confronted with the undeniable historical reality that the Muslim community was in fact ruled by three other men— Abu Bakr, Umar, and Uthman—before its choice fell upon Ali. This is how Hilli's commentator deals with the problem.

[Commentary] There are differing opinions regarding the appointment of the Imam. Some claim that after the Messenger of God the Imam was Abbas ibn Abd al-Muttalib because he was his heir. And most Muslims affirm that he was Abu Bakr because the people chose him. And the Shiᶜites maintain that he was Ali ibn Abi Talib because of the designation which came down directly from God and His Messenger to him, and that is the truth. And the author [that is, Hilli] has proved Ali's right in several ways: first, that unbroken tradition of the very words of the Prophet which the Shiᶜites quote regarding the right of Ali, and from which certitude can be elicited, namely, "Greet him as the chief of the believers" and "You are the successor after me," and other words which prove what we intended, to wit, that he is the Imam. (Hilli, *The Eleventh Chapter*, 191–192)

To view the Shiᶜite claims from the Sunni side of the Islamic community, we can turn to the popular theological manual by the Sunni scholar al-Nasafi (d. 1114 C.E.).

The objection may be raised that it is related of the Prophet, upon whom be God's blessing and peace, that he once said to Ali, with whom may God be pleased: "You are to me the same as Aaron was to Moses— on both of whom be blessings and peace—save that there will be no prophet after me." Now as the deputyship of Aaron admitted no possibility of substitution, so (the Shiᶜites claim) is the case here (between Muhammad and Ali).

The Sunni response in this instance is not to deny that the Prophet made the statement but to invoke the circumstances under which it was pronounced.

The reply is that the Prophet's honoring him was not in the way you [that is, the Shiᶜites] take it, for (it is common knowledge that) the

Prophet, upon whom be God's blessing and peace, appointed Ali as his deputy over Medina while he went out on one of his raids, and as a result the evilly-disposed said: "Look, the Prophet has turned his back upon him and confined him to the house." This grieved Ali so the Prophet said to him: "You are to me the same as Aaron was to Moses." Another indication (that their interpretation is false) is the fact that Aaron died before Moses, so it would only be sound if he had said: "You are to me the same as Joshua son of Nun," for Joshua was the real successor to Moses.

This was one of the contentions of the moderate Shiʿa who looked upon Ali as the designated and so the only legitimate successor to Muhammad. There were others, however, who would have put Ali above or beside Muhammad in the ranks of the Messengers.

One group of the Rafidites [that is, one of the radical Shiʿite sects] teaches that the revelations (brought by Gabriel) were meant for Ali, with whom may God be pleased, but that Gabriel, on whom be peace, made a mistake. Another group of them teaches that Ali was associated with Muhammad in the prophetic office. All these are disbelievers for they disavow both the text of the Quran and the consensus of the community, for God has said: "Muhammad is God's Messenger" (Quran 48:29). Some of them teach that Ali was more learned than the Apostle of God and is in the position (with regard to him) that al-Khidr held to Moses [that is, the mysterious figure who serves Moses as mentor in Quran 18:66–83]. The answer to this is that saying of the Prophet which shows such knowledge as Ali had was from the teaching of the Prophet (who said): "I am the city of learning and Ali is its gate."

Another indication (of the unsoundness of their teaching) is the fact that Ali was a Saint but the Apostle of God was a Prophet, and a Prophet ranks higher than a Saint. As for al-Khidr, on whom be peace, he had direct knowledge (of things divine) for God said: ". . . whom We taught knowledge such as We have" (Quran 18:66). He means there inspired knowledge, but even so Moses was superior to him since he had a body of religious Law and a Book, and he who has a religious Law and a Book is superior. A case in point is that of David and Solomon, where David is superior.

Another group of them teaches that there never is a time when there is no Prophet on earth, and that this prophetic office came by inheritance to Ali, with whom may God be pleased, and his progeny, so that anyone who does not regard obedience to him (and his progeny) as an incumbent duty is in unbelief. The truly orthodox people [that is, the Sunnis] teach that there is no Prophet after our Prophet, for this is proved by God's words "and seal of the Prophets" (Quran 33:40). It is related on the authority of Abu Yusuf that the Prophet said: "If a pretender to prophecy comes forward laying claim to the prophetic office, should anyone demand from him proof (of his mission), he [the one who requested proof] would thereby show himself to be in unbelief, for he would have disavowed the text of Scripture." The same is true of anyone who has doubts about him, for one demands a proof in order to make clear what is true from what is false, but if anyone lays claim to the prophetic office after Muhammad, upon whom be blessing and peace, his claim cannot be other than false." (Nasafi, *The Sea of Discourse on Theology*) [JEFFERY 1962: 445–446]

14. The Pool of Khum

*A more detailed version of how the Shi*c*ites explained the events surrounding the designation of Ali as Imam is provided by al-Majlisi (d. 1700 C.E.). Although he comes late in the tradition, he reproduces a standard Shi*c*ite contextual exegesis of the Quranic passage in question.*

When the ceremonies of the (farewell) pilgrimage were completed, the Prophet, attended by Ali and the Muslims, left Mecca for Medina. On reaching the Pool of Khum he halted, although that place had never before been a stopping place for caravans, because it had neither water nor pasturage. The reason for encampment in such a place (on this occasion) was that illustrious verses of the Quran came powerfully upon him, enjoining him to establish Ali as his successor. He had previously received communications to the same effect, but not expressly appointing the time for Ali's inauguration, which, therefore, he had deferred lest opposition be excited and some forsake the faith. This was the message from the Most High in Sura 5:67:

> "O Messenger, publish what has been sent down to you from
> your Lord, for if you do not, then you have not delivered His
> message. God will protect you from men; surely God guides
> not unbelieving people."

Being thus peremptorily commanded to appoint Ali his successor, and threatened with penalty if he delayed when God had become his surety, the Prophet therefore halted in this unusual place, and the Muslims dismounted around him. As the day was very hot, he ordered them to take shelter under some thorn trees. Having ordered all the camel-saddles to be piled up for a pulpit or rostrum, he commanded his herald to summon the people around him. When all the people were assembled he mounted the pulpit of saddles, and calling to him the Commander of the Believers [that is, Ali], he placed him on his right side. Muhammad now rendered thanksgiving to God, and then made an eloquent address to the people, in which he foretold his own death, and said: "I have been called to the gate of God, and the time is near when I shall depart to God, be concealed from you, and bid farewell to this vain world. I leave among you the Book of God, to which if you adhere, you will never go astray. And I leave with you the members of my family, who cannot be separated from the Book of God until both join me at the fountain of al-Kawthar."

He then demanded, "Am I not dearer to you than your own lives?" and was answered by the people in the affirmative. He then took the hands of Ali and raised them so high that the white (of his shirt) appeared and said, "Whoever receives me as his master (or ally), then to him Ali is the same. O Lord, befriend every friend of Ali, and be the enemy of all his enemies; help those who aid him and abandon all who desert him."

It was now nearly noon, and the hottest part of the day. The Prophet and the Muslims made the noon prayer, after which he went to his tent, beside which he ordered a tent pitched for the Commander of the Believers. When Ali was rested Muhammad commanded the Muslims to wait upon Ali, congratulate him on his accession to the Imamate, and salute him as the Commander. All this was done by both men and women, none appearing more joyful at the inauguration of Ali than did Umar. (Majlisi) [WILLIAMS 1971: 63–64]

15. The Martyrdom of Husayn

At the death of Ali by an assassin's hand in 661 C.E. the fortunes of his descendants and of the "party" that had grown up around them seemed uncertain. Ali's eldest son Hasan appeared little inclined to enter the deadly game of politics, and when Ali's rival Mu^cawiya of the wealthy and powerful Banu Umayya—Uthman too had been a member, and Abu Sufyan was their leader during the Prophet's days in Mecca—was declared Caliph in Jerusalem in 661 C.E., Hasan allowed himself to be persuaded to abdicate *his claim in favor of the Umayyad. He died in an easeful retirement in Medina in 669 C.E., possibly poisoned, as the Shi*ites claimed, and the responsibility for the Alids' fortunes fell upon his brother Husayn.*

*Nothing is heard of Husayn during the relatively long reign of Mu*awiya (661–680 C.E.), but when the Caliph died and contrived to have his son Yazid declared his successor, Husayn publicly refused to acknowledge him. He had some support among the Shi*a of Kufa and allowed himself to be persuaded to set out, accompanied by only a few troops and encumbered by the women and children of his family, across the steppe to lead the anti-Umayyad insurrection in Iraq. The Umayyads were aware he was on his way and Ubaydallah ibn Ziyad, the governor of Iraq, dispatched a force under the somewhat reluctant Umar ibn Sa*d to intercept him. The fateful encounter occurred at a place called Karbala on the Euphrates north of Kufa. The date was the 10th of the month of Muharram, forever thereafter a Shi*ite holy day (see chapter 6 below).*

Husayn continued and the vanguard of Ubaydallah's cavalry met him. When he saw them he turned aside toward Karbala. He positioned himself with his rear against reeds and grass so that he would have to fight from only one direction. Then he stopped and put up his tents. His followers were forty-five horsemen and a hundred foot soldiers. . . .

Then Umar ibn Sa*d fought against him. All Husayn's followers were killed, among whom were more than ten young men from his family. An arrow came and struck his baby son while he had him in his lap. He began to wipe the blood from him, saying, "O God! Judge between us and a people who asked us to come so that they might help us and then killed us." He called for a striped cloak, tore it and put it on. He took out his sword and fought until he was killed. A man of the tribe of Madhhij killed him and cut off his head. He took it to Ubaydallah. . . .

Ubaydallah sent him to (the Caliph) Yazid ibn Mu*awiya, and with him he sent the head. He put Husayn's head in front of him. With him was Abu Barzah al-Aslami [a Companion of the Prophet]. Yazid began to poke at the mouth with a cane. . . . Abu Barzah cried out to him, "Take your cane away. How often have I seen the Messenger of God kiss that mouth!"

Umar ibn Sa*d had sent Husayn's womenfolk and family to Ubaydallah. The only male member of the "People of the House" of Husayn ibn Ali who had survived was his son Ali who had been sick and had rested with the women. Ubaydallah ordered him to be killed but (Husayn's sister) Zaynab threw herself on him and said, "By God! He will not be killed until you first kill me." Ubaydallah had pity on her and refrained from killing the young lad. He equipped them for a journey and sent them to Yazid.

When they came to Yazid, he gathered together the Syrians who used to attend him. When the Syrians came to him and congratulated him on his victory, one of them, who was blue-eyed with a fair complexion, said, as he looked at one of their young women, "Commander of the Faithful, give that one to me." Zaynab said, "No, by God! There is no such honor possible for you or for him unless he leaves the religion of God." The blue-eyed man repeated his request but Yazid said to him, "Desist from this." (Tabari, *Annals* 2.216) [TABARI 1990: 75–76]

This is the rather spare account offered by the historian Tabari, himself a Shiᶜite, and it is immediately followed by a great many pages of alternative accounts. Most of them supply additional emotional details, like this one on the immediate aftermath of Husayn's death, derived from Abu Mikhna, who had gotten it from an eyewitness.

I looked at those women. As they passed (the slaughtered) Husayn and the members of his family and his sons, they shrieked and tore at their faces. I turned my horse toward them. I had never seen a sight of women more beautiful than the sight I saw of those woman. . . . Among the things that I will never forget: I will never forget the words of Zaynab, the daughter of Fatima, as she passed the prostrate body of her brother Husayn. She was saying, "O Muhammad! O Muhammad! May the angels of heaven bless you. Here is Husayn in the open, stained with blood and with limbs torn off. O Muhammad! Your daughters are prisoners, your progeny are killed, and the east wind blows dust over them." By God! She made every enemy and friend weep. (Tabari, *Annals* 2.370) [TABARI 1990: 164]

Or again, with even more pathetic detail:

I was with Yazid ibn Muᶜawiya in Damascus when Zahr ibn Qays arrived. . . . "O Commander of the Faithful, I bring good news of God's victory and support. Husayn ibn Ali came against us with eighteen men of his House and sixty of his Shiᶜa. We went out to meet them and asked them to surrender. . . . They chose to fight rather than surrender. We attacked them as the sun rose and surrounded them on every side. Eventually our swords took their toll of the heads of the people; they began to flee without having any refuge; they sought refuge from us on the hills and in the hollows as doves seek refuge from a hawk. By God! Commander of the Faithful, it was only a time for the slaughtering of animals, or for a man to take his siesta before we had come upon the last of them. There were their naked bodies, their bloodstained clothes, their faces thrown in the dust. The sun burst down on them; the wind scattered dust over them; their visitors in this deserted place were eagles and vultures. (Tabari, *Annals* 2.374–375) [TABARI 1990: 169]

*It is apparent that already by the time of Tabari the slaughter of Husayn and his family—his son Ali was the only male survivor—had caught the popular imagination. The Shi*ites had unwittingly been provided with the first and still the most preeminent martyr to their cause (see chapter 6 below).*

16. The "People of the House"

The expression "people of the house" occurs three times in the Quran, but one instance in particular caught the attention of the later Muslim commentators. In Sura 33 there are a number of admonitions apparently addressed to the wives or "women" of the Prophet, and in this context Quran 33:33 reads:

And God only wishes to remove all abominations from you, O people of the house, and purify you thoroughly. (Quran 33:33)

*What ostensibly refers to the Prophet's wives may have quite another point of reference, however. In early Islamic and pre-Islamic times the preeminent "People of the House" were the Quraysh—"house" is understood to refer, as it does in every instance in the Quran, to the Meccan Ka*ba. *If this was the original meaning of the verse, it was soon overwhelmed by another, quite political understanding of it: the "house" in question was Muhammad's own family, and the "People of the House" were Ali's family or, more precisely, Ali, Fatima, and their children, Hasan and Husayn. Prophetic sayings soon began to collect around this verse, most notably the "tradition of the cloak": when this verse was revealed, Muhammad took his cloak, spread it over Ali, Fatima, Hasan, and Husayn, and said, "O God, these are the people of my house whom I have chosen; take the pollution from them and purify them thoroughly." Thus the offspring of Ali and Fatima began to be regarded as constituting a divinely chosen and divinely blessed "Holy Family" of Islam.*

*The origins of this type of interpretation of Quran 33:33 go back to early Umayyad times and reflect the contest for the Caliphate between Ali and the House of Umayya that began with the murder of Uthman and the subsequent struggle between Ali and Mu*awiya. *The decisive defeat and*

death of Ali's son Husayn at Umayyad hands at Karbala in Iraq (680
C.E.), along with the passive attitude of Husayn's own son Ali, called Zayn
al-Abidin (d. 712 C.E.), and his grandson, Muhammad al-Baqir (d. 731
C.E.), kept Alid expectations at a low level during most of the Umayyad
era. But there were stirrings, though in a somewhat different direction. A
rebel named Mukhtar had attempted to raise the banner of Alid legitimacy,
not, however, in the name of Hasan's or Husayn's sons, but in support of
another of Ali's offspring, Muhammad ibn al-Hanafiyya, "son of the Ha-
nafite woman." Muhammad ibn al-Hanafiyya died sometime around 700
C.E. or shortly thereafter. Later the story circulated that he was "the
Mahdi"—he was the first Muslim to be given that messianic title—and
that he had not died but simply disappeared on a hill near Medina called
Jabal Radwa.

Nothing came of these early attempts at insurrection against the Caliphate, now under the apparently firm control of the House of Umayya,
but a new claim had been lodged, and it finally came to term in 749 C.E.
when rebels in eastern Iran collected support around Abu al-Abbas, a descendant of the Prophet's paternal uncle. The revolt was successful: in 749
C.E. the last Umayyad was toppled and Abu al-Abbas al-Saffah assumed
the Caliphate.

Abu al-Abbas was not an Alid nor did he claim to be. His proof of
legitimacy lay elsewhere, in the testimony that Ibn al-Hanafiyya's son, and
Ali's grandson, Abu Hashim (whom the Umayyads had under detention in
Damascus) had "bequeathed" his claim to the office to the father of Abu
al-Abbas. This legacy eventually passed to Abu al-Abbas himself, who thus
ruled as the legitimate Alid "heir." There were far more legitimate Alids
abroad in the mid-eighth century, of course, and one of them, Muhammad
ibn Abdullah, surnamed "the Pure Soul," began to assert himself in Medina
at the time of Mansur (r. 754–775 C.E.). Muhammad ibn Abdullah was
not a newcomer to the political stage. His father, himself a grandson of
Hasan ibn Ali ibn Abi Talib, had already put him forward as the Mahdi,
the savior of Islam. After the death of al-Walid II in 744, when the Umayyad dynasty was clearly tottering to its ruin, Muhammad ibn Abdullah's
father asked other family members to swear allegiance to his son before the
Kaʿba in Mecca in the course of the annual pilgrimage. It was done and,
the story went on, among those who took the oath were Abu al-Abbas and
his brother al-Mansur.

True or not, there was no place for "the Pure Soul" in the political
plans of either Abu al-Abbas or Mansur, and at the accession of the latter
in 754 C.E. Muhammad ibn Abdullah refused to take the oath of allegiance to the new Caliph. Mansur reacted with force, first by arresting any

members of the family he could lay hold of and then by sending an army into the Hijaz, the heart of whatever support Muhammad ibn Abdullah possessed. In a battle about Medina in December of 762 C.E. the great-grandson of Hasan ibn Ali was slain and his Medinese followers routed.

In an exchange of letters between Mansur and Muhammad ibn Abdullah before their fatal confrontation, the Alid claims to the rule of the community are spelled out in new detail; in consequence, so is Mansur's shifting of the legitimist grounds for his own house. "Our father Ali was the heir (of the Prophet) and the Imam; how could you inherit his title while his descendants are still alive?" Muhammad argued. "We are descended from the Prophet's . . . daughter Fatima in Islam." This of course ruled out the Abbasids' appeal to an inheritance from Muhammad ibn al-Hanafiyya who was obviously not a "Fatimid." To which Mansur pointedly replied that it was not Fatima who grounded the Abbasids' claim but the Prophet's uncle himself, al-Abbas. "God has not given to women the same status he has given to (paternal) uncles and to fathers. . . . For he gave the uncle equal status with the father."

What was first put forward by Mansur became the official doctrine of the Abbasid house under Mansur's son al-Mahdi (r. 775–785 C.E.). The new revisionist version of Abbasid claims is explicitly set out in an anonymous treatise called "Reports of the Abbasid Regime, together with Reports of Abbas and His Sons."

The organization of the Abbasid Shiᶜa originated in Muhammad ibn al-Hanafiyya. . . . This went on until the time of al-Mahdi. Al-Mahdi bade them, however, to establish the Imamate on al-Abbas ibn Abd al-Muttalib, telling them that the *imama* belonged to Abbas, the prophet's paternal uncle . . . since he was the most worthy of all men to succeed him and was his nearest kinsman. (*Akhbar al-dawla al-abbasiyya* 165–166)

17. The Shiᶜite Succession

In the view of the Sunni community the Muslim "partisans" par excellence were the Shiᶜites. It was not, however, the latter's partisanship for Ali, a revered figure for all Muslims, that made them suspect in Sunni eyes, but rather their rejection of what was understood to be a community consensus, as the Sunni philosopher and historian Ibn Khaldun (d. 1406 C.E.) explains in his Prolegomenon to History.

Ali is the one whom Muhammad appointed (as head of the community). The Shiᶜites transmit texts (of Prophetic traditions) in support of this belief, which they interpret so as to suit their tenets. The authorities on the Prophetic tradition and the transmitters of the religious law do not know these texts. Most of them are supposititious, or some of their transmitters are suspect, or their true interpretation is very different from the wicked interpretation that the Shi°a give them. (Ibn Khaldun, *Muqaddima* 3.25) [IBN KHALDUN 1967: 1:403]

Though the Shi°ites agreed on the general principle of the Imamate—that it was, for example, a spiritual office passing by designation from Ali through the line of his descendants—they eventually fell into schismatic disputes on who precisely was the designated heir. By the fourteenth century Ibn Khaldun could look back and trace an elaborately sectarian Shi°ite heresiography. The first issue to divide them was the matter of the Caliphs who preceded Ali, the other three among the four "Rightly Directed Ones" (rashidun), as the Sunnis called them. The Umayyad Uthman (r. 644–656 C.E.) was totally unacceptable, but what of Abu Bakr and Umar? Were they usurpers or simply inferior tenants of the office?

Some Shi°a hold the opinion that those texts [that is, the texts supporting Ali's claim to the Imamate] prove both the personal appointment of Ali and the fact that the Imamate is transmitted from him to his successors. They [that is, this group of Shi°ites] are the Imamites. They renounce the two shaykhs (Abu Bakr and Umar) because they did not give precedence to Ali and did not render an oath of allegiance to him, as required by the texts quoted. The Imamites do not take the Imamates of Abu Bakr and Umar seriously. But we do not want to bother with transmitting the slanderous things said about Abu Bakr and Umar by Imamite extremists. They are objectionable in our opinion and (should be) in theirs.

Other Shi°ites say that these proofs require the appointment of Ali not in person but in so far as his qualities are concerned. They say that people commit an error when they do not give the qualities their proper place. They are the Zaydi (Shi°a). They do not renounce the two shaykhs Abu Bakr and Umar. They do take their Imamates seriously, but they say that Ali was superior to them. They permit an inferior person to be the Imam, even though a superior person may be alive at the same time.

Then there is the far more divisive question of the legitimate succession among Ali's descendants. Here too the Imamite and the Zaydi Shi°a differ.

The Shi‘a differ in opinion concerning the succession to the Caliphate after Ali. Some have it passed on through the descendants of Fatima [one of Ali's wives and the daughter of Muhammad] in succession, through testamentary designation. . . . They are called "Imamites," with reference to their statement that knowledge of the Imam and the fact of his being appointed are an article of faith. That is their fundamental tenet.

Others consider the descendants of Fatima the (proper) successors to the Imamate, but through the selection of an Imam from among the Shi‘a. The conditions governing the selection of that Imam are that he have knowledge, be ascetic, generous and brave, and that he go out to make propaganda for his Imamate. They who believe this are "Zaydis," so named after the founder of the sect, Zayd son of Ali son of Husayn, the grandson of Muhammad. He [that is, Zayd; d. 740 C.E.] had a dispute with his brother Muhammad al-Baqir [d. 731 C.E.] concerning the condition that the Imam had to come out openly. Al-Baqir charged him with implying that, in the way Zayd looked at it, their father Ali Zayn al-Abidin [d. ca. 712 C.E.] would not be an Imam because he had not come out openly and had made no preparation to do so. . . . When the Imamites discussed the question of the Imamates of the two shaykhs Abu Bakr and Umar with Zayd, and noticed that he admitted their Imamates, they disavowed him and did not make him one of the Imams. On account of this they are called "Rafidites" or "Disavowers." . . .

There are also Shi‘a sects that are called "Extremists." They transgress the bounds of reason and the faith of Islam when they speak of the divinity of the Imams. They either assume that the Imam is a human being with divine qualities, or they assume that he is God in human incarnation. This is a dogma of incarnation that agrees with the Christian tenets regarding Jesus. . . . Some Shi‘a extremists say that the perfection of the Imam is possessed by nobody else. When he dies his spirit passes over to another Imam, so that this perfection may be in him. This is the doctrine of metempsychosis. (Ibn Khaldun, *Muqaddima* 3.26) [IBN KHALDUN 1967: 1:404–405]

18. Awaiting the Hidden Imam

Ibn Khaldun continues with his exposition of Shi‘ism.

Some Shi‘a extremists stop (*waqafa*) with one of the Imams and do not continue (the succession). They stop with the Imam whom they consider to have been appointed last. They who believe this are the "Waqifites." Some of them say that the Imam is alive and did not die.

This general typology of "Waqifite" Shiʿites brings Ibn Khaldun to an important feature of developed Shiʿism, the doctrine of the "Hidden Imam."

The extremist Imamites, in particular the Twelvers, hold a similar opinion. They think that the twelfth of their Imams, Muhammad ibn al-Hasan al-Askari, to whom they give the epithet of "The Mahdi," entered the cellar of their house in al-Hilla (in Iraq) and was "removed" [or "concealed"] when he was imprisoned there with his mother. He has remained there "removed" [since sometime after 874 C.E.]. He will come forth at the end of time and will fill the world with justice. The Twelver Shiʿa refer in this connection to the Prophetic tradition found in the collection of al-Tirmidhi regarding the Mahdi.

That tradition reads:

The world will not be destroyed until the Arabs are ruled by a man from my family, whose name shall tally with my name.

The text of Ibn Khaldun continues:

The Twelver Shiʿites are still expecting him to this day. Therefore they call him "the Expected One." Each night after the evening prayer they bring a mount and stand at the entrance to the cellar [where the Mahdi was "removed"]. They call his name and ask him to come forth openly. They do so until the stars are out. Then they disperse and postpone the matter to the following night. They have continued the custom to this time. (Ibn Khaldun, *Muqaddima* 3.26) [IBN KHALDUN 1967: 1: 406–408]

This is the account of a Sunni historian. If we return to the beginning of the process, we can understand somewhat better what gave rise to this position, which became normative among the great majority of Shiʿites.

The Shiʿites were the party of both hope and despair in the Islamic community: a hope that the Prophet's message would establish God's justice on earth, and despair that the community as presently constituted could achieve that goal. "As presently constituted" meant governance by the illegitimate Caliphs rather than the Imams, the divinely designated, divinely inspired, and divinely guided descendants of Ali.

Those Imams had little ground for hope in the ninth century. As we shall soon see, there had been a major schism in the Shiʿa over the succession to the Imamate among the sons of Jaʿfar al-Sadiq (d. 765 C.E.), and even the main body of the movement, those moderates called "Imamites" who supported the line from Ja'far's son Musa al-Kazim (d. 800 C.E.), must have grown despondent when the eleventh in that succession, Hasan al-Askari, died in 874 C.E., persecuted by the Sunni authorities, apparently without issue. A number of different views were put forward as a result, among them that there was indeed an infant son but that he had been kept in concealment because of the danger and difficulty of the times. The Shi'ite authority al-Nawbakhti, writing in the beginning of the tenth century, describes what came to be the majority opinion among Shi'ites.

We have conformed to the past tradition and have affirmed the Imamate of al-Askari and accept that he is dead. We concede that he had a successor, who is his own son and the Imam after him until he appears and proclaims his authority, as his ancestors had done before him. God allowed this to happen because the authority belongs to Him and He can do all that He wills and He can command as He wishes concerning his [that is, the Imam's] appearance and his concealment. It is just as the Commander of the Faithful (Ali) said: "O God, you will not leave the earth devoid of a Proof of Your own for mankind, be they manifest and well known, or hidden and protected, lest Your Proof and Your signs are annulled."

This then is what we have been commanded to do and we have received reliable reports on this subject from the past Imams. It is improper for the slaves of God to discuss divine affairs and pass judgment without having knowledge and to seek out what has been concealed from them. It is also unlawful to mention his [that is, the concealed Imam's] name or ask his whereabouts until such times as God decides. This is so because if he, peace be upon him, is protected, fearful and in concealment, it is by God's protection. It is not up to us to seek for reasons for what God does. . . . The reason is that if what is concealed were revealed and made known to us, then his and our blood would be shed. Therefore, on this concealment, and the silence about it, depends the safety and preservation of our lives. (Nawbakhti, *The Sects of the Shi'a* 92) [SACHEDINA 1981: 50]

Nawbakhti wrote during the concealment of the Imam, when there was some expectation that he might indeed emerge from it in some ordinary political sense and assert his claim. But as time passed there was no appearance, and at the end of a normal life span, when the hidden Imam could no longer be thought to be alive in any purely human sense, some adjustment in thinking had to be made. What it was is apparent in al-Mufid (d. 1022 C.E.), another Shi'ite authority, writing a century after Nawbakhti.

When al-Askari died, his adherents were divided into fourteen factions, as reported by al-Nawbakhti, may God be pleased with him. The majority among them affirm the Imamate of his son, al-Qa'im al-Muntazar [The Awaited Redresser of Wrongs, a messianic title]. They assert his birth and attest his (formal) designation by his father. They believe that he was someone named after the Prophet and that he is the Mahdi of the People. They believe that he will have two forms of concealment, one longer than the other. The first concealment will be the shorter, and during it the Imam will have deputies and mediators. They relate on the authority of some of their leaders that al-Askari had made him [that is, his son and successor] known to them and shown them his person. . . . They believe that the Master of the Command is living and has not died, nor will he die, even if he remains for a thousand years, until he fills the world with equity and justice, as it is now filled with tyranny and injustice; and that at the time of his reappearance he will be young and strong in (the frame of) a man of some thirty years. They prove this with reference to his miracles and take these as some proofs and signs (of his existence). (al-Mufid, *Ten Chapters on the Concealment*) [SACHEDINA 1981: 58]

In the developed form of this tradition, the young son of al-Askari went into concealment, perhaps at his father's death in 874 C.E., perhaps even earlier. During that interval the community—that is, the faithful Shi^c*ite remnant—was under the charge of four agents, as the theologian Nu*^c*mani (d. 970 C.E.) explains.*

As to the first concealment, it is that occultation in which there were the mediators between the Imam and the people, carrying out (the orders of the Imam), having been designated by him, and living among the people. These are eminent persons and leaders from whose hands have emanated cures derived from the knowledge and recondite wisdom which they possessed, and the answers to all the questions which were put to them about the problems and difficulties (of religion). This is the Short Concealment, the days of which have come to an end and whose time has gone by. (Nu^cmani, *The Book of the Concealment* 91) [SACHEDINA 1981: 85–86]

The last of these four agents died in 941 C.E. and then there began the Complete Concealment, which will end only with the eschatological appearance, or better, the reappearance of the Mahdi Imam. And until that occurs, the direction of the community rests, as it came to be understood, in the hands of the Shi^c*ite jurists. The return of the Mahdi-Imam must once have been a vivid expectation among the Shi*^c*ites, but as occurred among* *the Jews regarding the Messiah, and among the Christians on the Second Coming of Christ, so too the Shi*ites relaxed the immediacy of the event into the indefinite future, as is summed up in the tradition attributed to the fifth Imam, Muhammad al-Baqir (d. 732 C.E.). He was asked about a saying of Ali that the Shi*ites' time of trial would last seventy years, and his response both explains the delay and counsels, and so many had before and after, that "no man can know the day or the hour."*

God Most High had set a time to seventy years. But when (Ali's son) Husayn was killed (at Karbala in 680 C.E.), God's wrath on the inhabitants of the earth became more severe and that period was postponed up to a hundred and forty years. We had informed you about this, but you revealed the secret. Now God has delayed (the appearance of the Mahdi) for a further period for which He has neither fixed a time nor has He informed us about it, since "God blots and establishes whatsoever He will; and with Him is the essence of the Book." (Tusi, *The Book of the Concealment* 263) [SACHEDINA 1981: 152–153].

*But despite the advice not to concern itself with such matters, the unanimous Shi*ite tradition knows at least the day and the month of the return of the Hidden Imam: the Mahdi will return on the anniversary of Husayn's martyrdom on the tenth day of the month of Muharram (see chapter 6).*

Ibn Khaldun had ended his account with a passing reference to the ritual of awaiting, at al-Hilla in Iraq, the return of the Hidden Imam to the very house from which he had originally gone into "occultation." We have an eyewitness report of the same ceremony from the traveler Ibn Battuta written ca. 1355 C.E.

Near the principal bazaar of [al-Hilla] there is a mosque, over the door of which a silk curtain is suspended. They call this the "Sanctuary of the Master of the Age." It is one of their customs that every evening a hundred of the townsmen come out, carrying arms and with drawn swords in their hands, and go to the governor of the city after the afternoon prayer; they receive from him a horse or mule, saddled and bridled, and [with this they go in procession] beating drums and playing fifes and trumpets in front of this animal . . . and so they come to the Sanctuary of the Master of the Age. Then they stand at the door and say, "In the name of God, O Master of the Age, in the name of God come forth! Corruption is abroad and tyranny is rife! This is the hour for thy advent, that by thee God may divide the True from the False." They continue to call in this way, sounding the trumpets and drums and fifes, until the hour of the sunset prayer. For they assert that Muhammad ibn al-Hasan al-Askari entered this mosque and disappeared from sight in it, and that he will emerge from it since he is, in their view, the "Expected Imam." (Ibn Battuta, *Travels*) [IBN BATTUTA 1959–1962: 325]

Disappointed by history, the Shi c*ites eventually turned to Gnosticism. They became the purveyors of a hidden wisdom (hikma), a kind of particularist and underground sunna transmitted, generation after generation, by infallible Imams of the Alid house or by their delegates. In fully developed Shi*c*ism, which found its most lasting base by connecting itself with Persian nationalism, the entire range of Gnostic ideas is on display: the exaltation of wisdom (hikma) over science (ilm); a view of historical events as reflection of cosmic reality; and a concealed (batin) as opposed to an "open" (zahir) interpretation of Scripture. As we shall see in chapters 7 and 8 below, it was simply a matter of time before Shi*c*ite Gnosticism found its siblings within Sufism and philosophy.*

19. "Twelvers" and "Seveners" among the Shi*c*ites

*There were many branches of Shi*c*ites, as Ibn Khaldun describes in detail, but the two most important of them, in terms of the numbers of adherents they could command and the political power they could from time to time wield, were the Imamites called "Twelvers"—the term came to be almost synonymous with "Imamite"—and another group called either Isma*c*ilis or "Seveners." Ibn Khaldun explains:*

The Imamites consider the following as successors to the Imamate after Ali [d. 661 C.E.] . . . by designation as heirs: Ali's son Hasan [d. 669 C.E.], that latter's brother Husayn [d. 680 C.E.], Husayn's son Ali Zayn al-Abidin [d. 712 C.E.], the latter's son Muhammad al-Baqir [d. 731 C.E.], and his son Ja*c*far al-Sadiq [d. 765 C.E.]. From there on they split into two sects. One of them considers Ja*c*far's son Isma*c*il [d. 760 C.E.] as Ja*c*far's successor to the Imamate. They recognize Isma*c*il as their Imam and they are called Isma*c*ilis. The other group considers Ja*c*far's other son, Musa al-Kazim [d. 799 C.E.], as Ja*c*far's successor in the Imamate. They are the Twelvers because they stop the succession with the twelfth Imam [that is, Muhammad al-Mahdi, mentioned above]. They say that he remains "removed" until the end of time.

*That the Shi*c*ite "designation" was an indelible one and signaled, like the Christians' laying on of episcopal hands, the transmission of an irrevocable spiritual gift is clear from what follows.*

The Isma͑ilis say that the Imam Isma͑il became Imam because his father Ja͑far designated him to be his successor. Isma͑il died before his father, but according to the Isma͑ilis the fact that he was designated by his father as his successor means that the Imamate should continue among *his* successors. . . . As they say, Isma͑il's successor as Imam was his son Muhammad the Concealed One. He is the first of the Hidden Imams. According to the Isma͑ilis, an Imam who has no power goes into hiding. His missionaries remain in the open, however, in order to establish proof (of the Hidden Imam's existence) among mankind.

The Isma͑ili Imam did not, however, recede into some remote metaphysical outback. Sometime about 900 C.E. a certain Ubaydallah appeared in North Africa and convinced enough people that he was the great-grandson of Muhammad "the Concealed One" to carry him to power and his successors to rule over Muslim North Africa and Egypt under the dynastic name of Fatimids. Ibn Khaldun wryly concludes:

The Isma͑ilis are called such with reference to their recognition of the Imamate of Isma͑il. They are also called "Esotericists" (*batiniyya*) with reference to their speaking about the *batin*, that is, the hidden, Imam. They are also called "heretics" because of the heretical character of their beliefs. (Ibn Khaldun, *Muqaddima* 3.25) [IBN KHALDUN 1967: 1:412–413]

Ibn Khaldun's "Esotericists"—the title al-batiniyya might equally well be translated "Gnostics"—were a subdivision of the Shi͑ite movement who, unlike the main body of the Shi͑ah in the Middle Ages, had a political program for overthrowing the Sunni Caliph and replacing him with a revolutionary Mahdi-Imam. They were not successful, but they had access to and put to effective use the entire Gnostic apparatus of cosmic history, in which the Shi͑ite Imams became the Gnostic Aeons; a secret revelation of the "realities" that lay hidden in the concealed (batin) rather than the evident sense of Scripture; an Imam-guide who possessed an infallible and authoritative magisterium (ta͑lim); and an initiated elite that formed, in the Isma͑ili case, the core of an elaborate political underground. At their headquarters in Cairo, a city that the Isma͑ili Fatimids founded in 969 C.E., agents were instructed in the Isma͑ili gnosis and program, and were sent forth with the "call" of the Mahdi-Imam to cells and cadres that had been set up in the caliphal lands in Iraq and Iran.

For the Isma͑ilis, the Imam was not a political corollary of a religious system but an integral part of the religious system itself. In the famous Shi͑ite tradition already cited, Muhammad, upon his return from his "as-

cension" to the highest heavens where the truths of creation were revealed
to him, cast his mantle over his daughter Fatima and his grandsons Hasan
and Husayn and so signified the transmission of those same truths to his
Fatimid-Alid descendants. Thus it was the Imam and he alone who held,
at least in theory—every Sufi and philosopher from the twelfth century onward claimed the same privilege—the key to ta'wil, the allegorical exegesis
of Scripture that penetrated the surface meaning to the Truths beneath.

The intellectual defense of Sunnism against this claim was undertaken by al-Ghazali in a series of tracts that mounted a frontal attack on
"the Gnostics" and their infallible Imams. But the issue appears in all its
complexity in a more personal statement, his Deliverer from Error, which
describes his own investigation of the competing claims upon the faith of the
Muslim. Faith tied to simple acceptance on the authority of others was insufficient for Ghazali; it could be shaken by the conflicting claims put forward by different parties and sects within Islam and by the equally strong
adherence to their own faith by the Christians and Jews. Unless he was prepared to lapse into an agnostic skepticism, as Ghazali was not, there had
to be some other way for the seeker after truth.

The attraction of "authoritative instruction" in an age of growing
skepticism was undeniable, and Ghazali could reply that if such were the
answer, then it was far preferable to accept the infallible teaching of the
Prophet than the doctrine of some derivative Imam, whose teachings in any
event turned out to be some debased form of Greek philosophy, "some trifling
details from the philosophy of Pythagoras." But neither can really cure the
malady: it is part of the human condition to doubt and to disagree, and
on the rational level the only solution is not to throw oneself on the authority of another but to work out an answer with patience and intelligence, an answer based equally on the Quran and the principles of right
reason. The solution is, in short, Ghazali's own rigorous version of an
Islamic theology (see chapter 8 below).

20. A Juridical Portrait of the Sunni Caliph

By the eleventh century, amid the rising tide of Isma'ilism, Sunni Muslim
jurists had come to a consensus on their understanding of the Caliphate,
and the lawyer Mawardi (d. 1058 C.E.) was able to lay out the duties of
the office and the qualifications of its tenants with all the clarity typical
of a closed issue. It was closed in another sense as well: Mawardi was
writing at almost precisely the point when the actual office of Caliph had
lost most of its real powers to quite another official, the Sultan (see below).

God, whose power be glorified, has instituted a chief of the community as a successor to Prophethood and to protect the community and assume the guidance of its affairs. Thus the Imamate is a principle on which stand the bases of the religious community and by which the general welfare is regulated, so that the common good is assured by it. Hence rules pertaining to the Imamate take precedence over any other rules of government. . . . The Imamate is placed on earth to succeed the Prophet in the duties of defending Religion and governing the World, and it is a religious obligation to give allegiance to that person who performs those duties. . . .

Thus the obligatory nature of the Imamate is established, and it is an obligation performed for all by a few, like fighting in a Holy War, or the study of the religious sciences, and if no one is exercising it, then there emerge two groups from the people: the first being those who should choose an Imam from the community, and the second those who are fitted to be the Imam, of whom one will be invested with the Imamate. As for those of the community who do not belong to either of those two categories, there is no crime or sin if they do not choose an Imam. As to those two categories of people, each of them must possess the necessary qualifications. Those relating to the electors are three:

1. Justice in all its characteristics.

2. Knowledge sufficient to recognize who is worthy to be Imam by virtue of the necessary qualifications.

3. Judgment and wisdom to conclude by choosing the best person, who will best and most knowledgeably direct the general welfare.

As for those persons fitted for the Imamate, the conditions related to them are seven:

1. Justice in all its characteristics.

2. Knowledge requisite for independent judgment about revealed and legal matters.

3. Soundness of the senses in hearing, sight and speech, in a degree to accord with their normal functioning.

4. Soundness of the members from any defect that would prevent freedom of movement and agility.

5. Judgment conducive to the governing of subjects and administering matters of general welfare.

6. Courage and bravery to protect Muslim territory and wage the Holy War against the enemy.

7. Pedigree: he must be of the tribe of the Quraysh, since there

has come down an explicit statement on this, and the consensus has agreed. There is no need of taking account of Dirar ibn Amr, who stood alone when he declared that anyone could be eligible. The Prophet said: "The Quraysh have precedence, so do not go before them," and there is no pretext for any disagreement, when we have this clear statement delivered to us, and no word that one can raise against it.

There is some further discussion of the manner of electing an Imam/ Caliph, but as a matter of fact the Caliphate had been an inherited office within two families, the Umayyads and the Abbasids, uninterruptedly from 661 C.E. to the time of Mawardi's writing, a reality that is briefly averted to and approved.

If the Imamate has been conferred through the designation by the previous Imam of his successor, the consensus is that this is lawful because Abu Bakr designated Umar and Umar designated the electors of his successors. (Mawardi, *The Ordinances of Government*) [WILLIAMS 1971: 84–86]

21. The Powers of the Caliph-Imam

As the guardian and transmitter of the Apostolic tradition, the Christian bishop had enormous spiritual powers over his community, and the bishops of Rome claimed that in their case those same powers extended over the entire flock of Christ. But no Christian "overseer" ever possessed the plenitude of what Ibn Khaldun called "the royal power" and "the religious power" that he attributed to the office of the Caliph. As Ibn Khaldun explains, the Caliph held both of the "two swords" of temporal and spiritual authority in his single hand.

It has become clear that to be Caliph in reality means acting as a substitute for the Lawgiver (Muhammad) with regard to the preservation of the religion and the political leadership of the world. The Lawgiver was concerned with both things, with religion in his capacity as the person commanded to transmit the duties imposed by the religious laws to the people and to cause them to act in accordance with them, and with worldly political leadership in his capacity as the person in charge of the (public) interests of human civilization. (Ibn Khaldun, *Muqaddima* 3.29) [IBN KHALDUN 1967: 1:448]

We can observe the early Caliphs acting in exactly this fashion. In his brief tenure of the office (632–634 C.E.) Abu Bakr bade his fellow Muslims take up arms against those who sought to withdraw from the community at the death of the Prophet. Immediately after him Umar (634–644 C.E.) began to set in place many of the long-term institutions of the young Islamic state.

Abu Ja᷾far said: Umar was the first to fix and write the date (according to the Muslim era), according to what al-Harith told me, having heard it from Ibn Sa᷾d, on the authority of Muhammad ibn Umar in the year 16 (A.H.) in the month of First Rabi᷾ (March 637 C.E.). And I have already mentioned the reason for writing this and how the affair was. Umar, may God be pleased with him, was the first to date letters and seal them with clay. And he was the first to gather people before a prayer-leader to pray special prayers with them at night in the month of Ramadan, and he wrote concerning this to the provinces and commanded them to do likewise.

The most far-reaching of these measures of Umar was his exercising the "royal power" and establishing the first instruments of state to regulate the affairs of a rapidly expanding Islamic empire.

I heard from al-Harith, who heard from Ibn Sa᷾d, who heard from Muhammad ibn Umar, who heard from A᷾idh ibn Yahya, on the authority of Abu'l-Huwayrith, on the authority of Jubayr ibn al-Huwayrith ibn Nuqayd, that Umar ibn al-Khattab, may God be pleased with him, consulted the Muslims concerning the drawing up of registers, and Ali ibn Abi Talib said to him, "Share out every year whatever property has accumulated to you and do not retain anything." Uthman ibn Affan said, "I see much property, which suffices for all the people and which cannot be counted until you distinguish between those who have taken (from it) and those who have not. I do not like things to be in disorder." Al-Walid ibn Hisham ibn al-Mughira said to him, "O Commander of the Faithful, I have been to Syria and seen their kings, and they drew up a register and formed a legion. You should draw up a register and form a legion."

What was in question here was a list of pensioners, a register or diwan of those to whom the spoils of the new Islamic conquests would be distributed in order. Those spoils were now considerable, which explains the controversy about precedence that followed.

Umar summoned Aqil ibn Abi Talib and Makhrama ibn Nawfal and Jubayr ibn Mut'im, who were genealogical experts of the tribe of Quraysh, and he said to them, "Write down the people according to their ranks!" And they wrote, beginning with the Banu Hashim [that is, Muhammad's own family], then after Abu Bakr and his family and then Umar and his family, that is, following the order of succession to the Caliphate. When Umar looked at it he said, "I wish to God it were as you have written, but rather begin with the kin of the Prophet of God, may God bless and save him, and then continue in order of nearness to him until you place Umar where God has placed him."

I heard from al-Harith . . . from . . . from Usama ibn Zayd ibn Aslam, on the authority of his father, on the authority of his grandfather, who said: I was present with Umar ibn al-Khattab, when the writing (of the ranking order) was shown to him, with the Banu Taym after the Banu Hashim and the Banu Adi after the Banu Taym. And I heard him say, "Put Umar in his proper place." . . . And the Banu Adi [that is, Umar's kin] came to Umar and said, "You are the successor of the Prophet of God!" And he answered, "Rather I am the successor of Abu Bakr, and Abu Bakr was the successor of the Prophet of God." And they objected, "Why do you not put yourself where these people [that is, the genealogists] have ranked you?" And Umar said, "Well done, O Banu Adi! Do you want to feed off me? Do you want me to sacrifice my honor to you? No, by God, not until your turn comes, even though the register closes with you and you are written as the last among the people."

"I have two masters (Muhammad and Abu Bakr) who followed a certain path (Umar continued), and if I forsake them, I shall be forsaken in turn. Whatever bounty we have gotten in this world, and whatever reward we expect from God in the next world for our good deeds, is from Muhammad alone. He is our nobility, and his kin are the noblest of the Arabs; and as for the rest, they rank in order of their nearness to him. Indeed, the Arabs are ennobled with the Prophet of God, and perhaps some of them have many ancestors in common with him. As for us, it is clear that our genealogical lines coincide, and there are few ancestors that we do not share going right back to Adam. But for all that, I tell you, by God, if the non-Arabs come with deeds, and we come without them, on the Day of Judgment they will be nearer to Muhammad than we. Let no man take pride in his ancestry, but let him do God's work, and if any man's deeds fall short, his pedigree will not help him." (Tabari, *Annals* 1.2750–2752)

22. The Delegation of the Royal Power: The Sultanate

The "royal" or secular powers of the Caliph do not directly concern us here, and they were in any event "delegated" to other, more powerful figures in Islamic history, ministers who rose to dominate a Caliph or generals who simply cowed him. These de facto rulers of the Islamic commonwealth were generally known as "Sultans" and were even more often former Turkish warlords to whom the Caliphs owed the safety of their own house and the protection of the "Abode of Islam." The Caliph could only hope that the Sultan who lorded it over his own narrow base of operations around Baghdad might be Sunni and sympathetic and capable of controlling his own troops, as they often in fact were. It fell then to the Islamic lawyers to convert this rather naked usurpation of power into a form of "delegation" and make theory of a necessity. Thus Ibn Jamaᶜa (d. 1335 C.E.).

The Imam of the Muslims has the right to delegate authority over any region, country, area or province to whoever is able to hold general authority there, because necessity demands it—not least in a far country. . . . If it is to be a general delegation of power, such as is customary for sultans and kings in our own time, it is lawful for the delegate then to appoint judges and governors and rule the armies, with full disposition of the wealth from all quarters, but not to have anything to do with a region over which he is not delegated, because his is a particular government. The same qualifications apply to the delegate ruler when the Imam selects him that would apply to his own office, except that of Qurayshi descent, because he is standing in the Imam's place.

If a king attains power by usurpation and force in a (Muslim) country, then the Caliph should delegate the affairs of that place to him, in order to call him to obedience and avoid a split with him, lest there be disunity and the staff of the community be broken. In this way usurpation becomes legitimate government, issuing effective orders. (Ibn Jamaᶜa, *Statutes*) [WILLIAMS 1971: 91–92]

Ibn Khaldun, who knew well enough how to speak like a lawyer, here chooses to write like a historian.

When royal authority is firmly established in one particular family and tribe supporting the dynasty, and when that family claims all royal authority for itself and keeps the rest of the family away from it, and when the children of that family succeed to the royal authority in turn, by appointment, then it often happens that their wazirs [that is, their ministers] and entourage gain power over the throne. This occurs most often when a little child or a weak member of the family is appointed successor by his father and made ruler by his creatures and servants. It becomes clear that he is unable to fulfill the functions of ruler. Therefore they are fulfilled by his guardian, one of his father's wazirs, someone from his entourage, one of his clients, or a member of his tribe. That person gives the impression that he is guarding the power of the (child ruler) for him. Eventually it becomes clear that he exercises the control, and he uses the fact as a tool to achieve royal authority. He keeps the child away from his people. He accustoms him to the pleasures of his life of luxury and gives him every opportunity to indulge in them. He causes him to forget to look at government affairs. Eventually he gains full control over him. He accustoms the child ruler to believe that the ruler's share in royal authority consists merely in sitting on the throne, shaking hands, being addressed as "Sire" and sitting with the women in the seclusion of the harem. All exercise of actual executive power, and the personal handling and supervision of matters that concern the ruler, such as inspection of the army, finances, and defense of the border regions, are believed to belong to the wazir. He defers to him in all these things. Eventually, the wazir definitely adopts the coloring of the leader, of the man in control. The royal authority comes to be his. He reserves it for his family and his children after him. (Ibn Khaldun, *Muqaddima* 3.19) [IBN KHALDUN 1967: 1:377–378]

23. The Religious Powers of the Caliph

The Muslim's agreeably tolerant attitude of suspending judgment on the moral conduct of one's neighbor (see below) had some extremely disagreeable political implications that were, in fact, the chief point in the discussions of the Caliphate. Postponement of judgment, as it was called, effectively removed the religious and moral issue from the political life of the Islamic empire. Its acceptance marked another stage in the secularization of the Caliphate, whose tenants could no longer be challenged on the grounds of their personal morality. The predestination argument led in the same direction—de facto was in fact de Deo. The predestination versus free will argument eventually drifted off in another direction, into the metaphysical thicket of atoms, accidents, and "acquisition." But the "postponement" thesis held because it represented some kind of ill-shaped Muslim consensus that custom and the community were more important than tossing dead sinners into hell and live ones out of office or out of the community.

To return to the religious powers of this primary political authority in Islam, they are described in brief by Ibn Khaldun.

It should be known that all the religious functions of the religious law, such as (leadership of) prayer, the office of judge, the office of mufti, the Holy War, and market supervision fall under the "Great Imamate," which is the Caliphate. The Caliphate is a kind of great mainspring and comprehensive basis, and all these functions are branches of it and fall under it because of the wide scope of the Caliphate, its active interest in all conditions of the Muslim community, both religious and worldly, and its general power to execute the religious laws relative to both (religious and worldly affairs). (Ibn Khaldun, *Muqaddima* 3.29) [IBN KHALDUN 1967: 1:449]

What Ibn Khaldun saw as powers, the lawyer Ibn Jamaᶜa (d. 1333 C.E.) saw as the Caliph's duties, though both men were writing in an age when the holders of that office had little capacity for either exercising their powers or effectively fulfilling their duties.

As for the ten duties of the ruler to the subjects, the first is to protect the Muslim heritage and defend it, whether in every region, if he is Caliph, or in his own country if he is delegated over it, and to struggle against idolators and put down rebels. . . .

The second is to guard the religion in its principles and beliefs, and put down innovation and heretics and encourage the religious sciences and the study of the Law, venerate learning and religious scholars and raise places from which the light of Islam may shine. . . .

The third is to uphold the rites of Islam, such as the obligation of prayer and the congregational prayers and the call to prayer and performance of it, and the sermons and leadership of the prayers, and the matter of the fast and the feasts, and keeping the calendar, and the pilgrimage; and part of the last is facilitating the pilgrimage from all the districts, and keeping the roads clear and giving people security on the way and appointing people to look after them.

The fourth is to make the final decisions on court cases and sentences, by appointing governors and judges, so as to reduce contentiousness. . . .

The fifth is to wage the Holy War himself and with his armies at least once a year. . . .

The sixth is to apply the punishments imposed by the Law, and make no distinction when doing so between the powerful and the weak. . . .

The seventh is to collect the alms tax and the tribute from those who are to pay it [that is, the People of the Book] and the booty and the land tax, and to use it as the Law stipulates. . . .

The eighth is to supervise pious and family foundations, keep bridges and roads in good repair and make smooth the ways of welfare.

The ninth is to supervise the division and distribution of booty. . . .

The tenth is justice in the ruler in all his affairs. (Ibn Jamaᶜa, *Statutes*) [WILLIAMS 1971: 93–94]

The Caliph, it is clear, was the executor of the religious law and, unlike Muhammad whose "successor" he was, neither the maker of new laws nor the interpreter of the old. The earliest Caliphs may have exercised some of those religious functions in fact. They certainly led prayers when their personal security permitted it, conducted military campaigns, and acted as judges for the community. But rather quickly in that rapidly expanding empire others did them in the Caliph's stead: ministers, bureaucrats, and specialists, like the "mufti" on Ibn Khaldun's list—literally, "one capable of pronouncing a fatwa," *that is, a legal opinion which, if it was not binding, certainly constituted a legal precedent.*

The paradox of a ruler who possessed no direct religious powers governing a community whose common bond was the acceptance of Islam found its palliative in the growth of a body of Islamic Law that, from the ninth century onward, the Caliphs had to accept as normative. The Law was administered, as Muslim affairs had been from the beginning, by a judge or qadi *who was a caliphal appointee, and so an agent of government; but the actual control of the Law, its codification and subsequent modification, was in the hands of a body of jurisprudents known collectively as "the learned" or* ulama.

24. The Five Pillars of Islam

However they viewed it, the work of the jurisprudents had the effect of fashioning an answer to the question of what precisely constituted a Muslim. The Quran had provided the broad answer, the worship of one unique God, surely, and a salutary fear of the imminence of the Last Judgment; in the meantime the Muslim was commended to the practice of prayer, fasting, and almsgiving. It remained for the lawyers, working on the great body of Prophetic tradition, to supply the modalities and details.

It is narrated on the authority of Ibn Abbas that a delegation of (the tribe of) Abd al-Qays came to the Messenger of God, may peace be upon him, and said: Messenger of God, truly ours is a tribe of (the clan) Rabiʿa and there stand between you and us the unbelievers of Mudar and we find no freedom to come to you except in the Sacred Month. Direct us to an act which we should ourselves perform and invite those who live beside us (to perform). Upon this the Prophet remarked: I command you four things and prohibit to you four acts. (The prescribed acts are): Faith in God, and then he explained it for them and said: Testifying the fact that there is no god but the God, that Muhammad is the Messenger of God, establishment of prayer, payment of the alms-tax, and that you pay one-fifth of the booty fallen to your lot. And I prohibit you to use the round gourd, wine jars, wooden pots, or skins for wine. (Muslim, *Sahih* 1.7.22)

The prohibition against gourds, wine jars, wooden pots, and skins for wine may have been directed against a particular penchant of the Abd al-Qays for drinking. They had no role in the sequel, in any event. What was much more important, at least as far as the bedouin tribes outside Mecca were concerned, was the alms-tax, as this tradition from the era just following upon the death of the Prophet reveals.

It is narrated on the authority of Abu Hurayra that when the Messenger of God, may peace be upon him, breathed his last and Abu Bakr was appointed as his Caliph after him, those among the Arabs who wanted to become apostates apostatized. Umar ibn al-Khattab said to Abu Bakr: Why would you fight against the people when the Messenger of God declared: "I have been directed to fight against people so long as they do not say: There is no god but the God. . . ." Upon this Abu Bakr said: By God, I would definitely fight against him who separated prayer from the alms-tax, for it [that is, the alms-tax] is the obligation upon the rich. By God, I would even fight against them to secure the hobbling-cord which they used to give to the Messenger of God (as alms-tax) but now they have withheld it. Umar ibn al-Khattab remarked: By God, I found nothing but the fact that God opened the heart of Abu Bakr for fighting (against those who refused to pay the alms-tax) and I fully recognized that (his stand) was right. (Muslim, *Sahih* 1.9.29)

Adherence to Islam, as is already clear from the Quran, was more than a simple profession of faith in God and His Prophet; it also required acts: the ritual acts of prayer, fasting, and pilgrimage (see chapter 6

below), and the social and political act of paying the alms-tax. Fasting and
the pilgrimage do not occur as part of the obligations mentioned in the
traditions cited above, but they are certainly prescribed in the Quran, at
2:183, for example, and 2:196–197, and they are included in this sum-
mary tradition setting out the five Pillars of Islam.

It is narrated on the authority of Abdullah ibn Umar that the Messenger of God, peace be upon him said: (The superstructure of) Islam
is raised on five (pillars): testifying that there is no god but the God, that
Muhammad is His servant and Messenger, and the establishment of
prayer, payment of the alms-tax, pilgrimage to the House (of God at
Mecca), and the fast of (the month of) Ramadan. (Muslim, *Sahih* 1.6.20)

25. Moral Islam

The theologians and lawyers occasionally attempted to fashion a basic list
of Muslim beliefs, perhaps on the model of Christianity, but for most
Muslims Islam remained a matter of moral and social behavior rather than
the acceptance of dogma.

From Abu Hurayra, with whom may God be pleased, who said:
Said the Apostle of God, upon whom be God's blessing and peace: "Do
not envy one another; do not vie with one another; do not hate one
another; do not be at variance with one another; and do not undercut
one another in trading, but be servants of God, brothers. A Muslim is
a brother to a Muslim. He does not oppress him, nor does he forsake
him, nor deceive him nor despise him. God-fearing piety is here," he
said pointing to his breast. "It is enough evil for a man that he should
despise his brother Muslim. The blood, property and honor of every
Muslim is inviolable to a fellow Muslim." Muslim relates this tradition.
(Nawawi, *The Forty Traditions*, no. 35) [JEFFERY 1962: 157]

From Abu Hurayra, with whom may God be pleased, who said:
Said the Apostle of God, upon whom be God's blessing and peace: "In
truth God, may He be exalted, has said: 'Whoever acts with enmity
toward a friend of Mine, against him will I declare war. No servant of
Mine draws near to Me with anything I like more than that which I have
laid upon him as an incumbent duty, and a true servant of Mine will
continue drawing near to Me with supererogatory acts of worship so
that I may love him. Then when I am living with him, I am his hearing
with which he hears, his seeing with which he sees, his hand with which

he takes things, his foot with which he walks. If he asks of Me, I will surely give him, and if he takes refuge with Me, I will surely give him refuge.'" (Nawawi, *The Forty Traditions*, no. 38) [JEFFERY 1962: 158–159]

26. Alms and Charity

One of the Pillars of Islam and so an obligation binding upon every Muslim, was the paying of a statutory alms-tithe. The complex subject of tithing, how much, to whom, from whom, and for what purpose, is discussed at length in Muslim law books, but there are two Prophetic traditions in al-Nawawi's summary collection that look at alms not in their legal aspect but as a function of the virtue of charity.

From Abu Dharr, with whom may God be pleased, who said that some from among the Companions of the Apostle of God, upon whom be God's blessing and peace, said to the Prophet, upon whom be God's blessing and peace: "O Apostle of God, the rich take off all the rewards. They say prayers just as we do, they fast just as we do, but they can give in charity out of the superabundance of their wealth (and so surpass us in storing up merit)." He said: "Has not God appointed for you that you should give in charitable alms? Truly, in every ejaculation 'Glory be to God!' there is such an alms, in every 'God is the greatest!', in every 'Praise be to God!', in every 'Hallelujah!', in every bidding what is right and forbidding the doing of what is wrong; even when one of you has sex with his wife, there is an alms in that." They said: "O Apostle of God, (do you mean to say that) when one of us satisfies his desires (with his wife), there will be a reward for that?" He answered: "What do you think? Had He put it among the things forbidden, it would have been sinful for one, so when He put it among the allowable things, there was a reward for it also." Muslim relates this tradition. (Nawawi, *The Forty Traditions*, no. 25) [JEFFERY 1962: 153]

From Abu Hurayra, with whom may God be pleased, who said: Said the Apostle of God, upon whom be God's blessing and peace: "An alms is due each day that the sun rises from every finger-joint of all the people. If you straighten out some trouble between two individuals, that is an alms. If you help a man with his beast, mounting him thereon or hoisting up onto it his luggage, that is an alms. A good work is an alms. In every step you take in walking to prayer there is an alms.

Whenever you remove something harmful from the path, that is an alms." Al-Bukhari and Muslim both relate this tradition. (Nawawi, *The Forty Traditions*, no. 26) [JEFFERY 1962: 153]

27. The Sixth Pillar: War in the Path of God

As we have already seen in chapter 2 above, the Quran itself had given Muslims license to resort to force against their oppressors, and even, in Quran 2:217, to employ violence during one of the "sacred months" when the "Truce of God" was universally recognized to prevail. The point is clear: it was permissible to fight for God's cause, even in previously banned time, on the principle of a higher good's being served. It was a taking of sides, and the test was a profession of faith in the Lord God of all.

It is reported on the authority of Abu Hurayra that the Messenger of God said: I have been commanded to fight against people so long as they do not declare that there is no God but the God, and he who professed it was guaranteed the protection of his property and life on my behalf, except for the right, and his affairs rest with God. (Muslim, *Sahih* 1.9.30)

So reads an early tradition reported of Muhammad, justifying the militant quality of his calling—"I have been commanded"—and the test that qualifies one for membership in and protection of the community of Muslims. In this version that test has but a single article, belief in the one true God. However, the same authority is immediately invoked to report another, which adds a second clause.

It is reported on the authority of Abu Hurayra that he heard the Messenger of God say: I have been commanded to fight against people until they testify the fact that there is no god but the God, and believe (in me) that I am the Messenger (from the Lord), and in all that I have brought. And when they do it, their blood and riches are guaranteed protection on my behalf except where it is justified by law, and their affairs rest with God. (Muslim, *Sahih*, 1.9.31)

Islam was an activist faith, as the Prophet had demonstrated in both his words and deeds, and the theme of "striving on the path of God" runs throughout the Quran. In some instances the "striving" was a personal one against sin or toward perfection; in others the context was social or commu-nal—in short, as part of a "Holy War" in the quite literal sense of armed combat, what came to be called jihad.

Thus there came into being another candidate for inclusion among

the basic prescriptions of Islam, the "striving in the path of God" com-
manded to Muhammad and, in fact, to all Muslims. The following tradi-
tion reported after the Prophet's death appears to reflect some kind of debate
in the community on just how widely that obligation extended. In this
tradition at least, war in God's name is quite explicitly denied parity with
the other Pillars of Islam.

It is reported on the authority of Ta'us that a man said to Abdullah
ibn Umar: Why don't you carry out a military expedition? Upon which
he replied: I heard the messenger of God, may peace be upon him, say:
In truth Islam is founded on five (pillars): testifying that there is no god
but the God, establishment of prayer, payment of the alms-tax, the fast
of Ramadan, and pilgrimage to the House. (Muslim, *Sahih* 1.6.21)

Whether or not jihad *was formally one of the Pillars—and the law-*
yers continued to debate the question—militancy on behalf of the cause of
Islam, or better, of God, was a fundamental duty, as the Quran itself leaves
no doubt.

Fight those in the way of God who fight you, but do not be aggres-
sive: God does not like aggressors. And fight those wheresoever you find
them, and expel them from the place they had turned you out from.
Oppression is worse than killing. Do not fight them by the Holy Mosque
unless they fight you there. If they do, then slay them: such is the
requital for unbelievers. But if they desist, God is forgiving and kind.

Fight them until sedition comes to an end, and the Law of God
(prevails). If they desist, then cease to be hostile, except against those
who oppress. (Quran 2:190–193)

Enjoined on you is fighting, and this you abhor. You may dislike
a thing, yet it may be good for you; or a thing may haply please you but
may be bad for you. Only God has knowledge, and you do not know.
(Quran 2:216)

Those who barter the life of this world for the next should fight in
the way of God. And We shall bestow on who fights in the way of God,
whether he is killed or is victorious, a glorious reward.

What has come upon you that you fight not in the cause of God and
for the oppressed, men, women and children, who pray, "Get us out of
this city, O Lord, whose people are oppressors; so send us a friend by
Your will, and send us a helper."

Those who believe fight in the way of God; and those who do not
fight only for the powers of evil; so you should fight the allies of Satan.
Surely the stratagem of Satan is ineffective. (Quran 4:74–76)

28. "There Is No Compulsion in Religion"

The Holy War or jihad was fought against unbelievers living in the "Abode of War," that is, the territories outside the political control of the Muslim community. But within the "Abode of Islam" itself lived others who did not accept either the Quran or the Prophet yet were not heathens or polytheists. These were the "People of the Book," the "Scriptuaries" who practiced Judaism, Christianity, and, it will appear, Zoroastrianism. They were not required to embrace Islam; the proof-text is this verse of the Quran.

There is no compulsion in matters of faith. Distinct now is the way of guidance from error. He who turns away from the forces of evil and believes in God, will surely hold fast to a handle that is strong and unbreakable, for God hears all and knows every thing. (Quran 2:256)

The interpretation of this famous verse was fairly standard, despite a great deal of uncertainty about the circumstances of its revelation.

Wahidi (d. 1076 c.e.) relates on the authority of Saʿid ibn Jubayr, who related on the authority of Ibn Abbas: When the children of a woman of the Helpers [that is, early Medinese converts to Islam] all died in infancy, she vowed that if a child were to live, she would bring it up as a Jew. Thus when the Jewish tribe of al-Nadir was evicted from Medina, there were among them sons of the Helpers. The Helpers said, "O Messenger of God, what will become of our children?" Thus God sent down this (above cited) verse. Saʿid ibn Jubayr said: "Therefore whoever wished to join them did so and whoever wished to join them did so likewise." According to Mujahid, this (same) verse was sent down concerning a man who had a black male servant called Subayh. The man wished to compel his servant to enter Islam. Al-Suddi said that the verse was sent down concerning a man of the Helpers known as Abu al-Husayn who had two sons. One day merchants from Syria came to Medina to sell oil. The sons of Abu al-Husayn came to the merchants, who converted them to Christianity. They then went to Syria with the merchants. When Abu al-Husayn knew this, he came to the Prophet and asked: "Shall I pursue them?" God then sent down "There is no compulsion in religion." The Messenger of God said: "May God banish them! They are the first two who rejected faith." Mujahid said: "This was before the Messenger of God was commanded to fight against the People of the Book. God's saying 'There is no compulsion in religion' was abrogated and he was commanded to fight against the People of the Book in the Sura 'Repentance' (9:29)." . . .

According to other traditions, the verse was revealed in reference to the People of the Book, who should not be compelled to enter Islam so long as they pay the tribute. The verse is, therefore, not abrogated (by 9:29). Tabari (d. 923 C.E.) relates on the authority of Qatada: "Arab society was compelled to enter Islam because they were an unlettered community, having no book which they knew. Thus nothing other than Islam was accepted from them. The People of the Book are not to be compelled to enter Islam if they submit to paying the (tribute of the) poll-tax or the land-tax." . . .

Razi (d. 1209 C.E.) . . . comments: "This (verse) means that God did not rest the matter of faith on compulsion or coercion but rather based it on free will and the ability to choose. . . . This is what is intended here when God made clear the proofs of the Divine Unity. He said that there is no longer any excuse for a rejecter of faith to persist in his rejection. That he should be forced to accept faith is not lawful in this world, which is a world of trial. For coercion and compulsion in the matter of faith is the annulment of the meaning of trial and test." [AYOUB 1984: 252–254]

CHAPTER 4

The Word of God
and Its Understanding

The founding document of Islam is the Quran or The Recitation. *It is a composite work in which the revelations given by God through the angel Gabriel to Muhammad over the last twenty-two years of his life are collected into 114 suras or chapters. The* suras *vary greatly in length and are not arranged in chronological order; indeed, purely chronological considerations might invite one to read the book from its end to its beginning.*

Many of the suras *that appear to be early ones show a manner and an elevation of style not unlike that of the Jewish prophets as they admonish men to reform, or, as we shall see in chapter 8 below, warn of the judgment of eternity. The later* suras, *those revealed at Medina after 622 C.E., are longer and contain detailed regulations for the conduct of the already converted. For the Muslim it is God alone who speaks in the Quran; no other voice is heard in direct discourse. Much of the Quran is, indeed, about God, in Arabic* Allah, *and man's relationship to Him. But there is also much about prophecy and Prophets, the consequences of men's rejecting them in the past and the need to accept Muhammad as a genuine Prophet* (nabi) *and Messenger* (rasul) *of God.*

1. A Muslim History of Prophecy

The Quran is not only a "guidance" for the Muslims (2:185); it is also a history of God's past attempts to warn His people. It abounds with tales of other Prophets and other Books, notably the Tawra *given through Moses to the Jews and the* Injil *sent through Jesus to the Christians.*

We sent down the Torah which contains guidance and light, in accordance with which the prophets who were obedient to God gave instruction to the Jews, as did the rabbis and the priests, for they were the custodians and witnesses of God's writ. . . . Later in the train (of prophets), we sent Jesus son of Mary, confirming the Torah which had been sent down before him, and gave him the Gospel containing guidance and light for those who preserve themselves from evil and follow the straight path. . . . And to you We have revealed the Book containing the truth, confirming the earlier revelations, and preserving them. (Quran 5:44–48)

The Quran, then, is a book like those other Books, and its bearer, Muhammad, a Messenger in the tradition of Moses and Jesus—but, for all that, merely a messenger. God's word rests far above his merely mortal powers.

When Our clear messages are recited to them, those who do not hope to meet Us say: "Bring a different Quran, or make amendments in this one." Say: It is not for me to change it of my will. I follow only what was revealed to me. If I disobey my Lord, I fear the punishment of an awful Day. (Quran 10:15)

Muhammad is only a Messenger, and many a Messenger has gone before him. So what if he dies or is killed! Will you turn back and go away in haste? He who turns back and goes away in haste will do no harm to God. (Quran 5:144)

These notions all became commonplaces in the Islamic tradition, as is evident in this version of Sacred History, the details supplied and the lacunae filled in, by the literary virtuoso Jahiz (d. 886 c.e.).

When the situation becomes dangerous because the ancient traditions no longer inspire men's complete confidence, God sets a term at the end of each period of time, a sign to renew the strength of the traditions and renew the teaching of the Messengers when it grows faint. In this manner Noah renewed the traditions dating from the period between Adam and himself by giving true testimony and producing effective signs, so as to safeguard the traditions from corruption and protect them from damage. The (Prophetic) traditions and proofs of earlier generations had not been entirely obliterated or destroyed, but when they were about to be, God sent His signs so that His proofs might not disappear from the earth. That is why the end-time of a period is called "the enfeeblement." There is, however, an unmistakable difference between bending and breaking. Then God sent Abraham at the end of the second period, namely, that between the time of Noah and himself; this was the longest "enfeeblement" the world had yet experi-

enced, for Noah remained among his people, expounding and reasoning
and explaining, for 950 years, and the first of His signs was also the
greatest, namely, the Flood, in which God drowned all the people of the
earth except Noah and his followers. . . .

Then the Prophets followed one after the other in the period between Abraham and Jesus. Because their proofs followed one upon the
other, their signs clear, their acts numerous, and their deeds well
known, because all of that took deep root in people's hearts and souls
and the whole world spoke of it, their teachings were neither over-
turned nor diminished nor corrupted during the entire period from
Jesus to the Prophet (Muhammad). But when they were on the point of
becoming weakened, enfeebled, and spent, God sent Muhammad, who
renewed the teachings of Adam, Noah, Moses, Aaron, Jesus, and John
(the Baptist), and gave further detail to them; for Muhammad is righteous, and his witness is true, declaring that the Hour was at hand and
that he was the seal of the Prophets. We knew then that his proofs
would endure until the term set for it by God. (Jahiz, *The Proofs of
Prophecy* 133–134)

*Almost any educated Muslim could write such a Quran-based sum-
mary. Witness this example from the Muslim theologian al-Nasafi (d.
1114 C.E.), who is careful to draw the distinction between private or
personal written revelations—what he calls the "Scrolls"—and the
"Books," the four revealed codes of Law.*

It must be recognized that all the books (of Scripture) which God
has sent down (by revelation) to the Prophets and Apostles are the
uncreated word of God. Of these there were one hundred Scrolls and
four Books. (Of the Scrolls) God sent fifty to Seth the son of Adam, on
whom be peace. Thirty were sent to Idris [that is, Enoch], on whom be
peace; ten to Abraham, on whom be peace; and ten to Moses, on whom
be peace, before the Torah was sent down to him. It was called "The
Book of Naming" and was revealed before the drowning of the Pharaoh;
then God sent down the Torah after the drowning of the Pharaoh. Later
God sent down the Psalter to David, upon whom be peace, and then He
sent down the Gospel to Jesus, on whom be peace, who was the last of
the Prophets among the Children of Israel. Then God, may He be
praised and exalted, sent down the Quran to Muhammad, upon whom
be God's blessing and peace, who is the last of the Messengers. Anyone
who disavows a (single) verse in any of these Scriptures is in unbelief.

Should anyone say: "I believe in all the Messengers," and then disavow one of the Messengers about whom there is no (Scriptural) text,

saying, "this one does not belong among them," he would not be in a state of unbelief, but he would be in heresy. This holds so long as he does not enter another religion, but if he enters another religion he is an apostate and may be killed. . . . Be it known, moreover, that the Prophets, upon whom be peace, are 124,000, and the Messengers among them are 313, according to the tradition transmitted from Abu Dharr, with whom may God be pleased, going back to a statement of the Messenger of God, upon whom be God's blessing and peace. In some of the Prophetic traditions the (number of the) Prophets is given as a thousand thousand, or two hundred thousand and more, but the correct thing in this matter is for you to say, "I believe in God and in all the Prophets and Messengers, and in all that has come from God by way of revelation according as God willed." By thus doing you will not affirm someone to be a Prophet who was not, nor will you affirm someone not to be a Prophet who was. (Nasafi, *Sea of Discourse on Theology*) [JEFFERY 1962: 447–448]

2. Did the Jews and Christians Tamper with Scripture?

The Quran has no doubts that the earlier books given to the Jews and Christians were genuine revelation, and as such, they must have referred to the coming of the Prophet of Islam (Quran 7:157; 61:6; 3:81), much as Jesus was foreseen in the Old Testament. A search of those Scriptures failed to reveal any clear reference to Muhammad, however, which left to Muslim apologists the task of vindicating the Quran and demonstrating that the Jews and Christians had in fact tampered with the texts of the Books of God. One of the first to attempt such a demonstration in a systematic fashion was the Muslim theologian Juwayni (d. 1085 C.E.), in his work entitled The Noble Healing.

Certain clear passages in the Quran, whose information cannot be doubted, show that the texts of the Torah and the Gospel make mention of the Prince of Apostles, that the prayers of God were upon him. It is this motive that has induced Muslim scholars to declare that the texts were altered. The Jews and Christians in fact deny this announcement of the Prophet, and summon to their aid arguments which are like "a mirage in the desert. The thirsty man supposes it is water, but when he comes up to it, he finds that it is nothing" (Quran 24:39). . . .

What astonishes me is that the Jews and the Christians have conceded the fact of the alteration and at the same time regard as senseless someone who speaks of it as a possibility. They defend the impossibility of such a thing after agreeing that it did in fact take place. Listen to this ignorance. According to them, the affirmation of the fact of alteration is conditional to its possibility; but the conditions of such a possibility involve editing copies of the Torah and the Gospel dispersed all over the face of the earth, and of being assured of the willingness of each individual of the two religions, scholars, ascetics, the devout and the pious as well as the sinner, and of their agreement on one single opinion and one common expression, despite the wide differences of opinion. . . .

My position, then, with the aid of God, is that most of the errors that occur in the sciences arise from the fact that arguments are accepted without examination and without reason's making a careful examination of their premises. We shall mention the defects in this argument (of the Jews and Christians) and show wherein the carelessness of their authors lies.

Juwayni first takes up the circumstances that show the possibility of altering the Torah.

The Torah which is presently in the hands of the Jews is that which was written by Ezra the scribe after the troubles that Nabuchadnezzar imposed upon them. This latter wrought carnage among the groups of religious Jews, sparing only isolated groups, whose small number allows us to disregard them. He gave over their wealth as booty to his troopers and soldiers and he destroyed their books. Ignorant of the norms of their religious law, he [here, it seems, Antiochus IV] had decided in favor of the corrupt state of the practices of this law: he put up an idol in their place of worship and made public announcement by a herald warning against even a mention of the law. Things remained in this state until an entire generation had passed away. Then those who were in exile found some leaves of the Torah; they took refuge in caves and made pretenses in order to be able to read them in secret.

This (present Torah copy) Ezra wrote 545 years before the mission of the Messiah, upon whom be peace, and when there was not a single Christian upon the earth. It was at this moment that the alteration of the text was possible since it was not a question of reediting copies of the Torah scattered all over the world, as has been said, nor of counting on the willingness of individuals from different factions, nor were copies of the Torah in the hands of both Jews and Christians. In fact, they only came into Christian hands after they had been altered.

So there was only one doer of this deed, either Ezra himself or, if one puts it after Ezra, whoever it was who recopied Ezra's copy. More, an alteration on his part was possible from the fact that he was eager to see his power extended and by the fact that he was not credited with that kind of impeccability which would have prevented his commission of either light or serious faults. . . . It has been said that the love of power is the last thing to be made to leave the heads of the righteous, and power had considerable importance for the Israelites. And anyone who knows well the chronicles of world history and has followed their extraordinary developments finds there that men greater than Ezra have been moved by the love of power to act senselessly, rejecting the bonds of reason and of religion.

The Jews and the Christians can be convicted out of each other's mouth on the fact of alteration.

The reason why the Jews and Christians unanimously agree that the text was in fact altered is that the copies that each group has are clearly contradictory. . . . The motive for the difference is, according to the Christians, that the Torah testifies that the Messiah, on whom be peace, would be sent at the time he was, and the copies of the Torah in their hands support the truth of what they say. They maintain, then, that the Jews have changed their copies of the Torah to prevent the recognition of the mission of the Messiah, on whom be peace. The Jews for their part say that the Christians have changed their copies and that the Messiah, on whom be peace, will not come until the end of the seventh period, and their copies support the truth of what they say. Thus both parties agree that the text has been in fact changed, and each group puts a rope around the neck of the other.

For our part, we shall now mention the contradictions between the two versions: In the Jews' Torah, Adam, when he was 130 years old, begot Seth, and in the Christians', he was 230 years old when he begot Seth.

Juwayni then goes step by step through the age of the Patriarchs and shows the differences in the chronology of the Jewish and Christian versions of the Torah. He concludes:

These are the very expressions of the Torah, and you see how extraordinary and hateful is this divergence between the two religious groups. And they differ not on the kind of point where opinions vary according to the different points of view of scholars and there arise variations according to how much is assumed. Rather, each group maintains that its text came down to Moses, peace be upon him, and that is the very essence of the tampering.

Finally, there is the matter of the Samaritans' Torah. Its text differs from that in the hands of the two other religious groups, and on the basis of that fact alone one could make a very convincing argument for the fact that the texts were altered.

Juwayni next takes up the Gospels.

There is first of all the enormous error the Christians made in not carefully preserving what they had to transmit, and no reasonable man can hope to correct that. The reason why they fell into this error is that they were careless in a matter that required urgent attention, in times propitious to the alteration and loss of texts, and in the matter of an oral transmission.

Matthew says clearly in his Gospel that he composed it nine years after the Ascension of the Messiah, on whom be peace; as for John, he says explicitly that he assembled his text thirty or more years after the Ascension; likewise Mark, 12 years after the Ascension, and Luke 22, or according to others 20 years after the Ascension. That is the point made manifestly in the Gospels, and thence arises the error against which there is no defense; more, even if someone attempts to dissemble through the imagination, he cannot achieve what he sets out to do.

Juwayni's first point of attack on the Gospels is the contradictions between and the errors in Matthew and Luke's versions of the genealogy of Jesus. Then he takes up the varying versions of Peter's denial of Jesus, the prediction and the fact after the latter's arrest. He concludes on the matter of this second case:

But the event that took place was unique, as were the moment, the place and the circumstances of the act. But generally when the circumstances in two accounts are identical and yet the accounts differ, one is forced to conclude that one of the two is false. You see then the integrity in the transmission of these Gospels; and how ironic that they pretend that the Evangelists were immune to error and that they transmitted their Gospels from the time of the Messiah, on whom be peace, as one would who personally heard these narratives, preserving what he heard, and carefully keeping the order of the narrative and the very words. According to my opinion, they allowed a great deal of time to pass before composing the Gospels, and both forgetfulness and carelessness got the better of them.

There are other examples of differences among the Gospels, and Juwayni concludes with this one.

It is likewise extraordinary that Matthew had mentioned in his Gospel that when the Messiah was crucified and had rendered up his spirit, "the Temple was riven from top to bottom in two pieces, the earth quaked, the stones were shattered, tombs opened, and the bodies of the saints were resuscitated and left their tombs" [Matt. 27:51–53]. Those are his own words in his Gospel, and yet no other Evangelist mentions it. But if the facts which he narrated, and which are of such an extraordinary strangeness, took place as he described them, they would be great miracles which one would have great reason to report and which everyone near and far would have recognized. Even people who were incapable of carefully preserving the events of the life of the Messiah, upon whom be peace, nor of retaining the accounts, would have loved to have told of such facts and to immerse themselves in stories on this theme. . . .

All of which shows that Matthew lied or that the three other Evangelists have shown their carelessness by forgetting to mention these extraordinary facts. And they are well charged with negligence since they did not habitually forget. But it would be even stranger that they pretended not to have knowledge of the facts; in effect if such extraordinary miracles actually took place, everybody in the province, near or far, would have known, yes, and in other provinces as well. [JUWAYNI 1968: 40–83]

3. The Divine Origin of the Quran

The Messenger of the Quran may have been a mere mortal, but there was no doubt about the origin of the message he carried to men.

And this (Quran) is a revelation from the Lord of all the worlds, which the trusted spirit descended with to your heart that you may be a warner in clear Arabic. (Quran 26:192–195)

As the Quran instructs us, this quality of "trustworthiness" is shared by the heavenly Spirit—identified by the Islamic tradition as Gabriel— with God's chosen Messenger.

> This is indeed the word of an honored Messenger,
> Full of power, well-established with the Lord and
>   Master of the Throne,
> Obeyed and worthy of trust.

Your companion is not mad.
He had surely seen Him on the clear horizon.
And he is chary of making public what is unknown.
(Quran 81:19–24)

It is He who sent His Messenger with guidance and the true faith in order to make it superior to all other religions, though the idolaters may not like it. (Quran 9:33)

The message, the Quran also announces to the world, is not intended only for the pagans.

O People of the Book, Our Messenger has come to you announcing many things of the Scripture that you have suppressed, passing over some others. To you has come light and a clear Book from God, through which God will lead those who follow His pleasure to the path of peace, and guide them out of the darkness into light by His will, and to the path that is straight. (Quran 5:15–16)

O People of the Book, Our Messenger has come to you when Messengers had ceased to come long ago, lest you said: "There did not come to us any Messenger of good news or warnings." So now there has reached you a bearer of good tidings and of warnings; for God has the power over all things. (Quran 5:19)

This is the Book free of doubt and involution,
A guidance for those who preserve themselves from evil
And follow the straight path,
Who believe in the Unknown, and fulfill their
        devotional obligations,
And spend in charity of what We have given them;
Who believe in what has been revealed to you and what
        was revealed to those before you,
And are certain of the Hereafter.
They have found the guidance of their Lord and will
        be successful.
(Quran 2:1–5)

Thus does God Himself characterize the Book He has sent down to Muhammad, His servant, this very Book in which He is Himself speaking. How and under what circumstances that "sending down" took place are less easily accessible, though there are clues in that same Book.

It is not given to man that God should speak to Him, except by suggestion or indirectly, or send a Messenger to convey by His command whatsoever He please. He is all-high and all-wise.

And so We have revealed to you (Muhammad) the Spirit of Our command. You did not know what the Scripture was before, nor faith, and We made it a light by which We show the way to those of Our creatures as We please. (Quran 42:51–52)

And this Quran is not such as could be composed by anyone but God. It confirms what has been revealed before, and is an exposition of what is decreed for mankind, without any doubt, by the Lord of the worlds.

Do they say (of the Prophet) "He has composed it?" Say to them: "Bring a Sura like this, and call anyone apart from God you can to help you, if what you say is true." (Quran 10:37–38)

Do they say (of the Prophet): "He has forged (the Quran)?" Say: "Then bring ten Suras like it, and call upon anyone except God to help you, if what you say is true."

If they do not answer you, then know it has been revealed with the knowledge of God, and that there is no god but He. (Quran 11:13–14)

These were not the only objections raised by Muhammad's contemporaries. They demanded signs.

We have given examples of every kind of men in this Quran in various ways, and even then most men disdain every thing but disbelief. They say: "We will not believe you until you make a spring of water gush forth from the earth for us; or until you acquire an orchard of date palm trees and grapes, and produce rivers flowing through it, or let chunks of sky fall over us, as you assert." (Quran 17:89–92)

Behind such a request seems to be a more profound doubt: that Muhammad is but a man and thus ill qualified to be a heavenly Messenger.

Nothing prevented men from believing when guidance came to them, but they said: "Has God sent (only) a man as a messenger?" Say: "If angels had peopled the earth and walked about in peace and quiet, We would surely have sent to them an angel as a messenger." (Quran 17:94–95)

To which compare:

And they say: What sort of prophet is this who eats food and walks in the market places? Why was no angel sent to him to act as an admonisher with him? (Quran 25:7)

And:

Those who do not hope to meet us say: "Why are no angels sent down to us, or why do we not see our Lord?" (Quran 25:21)

4. Muhammad's Ascension into Heaven

However, there was a way, Muhammad was told by the Quraysh—whether in mockery or sincerity we cannot tell—by which their fellow Meccan could demonstrate his supernatural vocation.

And they say: "We will certainly not believe you until you . . . ascend to the skies, though we shall not believe in your having ascended till you bring down a Book for us which we can read." Say to them: "Glory be to my Lord! I am only a man and a Messenger." (Quran 17:95)

Thus Muhammad's opponents at Mecca, the doubting and not entirely unsophisticated Quraysh, demanded two signs validating his claim to prophecy: that he should ascend into heaven and that he should return to them with a book that was intelligible to them.

The response lay in the Quran itself. We have already noted in chapter 2 above the somewhat enigmatic reference in Sura 17:1 to a miraculous journey whereby Muhammad was carried by God at night from Mecca to another place eventually identified as Jerusalem. But according to the tradition, the voyage did not end there. The source is the Life of the Messenger of God.

One whom I have no reason to doubt told me on the authority of Abu Saʿid al-Khudri: I heard the Messenger say, "After the completion of my business in Jerusalem (on the occasion of the Night Journey) a ladder was brought to me finer than any I have ever seen. It was that to which the dying man looks when death approaches. My companion mounted it with me until we came to one of the gates of heaven called the Gate of the Watchers. An angel called Ismaʿil was in charge of it, and under his command were twelve thousand angels, each of them having (another) twelve thousand angels under his command." As he told the story the Messenger used to say, "and none knows the armies of God but He" (Quran 74:31). "When Gabriel brought me in, Ismaʿil asked who I was, and when he was told that I was Muhammad, he asked if I had been given a mission, and on being assured I had, he wished me well." . . .

. . . Then I was taken up to the second heaven and there were the two maternal cousins, Jesus, Son of Mary, and John, son of Zakariah. Then to the third heaven and there was a man whose face was as the moon at full. This was my brother Joseph, son of Jacob. Then to the fourth heaven and there was a man called Idris, "and We have exalted him to a lofty place" (Quran 19:56–57). Then to the fifth heaven and there was a man with white hair and a long beard; never before have I seen a more handsome man than he. This was the beloved among his people, Aaron, son of Imran. Then to the sixth heaven and there was a dark man with a hooked nose like the Shanuʾa. This was Moses, son of Imran. Then to the seventh heaven and there was a man sitting on a throne at the gate of the immortal mansion. Every day seventy thousand angels went in, not to come back until the Resurrection Day. Never have I seen a man more like myself. This was my father Abraham. (*Life* 268–270) [IBN ISHAQ 1955: 184–186]

5. The Night of Destiny

Was this heavenly ascension the occasion, then, when Muhammad received the Book? The text just cited does not seem to suggest it, but on the evidence of the Quran—and of the Bible and the Jewish tradition—Moses certainly received his Book on one single occasion. The Quranic evidence is not so certain for Jesus, but in his case too the Book appears to have been delivered once and for all. Muhammad's circumstances were patently different: both the Quran and the biographical traditions about the Prophet show the Quran being delivered chapter by chapter, and even occasionally verse by verse. It must have prompted remarks, since the Quran adverts to this quality that sets Muhammad apart from the other bearers of revelation.

We have divided the Quran into parts that you might recite it to men slowly, with deliberation. That is why We sent it down by degrees. (Quran 17:106)

The Muslim tradition certainly discussed the problem, chiefly in the context of the month of Ramadan, a holy month that the Quran itself closely associates with the act of revelation.

Ramadan is the month in which the Quran was revealed as guidance to man and clear proof of the guidance, and a criterion (of falsehood and truth). (Quran 2:185)

The Muslim commentator Zamakhshari (1134 C.E.) supplies additional details on this epochal event.

"In which the Quran was revealed": . . . The meaning of these words is: in which it *began* to be revealed. This occurred during the Night of Destiny. Some say that the Quran may have been sent down as a whole to the lowest heaven (on this night), and then later section by section to the earth. Others say that the meaning is "(the month of

Ramadan) on account of which the Quran was revealed." . . . The following is transmitted from the Prophet: the sheets (of writing) of Abraham came down on the first night of Ramadan; the Torah was sent down on the sixth night into the month; the Gospel the thirteenth, and the Quran after a lapse of twenty-four (nights into Ramadan). (Zamakhshari ad loc.)

The Quran returns to the same event in another verse, and once again the commentator fills out the narrative.

The perspicuous Book is a witness that We sent it down on a night of blessing—so that We could warn—on which all affairs are sorted out and divided as commands from Us. (Quran 44:2–5)

Most traditions say that the "night of blessing" is the same as the Night of Destiny (that is, the 24th of Ramadan), for God's word says: "Behold, We sent it (that is, the Quran) on the Night of Destiny" (Quran 97:1). Moreover, His words "on this night every wise bidding is determined" correspond with His words "In it the angels and the spirit descend, by the leave of their Lord, upon every command" (Quran 97:4). Finally, this also corresponds with his words "The month of Ramadan wherein the Quran was sent down" (Quran 2:185). According to most of the Prophetic traditions, the Night of Destiny falls during the month of Ramadan.

If one were to ask what is the significance of the sending down of the Quran on this night, I would respond: It is said that God first sent it down in its entirety from the seventh heaven to the lowest heaven. Then He commanded excellent writers to transcribe it on the Night of Destiny. Gabriel subsequently revealed it piece by piece to the Messenger of God. (Zamakhshari ad loc.)

6. The Heavenly Book

Islam shares with Judaism its belief in a heavenly prototype of Scripture, here called in the Quran's own words "the Mother of the Book," or so the lines were understood by the Muslim commentators.

I call to witness the clear Book, that we made it an Arabic Quran that you may perhaps understand. It is inscribed in the Mother of the Book with Us, sublime, dispenser of (all) laws. (Quran 43:2–4)

"Perhaps": This word expresses a wish, because there is a connection between this term and expressions of hoping. So we can say it means: We have created the Book in Arabic and not in any other language because We intended that the Arabs should understand it and not be able to say: "If only the verses of the Book had been sent forth clearly!"

The original text (of the Book) is the tablet corresponding to the words of God: ". . . it is a glorious Quran, in a well-preserved tablet" (Quran 85:21ff.). This writing is designated the "Mother of the Book" because it represents the original in which the individual books are preserved. They are derived from it by copying. (Zamakhshari ad. loc.)

Zamakhshari was here simply summarizing what the Quran itself asserts: that the Book of revelation is one and is preserved in Heaven. It contains all God's decrees and sums up all wisdom.

He has the keys of the Unknown. No one but He has knowledge; He knows what is on the land and in the sea. Not a leaf falls without His knowledge, nor a grain in the darkest recesses of the earth, nor any thing green or seared that is not noted in the clear Book. (Quran 6:59)

. . . There is not the weight of an atom on the earth and in the heavens that is hidden from your Lord, nor is there anything smaller or greater than this but is recorded in the clear Book. (Quran 10:61)

Do you not know that God knows whatever is in the heavens and the earth? This surely is in the Book; this is how God works inevitably. (Quran 22:70)

There is no calamity that befalls the earth or yourselves but that it was in the Book before We created them. This is how God works inevitably. (Quran 57:22)

It is this same Book whose exemplars were given to the earlier peoples of God's choice, to Moses for the Jews (Quran 28:43, 32:23, etc.) and to Jesus for the Christians (3:43, 19:31), and whose validity the Quran now confirms.

> And this is a revelation from the Lord of all the worlds,
> With which the trusted Spirit descended
> Upon your heart, that you may be a warner
> In clear Arabic.
> This was indicated in Books of earlier people.
> Was it not a proof for them that the learned men of Israel
> knew it?
> (Quran 26:191–197)

What We have revealed to you in the Book is the truth, and proves what was sent before it to be true. (Quran 35:31)

And all the more reason why those "People of the Book" should accept this new exemplar being revealed through the Messenger Muhammad.

Say to them: "O People of the Book, what reason have you for disliking us other than that we believe in God and what was sent down before us?" (Quran 5:59)

7. The Quran: Created or Uncreated?

It was the view that the Quran was in its primal form a book in heaven and thence was sent down to Muhammad, first whole and then in discrete revelations, that embroiled the Muslims' Scripture in an internal theological controversy that has little direct echo in either Judaism or Christianity.

If the Quran is the "speech" of God, His Word, then it is necessarily one of His attributes, a subject that provoked a lively interest among early Muslim theologians who were just beginning to explore the connection between essence and accidents as those Greek-defined notions were applied to God. It is difficult to say whether that interest antedated the debate or the debate provoked the interest in a conceptual system that helped the parties to argue or defend their positions. In any case, by the middle of the eighth century the issue had been broached. Indeed, it had gained such notoriety that in the 830s it became the benchmark of one of the few officially promulgated definitions of orthodoxy—and so of heresy—in Islam: the Caliph al-Ma'mun (813–833 C.E.) required Muslims to swear that the Quran was the created speech of God and threatened the recusants with imprisonment.

One who chose not to swear on that occasion was the jurist Ahmad ibn Hanbal (d. 855 C.E.), whose "profession of faith" includes the following article on the Quran.

The Quran is the Word of God and it is not created. It is not wrong to say, "It is not created," for God's Word is not separate from Him, and there is nothing of Him that is created. Beware of discussing this with those who speak about this subject and talk of the "creation of sounds" and such matters, and those who go midway and say "I don't know whether the Quran is created or uncreated, but it is God's Word." Such a one is guilty of a religious innovation, as is the one who says "It is created," for it is God's Word and that is not created. (Ahmad ibn Hanbal, *Creed*) [WILLIAMS 1971: 29]

In despite of Ma'mun and the theologians who may have had the caliphal ear at the time, it was the position of Ibn Hanbal—that the Quran is uncreated and eternal—that became the normative one in Islam.

But while Ibn Hanbal simply asserts it in the document just cited, later theologians were willing to argue the case at length and in detail. This, for example, is how the theological argument is integrated into the received accounts of the revelation of the Quran by al-Nasafi (d. 1114 C.E.) in his Sea of Discourse on Theology.

The Quran is God's speaking, which is one of His attributes. Now God in all of His attributes is One, and with all His attributes is eternal and not contingent, (so His speaking is) without letters and without sounds, not broken up into syllables or paragraphs. It is not He nor is it other than He. He caused Gabriel to hear it as sound and letters, for He created sound and letters and caused him to hear it by that sound and those letters. Gabriel, upon whom be peace, memorized it, stored it (in his mind) and then transmitted it to the Prophet, upon whom be God's blessing and peace, by bringing down a revelation and a message, which is not the same as bringing down a corporeal object and a form. He recited it to the Prophet, upon whom be God's blessing and peace, the Prophet memorized it, storing it up (in his mind), and then recited it to his Companions, who memorized it and recited it to the Followers, the Followers handed it on to the upright, and so on until it reached us. It is (now) recited by tongues, memorized by hearts and written in codices, though it is not contained by the codices. It may be neither added to nor taken from; just as God is mentioned by tongues, recognized by hearts, worshipped in places, yet He is not confined to existence in those places nor in those hearts. It is as He said, "Those who follow the Messenger, the unlettered Messenger, whom they find mentioned in the Torah and the Gospel which they have" (Quran 7:157), for they found (in those Books) only his picture, his description, not his person. Similarly, Paradise and Hell are mentioned, but they are not actually present among us. All this is according to the school of the truly orthodox. (Nasafi, *Sea of Discourse*) [JEFFERY 1962: 398]

8. "Bring a Sura Like It"

We have already seen the Quran's own response to accusations that it represents nothing more than the invention of Muhammad. Go, God challenges the doubters, and produce another Book like it.

This Quran is not such as could be composed by anyone but God. It confirms what has been revealed before, and is an exposition of what was decreed for mankind, without any doubt, by the Lord of the worlds.

Do they say (of the Prophet) "He has composed it"? Say to them: "Bring a Sura like this, and call anyone apart from God you can to help you, if what you say is true." (Quran 10:37–38)

The Quran, then, was not only of heavenly origin; it was, as a direct consequence of that origin, inimitable by mere men, Muhammad or any other, and so the challenge issued in this sura went unanswered. That fact remained the chief probative miracle of Islam, the "sign" that Muhammad resolutely refused to produce but that God produced for him and so verified His religion and His Prophet. The essayist al-Jahiz (d. 868 C.E.) reflects on this.

Muhammad had one unique sign, which affects the mind much in the same manner that (Moses') parting of the seas affected the eyes, namely, when he said to the Quraysh in particular and the Arabs in general—and they included many poets and orators, and eloquent, shrewd, wise, tolerant, sagacious, experienced, and farsighted men— "If you can equal me with but a single *sura*, my claims will be false and you will be entitled to call me a liar." Now it is impossible that among people like the Arabs, with their great numbers, the variety of their tastes, their language, their overflowing eloquence, and their remarkable capacity for elegant language, which has enabled them to describe . . . everything that crawls or runs, and in short everything that the eye can see and the mind picture, who possess every kind of poetic form, . . . the same people who were the first to show hatred toward him and make war, suffering losses themselves and killing some of his supporters, that among these people, I say, who were the fiercest in hatred, the most vengeful, the most sensitive to favor and slight, the most hostile to the Prophet, the quickest to condemn weakness and extol strength, no orator or poet should have dared take up the challenge.

Knowing everything we do, it is inconceivable that words should not have been their weapon of choice . . . and yet that the Prophet's opponents should have unanimously refrained from using them, at a time when they were sacrificing their possessions and their lives, and that they should not all have said, or that at least one of them should have said: Why do you kill yourselves, sacrifice your possessions, and forsake your homes, when the steps to be taken against him are simple and the way of dealing with him easy: let one of your poets or orators compose a speech similar to his, equal in length to the shortest *sura* he has challenged you to imitate, or the meanest verse he has invited you to copy? (Jahiz, *Proofs of Prophecy* 143–144)

9. The Earliest *Sura*

Scholars, medieval Muslim and modern Western, have for a long time been attempting to arrange the suras or chapters of the Quran in some kind of chronological order, chiefly in an attempt to integrate them into the biographical data on the life of the Prophet. As this quest proceeded, there have been various candidates for the earliest of the revelations, among them Sura 74.

> O you, enfolded in your mantle,
> Arise and warn!
> Glorify your Lord,
> Purify your inner self,
> And banish all trepidation.
> (Quran 74:1–5)

When we turn to the medieval Muslim commentators, we find a variety of opinions on which might have been the earliest sura.

It is maintained by some that this (74:1–5) was the first *sura* to be sent down. Jabir ibn Abdullah related (the following) from the Messenger of God: I was on Mount Hira (near Mecca) when someone called out to me, "Muhammad, you are the Messenger of God." I looked to the right and to the left but saw nothing. Then I looked up above me and there I saw something.—In the report according to (his wife) Aisha he says, "I glanced up above me and there I saw someone sitting on a throne between heaven and earth," meaning it was the angel Gabriel who had called out to him—"I was frightened," the tradition continues, "and returned to Khadija (Muhammad's first wife) and called out: 'Dress me in a mantle, dress me in a mantle!' Then Gabriel came and said, 'O you, enfolded in your mantle. . . .'"

From al-Zuhri it is related, on the other hand, that the first *sura* to come down was "Recite in the name of the Lord" down to the words of God "what he has not known" (Sura 96:1–5). (After the revelation of this *sura*) the Messenger of God became sad (because the revelations had ceased) and he began to climb to the tops of the mountains. Then Gabriel came to him and said, "You are the Prophet of God." And then Muhammad returned to Khadija and called out: "Dress me in a mantle and pour cold water over me!" Thereupon there came down the *sura* (which begins) "O you, enfolded in your mantle. . . ."

Still others say that the Prophet heard certain things from the (members of the tribe of) the Quraysh which displeased him, and that this caused him to grieve. Afterwards he was wrapped in his robe reflecting on what grieved him, as is customary with grieving people. Then he was commanded (through the present *sura*) to warn his countrymen continuously (of the punishment of God), even when they insulted him and caused him injury. (Zamakhshari *ad loc.*)

10. The Heart of the Quran: The "Throne Verse"

God's throne in heaven plays an important role in both Jewish and Muslim piety. In Islam the explicit mention of God's heavenly seat in the Quran set in train a whole series of speculations on both the throne and the verses in which it appeared.

God! There is no god but He, the living, the eternal, self-subsisting, ever sustaining. Neither does somnolence affect Him nor sleep. To Him belongs all that is in the heavens and the earth, and who can intercede with Him except by His leave? Known to Him is all that is present before men and what is hidden and that which is to come upon them, and not even a little of His knowledge can they grasp except what He wills. His Throne extends over the heavens and the earth, and He tires not protecting them: He alone is high and supreme. (Quran 2:255)

Qurtubi (d. 1273 C.E.) relates . . . on the authority of Muhammad ibn al-Hanifiyya: "When the Throne Verse was revealed, every idol and king in the world fell prostrate and the crowns of kings fell off their heads. Satans fled, colliding with one another in confusion until they came to Iblis [their chief]. . . . He sent them to find out what had happened, and when they came to Medina they were told that the Throne Verse had been sent down." . . .

Tabarsi (d. 1153 C.E.) relates on the authority of Abdullah ibn Umar that the Prophet said: "Whoever recites the Throne Verse after a prescribed prayer, the Lord of Majesty Himself shall receive his soul at death. He would be as if he had fought with the Prophet of God until he was martyred." . . . Ali also said: I heard the Messenger of God say, "O Ali, the chief of humankind is Adam, the chief of the Arabs is Muhammad, nor is there pride in this. The chief of the Persians is Salman [an early Persian convert to Islam], the chief of the Byzantines is Suhayb [A Christian convert among the Companions of the Prophet] and the chief of Abyssinia is Bilal [another convert and Islam's first muezzin]. The chief of the mountains is Mount Sinai, and the chief of the trees is the lote tree. The chief months are the sacred months and the chief day is Friday. The chief of all speech is the Quran, the chief of the Quran is the (second) Sura, 'The Cow,' and the chief of 'The Cow' is the Throne Verse. O Ali, it consists of fifty words and every word contains fifty blessings." [AYOUB 1984: 247–248]

11. The "Satanic Verses"

If speculation on the Quran's mention of the throne of God is essentially the work of piety, other verses in the Book raised enormously complex exegetical and legal questions. The following, for example, the so-called Satanic verses, occur in Sura 22 and are addressed to Muhammad.

We have sent no Messenger or Prophet before you with whose recitations Satan did not tamper. Yet God abrogates what Satan interpolates; then He confirms His revelations, for God is all-knowing, all-wise. This is in order to make the interpolations of Satan a test for those whose hearts are diseased and hardened. (Quran 22:52–53)

The occasion of the revelation of the present verse (22:52) is the following: As the members of the tribe of the Messenger of God turned away from him and took their stand in opposition to him, and as his relatives also opposed him and refused to be guided by what he brought to them, then, as a result of extreme exasperation over their estrangement, and of the eager desire and longing that they be converted to Islam, the Messenger of God hoped that nothing would be revealed to him that would make them shy away. . . . Now this wish persisted until the Sura called "The Star" (Sura 53) came down. At that time he (still) found himself with that hope in his heart regarding the members of his tribe. Then he began to recite (53:19–23):

> "Have you considered al-Lat and al-Uzza
> And Manat, the third, the other?
> Are there sons for you and daughters for Him?
> This is certainly an unjust apportioning.

"These are only names which you and your fathers have invented. No authority was sent down by God for them. They only follow conjecture and will-fulfillment, even though guidance had come already from their Lord."

When, however, he came to God's words "And Manat, the third, the other," Satan substituted something else conformable to the wish

that the Messenger of God had been harboring, that is, he whispered
something to him which would enable the Messenger to fulfill his wish.
In an inadvertent and misleading manner his tongue hurried on ahead of
him, so that he said: "These (goddesses) are the exalted cranes. Their
intercession (with God) is to be hoped for. . . ." Yet the Messenger of
God was not clear at this point until the protection (of God) reached
him and he became attentive again.

Some say that Gabriel drew his attention to what had happened,
or that Satan himself spoke these words and brought them to the people's hearing. As soon as the Messenger of God prostrated himself in
prayer at the end of the *sura*, all who were present did it with him and
felt pleased (that they had had their way). That the opportunity for
doing this would be given to Satan constituted a temptation and it was
God's test through which the hypocrites should increase in grievance
and injury, but the believers should increase in enlightenment and assur-
ance. (Zamakhshari *ad loc.*)

12. The Revelation and Its Copy

*The intrusion of these spurious verses into the Quran, followed by their
removal, is mirrored in reverse by the question whether our copies of the
Quran, its written exemplars, contain all the material revealed by God to
His Prophet. The text itself gives us no reason to think that such is not the
case, but the Muslim tradition preserves another recollection. As we shall
see shortly, the Shi*c*ite Muslims have charged that the received text was
indeed tampered with for sectarian reasons, but there are other, more fundamental cases of omissions that are more anomalous. The best known is
that of a verse which prescribed stoning as a penalty for adultery and which
was, on unimpeachable testimony, "memorized and recited" as part of the
Quran in Muhammad's own lifetime. Yet it occurs nowhere in the text of
the Book. If the "stoning verse" is the most celebrated example of genuine
revelation not incorporated into the "copy" of the Quran, it is not the only
one, as these canonically accepted traditions suggest.*

Ubayy reports: The Messenger of God said to me, "God has commanded me to instruct you in the reciting of the Quran." He then
recited "Did not those who rejected the Prophet among the People of
the Book and the associators. . . ." The verse continued, "Did the
offspring of Adam possess a wadi of property," or "Were the offspring
of Adam to ask for a wadi of property and he received it, he would ask

for a second, and if he received that, he would demand a third wadi. Only dust will fill the maw of the offspring of Adam, but God relents to him who repents. The very faith in God's eyes is the original belief, not Judaism or Christianity. Who does good, it will never be denied him." (Suyuti) [Cited by BURTON 1977: 82–83]

Ibn Abbas said, Did the offspring of Adam possess two wadis of wealth, he would desire a third. Only dust will fill the maw of the offspring of Adam, but God relents to him who repents. Umar asked, "What is this?" Ibn Abbas replied that Ubayy had instructed him to recite this (as part of the Quran). Umar took Ibn Abbas to confront Ubayy. Umar said, "We don't say that." Ubayy insisted that the Prophet had so instructed him. Umar then asked him, "Shall I write it into the copy in that case?" Ubayy said, "Yes." This was before the copying of the Uthman codices (without the verses in question) and on which the practice now rests. (Burhan al-Din al-Baji) [Cited by BURTON 1977: 83]

13. Uthman's Recension of the Quran

The assembled and ordered text of the Quran as we now possess it was the result of a cooperative work begun soon after the death of the Prophet. It was brought to completion by Uthman, an early companion of the Prophet and the third Caliph or head of the Muslim community (644–656 C.E.).

Zayd ibn Thabit said: Abu Bakr [Caliph 632–634 C.E.] sent for me at the time of the battle of al-Yamama, and Umar ibn al-Khattab [Caliph 634–644 C.E.] was with him. Abu Bakr said: Umar has come to me and said:

"Death was rampant at the battle of al-Yamama and took with it many of the reciters of the Quran. I fear lest death in battle also overtake the reciters of the Quran in the provinces and so a large part of the Quran be lost. I think you should give orders to collect the Quran."

"What," I asked Umar, "do you wish to do something which the Prophet of God himself did not do?"

"By God," replied Umar, "it would be a good deed."

Umar did not leave off urging me until at length God opened my heart to this and I thought as Umar did.

Zayd continued: Abu Bakr said to me: "You are a young man, intelligent, and we see no fault in you; more, you have already written down the revelation for the Prophet of God, may God bless and save him. Therefore go and seek the Quran and collect it."

By God, if he had ordered me to move a mountain, it would not have been harder for me than his order to collect the Quran. "What," I asked, "will you do something which the Prophet of God himself, may God bless and save him, did not do?"

"By God," replied Abu Bakr, "it would be a good deed."

Umar did not leave off urging me until at length God opened my heart to this as He had opened the hearts of Abu Bakr and Umar.

Then I searched out and collected the parts of the Quran, whether they were written on palm leaves or flat stones or in the hearts of men. Thus I found the end of the "Sura of Repentance" (Quran 9:129–130), which I had been unable to find anywhere else, in the possession of Abu'l-Khuzayma al-Ansari. These were the verses "There came to you a Prophet from amongst yourselves. It grieves me that you sin . . ." to the end.

The (collected) leaves remained in the possession of Abu Bakr until his death, then in Umar's for as long as he lived, and then with Hafsa, the daughter of Umar.

Anas ibn Malik said: Hudhayfa ibn al-Yaman accompanied Uthman [Caliph 644–656 C.E.] when he was preparing the army of Syria together with the army of Iraq to conquer Armenia and Azharbayjan. Hudhayfa was astonished by the differences in the (two armies') reading of the Quran, and said to Uthman, "O Commander of the Faithful, catch hold of this community before they begin to differ about their Book as do the Jews and the Christians."

Uthman sent to Hafsa to say, "Send us the leaves. We shall copy them in codices and return them to you."

Hafsa sent them to Uthman, who ordered Zayd ibn Thabit, Abdullah ibn al-Zubayr, Saʿid ibn al-As and Abd al-Rahman ibn al-Harith ibn Hisham to copy them into codices. Uthman said to the three of them who were of the tribe of the Quraysh, "If you differ from Zayd ibn Thabit on anything in the Quran, write it down according to the language of the Quraysh, for it is in their language that the Quran was revealed."

They did as he bade, and when they had copied the leaves into codices, Uthman returned the leaves to Hafsa. He sent copies of the codex which they made in all directions and gave orders to burn every leaf and codex which differed from it. (Bukhari, *Sahih* 3.392–394)

14. Who Put Together the *Suras*?

One striking feature of the Quran as we possess it is the fact that only one sura, Sura 9, also called "Repentance" or "Immunity," does not open with the formula "In the Name of God, the Compassionate, the Merciful." The following Prophetic tradition explains the anomaly and sheds some light as well on how the suras *might have been put together.*

Ibn Abbas said he asked Uthman what had induced him to deal with (Sura 8 called) "The Spoils," which is one of the medium-sized *suras*, and with (Sura 9 called) "Immunity," which is one with a hundred verses, joining them without writing the line containing "In the Name of God, the Compassionate, the Merciful," and putting it among the seven long *suras* (at the beginning of the Quran). When he asked again what had induced him to do that, Uthman replied: "Over a period of time *suras* with numerous verses would come down to the Messenger of God, and when something came down to him he would call one of those who wrote and tell him to put those verses in the *sura* in which such-and-such was mentioned, and when a (single) verse came down he would tell them to put it in the *sura* in which such-and-such is mentioned. Now 'The Spoils' was one of the first to come down in Medina, and 'Immunity' was among the last of the Quran to come down, and the subject matter of one resembled that of the other, so because the Messenger of God was taken (by death) without having explained to us whether it ('Immunity') belonged to it ('The Spoils'), I joined them without writing the line containing 'In the Name of God, the Compassionate, the Merciful,' and put it among the long suras." Ahmad ibn Hanbal, Tirmidhi, and Abu Dawud transmitted this tradition. (Baghawi, *Mishkat al-masabih* 8.3)

15. The Seven "Readings" of the Quran

The Quran, with its vowels unmarked in the manner of Semitic writing and transcribed in a still somewhat defective script—the Quran is the earliest Arabic literary text committed to writing—was open to different manners of reading and pronunciation. The Hebrew Bible had gone through similar uncertainties until its own textual standardization, and here we stand at the beginning of the same process as it affects the Quran.

Umar ibn al-Khattab said: I heard Hisham ibn Hakim ibn Hizam reciting the *sura* (called) "The Criterion" [that is, Sura 25] in a different manner from my way of reciting it, and it was the Messenger of God who taught me how to recite it. I nearly spoke sharply to him, but I delayed until he had finished, and then catching his cloak by the neck, I brought him to God's Messenger and said: "Messenger of God, I heard this man reciting 'The Criterion' in a manner different from that in which you taught me to recite it." He told me to let the man go and bade him to recite. When he recited it in the manner in which I had (earlier) heard him recite it, God's Messenger said, "Thus it was sent down." He then told me to recite it, and when I had done so he said, "Thus it was sent down. The Quran was sent down in seven modes of reading, so recite according to what comes most easily."

Ibn Abbas reported God's Messenger as saying, "Gabriel taught me to recite in one mode, and when I replied to him and kept asking him to give me more, he did so till he reached seven modes." Ibn Shihab said he had heard that these seven modes were essentially one, not differing about what is permitted and what is prohibited. (Baghawi, *Mishkat al-masabih* 8.3.1)

These Prophetic traditions represent the beginnings of one aspect of the textual study of the Quran in Islam, that devoted to a proper "reading" of the sacred text. Ibn Khaldun (d. 1406 C.E.), who stands at the end of the process, describes how it evolved.

The Quran is the word of God that was revealed to His Prophet and that is written down between the two covers of copies of the Quran. Its transmission has been continuous in Islam. However, the men around Muhammad transmitted it on the authority of the Messenger of God in different ways. These differences affect certain of the words in it and the manner in which the letters were pronounced. They were handed down and became famous. Eventually, seven specific ways of reading the Quran became established. Transmission of these Quranic readings with their particular pronunciation was also continuous. They came to be ascribed to certain men from among a large number of persons who had become famous as their transmitters. The Seven Quran Readings became the basis for reading the Quran. Later on other readings were occasionally added to the seven. However, they are not considered by the authorities on Quran reading to be as reliably transmitted (as the Seven).

The (Seven) Quran Readings are well known from books which deal with them. Certain people have contested the continuity of their transmission. In their opinion they are ways of indicating the pronunciation, and pronuciation is something which cannot definitely be fixed. This, however, they thought not to reflect upon the continuity of the transmission of the Quran (itself). The majority do not admit their view. The majority assert the continuity of the transmission of the Seven Readings. Others asserted the continuity of all Seven, save for certain fine points of pronunciation. . . . Quran readers continued to circulate and transmit these readings, until the knowledge of them was fixed in writing and treated systematically. (Ibn Khaldun, *Muqaddima* 6.10) [IBN KHALDUN 1967: 2:439–440]

The discipline of Quran readings is often extended to include also the discipline of Quran orthography, which deals with usage of the letters in copies of the Quran and with the orthography of the Quran. The Quran uses many letters that are used differently than is usual in writing. . . . When the divergences in the usage and norm of writing made their appearance, it became necessary to deal with them comprehensively. Therefore, they too were written down when scholars fixed the sciences in writing. (Ibn Khaldun, *Muqaddima* 6.10) [IBN KHALDUN 1967: 2:442]

16. Textual Corruptions? The Shiᶜite View

God had helped you during the Battle of Badr at a time when you were helpless. So act in compliance with the laws of God; you may well be grateful. (Quran 3:123)

Some Muslim scholars had difficulty with this particular verse in the transmitted Quran.

"When you were helpless . . .": al-Qummi and al-Ayyashi say according to (the Imam) Jaᶜfar al-Sadiq: They were not helpless, for the Messenger of God was among them. (Actually the following) came down: "When you were weak. . . ." Al-Ayyashi reports according to Jaᶜfar al-Sadiq that Abu Basir recited the verse in this manner in al-Sadiq's presence. Jaᶜfar said that God had not revealed the verse in that form, but what had come down was "When you were few. . . . " In a Prophetic tradition it is said that God never cast down His Messenger and so what had been revealed was "when you were few. . . ." In several reliable reports it is said that they numbered three hundred and thirteen. (Kashi *ad loc.*)

This kind of textual criticism may have had no other object than to express a reservation on what was considered an unlikely thing for God to

have said of His own Prophet. But in other instances the criticism is more
direct and more pointed—namely, that the text of God's Book had been
tampered with in order to promote one sectarian view at the expense of
another. The latter was most often the Shiᶜites or "Party of Ali," who
thought that spiritual leadership in the community had been reserved for
Muhammad's cousin Ali ibn Abi Talib and his descendants. Since the
Quran is silent on this claim, there were inevitably Shiᶜite charges of
tampering with the text.

. . . And the oppressors will now come to know through what
reversals they will be overthrown! (Quran 26:227)

Al-Qummi says: God mentioned their enemies and those who did
wrong against them. He has said (in 26:227), "Those who have done
wrong against the law of the family of Muhammad will (one day) know
what kind of turning upside down they will experience." This is the way
the verse was actually revealed. (Kashi *ad loc.*)

O Messenger, announce what has reached you from your Lord, for
if you do not, you will not have delivered His message. God will preserve you from men; for God does not guide those who do not believe.
(Quran 5:67)

"Announce what has reached you": That is, concerning Ali. According to the tradition of the authorities on doctrine, this verse was
actually revealed in this (extended) form [that is, including "concerning
Ali"].

"For if you do not . . .": If you discontinue the delivery of what has
been sent down to you concerning Ali's guardianship (over the believers), and you keep this secret, then it is as if you delivered none of the
message of the Lord concerning that which requires reconciliation.
Some also read: "His message concerning the confession of the unity of
God." . . .

"God does not guide those who do not believe": In the *Collection*
(of al-Tabarsi) it is said on the authority of Ibn Abbas and Jabir ibn
Abdullah that God commanded His Prophet to place Ali before men and
to (publicly) inform them of his guardianship (over them). The Prophet,
however, was afraid that they would say: "He is protecting his cousin,"
and that a group of his companions might find this distressing. The
present verse came down regarding this. On the following day, the
Prophet took Ali gently by the hand and said: "Whose protector I am,
their protector (also) is Ali." Then he recited the verse in question."
(Kashi *ad loc.*)

17. The Proofs of Prophecy

Among the voluminous works of the essayist al-Jahiz (d. 886 c.e.) is one entitled The Proofs of Prophecy. *In it he took up the question of why the earliest generations of Muslims did not, like the Christians, make a systematic collection of the various and many proofs of Muhammad's prophetic calling.*

Let us return to the question of the signs and tokens of the Prophet, and the arguments in favor of his proofs and testimonies. I say this: If our ancestors, who compiled written editions of the Quran, which up to that point had been scattered in men's memories, and united the people behind the reading of Zayd ibn Thabit, while formerly other readings were in free circulation, and established a text free from all additions and omissions, if those early Muslims had likewise collected the signs of the Prophet, his arguments, proofs, and miracles, the various manifestations of his wondrous life, both at home and abroad, and even on the occasion when he preached to a great multitude, to a crowd so large that its testimony cannot be questioned except by ignorant fools or the bigoted opponents (of Islam), if they had done so, today no one could challenge the truth of these things, neither the godless dualist, nor the stubborn materialist, not even the licentious fop, the naive moron, or callow stripling. This tradition of the Prophet would then have been as well known among the common people as among the elite, and all our notables would see the truth (of their religion) as clearly as they see the falsity (of the beliefs) of Christians and Zoroastrians. . . .

The first Muslims were led (to commit this omission) by their confidence in the manifest nature (of the acts of the Prophet); but we ourselves have come to this state because dunces, youths, madmen, and libertines lack the proper care and show themselves totally unconcerned, callow, and neglectful; also because, before acquiring even the elements of dialectical theology, they filled their heads with more subtleties than their strength can manage or their minds contain. (Jahiz, *The Proofs of Prophecy* 119)

18. Muhammad, the Seal of the Prophets

Christianity rested its claim upon a Messiah, an individual who was sent not so much to teach the Kingdom of God as to proclaim it in his own person. For the Christian, Jesus did not belong in the company of the

Prophets but was a unique figure in God's plan, the Son of God promised from the beginning and whose redemptive death required no sequel. With Islam we are back on biblical ground, however. As we have seen, Muhammad was announced as one of a line of Prophets stretching back to Adam and reaching forward through Abraham and Moses, David and Solomon, until it reached Jesus. And, according to the Quran, though he had predecessors, he would have no successor.

Muhammad is not the father of any man among you, but a Messenger of God and the seal of the Prophets. God has knowledge of every thing. (Quran 33:40)

The commentators took the verse as self-evident.

"But (he is) the messenger of God": Every messenger is the father of his religious community insofar as they are obliged to respect and honor him, and he is obliged to care for them and give them advice. . . .

"And the seal of the Prophets": . . . If one asks how Muhammad (as the Seal of the Prophets) can be the last Prophet when Jesus will come down at the end of time [that is, to announce the Day of Judgment and suffer death], then I reply that Muhammad's being the last of the prophets means that no one else will (afterwards) be active as a prophet; Jesus was active as a prophet before Muhammad. And when Jesus comes down he will do this because he devotes himself to the law of Muhammad and performs his prayer according to Muhammad's direction of prayer [that is, facing Mecca], as if he were a member of this community. (Zamakhshari *ad loc.*)

Another already cited verse opens the perspective somewhat, however.

We have sent no Messenger or Prophet before you with whose recitations Satan did not tamper. (Quran 22:52)

The second half of the verse requires its own exegesis, as we have already seen in connection with the "Satanic verses." Our concern here is with the opening phrase, which speaks to an important distinction.

"We have never sent any Messenger or Prophet . . . ": This is a clear proof that there is a difference between a "Messenger" (*rasul*) and a "Prophet" (*nabi*). It is related from the Prophet that once when he was asked about the Prophets, he replied: "There are one hundred and twenty-four thousand." And when he was then asked how many Messengers there were among those, he answered, "The great host of three hundred and thirteen." The distinction between the two is that a Messenger is one of the Prophets to whom the Book is sent down, together

with a miracle confirming it. A Prophet, on the other hand, who is not
an Apostle, is one to whom no book has been sent down, but who was
commanded only to restrain people on the basis of the earlier revealed
Law. (Zamakhshari *ad loc.*)

19. Muhammad among the Prophets

*The question mooted by Zamakhshari is in part exegetical—the occurrence
in the Quran of two distinct terms, "Messenger" and "Prophet"—but arises
as well from the need to separate and distinguish Muhammad from the
other Prophets, biblical and nonbiblical, mentioned in the Quran. Zamakhshari's criterion, that the Messenger is the recipient of a public revelation, which separates Muhammad from Jeremiah or Isaiah, for example,
and brackets him with Moses and Jesus, was not the only distinction possible. In the passage that follows, the comparison is straightforward, detailed, and obviously popular. The context is said to be a meeting between
Muhammad, who is accompanied by Umar, and the Jews of Medina. When
Umar praises Muhammad, the Jews retort that he must be talking about
Moses. Umar turns to Muhammad and asks, "Alas for my soul, was Moses
better than you?"*

Then the Messenger of God, may God bless him and grant him
peace, said: "Moses is my brother, but I am better than he, and I was
given something more excellent than he was." The Jews said: "This is
what we wanted!" "What is that?" he asked. They said: "Adam was
better than you; Noah was better than you; Moses was better than you;
Jesus was better than you; Solomon was better than you." He said: "That
is false. I am better than all these and superior to them." "You are?" they
asked. "I am," he said. They said, "Then bring a proof of that from the
Torah."

*Muhammad agrees but must invoke the assistance of one of his Jewish
converts, Abdullah ibn Salam, to check the Torah, presumably because this
latter could read Hebrew, while Muhammad was, as the Muslim tradition
maintained, "unlettered." The discussion continues:*

"Now why," Muhammad asked, "is Adam better than I?" "Because," they answered, "God created him with His own hand and
breathed into him of His spirit." "Adam," he then replied, "is my father,
but I have been given something better than anything he has, namely,
that every day a herald calls five times from the East to the West: 'I bear
witness that there is no god but the God and I bear witness that Muham-

mad is the Messenger of God.' No one has ever said that Adam was the Messenger of God. Moreover, on the Day of Resurrection the Banner of Praise will be in my hand and not in that of Adam." "You speak but the truth," they replied, "that is so written in the Torah." "That," he said, "is one."

Said the Jews: "Moses is better than you." "And why?" he inquired. "Because," they said, "God spoke to him four thousand four hundred and forty words, but never did He speak a thing to you." "But I," he responded, "was given something superior to that." "And what was that?" they asked. Said he: "Glory be to Him who took His servant by night (Quran 17:1), for He bore me up on Gabriel's wing until He brought me to the seventh heaven, and I passed beyond the Sidra tree of the Boundary at the Garden of Resort (Quran 53:14–15) till I caught hold of a leg of the Throne, and from above the Throne came a voice: 'O Muhammad, I am God. Beside me there is no other god.' Then with all my heart I saw my Lord. This is more excellent than that (given to Moses)." "You speak but the truth," they replied, "that is so written in the Torah." "That," he said, "makes two."

Noah is then similarly disposed of. "Well," said Muhammad, "that is three."

They said: "Abraham is better than you . . . God Most High took him as a friend." He answered, "Abraham was indeed the friend of God, but I am His beloved. Do you know why my name is Muhammad? It is because He derived it from His name. He is Al-Hamid, the Praiseworthy, and my name is Muhammad, the Praised, while my community are the Hamidun, those who give praise." "You speak but truly," they replied, "this is greater than that." "That is four."

"But Jesus," they said, "is better than you . . . because he mounted up to the pinnacle of the Temple in Jerusalem, where the satans came to bear him away, but God gave command to Gabriel who with his right wing smote them in their faces and cast them into the fire." "Nevertheless," he said, "I was given something better than that. I returned from fighting with the polytheists on the day of Badr exceedingly hungry, when there met me a Jewish woman with a basket on her head. In the basket there was a roasted kid, and in her sleeve some sugar. She said: 'Praise be to God who has kept you safe. I made a vow to God that if you returned safely from this warlike expedition I would not fail to sacrifice this kid for you to eat.' Then she set it down and I put my hand to it, which caused the kid to speak, standing upright on its four feet, and saying, 'Eat not of me, for I am poisoned.'" "You speak but true," they said. "That is five, but there remains one more, for we claim that Solomon was better than you."

"Why?" he asked. "Because," they said, "God subjected to him satans, jinn, men and winds, and taught him the language of the birds and insects." "Yet," he replied, "I have been given something superior to that. God subjected to me Buraq (the miraculous beast that bore Muhammad on the Night Journey), who is more precious than all the world. He is one of the riding-beasts of Paradise. . . . Between his eyes is written 'There is no god but the God. Muhammad is the Messenger of God.'" "You speak truly," they said, "we bear witness that there is no god but the God and that you are His servant and Messenger." (Suyuti, *Glittering Things*) [JEFFERY 1962: 334–336]

Finally, in the course of his Night Journey and Ascension to Heaven (see chapter 2 above), Muhammad was given sight of his fellow Prophets, whose physical appearance is relayed, on his authority, in his standard biography.

Al-Zuhri alleged as from Sa'id al-Musayyab that the Messenger described to his companions Abraham, Moses and Jesus as he saw them that night, saying: "I have never seen a man more like myself than Abraham. Moses was a ruddy faced man, tall, thinly fleshed, curly haired with a hooked nose as if he were of the Shanu'a. Jesus Son of Mary was a reddish man of medium height with lank hair and with many freckles on his face as though he had just come from a bath. One would suppose that his head was dripping with water, though there was no water on it. The man most like him among you is Urwa ibn Mas'ud al-Thaqafi." (*Life* 266) [IBN ISHAQ 1955: 183–184]

20. Avicenna on the Prophethood of Muhammad

For the philosophers among the Muslims, a prophet too is a philosopher in his understanding of God's eternal truths and moves to the higher stage of prophecy only upon turning toward society and converting those truths, or at least some of them, into an idiom comprehensible to the masses, who cannot philosophize and so need guidance on their path to happiness and salvation. So it is set forth by one of the most prominent among the philosophers: the physician, statesman, and polymath Ibn Sina (d. 1038 C.E.), or Avicenna as he came to be called in the West. In this passage from his Book of Deliverance it is first established that man is a social animal and will of necessity associate with other men and transact business. These transactions require a code of law, which in turn calls for a lawgiver, someone "in the position to speak to men and constrain them to accept the code; he must therefore be a man." Avicenna continues:

Now it is not feasible that men should be left to their own opinions in this matter so that they will differ each from the other, every man considering as justice that which favors him, and as injustice that which works against his advantage. The survival and complete self-realization of the human race requires the existence of such a lawgiver. . . .

It follows therefore that there should exist a prophet, and that he should be a man; it also follows that he should have some distinguishing feature which does not belong to other men, so that his fellows may recognize him as possessing something which is not theirs, and so that he may stand out apart from them. This distinguishing feature is the power to work miracles.

Such a man, if and when he exists, must prescribe laws for mankind governing all their affairs, in accordance with God's ordinance and authority, God inspiring him and sending down the Holy Spirit upon him. The fundamental principle upon which his (that is, the prophet's) code rests will be to teach them that they have One Creator, Almighty and Omniscient, whose commandments must of right be obeyed; that the Command must belong to Him who possesses the power to create and that He has prepared for those who obey Him a future life of bliss but wretchedness for such as disobey Him. So the masses will receive the prescriptions, sent down upon his tongue from God and the Angels, with heedful obedience. (Avicenna, *Book of Deliverance*) [AVICENNA 1951: 42–44]

There is little in this to suggest that Muhammad had either a unique role among the prophets or that the possibility of prophetic revelation ended with him. One can suggest that it is because these passages occur in the context of a discussion of metaphysics or theories of knowledge. But in one of his works, On the Proof of the Prophecies, *Avicenna explicitly takes up the case of the prophethood of Muhammad, for reasons he explains at the outset.*

You have asked—may God set you aright—that I sum up for you in a treatise the substance of what I said to you with a view to eliminate your misgivings about accepting prophecy. You are confirmed in these misgivings because the claims of the advocates of prophecy are either logically possible assertions that are treated as necessary without the benefit of (rigorous) demonstrative argument or even of (secondary) dialectical proof, or else impossible assertions on the order of fairy tales, such that the very attempt on the part of their advocate to expound them deserves derision.

Avicenna then gives his own succinct explanation of what prophetic revelation is and how it occurs.

Revelation is the emanation and the angel is the received emanating power that descends on the prophets as if it were an emanation continuous with the Universal Intellect. It is rendered particular, not essentially, but accidentally, because of the particularity of the recipient. Thus the angels have been given different names because (they are associated with) different notions; nevertheless, they form a single totality, which is particularized, not essentially, but accidentally, by the particularity of the recipient. The message, therefore, is that part of the emanation termed "revelation" which has been received and couched in whatever mode of expression is deemed best for furthering man's good in both the eternal and the corruptible worlds as regards knowledge and political governance, respectively. The Messenger is the one who conveys what he acquires of the emanation termed "revelation," again in whatever mode of expression is deemed best for achieving through his opinions the good of the sensory world by political governance and of the intellectual world by knowledge.

There immediately follows this curiously reticent conclusion.

This, then, is the summary of the discourse concerning the affirmation of prophecy, the showing of its essence, and the statements made about revelation, the angel and the thing revealed. As for the validity of the prophethood of our prophet, of Muhammad, may God's prayers and peace be upon him, it becomes evident to the reasonable man once he compares him with the other prophets, peace be on them. We shall refrain from elaboration here. (Avicenna, *On the Proof of Prophecies* 120–124) [LERNER & MAHDI 1972: 113–115]

21. The Clear and the Ambiguous in the Quran

The Bible is, in a sense, a long commentary upon itself, and Jesus too gave instruction to his disciples on how they were to understand his teaching, and particularly his parables. The reason in both instances is that the Word of God is not prima facie clear, or, if that sounds like an overbold statement, that it requires explanation. That much is clear from the Quran

*itself, which issued a warning about the problems and dangers in under-
standing the words of God, and thus provided an inviting peg upon which
later commentators might hang their own theories concerning Quranic
exegesis.*

He has sent down this Book which contains some clear verses that
are categorical [or "are from the Mother of the Book"] and others allegorical [or "ambiguous"]. But those who are twisted in mind look for
verses allegorical [or "ambiguous"], seeking deviation and giving them
interpretations of their own; but none knows their meaning except
God; and those who are steeped in knowledge affirm: "We believe in
them as all of them are from the Lord"; but only those who have wisdom
understand. (Quran 3:7)

*The following are the comments of Zamakhshari on these verses,
written in 1134 C.E.*

Categorical verses: namely, those whose diction and meaning are
sufficiently clear that they are preserved from the possibility of differing interpretations and ambiguity. "And others that are ambiguous,"
namely, those verses that are ambiguous in that they allow differing
interpretations.

The Mother of the Book: that is, the origin of the Book, since the
ambiguous verses must be traced back to it and harmonized with it.
Examples of such ambiguity include the following: "The vision reaches
Him not, but He reaches the vision; He is All-subtle, All-aware"
(6:103); or "Upon that day their faces shall be radiant, gazing upon their
Lord" (75:22); or "God does not command indecency!" (7:28) compared with "And when We desire to destroy a city, We command its
men who live at ease, and they commit ungodliness therein. Then the
command is realized against it, and We destroy it utterly" (17:16).

If one then asks whether the (meaning of the) entire Quran might
not be (clearly) determined, I answer that men would (then) depend on
it since it would be so easily accessible, and thus they would neglect
what they lack, namely, research and meditation through reflection and
inference. If they did that, then they would be neglecting the only way
by which we can attain to a knowledge of God and His unity. Again, the
ambiguous verses present a test and a means of distinguishing between
those who stand firm in the truth and those who are uncertain regarding
it. And great advantages, including the noble sciences and the profit of
higher orders of being, are granted by God when scholars stimulate each
other and so develop their natural skills, discovering the meanings of the

ambiguous verses and harmonizing these with the (clearly) determined verses. Further, if the believer is firmly convinced that no disagreement or self-contradiction can exist in God's words, and then he notices something that appears at least to be a contradiction, and he then diligently searches out some way of harmonizing it (with the clear verses), treating it according to a uniform principle, and by reflecting on it comes to an insight about himself and other things, and with God's inspiration he comes to an understanding of the harmony that exists between the ambiguous verses and the (clearly) determined verses, then his certainty grows and the intensity of his conviction increases.

As for those whose heart is swerving: these are the people who introduce innovations.

They follow the ambiguous part: that is, they confine their attention to the ambiguous verses, which give free rein to innovations without harmonizing them with the (clearly) determined verses. But these (same verses) likewise permit an interpretation which agrees with the views of the people of truth.

The following interpretation depends on how one divides—in our parlance, punctuates—the text: to wit, whether or not there should be a pause or semicolon after "except God." In Zamakhshari's first interpretation it is not in fact so punctuated, though he concedes the possibility.

And none knows its interpretation except God and those firmly rooted in knowledge: namely, only God and His servants who have firmly rooted knowledge, that is to say, those who are firm in knowledge and so "bite with a sharp tooth," come to the correct interpretation, according to which one must necessarily explain it. Some, however, place a pause after *except God* and begin a new sentence with *And those firmly rooted in knowledge . . . say*. Thus they interpret the ambiguous verses as those whose understanding God reserves to Himself alone as well as the recognition of whatever wisdom is contained in them, as, for example, the exact number of the executioners in Hell and similar questions. The first reading is the correct one, and the next sentence begins with *they say*, setting forth the situation of those who have a firmly rooted knowledge, namely, in the following sense: Those who know the meaning say *we believe in it*, that is, in the ambiguous verses.

All of them are from our Lord: that is, all the ambiguous verse as well as all the (clearly) determined verse (in the Quran) is from Him. Or (to put it another way), not only the ambiguous verses in the Book but also the (clearly) determined verses are from God, the Wise One, in whose words there is no contradiction and in whose Book there is no discrepancy. (Zamakhshari *ad loc.*)

One who preferred to read and punctuate this text as Zamakhshari had was the most straightforward Aristotelian produced in Islam, the Spanish philosopher Ibn Rushd or Averroes (d. 1198 C.E.). In his Decisive Treatise *he is developing an argument that since there is no absolute Muslim consensus on which Scriptural verses should be read literally and which allegorically, a certain latitude should be permitted in exegesis (see below). He then turns to this same verse, Sura 3:7.*

It is evident from what we have said (to this point) that a unanimous agreement cannot be established in (theoretical) questions of this kind, because of the reports that many of the believers of the first generation (of Muslims), as well as others, have said that there are allegorical interpretations which ought not to be expressed except to those who are qualified to receive allegories. These are those who "are firmly rooted in knowledge." For we prefer to place a stop after God's words "and those who are firmly rooted in knowledge" (and not before it), because if the scholars did not understand allegorical interpretation (but only God), there would be no superiority in their assent which would oblige them to a belief in Him not found among the unlearned. God has described them as those who believe in Him, and this can only refer to a belief which is based on (scientific or philosophical) demonstration; and this belief only occurs together with the science of allegorical interpretation. For the unlearned believers are those whose belief in Him is not based on demonstration; and if this belief which God has attributed to the scholars (in Quran 3:7) is peculiar to them, it must come through demonstration, and if it comes through demonstration, it only occurs together with the science of allegorical interpretation. For God the Exalted has informed us that those (verses) have an allegorical interpretation which is the truth, and demonstration can only be of the truth. That being the case, it is not possible for general unanimity to be established about allegorical interpretations, which God has made peculiar to scholars. This is self-evident to any fair-minded person. (Averroes, *The Decisive Treatise* 10) [AVERROES 1961: 53–54]

22. How the Muslim Should Read the Quran

Instruction on how to read the Quran began, not unnaturally, with the Prophet himself, as this tradition circulated under Muhammad's name spells out.

Abu Hurayra reported God's Messenger as saying: "The Quran came down showing five aspects: what is permissible, what is prohibited, what is firmly fixed, what is obscure, and parables. So treat what is permissible as permissible and what is prohibited as prohibited, act upon what is firmly fixed, believe in what is obscure, and take a lesson from the parables." (Baghawi, *Mishkat al-Masabih* 1.6.2)

Parables, this tradition would have us believe, are moral exempla, *and the Quran abounds in them, like the rather extended one in Quran 68:17–32. Muhammad too used parables in his own teaching, and there is one with interesting similarities to Jesus' parable of the sower (Matt. 13:1–23), and which has, like Jesus', its own attached exegesis.*

Abu Musa reported that the Messenger of God said: "The guidance and knowledge with which God has commissioned me is like abundant rain which fell on some ground. Part of it was good, and absorbing the water, it brought forth abundant herbage and pasture; and there were some hollows in it which retain the water by which God gave benefit to men, who drank, gave drink, and sowed seed. But some of it fell on another portion which consisted only of bare patches which could not retain the water or produce herbage. That [that is, the hollows] is like the one who becomes versed in religion and receives benefit from the message entrusted to me by God, so he knows for himself and teaches others; and (the bare patches) are like the one who does not show regard for that and does not accept God's guidance with which I have been commissioned." (Baghawi, *Mishkat al-Masabih* 1.6.1)

23. Quranic Exegesis

The already cited report in which Muhammad explains how the Muslim is to understand the Quran may seem somewhat schematic for a genuine Prophetic utterance. But the highly systematic, scholastic view of the sciences connected with reading and understanding the Quran that the Spanish social philosopher and historian Ibn Khaldun inserted in his Prolegomenon to History *in 1377* C.E. *is less cause for surprise.*

It should be known that the Quran was revealed in the language of the Arabs and according to their rhetorical methods. All the Arabs understood it and knew the meaning of the individual words and composite statements. It was revealed in chapters [that is, *suras*] and verses in order to explain the Oneness of God and the religious duties appropriate to the various occasions.

Some passages . . . are early and are followed by other, later passages that abrogate the earlier ones. The Prophet used to explain these things, as it is said, "So that you may explain to the people what was revealed to them" (Quran 14:46). He used to explain the unclear statements (in the Quran) and to distinguish the abrogating statements from those abrogated by them, and to inform the men around him of this sense. Thus the men around him became acquainted with the subject. They knew why individual verses were revealed and the situation that had required them, and this directly on Muhammad's authority. Thus the verse of the Quran "When God's help comes and the victory" (110:1) refers to the announcement of the Prophet's death, and similar things.

These explanations were transmitted on the authority of the men around Muhammad [that is, the "Companions of the Prophet"; see chapter 5 below] and were circulated by the men of the second generation (after him). They continued to be transmitted among the early Muslims, until knowledge became organized in scholarly disciplines and systematic scholarly works began to be written. At that time most of these explanations were committed to writing. The traditional information concerning them, which had come down from the men around Muhammad and the men of the second generation was transmitted farther. That material reached al-Tabari (d. 923 c.e.), al-Waqidi (d. 823 c.e.) and al-Tha'alibi (d. 1035 c.e.) and other Quran interpreters. They committed to writing as much of the traditional information as God wanted them to do.

The linguistic sciences then became technical discussions of the lexicographical meaning of words, the rules governing vowel endings, and style in the use of word combinations. Systematic works were written on these subjects. Formerly these subjects had been habitual with the Arabs, and so no recourse to oral and written transmission had been necessary with respect to them. Now, that was forgotten, and these subjects were learned from books by philologists. They were needed for the interpretation of the Quran, because the Quran is in Arabic and follows the stylistic technique of the Arabs. Quran interpretation thus came to be handled in two ways.

One kind of Quran interpretation is traditional. It is based on information received from the early Muslims. It consists of knowledge of the abrogating verses and of the verses that are abrogated by them, of the reasons why a verse was revealed, and the purposes of individual verses. All this can be known only through the traditions based on the

authority of the men around Muhammad and the men of the second
generation. The early scholars had already made complete compilations
on the subject. . . .

The other kind of Quran interpretation has recourse to linguistic
knowledge, such as lexicography and the stylistic form used for conveying meaning through the appropriate means and methods. This kind of
Quran interpretation rarely appears separately from the first kind. The
first kind is the one that is wanted essentially. The second made its
appearance only after language and the philological sciences had become
crafts. However, it has become preponderant, as far as certain Quran
commentaries are concerned. (Ibn Khaldun, *Muqaddima* 6.10) [IBN
KHALDUN 1967: 2:443–446]

24. Where Did the Muslim Commentators
Get Their Information?

*The schema laid out by Ibn Khaldun is an ideal one. Even in its far less
ideal forms, Quranic interpretation not only demanded linguistic skill,
but—since the Book is filled with historical allusions, chiefly from the
biblical tradition—required that the exegete possess a fund of information
about the Sacred Past. The Jews were a likely source, as even the earliest
Muslims understood.*

Abdullah ibn Amr reported that God's Messenger said: "Pass on
information from me, even if it is only a verse of the Quran; and relate
traditions from the Banu Isra'il, for there is no restriction." . . . Bukhari
transmitted this tradition. (Baghawi, *Mishkat al-Masabih* 2.1.1)

*Thus a well-known tradition attributed to the Prophet. Ibn Khaldun
concurred that such a transmission from Jewish sources had occurred, particularly when it came to fleshing out some of the narrative material in the
Quran, and he had the social theory to enable him to explain it.*

The early scholars' works (on the Quran) and the information they
transmit contain side by side important and unimportant matters, accepted and rejected statements. The reason is the Arabs had no books
or scholarship. The desert attitude and illiteracy prevailed among them.
When they wanted to know certain things that human beings are usually
curious to know, such as the reasons for existing things, the beginning
of creation, and the secrets of existence, they consulted the earlier
People of the Book and got their information from them. The People of
the Book were the Jews who had the Torah and the Christians who

followed the religion (of the Jews). Now the People of the Torah who lived among the Arabs at that time were themselves Bedouins. They knew only as much about these matters as is known to ordinary People of the Book. The majority of those Jews were Himyarites [that is, South Arabians] who had adopted Judaism. When they became Muslims, they retained the information they possessed, such as information about the beginning of creation and information of the type of forecasts and predictions. That information had no connection with the (Jewish or Christian) religious laws they were preserving as their own. Such men were Kaʿb al-Ahbar, Wahb ibn Munabbih, Abdullah ibn Salam, and similar people.

The Quran commentaries were filled with material of such tendencies transmitted on their authority; it is information that entirely depends on them. It has no relation to (religious) laws, such that one might claim for it the soundness that would make it necessary to act (in accordance with it). The Quran interpreters were not very rigorous in this respect. They filled the Quran commentaries with such material, which originated, as we have stated, with the People of the Torah who lived in the desert and were not capable of verifying the information they transmitted. However, they were famous and highly esteemed because they were people of rank in their religion and religious group. Therefore, their interpretation has been accepted from that time onward. (Ibn Khaldun, *Muqaddima* 6.10) [IBN KHALDUN 1967: 2:445–446]

25. The Outer and Inner Meanings of the Quran

A thinker whose opinions recur again and again in the work of Averroes is Ghazali (d. 1111 C.E.), the earlier Baghdad theologian and lawyer. Ghazali's scathing attack on the rationalist philosophy that was attracting some Muslim thinkers in the tenth and eleventh centuries was, despite its spirited defense by Averroes, the likely cause of its eventual repudiation in Islam. Ghazali too is willing to admit the allegorical interpretation of Scripture, though with considerably more caution than Averroes.

. . . The Prophet said: "Whoever interprets the Quran according to his own opinion will have his place in Gehenna." The people who are acquainted with only the outer sense of exegesis have for this reason discredited the mystics to the extent that these latter practice exegesis, because they explain the wording of the Quran in a manner other than according to the tradition of Ibn Abbas and the (traditional) commentators; and they further maintain that what is involved (in such interpretation) is a matter of unbelief. If the advocates of traditional exegesis are correct, then the understanding of the Quran consists in nothing else than knowing its external meaning. But if they are not right, then what is the meaning of the Prophet's words: "Whoever interprets the Quran according to his own opinion will have his place in Gehenna"?

It should be noted that whenever someone maintains that the Quran has no meaning other than that expressed by the external method of exegesis, then in so doing he is expressing his own limitations. With this avowal about himself he expresses something which is doubtless correct (for his own situation), but he is mistaken in thinking that the entire creation is to be regarded on his level, that is, restricted by his limitations and situation. The commentaries and traditions show that the meanings contained in the Quran exhibit a wide scope for experts in the field. Thus, Ali [the cousin and son-in-law of the Prophet and the fourth Caliph of Islam] said (that a specific meaning can be grasped) only when God grants to someone an understanding of the Quran. But if nothing else is involved except the traditional interpretation, this is not "understanding." Further, the Prophet said that the Quran had a literal meaning, an inner meaning, an end point and a starting point of understanding. . . . According to the opinion of some scholars, every verse can be understood in sixty thousand ways, and that what still remains unexhausted (of its meaning) is still more numerous. Others have maintained that the Quran contains seventy-seven thousand and two hundred (kinds of) knowledge. . . .

Ibn Mas῾ud said: Whoever wishes to obtain knowledge of his ancestors and descendants should meditate upon the Quran. This knowledge does not appear, however, if one restricts the interpretation of the Quran to its outer meaning. Generally speaking, every kind of knowledge is included in the categories of actions and attributes, and the description of the nature of the actions and attributes of God is contained in the Quran. These kinds of knowledge have no end; yet in the Quran is found (only) an indication of their general aspects. Thereby the degrees of the deeper penetration into the particulars of knowledge are traced back to the (actual) understanding of the Quran. The mere outer aspect of interpretation gives no hint of this knowledge. Rather, the fact is that the Quran contains indications and hints, which certain select people with (correct) understanding can grasp, concerning all that remains obscure in the more abstract way of thinking and about which men disagree regarding the theoretical sciences and rational ideas. How can the interpretation and explanation of the outer meaning of the Quran be adequate for this?

There are, according to Ghazali, additional reasons why one should not be limited to the mere literal meaning of God's word.

The Companions of the Prophet and the commentators disagree on the interpretation of certain verses and put forth differing statements about them which cannot be brought into harmony with one another. That all these statements were heard issuing from the mouth of the Messenger of God is patently absurd. One was obliged to understand one of these statements of the Messenger of God in order to refute the rest, and then it becomes clear that, as concerns the meaning (of the passage of the Quran in question), every exegete has expressed what appeared to him to be evident through his inferential reasoning. This went so far that seven different kinds of interpretations, which cannot be brought into harmony with one another, have been advanced concerning the letters at the beginning of (some of) the *suras*.

There arises, however, the danger of personal bias.

The prohibition (against interpretation according to personal opinion cited at the outset) involves the following two reasons for its having been sent down: The first is that someone may have a (personal) opinion about something, and through his nature as well as his inclination he may harbor a bias toward it and then interpret the Quran accordingly in order thereby to find arguments to prove that his view is the correct one. Moreover, the meaning (which he links to his view) would not at all have appeared to him from the Quran if he did not have some preconceived opinion and bias. Sometimes this happens consciously, as perhaps in the case of those who use individual verses of the Quran as arguments in support of a heretical innovation and thus know that this is not in accordance with what is meant by the verse. They want rather to deceive their opponents. Sometimes, however, it (also) happens unconsciously. For instance, when a verse admits various meanings, a man inclines in his understanding to what best accords with his own opinion and inclination and thus interprets according to his "individual opinion." That is, it is a person's "individual opinion" which drives one to such an interpretation.

Finally, there is the question of the notorious ambiguity of the Arabic language.

The second reason is that someone may come to an interpretation of the Quran prematurely on the basis of the literal meaning of the Arabic, without the assistance of "hearing" (from earlier sources) and the Prophetic tradition on what is involved in the passages of the Quran which are difficult to understand, on the obscure and ambiguous expressions which are found in the Quran, and on the abbreviations, omissions, implications, anticipations, and allusions which are contained in it. Whoever has not mastered the outer aspect of exegesis, but proceeds hastily to conclusions on the meaning (of the Quran) solely on the basis of his understanding of the Arabic language, he commits many errors and aligns himself thereby to the group of those who interpret the Quran according to individual opinion. Prophetic tradition and the "hearing" are indispensable for the outer aspects of exegesis, first of all in order to make one secure thereby against the opportunities for error, and also in order to extend the endeavor to understand and to reach conclusions. (Ghazali, *Revivification of the Sciences of Religion* 1.268)

26. Ghazali on the Sciences of Revelation

It is evident, then, from the differing opinions in the commentaries written on the subject—to say nothing of the received opinion that each verse of the Book "can be understood in sixty thousand ways"—that Muslims found a somewhat greater number of ambiguities in the Quran than the few classical instances cited by the exegetes. The whole range of learning that would eventually be brought to bear on elucidating them is next illustrated in textbook fashion by Ghazali.

The praiseworthy sciences have roots, branches, preliminaries, and completions. They (that is, the sciences of revelation) comprise, therefore, four kinds.

The "roots," of which there are (in this instance) four, constitute the first kind: (They are) the Book of God, the custom of the Prophet, the consensus of the (Muslim) community, and the traditions concerning the Companions of the Prophet (that is, his contemporaries). The consensus of the community is a "root" because it furnishes indications of the custom of the Prophet; as a "root" it is ranked third. The same is true of the traditions (of the Companions), which likewise provide indications of the custom of the Prophet. The Companions witnessed the inspiration and the sending down (of the Quran) and were able to comprehend much, through a combination of circumstances, which others were not able to observe. Sometimes the explicit statements (of revelation) do not contain something which can be observed through a combination of circumstances. For this reason the men of learning found it beneficial to follow the example of the Companions of the Prophet and to be guided by the traditions regarding them.

The "branches" constitute the second kind. This group deals with that which one comprehends on the basis of the "roots" mentioned above—and indeed cannot be gleaned from the external wording alone—through which the mind is awakened and understanding is thus expanded, so that one comprehends other meanings that are beyond the external wording. Thus one comprehends from the words of the Prophet, "the judge may not judge in anger," that he also would not judge when hungry, needing to urinate, or in the pains of sickness. The "branches" comprise two subtypes, the first of which deals with the requisites of the present world. This subtype is contained in the books of jurisprudence and is entrusted to the lawyers, who are thus the men of learning responsible for the present world. The second subtype deals with the requisites of the hereafter, thus the knowledge of the circumstances of the heart, its praiseworthy and blameworthy characteristics, that which is pleasing to God and that which is abhorrent to Him. . . .

The "preliminaries" constitute the third kind. They are the tools (of Scriptural exegesis) such as lexicography and grammar, which are naturally one tool for gaining knowledge of the Book of God and the custom of His Prophet. In themselves lexicography and grammar do not belong to the sciences of revelation; however, one must become engrossed in them for the sake of revelation because the latter appears in the Arabic language. Since no revelation comes forth without language, the mastery of the language concerned becomes necessary as a tool. Among the tools of this kind belongs also the skill of writing; however this is not unconditionally required since the Messenger of God was unlettered. If a man were able to retain in his memory everything he hears, then the skill of writing would become unnecessary. Yet, since people are not able to do this, in most cases the skill of writing is essential.

The "completions," that is, in relation to the study of the Quran, constitute the fourth kind. This group contains the following divisions: (1) that which is connected with the external wording, such as the study of the (various) readings and of the phonetics; (2) that which is connected with the meaning of the contents, such as traditional exegesis, where one must also rely on tradition since the language alone does not yield the meaning; and (3), that which is connected with the "decisions" of the Quran, such as a knowledge of the abrogating and abrogated (verses), the general and the particular, the definite and the probable, as well as the kind and manner, in the same way that one makes one decision in relation to others.

It is already apparent from the listing of the "roots" above that the extra-Quranic traditions attributed to the Prophet rank directly after the Quran itself as part of God's revelation. They too have their own proper sciences, as Ghazali now explains, and as we shall see in more detail in chapter 5 below.

The "completions" relating to the traditions of the Prophet and the historical narratives consist of: (1) the study of the authorities, including their names and relationships, as well as the names and characteristics of the Companions of the Prophet; (2) the study of the reliability of the transmitters (of those traditions); (3) the study of the circumstances under which the transmitters lived, in order to be able to distinguish between those who are unreliable and those who are reliable; and (4) the study of the life spans of the transmitters, through which that which is transmitted with defective chains of authorities can be distinguished from that which exhibits unbroken chains. (Ghazali, *Revivification of the Sciences of Religion* 1.254)

27. Allegorical Interpretation as a Resolution of Apparent Contradictions

Averroes (d. 1198 C.E.) begins his tract entitled The Decisive Treatise Determining the Nature of the Connection between Religion and Philosophy *by demonstrating, as we shall see, that the Quran not only permits but even commands the study of philosophy. Whatever the virtues of this exercise, the fact remained that for most Muslims there was a conflict between what they were told in the Book of God and what they read in the Greek and Muslim philosophers. It is to this point that Averroes then turns.*

Now since this religion is true and summons to the study which leads to the knowledge of the Truth, we the Muslim community know definitively that demonstrative study (that is, philosophy) does not lead to (conclusions) conflicting with what Scripture has given us; for truth does not oppose truth but accords with it and bears witness to it.

This being so, whenever demonstrative study leads to any manner of knowledge about any being, that being is inevitably either unmentioned or mentioned in Scripture. If it is unmentioned, there is no contradition, and it is the same case as an act whose category is unmentioned so that the (Muslim) lawyer has to infer it by reasoning from Scripture. If Scripture does speak about it, the apparent meaning of the words inevitably either accords or conflicts with the conclusions of (philosophical) demonstration about it. If this apparent meaning accords, there is no conflict. If it conflicts, there is a call for allegorical interpretation. The meaning of "allegorical interpretation" is: the extension of the significance of an expression from real to metaphorical significance, without forsaking therein the standard metaphorical practices of Arabic, such as calling a thing by the name of something resembling it or a cause or a consequence or accompaniment of it, or other such things as are enumerated in accounts of the kinds of metaphorical speech.

. . . Muslims are unanimous in holding that it is not obligatory either to take all the expressions of Scripture in their apparent (or external) meaning or to extend them all from the apparent meaning by means of allegorical interpretation. They disagree (only) over which of them should and which should not be so interpreted: the Ashʿarites [that is, certain dialectical theologians] for instance give an allegorical interpretation to the verse about God's directing Himself (Quran 2:29) and the Prophetic tradition about His descent (into this world), while the Hanbalites [that is, fundamentalist lawyers and traditionists] take them in their apparent meaning. . . .

It may be objected: There are some things in Scripture which the Muslims have unanimously agreed to take in their apparent meaning, others (which they have agreed) to interpret allegorically, and others about which they have disagreed; is it permissible, then, that demonstration should lead to interpreting allegorically what they (that is, the Muslims) have agreed to take in its apparent meaning, or to taking in its apparent meaning what they have agreed to interpret allegorically? We reply: If unanimous agreement is established by a method which is certain, such (a result) is not sound; but if (the existence of) agreement on those things is a matter of opinion, then it may be sound. This is why Abu Hamid (al-Ghazali) and Abuʾl-Maʿali (al-Juwayni) and other leaders of thought said that no one should be definitely called an unbeliever for violating unanimity on a point of interpretation in matters like these.

For Averroes, that unanimity which absolutely confines one to either a literal or an allegorical interpretation of a scriptural verse is only rarely achieved, particularly under the stringent conditions he posits. The absence of consensus of course gives considerable latitude to the exegete.

That unanimity on theoretical matters is never determined with certainty, as it can be on practical (or behavioral) matters, may be shown to you by the fact that it is not possible for unanimity to be determined on any question at any period unless that period is strictly limited by us, and all the scholars existing in that period are known to us, that is, known as individuals and in their total number, and the doctrine of each one of them on the question has been handed down to us on unassailable authority. And in addition to all this, unless we are sure that the scholars existing at the time were in agreement that there is not both an apparent and an inner meaning in Scripture, that knowledge of any question ought not to be kept secret from anyone, and that there is only one way for people to understand Scripture. But it is recorded in tradition that many of the first believers used to hold that Scripture had both an apparent and an inner meaning, and that the inner meaning ought not to be learned by anyone who is not a man of learning in this field and who is incapable of understanding it. . . . So how can it possibly be conceived that a unanimous agreement can be handed down to us about a single theoretical question, when we know definitely that not a single period has been without scholars who held that there are things in Scripture whose true meaning should not be learned by all people? (Averroes, *The Decisive Treatise* 7–9) [AVERROES 1961: 50–53]

28. Dull Masses and
Minds Tied Down to Sensibles

Almost from its appearance in the Jewish tradition, the practice of allegorical exegesis was accompanied by warnings that it was not appropriate for every believer, that it should be reserved for the mature and the learned. This appears sagacious enough, but it led, not too far down the path, to a profound distinction between "pure truth," the domain of the philosopher, on the one hand, and the crude and materialistic expressions by which the prophet, who certainly knew far better, was constrained to address the masses in Scripture. What follows is one expression of such a view, in this case from the Muslim philosopher Ibn Sina, or, as the West called him, Avicenna (d. 1038 C.E.).

As for religious law, one general principle is to be admitted, to wit, that religions and religious laws promulgated through a prophet aim at addressing the masses as a whole. Now it is obvious that the deeper truths concerning the real Unity (of God), to wit, that there is one Creator, who is exalted above quantity, quality, place, time, position and change, which lead to the belief that God is one without anyone to share His species, nor is He made of parts, quantitative or conceptual, that neither is He transcendent nor immanent, nor can He be pointed to as being anywhere—it is obvious that these deeper truths cannot be communicated to the multitude. For if this had been communicated in its true form to the bedouin Arabs or the crude Hebrews, they would have refused straightway to believe and would have unanimously proclaimed that the belief to which they had been invited was a belief in an absolute nonentity.

This is why the whole account of the Unity (of God) in religion is (expressed) in anthropomorphisms. The Quran does not contain even a hint to (the deeper truth about) this important problem, nor a detailed account concerning even the obvious matters needed about the doctrine of Unity, for a part of the account is apparently anthropomorphic, while the other part contains absolute transcendence [that is, the total unlikeness of God to His creation], but in general terms, without specification or detail. The anthropomorphic phrases are innumerable, but they [that is, the orthodox interpreters of the Quran] do not accept them as such. If this is the position concerning the Unity (of God), what of the less important matters of belief?

Some people may say: "The Arabic language allows wide use and metaphor; anthropomorphisms like the hand and the face (of God), His coming down in the canopies of clouds, His coming, going, laughter, shame, anger are all correct (linguistically); only the way of their use and their context show whether they have been employed metaphysically or literally." . . . Let us grant that all these (expressions) are metaphors. Where, then, we ask, are the texts which give a clear indication of pure Unity to which doubtlessly the essence of this righteous Faith— whose greatness is acclaimed by the wise men of the entire world— invites? . . .

Upon my life, if God the Exalted did charge a prophet that he should communicate the reality about these (theological) matters to the masses with dull natures and with minds tied down to pure sensibles, and then constrained him to pursue relentlessly and successfully the task of bringing faith and salvation to those same masses, and then, to crown all, He charged him to undertake the purifying training of all the souls so they may be able to understand these truths, then He has certainly

laid upon him a duty incapable of fulfillment by any man—unless the
ordinary man receives a special gift from God, a supernal power or a
divine inspiration, in which case the instrumentality of the prophet will
be superfluous.

But let us even grant that the Arabian revelation is metaphor and
allegory according to the usage of the Arabic language. What will they
say about the Hebrew revelation—a monument of utter anthropomorphism from beginning to end? One cannot say that that book is tampered with through and through, for how can this be with a book dis-
seminated through innumerable people living in distant lands, with
so different ambitions—like Jews and Christians with all their mutual
antagonisms?

All this shows that religions are intended to address the masses in
terms intelligible to them, seeking to bring home to them what tran-
scends their intelligence by means of metaphor and symbol. Otherwise,
religions would be of no use whatever. (Ibn Sina, *Treatise on Sacrifice*)
[RAHMAN 1958: 42–44]

29. The Pleasures of Paradise

*In the end, the Muslims had to face the same scriptural problems as the Jews
and Christians before them and resorted to the same forms of scriptural exegesis to solve them. Chief among those problems was the question of anthropomorphism in Scripture. It is not that the Quran is more anthropomorphic
than those other revelations, but rather that the Muslim was, from his view
of the origin and nature of the Book, somewhat less easy with allegorizing
God's words for whatever reason. And yet it was done. The Quran, for example, had a great deal to say about the afterlife, and assurances to the
pagans of Mecca of the physical reality of both Paradise and Gehenna are
part of the earliest revelations in the Quran, as we shall see in considerably
greater detail in chapter 8 below. Here we may simply note the words of
Sura 76, which dates from the early Meccan period of Muhammad's career.*

Was there not a time in the life of man when he was not even a
thing? Verily We created man from a sperm yoked (to the ovum) to
bring out his real substance, then gave him hearing and sight. We surely
showed him the way that he may be either grateful or deny. We have
prepared for unbelievers chains and collars and a blazing fire.

Surely the devotees will drink cups flavored with palm blossoms
from a spring of which the votaries of God will drink and make it flow
in abundance. Those who fulfill their vows and fear the Day whose evil

shall be diffused far and wide, and feed the needy for the love of Him, and the orphans and the captives, saying: "We feed you for the sake of God, desiring neither recompense nor thanks. We fear the dismal day calamitous from our Lord."

So God will protect them from the evil of that day, and grant them happiness and joy, and reward them for their perseverance with Paradise and silken robes where they will recline on couches feeling neither heat of the sun nor intense cold. The shade will bend over them, and low will hang clusters of grapes. Passed round will be silver flagons and goblets made of glass, and crystal clear bottles of silver, of which they will determine the measure themselves. There they will drink a cup flavored with ginger from a spring by the name of Salsabil. And boys of everlasting youth will go about attending them. Looking at them you would think they were pearls dispersed.

When you look around you will see delights and a great dominion. On their bodies will be garments of the finest silk and brocade, and they will be adorned with bracelets of silver; and their Lord will give them the purest draught to drink. (Quran 76:1–21)

The Muslim commentators approach these and other Quranic descriptions of Paradise in a number of different ways. Here, for example, is a cosmology, a laying out of the celestial geography of Paradise in the context of its creation, and into whose fabulous details have been integrated some of the themes of Islamic theodicy. Often this comes in the form of a vision (chapter 7 below), but here the details have been supplied in a rather straightforward manner, presumably on the authority of the Prophet, and relayed through his contemporary Ibn Abbas.

Ibn Abbas, may God be pleased with him, said that then (after the creation of the heavens) God created Paradise, which consists of eight gardens. . . . The eight gardens have gates of gold, jewel-encrusted and inscribed. On the first gate is written: "There is no God but the God and Muhammad is the Messenger of God." On the second is written: "The Gate of those who pray the five (liturgical daily) prayers, observing perfectly the ablutions and the prostrations." On the third is written: "The Gate of those who justify themselves by the purity of their souls." On the fourth gate is written: "The Gate of those who encourage the doing of what is approved and discourage the doing of what is disapproved." On the fifth gate is written: "The Gate of him who holds himself back from lusts." On the sixth gate is written: "The Gate of those who perform the Greater and Lesser Pilgrimage." On the seventh gate is written: "The Gate of those who go out on Holy War." On the eighth gate is written: "The Gate of those who desire," that is, those who avert their eyes (from unseemly things) and perform good works such as showing due affection to parents and being mindful of one's kin. By these gates will enter those whose works have been of the kind written on them. (Kisaʾi, *Stories of the Prophets*) [JEFFERY 1962: 172–173]

It is not always easy, or perhaps even useful, to connect a certain exegetical approach with a specific literary genre. The last passage cited above, which has a distinct homiletic flavor, occurs in a collection of narratives, the Stories of the Prophets. *The following sections of the homiletic* Arousing of the Heedless *by Abuʾl-Layth al-Samarqandi (d. 983 C.E.) easily combine a Quranically based moral exhortation—the individual Prophetic tradition has already glossed the Quran, and Samarqandi braids a catena of these texts to make his own point—with an undisguised interest in the fabulous elements of Paradise.*

It is related of Ibn Abbas, may God be pleased with him, that he used to say: In Paradise are dark-eyed maidens of the type called "toys," who have been created out of four things, from musk, ambergris, camphor and saffron, stirred into a dough with water of life. All the celestial maidens love them dearly. Were one of them to spit into ocean its waters would become sweet. On the throat of each of them is written: "He who would desire to have the like of me, let him do the works of obedience to my Lord." Mujahid said that the ground of Paradise is of silver, its dust of musk, the trunks of its trees are of silver, their branches of pearl and emerald, their leaves and fruits hang low so that he who would eat standing can reach them, and likewise he who would eat sitting or even lying can reach them. Then he recited: "Its fruit clusters hang low" (Quran 86:14), that is, its fruits are near so that both he who is standing and he who is sitting can reach them. Abu Hurayra, may God be pleased with him, said: "By Him who sent down the Book to Muhammad, upon whom be God's blessing and peace, the dwellers in Paradise increase in beauty and handsomeness as in this world the inhabitants increase in decrepitude." (Samarqandi, *Arousing the Heedless*) [JEFFERY 1962: 240–241]

There are problems with such anthropomorphisms, and they are raised, not unnaturally, by a Christian polemicist.

The sage Abuʾl-Fadl al-Haddadi has related to us . . . from Zayd ibn Arqam, who said: There came a man of the People of the Book to the Prophet, upon whom be God's blessing and peace, and said: "O Abuʾl-Qasim (that is, Muhammad), do you pretend that the inhabitants of the Garden (really) eat and drink?" "Surely," he replied, "by Him in whose hand is my soul, every one of them will be given the capacity of a hundred men in eating and drinking and having intercourse." The man said: "But someone who eats or drinks has a need of relieving himself, whereas Paradise is too fine a place for there to be in it anything so malodorous." Muhammad replied: "A man's need to relieve himself will be satisfied by perspiring, which will be as sweet-smelling as musk." (Samarqandi, *Arousing the Heedless*) [JEFFERY 1962: 243]

In the following passage the physical delights of Paradise begin to recede into the background, however, and the exegetical focus turns to the vision of God in the afterlife.

In another tradition it is related that God, may He be exalted, will say to His angels, "Feed my saints," whereupon various kinds of food will be brought, in every bite of which they will find pleasure different from that they found in any other. When they have had their fill of eating, God, may He be exalted, will say, "Give My servants drink," whereupon drinks will be brought, in which they will find a pleasure different from that which they found in any other. When they have finished, God, may He be exalted, will say to them: "I am your Lord. I have made My promise to you come true. Now ask of Me and I will give it to you." They will reply: "O our Lord, we ask that You should be well pleased with us." This they will say two or three times, where-upon He will say: "I am well pleased with you, but today I have an increase (for you). I shall favor you with a token of regard greater than all that." Then the Veil will be removed and they will look upon Him for such a period as God wills. Then they will fall on their faces in a prostration, remaining prostrated for such a time as God pleases, whereat He will say to them: "Raise your heads. This is no place for worshiping." At that they will quite forget all the other enjoyment they have been having, for to see their Lord is the most precious of all their joys.

We shall look somewhat more closely at this question of the vision of God in the afterlife in chapter 8 below, but Samarqandi knows very well that it presents a problem, and so he intervenes to offer a correction and his own interpretation.

The lawyer [that is, the author, Abu'l-Layth al-Samarqandi], may God have mercy on him, says: When he [presumably Muhammad, the source of the anonymous transmitted tradition] speaks about the Veil being lifted, he means the veil which is over them (that is, over the

glorified souls) which prevents them from seeing Him. As for his statement that they will look upon Him, some say (it means) that they will
look on a token such as they had not previously seen. Most of the
learned, however, say that it is to be taken according to its literal meaning, and that they will actually see Him, though we know not how, save
that it will not be in an anthropomorphic manner, just as here on earth
they knew Him, but not in an anthropomorphic manner. (Samarqandi,
Arousing the Heedless) [JEFFERY 1962: 242–243]

CHAPTER 5

The Quran, the Prophet, and the Law

However the historian might view it, the Quran presented itself as a divine revelation with a direct and explicit connection to those earlier and authentic revelations given to the Jews and the Christians, the Tawra and Injil, as Muhammad called them, and like those earlier Scriptures—there seems to have been some uncertainty about the contents of the Gospels—the Quran was intended to spell out what islam, "submission to the will of God," signified in terms of concrete human acts. Some small part of the Quranic injunctions is devoted to what might broadly be called ceremonial or liturgical acts: prayer, fasting, and the like. But where specific acts are prescribed or forbidden, most of them have to do with questions of personal status such as the treatment of heirs, women, slaves, and orphans; with the reformation of morals, criminal procedures, and the observance of binding contracts. Muhammad could address these issues as they arose in his small community of believers. We may suppose that there were at least some other prescriptions rendered by him that are not recorded in the Quran and, what is virtually certain, that Muhammad acted as sole judge and arbitrator for the community of Muslims.

There is implicit in all that Muhammad did and preached the notion that there is such a thing as an Islamic "way" (shariᶜa), which resembled the Jewish and the Christian "ways" in that it came from God, but which stood in sharp opposition to both the religious paganism and degenerate tribal custom of the contemporary Arabs of the "Era of Ignorance." But the Islamic "way" was no more explicit and formal than the random precepts of the Quran that defined it, and at Muhammad's death in 632 C.E., God's revelation was ended and the Quran had become forever a closed Book. At *that very moment, however, the Muslim community, which was endowed with only the most rudimentary religious and secular institutions, was poised at the beginning of an immense military and political expansion that would carry it within a short time from Spain to the Indus.*

We possess only the vaguest idea of how the Muslims conducted their legal affairs in the first century after the death of the Prophet. The Caliph was recognized as the chief judge (qadi) of the community, as Muhammad had been, and he delegated this judicial power to others in the provinces of the new Islamic empire. But how the qadis rendered their judgments to other Muslims—Muslim justice applied only to Muslims; Jews and Christians continued under their own juridical traditions—we can only surmise, though it was probably on the basis of local custom, caliphal instruction, their own understanding of the Quran and perhaps an embryonic sense of an Islamic "tradition."

There were those who found such pragmatic and even secular arrangements in God's own community unsettling, and out of that dissatisfaction, which was reinforced by political, financial, and tribal disenchantment with the current dynasty of Muslim rulers, there arose in certain traditionist circles the first debates over what it meant to be a Muslim and to pursue an Islamic "way" in all its ethical and legal implications. The results are sketchy, but we can observe that to validate their conclusions those early pioneers in Muslim jurisprudence (fiqh) appealed not only to the Quran, as might be expected in a revealed religion, but increasingly to "the customary practice (sunna) of the Prophet."

1. On the Usefulness of Tradition

By the ninth century, two hundred years after the death of the Prophet, the resort to tradition, and more specifically, to the Prophet's tradition, had become a central concern in shaping the behavioral contours of a Muslim life. The littérateur *al-Jahiz (d. 886 C.E.) offered his readers this explanation of the presence of a large body of "reports" (hadith) emanating from the Prophet that were circulating in Islam.*

God knows that man cannot of himself provide for his own needs, and does not intuitively understand the consequences of things without the benefit of the example of messengers, the books of his ancestors, and information about past ages and rulers. And so God has assigned to each generation the natural duty of instructing the next, and has made each succeeding generation the criterion of the truth of the information handed down to it. For hearing many unusual traditions and strange ideas makes the mind more acute, enriches the soul, and gives food for thought and incentive to look further ahead. More knowledge received orally means more ideas, more ideas mean more thought, more thought means more wisdom, and more wisdom means more sensible actions. . . .

Since God did not create men in the image of Jesus, son of Mary, John, son of Zachariah, and Adam, father of humankind, but rather He created them imperfect and unfit to provide for their own needs . . . He sent His Messengers to them and set up His Prophets among them, saying, "Man should have no argument against God after the Messengers" (Quran 4:163). But most men were not eyewitnesses to the proofs of His Messengers, nor did God allow them to be present at the miracles of His Prophets, to hear their arguments or to see their manner of working. And so it was needful that those who were present tell those who were absent, and the latter attend to the teaching of the former; and He needed to vary the characters and the motives of those who were doing the transmitting, to show to their hearers and the faithful generally that a large number of people with differing motives and contrasting claims could not all have invented a false tradition on the same subject without collusion and conspiring on the subject. . . . For if they had, it would be known and spoken of abroad . . . and men would have the greatest of proofs against God, as He said, "That man should have no argument against God after the Messengers"; for He would be enjoining on them obedience to His Messengers, faith in His Prophets and His Books, and belief in His heaven and His hell, without giving them proof of tradition or the possibility of avoiding error. But God is far above such. (Jahiz, *The Proofs of Prophecy* 125–126)

2. Scripture, Tradition, and the Law in Islam

His mildly rationalizing and utilitarian view of tradition in general and Islamic tradition in particular may have interested the more sophisticated readers of the cultured and clever Jahiz, but for most Muslims, "the tradition" or "the traditions" had quite another import: by Jahiz's day they already provided the basis of a great deal of Muslim belief and practice. In Arabic "a tradition" (hadith) and "the tradition" (sunna) mean two different things, neither entirely synonymous with what is understood by the

English term "tradition." "A tradition," when it is being used in its technical
sense, means a report of some saying or deed of the Prophet that is transmit-
ted on the witness and authority of one of the men or women around him,
the "Companions of the Prophet," as they came to be called. It will generally
be called here "a Prophetic tradition." "The tradition" is actually "the tra-
dition of the Prophet," that is, his customary behavior (sunna), his teaching
or example, as it is reflected in those just mentioned reports.

"The tradition of the Prophet" was as authoritative as the Quran for
Muslims, from both a legal and a doctrinal point of view, as indeed some
Prophetic traditions themselves assert.

Al-Irbad al-Sariya declared that God's Messenger got up and said:
"Does any of you, while reclining on his couch, imagine that God has
prohibited only what is to be found in the Quran? By God, I have
commanded, exhorted and prohibited various matters as numerous as
what is found in the Quran, or more numerous." (Baghawi, *Mishkat
al-Masabih* 6.1.2)

Aisha said: God's Messenger did a certain thing and gave permission for it to be done, but some people abstained from it. When God's
Messenger heard of it, he delivered a sermon, and after extolling God
he said: "What is the matter with people who abstain from a thing which
I do? By God, I am the one of them who knows most about God and
fears Him most." Bukhari and Muslim transmit this tradition. (Baghawi,
Mishkat al-Masabih 6.1.1)

That the earliest Muslims followed the example of their Prophet, "who
knows most about God," would seem to need little argument or demonstra-
tion. But there were other means of defining moral and legal action for a
Muslim, adherence to local custom, for example, or even resort to some kind
of analogical reasoning to elicit expanded or additional legal prescriptions
from the Quran's "clear declarations." It was in this more polemical context
that the role of "the Prophetic tradition" began to be argued in Islam. The
earliest and most powerful case for the role of the Prophet's own authentic
words and deeds, his "tradition," as the primary instrument for understand-
ing the legal material in the Quran was made by the pioneer Egyptian
Muslim jurist al-Shafi'i (d. 820 C.E.) in his Treatise on the Roots of
Jurisprudence. *The argument begins, as always, with the Book itself.*

Shafi'i said: God has placed His Messenger—(in relation) to His
religion, His commands and His Book—in the position made clear by
Him as a distinguishing standard of His religion. He did this by imposing

(on the earliest Muslims) the duty of obedience to him as well as pro-
hibiting disobedience to him. He has made his merits evident by associating belief in His Messenger with belief in Him. . . . He said:

> "They alone are true believers who believe in God and His
> Messenger, and when they are with him on a matter of com-
> mon concern, do not depart without obtaining his leave."
> (Quran 24:62)

Thus God prescribed that the perfect beginning of the faith to
which all things are subordinate shall be belief in Him and then in His
Messenger. For if a person believes only in Him and not in His Messenger, the name of the perfect faith will never apply to him until he
believes in His Messenger together with Him. (Shafiʿi, *Treatise*) [SHAFIʿI
1961: 109–110]

*On this principle that belief in God is necessarily accompanied by
belief in the Messenger of God, Shafiʿi then proceeds to bind the notion of
the Prophet's custom into the scriptural proof. This he does by understanding the concept of "wisdom," where it occurs in the phrase "the Book and the
Wisdom," as a reference to the words and deeds of the Prophet himself.*

Shafiʿi said: God has imposed the duty on men to obey His divine
commands as well as the tradition of His Messenger. For he said in His
Book:

> "Send to them, O Lord, a Messenger from among them to
> impart Your messages to them, and teach them the Book and
> the wisdom, and correct them in every way; and indeed, You
> are mighty and wise."   (Quran 2:129)

After citing a number of almost identical passages, Shafiʿi continues.

So God mentioned His Book, which is the Quran, and Wisdom,
and I have heard that those who are learned in the Quran, whom I
approve, hold that Wisdom is the tradition of the Prophet of God,
which is like what God Himself said; but God knows best! For the
Quran is mentioned first, followed by Wisdom; then God mentioned
His favor to mankind by teaching them the Quran and Wisdom. So it is
not permissible for Wisdom to be called here anything save the tradition
of the Messenger of God. For Wisdom is closely linked with the Book
of God, and God has imposed the duty of obedience to His Messenger,
and imposed on men the obligation to obey his orders. So it is not
permissible to regard anything as a duty save that set forth in the Quran

and the tradition of the Prophet. (Shafiʿi, *Treatise*) [SHAFIʿI 1961: 110–122]

That what Muhammad said and did reflected nothing but the will of God is easily demonstrated by Shafiʿi, by reference to passages like the following, for example.

O Prophet, fear God and do not follow the unbelievers and the hypocrites. But follow what is revealed to you from your Lord. Verily, God is All-knowing, All-wise. Truly, God is aware of the things you do. (Quran 33:1–2)

O Messenger, announce what has reached you from your Lord, for if you do not, you will not have delivered His message. God will preserve you from the mischief of men; for God does guide those who do not believe. (Quran 5:67)

In certifying that the Prophet guides mankind along a straightforward path—the path of God—and that he delivers His message and obeys His commands, as we have stated before, and in ordering obedience to him and in emphasizing all this in the (divine) communications just cited, God has given evidence to mankind that they should accept the judgment of the Messenger and obey his orders. (Shafiʿi, *Treatise*) [SHAFIʿI 1961: 118]

Shafiʿi's argument has now reached a crucial juncture.

Shafiʿi said: Whatever the Messenger has decreed that is not based on any (textual) command from God, he has done so by God's command. . . . For the Messenger had laid down a tradition (on matters) for which there is a text in the Book of God as well as for others concerning which there is no specific text. But what he has laid down in the Prophetic tradition God has ordered us to obey, and He regards our obedience to him (Muhammad) as obedience to Himself, and refusal to obey him as disobedience to Him for which no man will be forgiven; nor is an excuse for failure to obey the Prophet's tradition possible owing to what I have already stated and what the Prophet himself has said.

Shafiʿi then quotes a Prophetic tradition that seems aimed directly at Quranic fundamentalists.

Sufyan told us from Salim Abu al-Nadr, a freed slave of Umar ibn Ubaydallah, who heard Ubaydallah ibn Abi Rafiʿ related from his father that the Messenger had said: "Let me find no one of you reclining on his couch, and when confronted with an order of permission or prohibition from me, say: 'I do not know (if this is permitted or prohibited); we will follow only what we find in the Book of God.'" (Shafi'i, *Treatise*) [SHAFI'I 1961: 118–119]

In the wake of Shafi'i's arguments, both the Prophetic tradition and the discrete reports that constituted it began to be carefully studied by Muslim scholars, as Ibn Khaldun explains in his Prolegomenon to History, *written in 1377 C.E.*

It should be known that the sciences with which people concern themselves in cities and which they acquire and pass on through instruction are of two kinds: one that is natural to man and to which he is guided by his own ability to think, and a traditional kind that he learns from those who invented it.

The first kind comprises the philosophical sciences. They are the ones with which man can become acquainted through the very nature of his ability to think and concerning whose objects, problems, arguments and methods of instruction he is guided by his human perceptions, so that he is made aware of the distinction between what is correct and what is wrong in them by his own speculation and research, inasmuch as he is a thinking human being.

The second kind comprises the traditional, conventional sciences. All of them depend upon information based on the authority of the given religious law. There is no place in the intellect for them, save that the intellect may be used in connection with them to relate problems of detail with basic principles. Particulars that constantly come into being are not included in the general tradition by the mere fact of its existence. Therefore, such particulars need to be related (to the general principles) by some kind of analogical reasoning. However, such analogical reasoning is derived from the (traditional) information, while the character of the basic principle, which is traditional, remains valid [that is, unchanged]. Thus analogical reasoning of this type reverts to being tradition itself, because it is derived from it.

It is clear from Ibn Khaldun's remarks that he is not using "traditional" in the sense of "ordinary," "usual," or "the way things have always been done," but rather in the original sense of "handed down," and so, somewhat more awkwardly in English, of the "traditioned" sciences, where it is not so much a question of a science that had been handed down as of a science using "traditioned" data. All those data derive, as he next indicates, from the twin source of the Quran and the reported, or "traditioned," behavior of the Prophet.

The basis of all the traditional [that is, "traditioned"] sciences is the legal material of the Quran and the customary behavior (*sunna*) of the Prophet, which is the law given us by God and His Messenger, as well as the sciences connected with that material, by means of which we are enabled to use it. This, further, requires as auxiliary sciences the sciences of the Arabic language [that is, grammar, rhetoric, lexicography, etc.]. Arabic is the language of Islam and the Quran was revealed in it.

The different kinds of traditional sciences are numerous, because it is the duty of the responsible Muslim to know the legal obligations God placed upon him and upon his fellow men. The are derived from the Quran and the reported behavior of the Prophet, either from the text itself or through general consensus, or a combination of the two. Thus he must first study the explicit wording of the Quran. This is the science of Quran interpretation. Then he must study the Quran, both with reference to the manner in which it has been transmitted and related on the authority of the Prophet who brought it from God, and with reference to the differences in the readings of the Quran readers. This is the science of Quranic "reading."

Then he must study the manner in which the behavior of the Prophet is connected with its originator [that is, Muhammad], and he must discuss the transmitters who have handed it down. He must know their circumstances and their probity, so that the information he receives from them may be trusted and so that one may be able to know the part of it in accordance with whose implications one must act. These are the sciences of Prophetic tradition.

Then the process of evolving the laws from their basic principles requires some normative guidance to provide us with the knowledge of how that process takes place. This is the science of the principles of jurisprudence. After one knows the principles of jurisprudence, one can enjoy, as its result, the knowledge of the divine laws that govern the actions of all Muslims. This is jurisprudence proper.

Furthermore, the duties of the Muslim may concern either the body or the heart. The duties of the heart are concerned with faith and the distinction between what is to be believed and what is not to be believed. This concerns the articles of faith which deal with the essence and the attributes of God, the events of the Resurrection, Paradise, punishment and predestination, and entails discussion and defense of these subjects with the help of intellectual arguments. This is speculative theology [see chapter 8 below]. (Ibn Khaldun, *Muqaddima* 6.9) [IBN KHALDUN 1967: 2:436–438]

3. The Word of God Is One:
The Inspiration of the Prophetic Traditions

As we have already seen, there was no doubt in Muslim circles that the Quran was the inspired word of God. Likewise, for the Prophetic traditions, there is some internal testimony in a few of those reports that some at least of Muhammad's words were the result, and enjoyed the authority of, a divine inspiration. The following is reported on the authority of the Prophet's companion Ubayda.

The descent of inspiration was troublesome to the Prophet. His face would go ashen in color. One day inspiration came down on him (possibly just after the revelation of Sura 4:15) and he showed the usual signs of distress. When he recovered, he said: "Take it from me! God has appointed a way for the women: the non-virgin with the non-virgin and the virgin with the virgin. The non-virgin, one hundred strokes and death by stoning; the virgin, one hundred strokes and banishment for a year." (Bayhaqi) [Cited by BURTON 1977: 74]

The theologian al-Ghazali puts the Muslim position on the Prophetic traditions succinctly.

God does not have two words, one in the Quranic style which we are bidden to recite publicly, and called the Quran, while the other word is not Quran. God has but one word which differs only in the mode of its expression. On occasions God indicates His word by the Quran; on others, by words in another style, not publicly recited, and called the Prophetic tradition. Both are mediated by the Prophet. (Ghazali, *Mustasfa* 1.125) [Cited by BURTON 1977: 57]

4. Their Transmission

The Muslim tradition is unanimously agreed that parts at least of the Quran were written down, whether "on palm leaves or flat stones or in the hearts of men," during the Prophet's own lifetime. There is no such unanimity concerning the Prophetic traditions, however, as these two widely circulated reports testify.

Abdullah ibn Umar reported: We said, "O Prophet of God, we hear from you traditions which we cannot remember. May we not write them down?" "By all means write them down," he said.

Abu Hurayra reported: The Prophet of God came to us while we were writing down traditions and said, "What is this you are writing down?" We said, "Traditions which we hear from you." Said he, "A book other than the Book of God! Do you not know that it was nothing but the writing of books other than the Book of God that led astray the peoples who were before you?" We said, "Are we to relate traditions from you, O Prophet of God?" He replied, "Relate traditions from me; there is no objection to that. But he who intentionally speaks falsely on my authority will find a place in hell." [Cited by GUILLAUME 1924: 15–16]

5. Tendentious and Sectarian Traditions

*That some were in fact speaking falsely on the authority of the Prophet must have been apparent to everyone who looked into the matter of the Prophetic traditions. The reported words of the Prophet were important not merely for the understanding of the legal material in the Quran but also for the settling of various historical claims. The Shi*ites, for example, those parti-sans of the Imamate of Ali (see chapter 3 above), bolstered their claims to rulership in Islam not merely by charging that the text of the Quran had been deliberately tampered with; they also interpreted the extant text in a different fashion. How can one determine the truth or falsity of such a claim? This is the question posed by the essayist al-Jahiz (d. 886 C.E.) in his tract called* The Uthmanis.

The radical Shi'ites claim that God revealed several verses regard-ing Ali, notably the following: "Obey God, obey God's Messenger and those in authority among you" (Quran 4:62), in which "those in author-ity" refers to Ali and his descendants. In truth, if traditionists were agreed that this verse refers to Ali and his descendants, then we must accept it; but if it [that is, this reported interpretation] is spurious, transmitted on weak authority, it is not only weak but exceptional, and you cannot account it part of your evidence. A Prophetic tradition can derive from a single reliable source and be transmitted on equally sound authority, but it is still reckoned "exceptional" unless it is widely known and a matter of common knowledge. On the other hand, a tradition can be transmitted by two or three persons regarded by traditionists as weak authorities, and in that case it is weak by reason of the weakness of its transmitters; but it still cannot be described as "exceptional" as long as it is transmitted by three authorities. The only sure proof lies in tradi-tions that are transmitted in such a fashion that deliberate forgery or conspiracy to forge can be ruled out. These are the accepted Prophetic traditions.

A tradition is accepted not merely because of the number and reliability of its transmitters, but because it has been transmitted by a number of authorities whose motives and inclinations are so different that they could not have possibly conspired together to utter a forged Prophetic tradition. Then the compiler must satisfy himself that these different authorities transmitted the tradition through an equal number of transmitters of equally different motives and tendencies. If the final version then corresponds with the original, conviction is inescapable and doubt and suspicion are excluded.

Turning to the claim that in the verse "Obey . . ." God was referring to Ali to the exclusion of all the (other) Migrants, the report on which this interpretation rests does not fulfill these conditions or fit this description. Indeed, the commentators suggest that it refers rather to the Prophet's officers and governors, to Muslims in general or to the leaders of expeditions . . . and that it is an injunction to the people to obey the commanders of the army and submit to the civil administration (of the community). (Jahiz, *The Uthmanis* 115)

6. The Criticism of Traditions

Nor was sectarianism the only cause for the multiplication of Prophetic traditions, some of them of very doubtful authenticity. Within less than a hundred years after the death of Muhammad the "traditions of the Prophet" were being invoked ever more frequently and systematically in the elaboration of Islamic law. This new approach to Islamic law, which is typified in the Muslim jurisprudent al-Shafi'i (d. 820 C.E.), created a new demand for traditions, and the supply soon began to rise to meet it.

Some idea of the enormous number of traditions that were eventually credited to the Prophet may be gotten from the fact that when Muslim scholars sat down to collect these reports, one of them, al-Bukhari (d. 870 C.E.), had reputedly accumulated 600,000 such, of which only 7,275 were included in his anthology, a number that may perhaps be reduced to 4,000 or even 2,762 when repetitions are eliminated. Another scholar, Abu Dawud, used only 4,800 out of his collection of some 500,000 Prophetic traditions in his anthology.

One Muslim response to this unchecked growth in the number of Prophetic traditions was to do as Jahiz had done, to develop a more critical attitude toward these reports and to attempt to separate, if not the authentic from the spurious, then the "sound" from the "weak." The chief method of proceeding was to scrutinize the chain of transmitters that each tradition now self-consciously bore as a sign of its own authenticity. Ibn Khaldun (d. 1406 c.e.) describes the fully developed science of tradition criticism in the survey of the Islamic sciences that he incorporated into his Prolegomenon *to History.*

The purpose of the discipline is a noble one. It is concerned with the knowledge of how to preserve the traditions transmitted on their authority of the Master of the religious law [that is, Muhammad], until it is definite which are to be accepted and which are to be rejected.

It should be known that the men around Muhammad and the men of the second generation who transmitted the traditions were well known in the cities of Islam. There were transmitters in the Hijaz, in Basra and Kufa [the early Muslim garrison towns in Iraq], and then in Egypt and Syria. They were famous in their time. The transmitters in the Hijaz had fewer links in their chains of transmitters and they were sounder, because they were reluctant to accept (as reliable transmitters) those who were obscure and whose conditions were not known. . . .

At the beginning, knowledge of the religious law was entirely based on (oral) tradition. It involved no speculation, no use of opinion, and no intricate reasoning. The early Muslims occupied themselves with it, selecting the sound material, and thus eventually perfected it. Malik wrote the *Kitab al-Muwatta* according to the Hijazi tradition, in which he laid down the principal laws on the basis of sound, generally agree-upon (material). He arranged the work according to juridical categories. (Ibn Khaldun, *Muqaddima* 6.11) [IBN KHALDUN 1967: 2:452–453]

Another of the sciences of tradition is the knowledge of the norms that leading tradition scholars have invented in order to know the chains of transmitters, the (individual) transmitters, their names, how the transmission took place, their conditions, their classes, and their different technical terminologies. This is because general consensus makes it obligatory to act in accordance with information established on the authority of the Messenger of God. This requires probability for the assumption that the information is true. Thus the independent student must verify all the means by which it is possible to make such an assumption.

He may do this by scrutinizing the chains of transmitters of traditions. For that purpose one may use such knowledge of the probity, accuracy, thoroughness and lack of carelessness or negligence as the most reliable Muslims describe a transmitter as possessing. Then, there are the differences in rank that exist among the transmitters. Further, there is the way the transmission took place. The transmitter may have heard the *shaykh* (dictate the tradition), or he may have read it (from a book) in his presence, or he may have heard it read (by another) in the presence of the *shaykh* or the *shaykh* may have written it down for him, or he may have obtained the approval of the *shaykh* for written material, or he may have obtained his permission to teach certain materials. (Ibn Khaldun, *Muqaddima* 6.11) [IBN KHALDUN 1967: 2:448–449]

7. The Categories of Traditions

This careful scrutiny of the transmitters of any given tradition allowed the scholar to categorize the tradition in question and to rate it according to the criteria he had set up.

There are differences with regard to the soundness or acceptability of the transmitted material. The highest grade of transmitted material is called "sound" (by the tradition scholars). Next comes "good." The lowest grade is "weak." The classification of traditions also includes "missing the original transmitter on Muhammad's authority," "missing one link," "missing two links," "affected with some infirmity," "unique," "unusual" and "unique and suspect." In some cases there is a difference of opinion as to whether such traditions should be rejected. In other cases, there is general agreement that they should be rejected. The same is the case with traditions with sound chains. In some instances there is general agreement as to their acceptability and soundness, whereas, in other instances, there are differences of opinion. Tradition scholars differ greatly in their explanation of these terms. (Ibn Khaldun, *Muqaddima* 6.11) [IBN KHALDUN 1967: 2:449–450]

8. The Companions of the Prophet

The passing-down of reports on the excellence of the generation of Muhammad's contemporaries was not simply an exercise in piety since it was these worthies who were the eyewitness generation and so stood behind every tradition attributed to the Prophet. And it was their character rather than the acuity of their sight or hearing that guaranteed what they transmitted.

The best of mankind after these [that is, after the early Caliphs and the veterans of the battle of Badr] are the Companions of God's Messenger from the period during which he was among them. Anyone who knew him for a year or a month or a day or an hour, or even saw him,

is of the Companions, to the extent that he was with him, took precedence with him, heeded his words and regarded him. The least of these
in companionhood is better than the generation which did not see him.
If they should come before God with all their works like those who were
the associates of the Prophet—God bless him and give him peace—and
beheld him and listened to him, the one who saw him with his own eye
and believed in him even for a single hour is better for his association
than all who followed after, even if they should have performed all the
(requisite) good works. (Ahmad ibn Hanbal, *Creed*) [WILLIAMS 1971: 31]

9. Contradictory Traditions

Careful scrutiny of the external transmission mechanisms of a Prophetic tra-
dition was not the only way of investigating Prophetic traditions in Islam.
Some attention was also given to the matter of the tradition itself, and par-
ticularly to the question of contradictory traditions. Al-Shafiʿi himself ad-
dressed the problem.

As to contradictory Prophetic traditions where no indications exist
to specify which is the abrogating and which is the abrogated tradition,
they are all in accord with one another and contradiction does not really
exist among them. For the Messenger of God, being an Arab by tongue
and by country, may have laid down a general rule intended to be
general and another general rule intended to be particular. . . . Or a
certain question may have been asked to which he gave a concise answer, leading some of the transmitters to relate the tradition in detail
and others in brief, rendering the meaning of the tradition partly clear
and partly vague. Or (it may happen) that the transmitter of a certain
tradition related the answer he heard from the Prophet without knowing what the question had been, for had he known the question he
would have understood the answer clearly from the reasoning on which
the answer was based.

The Prophet may have likewise laid down a tradition covering a
particular situation and another covering a different one, but some of
those who related what they had heard failed to distinguish between the
two differing situations for which he had laid down the traditions. . . .
He may have also provided a tradition consisting of an order of permission or prohibition the wording of which was general, and he may have
provided a second specifying tradition which made it evident that his
order of prohibition was not intended to prohibit what he made lawful,

nor that his order of permission made lawful what he prohibited. For all possibilities of this kind parallel examples exist in the Book of God. (Shafi͑i, *Treatise*) [SHAFI͑I 1961: 180–181]

10. The Canonical Collections

We return to Ibn Khaldun's survey of the science of tradition. He now describes the five standard collections of traditions that had gained the cachet of authority in Islam.

There was Muhammad ibn Isma͑il al-Bukhari (d. 870 C.E.), the leading tradition scholar of his time. In his *Musnad al-Sahih* he widened the area of tradition and published the orthodox traditions according to subject. He combined all the different ways of the Hijazis, Iraqis and Syrians, accepting the material upon which they all agreed, but excluding the material concerning which there were differences of opinion. He repeated a given tradition in every chapter upon which the contents of that particular tradition had some bearing. Therefore his traditions were repeated in several chapters, because a single tradition may deal with several subjects, as we have indicated. His work thus comprised 7,200 traditions, of which 3,000 are repeated. In each chapter he kept separate the (different) recensions (of the same tradition), with the different chains of transmitters belonging to each.

Then came the imam Muslim (d. 875 C.E.). . . . He composed his *Musnad al-Sahih*, in which he followed Bukhari, in that he transmitted the material that was generally agreed upon, but he omitted the repetitions and did not keep the (different) recensions and chains of transmitters separate. He arranged his work according to juridical categories and the chapter headings of jurisprudence.

How elaborate these judicial categories were may be seen from a glance at Bukhari's Sahih. The whole work is divided into ninety-seven "books." The first contain traditions on the beginning of revelation, on faith and knowledge. The next thirty books are given over to traditions connected with ablution, prayer, alms, pilgrimage, and fasting. These are followed by twenty-two books on matters of business, trusteeship, and in general with conditions of employment and various legal matters. There are three books of traditions on fighting for the faith and dealing with subject peoples, followed by one on the beginning of creation. The next four collect traditions on the Prophets and the admirable traits of various contemporaries of

Muhammad, including some account of the Prophet's life up to the Hijra, and the next book follows his career at Medina. There are two books with exegetical traditions on the Quran. The three following deal with marriage, divorce, and the maintenance due to one's family. From here to Book 95 various subjects are treated, among which are such matters as food, drink, clothing, seemly behavior, medicine, invitations, vows, the expiation of broken vows, blood revenge, persecution, the interpretation of visions, civil strife, and the trials before the end of the world. Book 96 stresses the importance adhering to the Quran and the Sunna, and the last book, which is fairly lengthy, addresses itself chiefly to theological questions on the subject of the Unity of God.

We return once more to the text of Ibn Khaldun.

Scholars have corrected the two authors [that is, Bukhari and Muslim], noting the cases of sound traditions not (included in their works). They have mentioned cases where they have neglected (to include traditions which, according to) the conditions governing the inclusion of traditions in their works (should have been included).

Abu Dawud (d. 888 C.E.) . . . al-Tirmidhi (d. 892 C.E.) . . . and al-Nasaʾi (d. 915 C.E.) wrote tradition works which included more than merely "sound" traditions. Their intention was to include all traditions that amply fulfilled the conditions making them actionable traditions. They were either traditions with few links in the chain of transmitters, which makes them sound, as is generally acknowledged, or they were lesser traditions, such as (the category of) "good" traditions and others. It was to serve as a guide to orthodox practice. (Ibn Khaldun, *Muqaddima* 6.11) [IBN KHALDUN 1967: 2:454–455]

11. The Derivation of God's Commands

The Quran, since it was the word of God, and since it obviously included in its contents a great many prescriptions pertaining to conduct, was also the Law of God. There is no doubt that Muslims thought so from the beginning, or that the Prophet's own extra-Quranic teaching and example counted heavily in the early community's efforts at living the life of a believer. That much we can assume; it fell to later Muslims, who lived within a long-established and fully defined version of that life, to explain to themselves just how that had come about. The first example comes from a lawyer, al-Shafiʿi (d. 820 C.E.), who was himself involved in defining the Islamic law.

Shafi'i said: The sum total of what God declared to His creatures in His Book, by which He invited men to worship Him according with His prior decision, falls in various categories.

One such category is what He declared to His creatures textually (in the Quran), such as the aggregate of duties owed him, namely, that they shall perform the prayer, pay the alms-tax, perform the pilgrimage and observe the fast (of Ramadan); and likewise that He has forbidden disgraceful acts, in both public and private, such as the explicit prohibition of adultery, the drinking of wine, eating the flesh of dead things and of blood and pork; and finally He has made clear to them how to perform the duty of ablution as well as other matters stated explicitly in the Quran.

A second category consists in those acts the obligation of which He established in His Book but whose manner of performance He made clear by the discourse of His Prophet. The number of prayers (to be said each day), and the (amount) of the alms-tax and their time (of fulfillment) are cases in point, but there are similar cases revealed in His Book.

A third category consists of what the Messenger of God established by his own example or exhortation, though there is no explicit rule on them defined by God (in the Quran). For God has laid down in His Book the obligation of obedience to His Prophet and recourse to his decision. So he who accepts a duty on the authority of the Prophet of God accepts it by an obligation imposed by God.

A fourth category consists in what God commanded His creatures to seek through personal initiative (devoted to study of the Quran or the traditions of the Prophet) and by it put their obedience to the test exactly as He tried their obedience by the other duties which He ordered them to fulfill, for the Blessed and Most High said: "And We shall put you on trial in order to know those of you who strive and endure, and We will test your accounts" (Quran 47:33). (Shafi'i, *Treatise*) [SHAFI'I 1961: 67–68]

The same process is described five and a half centuries later by Ibn Khaldun (d. 1406 c.e.), now writing less as a lawyer than as a self-conscious historian.

The basic sources of legal evidence are the Book, that is, the Quran, and then the Prophetic traditions, which clarify the Quran. At the time of the Prophet the laws were received directly from him. He possessed the Quranic revelation, and he explained it directly. No transmission, speculation or analogical reasoning was necessary. After the Prophet's death direct explanation was no longer possible. The Quran was preserved through a general and continuous transmission. As for the Prophetic tradition, the men around Muhammad all agree that it was necessary to act in accordance with whatever of it has reached us, as statement or practice, through a sound report that can be trusted to be truthful. It is in this sense that legal evidence is determined by the Quran and the Prophetic tradition.

Then general consensus took its place next to them. The men around Muhammad agreed to disapprove of those who held opinions different from theirs. They would not have done that without some basis for doing so, because people like the men around Muhammad do not agree upon something without a valid reason. In addition, the evidence attests the infallibility of the whole group. Thus, general consensus became a valid proof in legal matters.

Then we looked into the methods according to which the men around Muhammad and the early generations made their deductions from the Quran and the Prophetic tradition. It was found that they compared similar cases and drew conclusions from the analogy, in that they either all agreed or some of them made concessions in this connection to others. Many of the things that happened after the Prophet are not included [or are not covered] in the established texts. Therefore they compared and combined them with the established indications that are found in the texts, according to certain rules that governed their combinations. This assured the soundness of their comparison of two similar cases, so that it could be assumed that one and the same divine law covered both cases. This became another kind of legal evidence, because the early Muslims all agreed upon it. This is analogy, the fourth kind of evidence. (Ibn Khaldun, *Muqaddima* 6.13) [IBN KHALDUN 1967: 3:23–24]

12. On Consensus

*Both Shafi*c*i and Ibn Khaldun were discussing what had come to be called the "roots of the law," that is, the sources from which authoritative legal prescriptions may be derived. The Quran is obviously one such source, and in its case the problem was not one of validation but of interpretation (see chapter 3 above). As for the Prophetic traditions and indeed for certain practices that find no authority in either the Quran or those same traditions, Ibn Khaldun rests heavily on the principle of consensus, which he* *pushes back into the "Apostolic age" of Islam, that "generation of men around Muhammad" who "agreed to disapprove of men who held opinions different from theirs." Shafi*^c*i too had something to say about this principle of consensus, and it is not very different from what Ibn Khaldun said nearly seven centuries after him.*

Al-Shafi^ci said, may God have mercy on him: Someone said to me: I have understood your rule concerning the prescriptions of God and the prescriptions of the Prophet, may God bless and save him, and I have understood that whoever follows the Prophet follows God in that God has enjoined obedience to His Prophet. There is also proof of what you say, that no Muslim who knows a Quranic text or a Prophetic tradition may maintain the contrary of either of them, and I have understood that this too is a prescription of God. But what is your proof for following that on which the people are agreed when there is no text to that effect, either as a revelation from God or as a tradition handed down from the Prophet? Do you believe, as some do, that their consensus can only rest on a firm Prophetic tradition, even when that latter has not been handed down?

I answered him: That on which they are in agreement and say that it is a tradition handed down from the Prophet is as they say, if it please God. . . . We maintain what they maintain, following their authority, because we know that even though the tradition of the Prophet may be forgotten by some of them, it cannot be forgotten by all of them, and we know that all of them cannot come to agree on something contrary to the Prophetic tradition, or on any error, please God.

His anonymous questioner requires a proof and Shafi^c*i cites a Prophetic tradition to him.*

There are three things which cannot be resented by the heart of a Muslim: sincerity of action for God, good advice to the Muslims, and keeping close to the community of the Muslims. . . .

It was then asked, what is the meaning of the Prophet's command to keep close to the community?

Shafi^c*i explains, and his explanation suggests that the consensus did not concern merely the first generation of Muslims, those "Companions of the Prophet," on whom so much of the validation of Islamic law rests, but extended into the entire community of believers.*

I said, Shafi^ci continued, there is but one meaning to it. . . . Since the community of the Muslims is scattered in different countries, one could not keep close to the physical community whose members were

scattered, and besides, they were found together with Muslims and unbelievers, with pious men and sinners. Thus it could not mean a physical
"closeness" since that was not possible, and because physical nearness
would in itself effect nothing, so that there is no meaning in "cleaving
to the collectivity" except in agreeing with them in what they make
lawful and forbidden, and obedience in both these matters. He who
maintains what the community of the Muslims maintains is keeping
close to the community, and he who deviates from what the community
of the Muslims maintains deviates from that community to which he is
commanded to remain close. Error arises in separation. In the community there can be no total error concerning the meaning of the Book, of
the Prophetic tradition, or of analogical reasoning, please God. (Shafiʿi,
Treatise) [SHAFIʿI 1961: 285–287]

13. Personal Initiative in the Law

*Of all the "roots" of the law, it was the one known as "taking personal
initiative" that provoked the most resistance in conservative legal circles.
The Quran and the Prophetic tradition both came to be regarded as a form
of God's revelation, as we have seen, and the consensus of the community
could be seen as the working out of that revelation in social terms: the community would not err on God's and His Prophet's intentions, particularly
since there were diffused throughout that community of Muslims so many
well-attested and agreed-upon Prophetic traditions that exemplified those
intentions. But "personal initiative" was a more nakedly personal judgment
on the divine intention, an attempt on the part of a jurist to advance his
own reasoned opinion where the Quran provided no text, and the tradition
and consensus no guidance. Shafiʿi accepted it, but under limited circumstances and with a prescribed methodology, namely, analogy, which for
him and for most jurists was the only acceptable way of exercising personal
initiative in the law.*

On all matters touching the Muslim there is either a binding decision (based on the Quran or the tradition) or an indication as to the right
answer. If there is a decision, it should be followed; if there is no
indication as to the right answer, it should be sought by personal initiative, and that is the same as analogy.

Shafiʿi chose to write his Treatise on the Roots of Jurisprudence *in
the form of a dialogue, and at this point his imaginary interlocutor has a
great many questions and problems about this personal approach to the
law.*

He asked: If the scholars apply analogy correctly, will they arrive at the right answer in the eyes of God? And will it be permissible for them to disagree through analogy? Have they been ordered to seek one or different answers for each question? What is the proof for the position that they should apply analogy on the basis of the literal rather than the implicit meaning (of a precedent), and that it is permissible for them to disagree in their answers . . . ?

Shafi῾i does not answer directly; he prefers, in his pedagogical fashion, to return and review the general elements in the law and our knowledge of it.

Legal knowledge is of various kinds. The first consists of the right decisions in both the literal and implied senses; the other, of the right answer in the literal sense only. The right decisions in the first instance are those based either on God's command (in the Quran) or on a tradition from the Messenger related by the public from an earlier public. These two [that is, the Quran and the Prophetic tradition] are the two sources by virtue of which the lawful is to be established as lawful and the unlawful as unlawful. This is the kind of knowledge of which no one is allowed to be either ignorant or doubtful.

Second, the legal knowledge of the specialists consists of Prophetic traditions related by a few and known only to scholars, but others are under no obligation to be familiar with it. Such knowledge may be found among all or a few of the scholars, and it is related by a reliable transmitter from the Prophet. This is the kind of knowledge which is binding on scholars to accept, and it constitutes the right decision in the literal sense insofar as we accept the validity of the testimony of two. This is right only in the literal sense, because it is possible that the evidence of the two witnesses might be false.

Third, there is legal knowledge derived from consensus.

And finally, we come to legal knowledge derived from personal initiative by way of analogy, by virtue of which right decisions are sought. Such decisions are right in the literal sense only to the person who applies the analogy but not to the majority of scholars, since nobody knows what is hidden except God.

The other asked: If legal knowledge is derived through analogy, provided it is rightly applied, should those who apply analogy agree on most of the decisions, although we may find them disagreeing on some?

Shafi῾i replied: Analogy is of two kinds: the first, if the case in question is similar in principle to the precedent, no disagreement of this kind is permitted. The second, if the case in question is similar to several precedents, analogy must be applied to the nearest in resemblance and the most appropriate. But in this instance those who apply analogy are likely to disagree (in their answers).

The other asked: Will you give examples . . . ?

Shafi'i replied: If we were in the Sacred Mosque (at Mecca) and the Ka'ba is in sight, do you not say that we should face it in prayer with certainty? . . .

The other replied: That is right.

Shafi'i asked: Are we not under obligation to face the Sacred House in prayer no matter where we happen to be?

That is right.

Do you hold that we could always face the Sacred House correctly?

No, he replied. Not always as correctly as when you were able to see the Sacred House; however, the duty imposed on you was fulfilled [that is, however imperfectly we may have faced the now invisible Ka'ba].

Shafi'i asked: Is, then, our obligation to seek the unknown object different from our obligation to seek the known object?

That is right. . . . On what ground do you hold that the exercise of personal initiative is permitted?

Shafi'i replied: It is on the basis of God's saying:

"From whatever place you come out, turn your face in the direction of the Holy Mosque; and wherever you may be, turn your faces in its direction."   (Quran 2:145)

Regarding him who wishes to face the Sacred Mosque in prayer and whose residence is at a distance from it, legal knowledge instructs us that he can seek out the right direction through personal initiative on the basis of certain indications (guiding) toward it. For he who is under obligation to face the Holy House and does not know whether he is facing in the right or wrong direction may be able to face toward the right one through certain indications known to him which help him to face it as accurately as he can, just as another person may know other indications which help to orient him, though the direction found by each person may be different. . . . Let us assume that you and I know the direction of this road, and that I hold that the prayer-direction is this way and you disagree with me. Who should follow the opinion of the other?

The other replied: Neither is under an obligation to follow the other.

What should each one do then?

The other replied: If I hold that neither should pray until he is certain (of the direction), both might not know it with certainty. Then either the prayer obligation should be abandoned, or the prayer-direction obligation waived so that each can pray in whatever direction he wishes. But I am not in favor of either of those two options. I am rather bound to hold that each one should pray in the direction he believes right and he would be under no obligation to do otherwise. . . .

Shafiʿi replied: You have held that prayer is permissible despite your awareness that one of them is in error; it is even possible that both of them were in error. I have added (the general principle that) such a distinction would be binding on you in the cases of legal witnesses and analogical deduction.

The other replied: I hold that such an error is inevitable but it is not intentional. . . .

Shafiʿi said: It is clear to those of you who are certain of truthful information that personal initiative should never be resorted to except in seeking an unknown object by means of certain indications, although it is permissible for those who exercise such initiative to disagree in their decisions.

The other asked: How is personal initiative to be exercised?

Shafiʿi replied: God, glorified and praised be He, has endowed men with reason by which they can distinguish between differing viewpoints, and He guides them to the truth either by (explicit) texts or by indications (through which they may exercise judgment).

Will you give an example?

God erected the Sacred House and ordered men to face it in prayer when it is in sight, and to seek its direction (by personal initiative) when they are at a distance from it. And He created for them the heaven and the earth and the sun and the moon and the stars and the seas and the mountains and the wind (as guiding indications). For God said:

> "It is He who has appointed for you the stars, that by them you might be guided in the darkness of land and sea." (Quran 6:97)

And He said:

> "And by landmarks and by the stars they might be guided." (Quran 16:16)

Thus God instructed men to be guided by the stars and other indicators, and by His blessing and help they know the direction of the Sacred House. . . . Thus men should seek, through the reasoning power that God has implanted in them, the direction in which He made it incumbent upon them to face in prayer. If it is thus sought, through their reasoning power and the indications (pointing to it), men can fulfill their duty. (Shafiᶜi, *Treatise*) [SHAFIᶜI 1961: 288–303]

If we move forward four centuries, we discover that Shafiᶜi's carefully wrought argument has come to rest in summary form in the legal hand-books, in this instance that written by the Syrian jurist Ibn Qudama (d. 1223 C.E.). It occurs under the heading "The Conditions of Prayer," in the subsection "Facing the Prayer-Direction."

The traveller who is making a supererogatory prayer while mounted may pray in whatever direction he happens to be; likewise, the Muslim who is incapable of turning toward the Kaᶜba, by reason of danger or for some other reason, should make his prayer however he is able. But outside these two cases, no prayer is meritorious unless it is made in the direction of the Kaᶜba. The Muslim who is in the vicinity should turn toward the Kaᶜba itself; if he is at a distance, he should pray in its direction.

The Muslim who is ignorant of the direction of the Kaᶜba and is in an inhabited area, should inform himself and base himself on the prayer-niches of the Muslims (there); he is bound, in case of error, to begin the prayer over. When two Muslims must determine the direction on their own personal initiative and they are in disagreement, neither is bound to follow the other. The blind man and uneducated should follow the advice of whoever seems most worthy of confidence. (Ibn Qudama, *The Conditions of Prayer*) [IBN QUDAMA 1950: 22–23]

We return to Shafiᶜi's Treatise, *where he now sets down some sum-mary cautions on the use of personal initiative in the law.*

Nobody should apply analogy unless he is competent to do so through his knowledge of the commands of the Book of God; its pre-scribed duties and its ethical discipline, its abrogating and abrogated communications, its general and particular rules, and its right guidance. Its ambiguous passages should be interpreted by the tradition of the Prophet; if no tradition is found, then by the consensus of Muslims; if no consensus is possible, then by analogical deduction.

No one is competent to apply analogy unless he is conversant with the established Prophetic tradition, the opinions of his predecessors, the consensus and disagreement of the people, and has adequate knowledge of the Arab tongue. Nor is he regarded as competent in analogical reasoning unless he is sound in mind, able to distinguish between closely parallel precedents, and is not hasty in expressing an opinion unless he is certain of its correctness. Nor shall he refrain from listening to the opinions of those who may disagree with him. [SHAFIᶜI 1961: 306–307]

Shafiᶜi has enumerated some of the skills required of the Muslim lawyer if he is to exercise "personal initiative." Ibn Khaldun covers much the same ground.

The transmitted traditions which constitute the "Prophetic tradition" need verification through an investigation of the ways of transmission and the probity of the transmitters, so that the likelihood of the truthfulness of the transmitted information, which is the basis for the necessity to act in accordance with it, becomes clear. This is also one of the basic subjects of the discipline of jurisprudence. Added to this is the knowledge of abrogating and abrogated traditions, when two traditions are contradictory and the earlier one of the two is taught. This too is another subject of jurisprudence. After that there comes the study of the meaning of words. This is because one depends upon knowledge of the conventional meanings of single or composite utterances, for deriving ideas in general from word combinations in general. The philological norms needed in this connection are found in the sciences of grammar, inflection, syntax and style. . . .

Next, the study of analogy is a very important basis for this discipline. It helps to ascertain the correctness of both principal and special aspects of laws depending on reasoning and analogy; to examine the particular characteristic of a case on which the law is considered probably to depend, as to whether it exists in the principle; and to find out whether that characteristic exists in the special case without anything contradicting it, which would make it impossible to base the law upon it. (Ibn Khaldun, *Muqaddima* 6.13) [IBN KHALDUN 1967: 3:24–27]

14. Legal Knowledge and Legal Obligations

The Islamic law is not simply a body of theory; it is also a code of action defining which among human acts are permissible and which forbidden. In short, it imposes obligations, and Shafiᶜi in his Treatise undertakes to explain how those obligations differ for different segments of the Muslim community.

Someone asked me: What is legal knowledge and how much should men know of it?

Shafiʿi replied: Legal knowledge is of two kinds: one is for the general public, and no sober and mature person should be ignorant of it. . . . For example, that the daily prayers are five, that men owe to God to fast in the month of Ramadan, to make the pilgrimage to the Holy House whenever they are able, and to pay the legal alms in their estate; that He has prohibited usury, adultery, homicide, theft, wine, and everything of that sort which He has obligated men to comprehend, to perform, to pay in their property, and to abstain from because He has forbidden it to them.

This kind of knowledge may be found textually in the Book of God or may be found generally among the people of Islam. The public relates it from the preceding public and ascribes it to the Messenger of God, no one ever questioning its ascription or its binding force upon them. It is the kind of knowledge that admits of error neither in its narrative nor in its interpretation; it is not permissible to question it.

He asked: What is the second kind?

Shafiʿi replied: It consists of the detailed duties and rules obligatory on men, concerning which there exists neither a text in the Book of God nor, regarding most of them, a Prophetic tradition. Whenever a Prophetic tradition does exist in such a case, it is of the kind that is related by few authorities, not the public, and is subject to different interpretations arrived at by analogy. (Shafiʿi, *Treatise*) [SHAFIʿI 1961: 81–82]

15. The Collective Obligation

In addition to the obligation common to every individual and that binding only on specialists, Shafiʿi continues, there is a third type of legal obligation, collective in nature, which rests upon the Muslim community as a whole but not upon every individual within it.

There is a third kind of knowledge. . . . The public is incapable of knowing this kind of knowledge, nor can all specialists obtain it. But those who do obtain it should not neglect it. If some can obtain it, the others are relieved of the obligation of obtaining it, but those who do

obtain it (and perform the consequent obligation), they will be rewarded.

*The classic example of a "collective obligation" is that of the Holy
War (see chapter 3 above), to which Shafiʿi now turns.*

God has imposed the duty of Holy War, as laid down in His Book
and uttered by His Prophet's tongue. He stressed the calling to Holy
War as follows:

> "God has verily bought the souls and possessions of the faith-
> ful in exchange for Paradise. They fight in the way of God
> and kill and are killed. This is a promise incumbent on Him,
> as in the Torah, so the Gospel and the Quran. And who is
> more true to his promise than God? So rejoice at the bargain
> you have made with Him; for this will be triumph supreme."
> (Quran 9:111)

*A number of other Quranic passages on the subject are cited. Then
Shafiʿi resumes:*

These communications mean that the Holy War, and rising up in
arms in particular, is obligatory for all able-bodied believers, exempting
no one, just as prayer, pilgrimage and alms are performed, and no
person is permitted to perform the duty for another, since performance
by one will not fulfill the duty for another.

They may also mean that the duty of Holy War is a collective duty
different from that of prayer: Those who perform it in a war against the
polytheists will fulfill the duty and receive the supererogatory merit,
thereby preventing those who remained behind from falling into error.

But God has not put the two categories of men on an equal foot-
ing, for He said:

> "Such believers who sit at home—unless they have an in-
> jury—are not the equals of those who fight in the path of
> God with their possessions and their selves. . . . God has
> promised the best of things to both, and He has preferred
> those who fight to those who sit at home by granting them a
> mighty reward."   (Quran 4:97)

He asked: What is the proof for your opinion that if some people
perform the duty, the others would be relieved of the punishment?

It is in the communication I have just cited. . . . God said: "Yet to
each God has promised the best of things." Thus God promised "the best

of things" for those who stayed behind and could not go to the Holy
War, although He clearly specified His preference for those who went
to the Holy War over those who stayed at home. If those who stayed at
home were in error, while others were fighting, they would be committing a sin, unless God forgives them, rather than receiving "the best
of things." (Shafi⁣ʿi, *Treatise*) [SHAFIʿI 1961: 82–86]

16. The Evolution of Islamic Jurisprudence

*The early evolution of Islamic law took place in widely scattered centers
across the Islamic world. Not even Shafiʿi's attempts at imposing a kind of
order on its development eradicated or even inhibited the continued growth
of different schools of legal interpretation, each of them recognized as
orthodox and legitimate by the others. Thus the Shafiʿite, Malikite, Ha-
nafite, and Hanbalite schools founded by and named after early masters of
Islamic jurisprudence flourished and continued to flourish among Muslims.
They differ on specific points of theory and practice, but their differences
are not very substantial, nor do their practices much differ from the positive
precepts of Shiʿite law, though this latter has a considerably divergent view
of what lawyers call "the roots of jurisprudence." The four major Sunni
schools recognized, with varying degrees of enthusiasm, the Quran, the
sunna of the Prophet (as expressed in the* hadith*), the consensus of the
community, and a measure of personal interpretation (ijtihad) as the basis
of the shariʿa; the Shiʿites, on the other hand, relied heavily upon the
infallible teachings of the Imams and rejected the consensus of the community out of hand.*

   *All these matters are addressed by Ibn Khaldun, who gave over a part
of his* Prolegomenon to History *to a description of the origin and evolution of the various sciences found in Islam. Some of these are what he calls
"speculative," that is, they rely on the unaided use of the human intellect
for their development and understanding. Others, as we have seen, are
"traditioned" and are essentially the elaboration of revealed data given in
the Quran and the Prophetic traditions. The former are by and large the
legacy of Hellenism in Islam, while the latter are an Arab creation and are
indigenous to Islam.*

   *Primary among the "traditioned" sciences is the one called jurispru-
dence (fiqh).*

   Jurisprudence is the knowledge of the classification of the laws of
God, which concern the actions of all responsible Muslims, as obliga-

tory, forbidden, recommendable, disliked, or permissible. These laws
are derived from the Quran and the Prophetic traditions and from the
evidence the Lawgiver [that is, Muhammad] has established for a knowledge of the laws. The law evolved from the whole of this evidence is
called jurisprudence.

*And then, as he does for all the sciences under discussion, Ibn Khal-
dun launches into a capsule history of the discipline.*

The early Muslims evolved the laws from that evidence, though
unavoidably they differed in the interpretation of it. The evidence is
mostly derived from texts; the texts are in Arabic. In many instances,
and particularly with regard to legal concepts, there are celebrated differences among them as to the meaning implicit in the words. Furthermore, the Prophetic traditions differ widely in respect of the reliability
of the recensions; their legal contents, as a rule, are contradictory.
Therefore a decision is needed. This makes for differences of opinion.
Furthermore, evidence not derived from texts causes still other differences of opinion. Then there are new cases which arise and are not
covered by the texts. They are referred by analogy to things that are
covered by the texts. All this serves to stir up unavoidable differences
of opinion, and this is why differences of opinion occurred among the
early Muslims and the religious leaders after them.

Moreover, not all the men around Muhammad were qualified to
give legal opinions. Not all of them could serve as sources for religious
practice; that was restricted to men who knew the Quran and were
acquainted with the abrogating and the abrogated, the ambiguous and
the unambiguous verses, and with all the rest of the evidence that can
be derived from the Quran, since they have learned these matters
from the Prophet directly, or from their higher ranking colleagues who
had learned it from him. These men were called "readers," that is, men
who were able to read the Quran. (Ibn Khaldun, *Muqaddima* 6.14) [IBN
KHALDUN 1967: 3:3–4]

17. The Classical Schools

*Ibn Khaldun continues his survey of the evolution of Islamic jurisprudence,
told, as was usual for him, from the perspective of a social historian.*

It continued to be that way at the beginning of Islam. Then the
cities of Islam grew, and illiteracy disappeared from among the Arabs
because of their constant occupation with the Quran. Now the develop-

ment of jurisprudence from its sources took place. Jurisprudence was perfected and came to be a craft and science. The Quran readers were no longer called Quran readers but jurists (*fuqaha*) and religious scholars (*ulama*).

The ulama *were at first unofficial and unorganized students of the "traditions of the Prophet," but with the institution and spread of law schools* (madrasas), *each supported by a permanent and inalienable endowment* (waqf), *the* ulama *acquired a remarkable power and cohesiveness. The jurisprudents had their differences, of course, on both detail and theory, which in time resolved themselves into four major* madhhabs, *variously rendered as "rites" or "schools," and representing somewhat different methods of parsing the basic legal texts of Sunni Islam. In the end they agreed to differ, however, and, more importantly, to accept each other's orthodoxy.*

The jurists developed two different approaches to jurisprudence. One was the use of opinion [or reasoning] and analogy; it was represented by the Iraqis. The other was the use of Prophetic traditions; it was represented by the Hijazis. . . . Few traditions circulated among the Iraqis. Therefore they made much use of analogy and became skilled in it. That gave them the name of the "representatives of opinion." Their chief, around whom and whose followers their school centered, was the imam Abu Hanifah [d. 767 C.E.]. The leader of the Hijazis was Malik ibn Anas [d. ca. 795 C.E.] and, after him, al-Shafiʿi [d. 820 C.E.].

Later on, a group of religious scholars disapproved of analogy and rejected its use. They were the Zahirites [literally, "partisans of the plain (or 'open') sense"]. They restricted the sources of the law to the texts and the general consensus. . . . The leader of this school was Dawud ibn Ali [d. 884 C.E.] and his son and their followers. . . . The Zahirite school has become extinct today as the result of the extinction of their religious leaders and the disapproval of their adherents by the great mass of Muslims. . . .

. . . The Alids [that is, the Shiʿites] invented their own school and had their own jurisprudence. They based it on their dogma requiring abuse of some of the men around the Prophet and upon their stated opinion concerning the infallibility of the Imams and the inadmissibility of differences in their statements [see chapter 3 above]. All these are futile principles. The Kharijites similarly had their own school. The great mass did not approve of these schools but greatly disapproved them and abused them. Nothing is known of the opinions of these schools. Their books have not been transmitted; no trace of them can

be found except in regions inhabited (by them). The books of the Shi'a
are thus found in Shi'ite countries and wherever Shi'ite dynasties exist,
in the West, the East and in the Yemen. The same applies to the Kharijites. . . .

Malik ibn Anas was followed by al-Shafi'i. He traveled to Iraq after
Malik's time. He met the followers of the imam Abu Hanifah and
learned from them. He combined the approach of the Hijazis with those
of the Iraqis. He founded his own school and opposed Malik on many
points. Malik and al-Shafi'i were followed by Ahmad ibn Hanbal [d. 855
C.E.]. He was one of the highest ranking scholars of the Prophetic traditions. His followers studied with those of Abu Hanifah, notwithstanding
the abundant knowledge of Prophetic traditions they themselves possessed. They founded another school. (Ibn Khaldun, *Muqaddima* 6.14)
[IBN KHALDUN 1967: 3:4–8]

18. The End of the Age of the Fathers

*Just as a consensus developed among medieval Christians that the line of
the "Fathers of the Church" had come to an end sometime in the era of John
of Damascus (d. ca. 750 C.E.), the Muslims too reflectively closed what was
called "the gate of independent judgment" and denied later scholars the
same freedom enjoyed by earlier Muslim lawyers to derive fresh legal principles from the data of the Quran and the Prophetic traditions. The phrase
"closing the gate" has an ominous ring. However, it should be understood
not as the death of an intellectual enterprise but as a herald of the advent
of scholasticism, when scholars had to couch their legal speculations in the
form of commentary and explication on an established body of masters, in
this case the developed doctrine of the canonical schools.*

*Well into the era of scholasticism, Ibn Khaldun attempts to explain
why this had occurred.*

These four authorities [that is, Malik ibn Anas, Abu Hanifah, al-
Shafi'i, and Ahmad ibn Hanbal] are the ones recognized by tradition in
Muslim cities. Tradition-bound people obliterated all other authorities
and scholars no longer admitted any differences of opinion. The technical terminology became very diversified, and there are obstacles preventing people from attaining the level of independent judgment. It was
also feared that the existence of differences of opinion might affect
unqualified people whose opinion and religion could not be trusted.
Thus, scholars came to profess their inability to apply independent judg-

ment and had the people adopt the tradition of the authorities mentioned and of the respective group of adherents of each. They also
forbade one to modify his traditional allegiance (to one of these four
schools) because that would imply frivolity. All that remained after basic
textbooks had been produced and the continuity of their transmissions
had been established was to hand down the respective school traditions
and, for each individual adherent, to act in accordance with the traditions of his school. Today jurisprudence means this and nothing else.
The person who would claim independent judgment nowadays would
be frustrated and have no adherents. (Ibn Khaldun, *Muqaddima* 6.12)
[IBN KHALDUN 1967: 3:8–9]

19. Abrogation in Islamic Law

As both Shafi^c*i and Ibn Khaldun pointed out more than once, there was no
more troublesome issue in Islamic law than that of abrogation, the annulment of one divine ordinance and the substitution of another such in its
place, "so that what is lawful may become unlawful and what is unlawful
may become lawful," as Tabari says. The question is in fact raised by the
Quran itself.*

When we cancel a message [or "verse"] or throw it into oblivion,
We replace it with a better one or one similar. Do you not know that
God has power over all things? (Quran 2:106)

When we substitute a revelation for another revelation—God
knows best what He reveals—they say, you (Muhammad) have made it
up. (Quran 16:101)

This is Shafi^c*i's view of the passages and the principle behind them.*

God indeed created mankind for whatever His established knowledge desired in creating it and for whatever its destiny should be. There
is no reversal at all in His judgment, He being swift of reckoning. And
He revealed to them the Book that explains everything as a guide and a
mercy. In it He laid down some duties which He confirmed and others
which He abrogated, as a mercy to His people so as to lighten their
burden and to comfort them in addition to the favors which He had
begun to bestow upon them. For the fulfillment of the duties which He
confirmed, He rewarded them with Paradise and with salvation from
His punishment. His mercy has included all of them in what He confirmed and what He abrogated. Praise be to Him for his favors. (Shafi^ci,
Treatise) [SHAFI^cI 1961: 123]

The principle that one verse of the Quran may abrogate or cancel another, for all its intrinsic interest to the theologian, was not the crucial point with regard to Islamic law, however. For the lawyers the more troublesome question was whether a tradition reported from and attributed to the Prophet could replace a Quranic prescription. At first there was resistance to the notion that one of the Prophet's sayings could invalidate a Quranic prescription, as appears in what Shafiᶜi says next.

God has declared that He abrogated revelations of the Book only by means of other revelations in it; that the Prophetic tradition cannot abrogate the Book but that it should only follow what is laid down in the Book, and that the Prophetic tradition is intended to explain the meaning of a revelation of a general nature set forth in the Book. For God said:

> "When Our clear messages are recited to them, those who do not hope to meet Us say: 'Bring a different Quran, or make amendments in this one.' Say: 'It is not for me to change it of my will. I follow only what was revealed to me. If I disobey my Lord, I fear the punishment of an awful Day.'" (Quran 10:15)

Thus God informed men that He had commanded His Prophet to obey what was revealed to him but that he did not empower him to alter (the Book) of his own accord. (Shafiᶜi, *Treatise*) [SHAFIᶜI 1961: 123–124]

And what of the Prophetic tradition itself? May it too be abrogated? Shafiᶜi replies:

In like manner the tradition of the Prophet states: Nothing can abrogate it except another tradition of the Prophet. If God were to address to His Messenger a revelation on a matter on which Muhammad had provided a tradition different from what God had addressed to him, the Prophet would (then) provide a tradition in conformity with whatever God had revealed to him, and thus he would make clear to men that he was providing a tradition that abrogated one earlier or contrary to it. (Shafiᶜi, *Treatise*) [SHAFIᶜI 1961: 125]

But lawyers know that neither life nor law is so simple.

Someone may ask: It is possible to assume that there was a transmitted tradition which was abrogated, while the abrogating tradition was not transmitted?

Shafiᶜi replied: That is impossible. . . . Were this possible the entire Prophetic tradition might be abandoned by men, for they would then say, "Perhaps it was abrogated." No duty has ever been abrogated unless it was replaced by another. The abrogation of the prayer-direction toward Jerusalem by another in the direction of the Ka'ba is a case in point. (Shafi'i, *Treatise*) [SHAFI'I 1961: 126]

But the importance given to those divinely certified traditions by legal scholars—and Shafi'i was chief among them—eventually prevailed, and what passed into Muslim orthodoxy was the principle that the Quran could be abrogated by both the Quran and the tradition of the Prophet. The argument is laid out with great clarity by Ghazali (d. 1111 C.E.).

There is no dispute concerning the view that the Prophet did not abrogate the Quran on his own authority [cf. Quran 10:16: "And when Our clear revelations are recited to them, they who look not for the meeting with Us say: Bring a Quran other than this, or change it. Say (O Muhammad): It is not for me to change it of my own accord. I only follow that which is inspired in me . . ."], He did it in response to revelation [cf. Quran 53:3–4: "Nor does he speak of his own desire. It is nothing but an inspiration that is inspired"]. The abrogating text in such cases is not worded in the Quranic style.

Even if we consider the Prophet capable of abrogating the Quran on the basis of his own reflection, the authority to exercise his discretion derived from God. Thus God does the actual abrogating, operating through the medium of His Prophet. Consequently, one should hold that the rulings of the Quran may (also) be abrogated by the Prophet, rather than solely by (another verse of) the Quran. Although the inspiration in these cases is not Quranic inspiration, the word of God is nonetheless one, and God's word is both the abrogating and the abrogated. God does not have two words, one in the Quranic style which we are bidden to recite publicly, and called the Quran, while the other word is not Quran. God has but one word which differs in the mode of its expression. On occasions God indicates His word by the Quran; on others, by words in another style, not publicly recited, and called the Prophetic tradition.

Both are mediated by the Prophet. In each case the abrogator is God alone who indicates the abrogation by means of His Prophet, who instructs us of the abrogation of His Book. Thus none other but the Prophet is capable of manifesting; none other but God of initiating. Were God in this manner to abrogate a verse by the instrumentality of His Prophet, and subsequently to bring another verse similar to the one that had been abrogated, He would have made good His promise (in

Sura 2:106). . . . God did not mean to say that He proposed to bring a verse superior to the first. No part of the Quran is superior to another. He meant to state that He would bring a ruling superior to the first, in the sense of its being easier to perform, or richer in terms of reward. (Ghazali, *Mustasfa* 1.125) [Cited by BURTON 1977: 57]

20. The Case of the Woman Taken in Adultery

This issue of abrogation leads us back to one of the more celebrated incidents recorded in the Gospel of John, that of the woman who was seized in an adulterous act and was then brought to Jesus as a test case.

Jesus bent over and began writing with his finger on the ground. When they continued to press their question, he stood up straight and said, "The one of you who is sinless shall throw the first stone." Then once again he bent over and continued writing on the ground. When they heard what he said, one by one they went away, the eldest first. And Jesus was left alone with the woman still standing there in front of him. Jesus stood up and said to the woman, "Where are they? Has no one condemned you?" She answered, "No one, sir." Jesus said, "Nor do I condemn you. You may go; do not sin again." (John 8:6–11)

There is a somewhat similar incident that is told of Muhammad, though here a very different point is being made. The story occurs in a tradition going back to Umar and is preserved in Bukhari's collection of "sound traditions."

(According to Umar): "They brought to the Prophet, on whom be God's blessing and peace, a Jew and a Jewess who had committed fornication. He said to them, 'What do you find in your Book?' They said, 'Our rabbis blacken the faces of the guilty and expose them to public ridicule.' Abdullah ibn Salam [a Jewish convert] said, 'Messenger of God, tell the Jews to bring the Torah.' They brought it but a Jew put his hand over the verse which prescribes stoning and began to read what came before and after it. Ibn Salam said to him, 'Raise your hand,' and there was the verse about stoning beneath his hand. The Messenger of God gave the order and they were stoned." Ibn Umar added: "They were stoned on the level ground and I saw the man leaning over the woman to shield her from the stones." (Bukhari, *Sahih*, 4.300.309)

As we have already seen in chapter 3 above, one of the recurrent charges leveled by Muhammad against the Jews, and echoed in the Quran, was that of the falsification of Scripture, and in the example just cited the Prophet shows his fidelity to the Torah-prescribed penalty of stoning, despite the Medinese Jews' attempt to conceal it. The Quran too is explicit on the matter of adultery and fornication, though in a somewhat unexpected way.

The adulterer and the adulteress should be flogged a hundred lashes each, and no pity for them should deter you from the law of God, if you believe in God and the Last Day, and the punishment should be witnessed by a body of believers. (Quran 24:2)

Stoning, then, as a penalty for adultery is nowhere mentioned in the Quran, though the punishment is prescribed by the Torah and was apparently enforced by Muhammad. The reconciliation was effected through an already cited Prophetic tradition related on the authority of Ubada, and in this case the divine inspiration for Muhammad's utterance is carefully underlined.

The descent of inspiration was troublesome to the Prophet. His face would go ashen in color. One day inspiration came down upon him and he showed the usual signs of distress. When he recovered he said: "Take it from me! God has appointed a way for the women: the non-virgin with the non-virgin and the virgin with the virgin. The non-virgin, one hundred strokes and death by stoning; the virgin, one hundred strokes and banishment for a year." [BURTON 1977: 74]

Put in this fashion, a Prophetic tradition would simply have abrogated the Quran. But some at least must have had reservations since another set of traditions, this time reported of Muhammad's companion and the second Caliph of Islam, Umar ibn al-Khattab, suggested that a stoning penalty actually had been revealed as part of the Quran, though it was not in the present copies. According to Umar:

God sent Muhammad with the truth and revealed to him the Book. Part of what God revealed was the stoning verse. We used to recite it and we memorized it. The Prophet stoned and we have stoned after him. I fear that with the passage of time some will say, "we do not find stoning in the Book of God," and will therefore neglect a divine injunction which God revealed. Stoning is a just claim. [BURTON 1977: 77–78]

Why then did not Umar add it to the text of the Quran?

By Him who holds my soul in His hand! Except that men would say "Umar has added it to the Book of God" I would write it in with my own hand: "The married man and the married woman, when they fornicate, stone them outright." [BURTON 1977: 78]

We are even told where this verse would have occurred.

Ubayy asked Zirr ibn Hubaysh, "How many verses do you recite in the *sura* (called) "The Clans" (Sura 33)?" Zirr replied, "Seventy-three verses." Ubayy asked if that was all. "I have seen it," he said, "when it was the same length as (the Sura called) "The Cow" (Sura 2). It contained the words: 'The married man and the married woman, when they fornicate, stone them outright, as an exemplary punishment from God. God is Mighty, Wise.'" [BURTON 1977: 80]

The question finally comes to rest, all controversy aside, in a jurist's manual of the thirteenth century, in a section on Quranically prescribed penalties. The author is the Syrian al-Nawawi (d. 1277 C.E.).

Fornication: This consists of introducing the male organ into the vagina of a forbidden woman without any ambiguity or doubt, or into the anus of a man or woman as well, according to our (Shafiʿite) school, and it receives a prescribed penalty, regardless of whether it was done for payment or by consent, and is applied as well for (relations with) a woman within the forbidden degrees of kinship or marriage, even if a marriage was performed. The guilty person must be adult, sane, and aware that it was wrong. Drunkenness is no excuse.

1. The prescribed penalty of an adult free Muslim or member of a "protected community" [e.g., a Jew or a Christian], who has consummated a legal marriage previous to the act, is stoning to death. If one of the two partners has not (contracted a marriage), it does not lessen the guilt of the other.

2. The prescribed penalty of a fornicator who is not an adult and free or who has never married is one hundred lashes and banishment for one year, and if the Imam [that is, the ruler] designates a place of banishment, that must be accepted.

3. For a slave the prescribed punishment is fifty lashes and banishment for half a year. (Nawawi, *The Goal of Seekers*) [WILLIAMS 1971: 150–151]

21. Crimes and Their Penalties in the Quran

As for the thief, whether man or woman, cut off his hand as a punishment from God for what he has done. (Quran 5:38)

The Quran had, then, like the Bible, its own list of crimes and the punishments specified for each. In such cases of Quranically prescribed pen-

alties there was, of course, no room for a judge's discretion, no matter how harsh they might seem. The following legal definitions of certain crimes— the Quran does not so much define the crimes as name them—and their prescribed penalties is from a manual written by the jurisprudent al-Na- wawi (d. 1277 C.E.).

Crimes punishable by amputation: For theft the amount necessi- tating punishment by amputation is (at least) of equal value to a quar- ter of a (gold) dinar. Two persons stealing together must have stolen twice the minimum amount. There is no amputation if what was stolen was impurity [which cannot constitute property], such as wine, or a pig or dog, or the skin of an animal not ritually slaughtered. But if the container of the wine was worth the minimum amount, amputation follows.

Theft by a minor, an insane person, or one forced against his will is not punished by cutting off the hand, but cutting may be performed on members of a "protected community" [e.g., a Jew or a Christian], subject to our laws. The right hand is cut off for the first offense, even if more than one theft was involved, the left foot for the second, the left hand for the third, and the right foot for the fourth. . . .

Sins not punishable by a prescribed penalty or expiation may be punished by imprisonment, beating, slapping, or threatening. The na- ture of this is at the discretion of the ruler or his deputy. (Nawawi, *The Goal of Seekers*) [WILLIAMS 1971: 151]

22. Divorce in Islamic Law

Like the Jewish legal tradition, Muslim law recognized without debate the possibility of dissolving a marriage contract and devoted most of its atten- tion to regulating and defining the grounds for such action, how it was to be performed in a valid fashion, and what were its legal consequences. And of these latter it was the establishment of paternity after the divorce and the conditions of the marriage settlement that attracted the most concern. The Quran is already quite detailed on the matter.

Those who swear to keep away from their wives (with intent to divorce) have four months of grace; then if they reconcile (during this period), surely God is forgiving and kind. And if they are bent on di- vorce, God hears all and knows everything. (Quran 2:226–227)

If the husband's waiting period is to prevent rash or hasty action, that prescribed for the wife is to insure that, if she is pregnant, the father may be identified.

Women who are divorced have to wait for three monthly periods, and if they believe in God and the Last Day, they must not hide unlawfully what God has formed within their wombs. Their husbands would do well to take them back in that period, if they wish to be reconciled. Women also have recognized rights as men have, though men are over them in rank. But God is all-mighty and all-wise.

Divorce must be pronounced twice, and then a woman must either be retained in honor or released in kindness. And it is not lawful for you [that is, the husband] to take anything of what you have given them. . . .

Divorce is (still revocable) after two pronouncements, after which they must either keep them [that is, the men's wives] honorably or part with them in a decent way. You are not allowed to take away the least (part) of what you have given your wives, unless both of you fear that you would not be able to keep within the limits set by God. . . .

If a man pronounces divorce again [that is, for the third time], she becomes unlawful for him (for remarriage) until she has married another man. Then if this latter divorces her, there is no harm if the (original) pair unite again if they think they will keep within the bounds set by God and made clear for those who understand.

When you have divorced your wives, and they have reached the end of the period of waiting, then either keep them honorably or let them go with honor, and do not detain them with the intent of harassing lest you should transgress. (Quran 2:228–231)

What seems to be chiefly envisioned here is the restraint of the financial manipulation of women, perhaps through prolonging the action of pronouncing the triple formula of divorce, since only the husband could initiate the divorce, or even of coercing the women to buy themselves out of the contract.

A number of Prophetic traditions show other sides of the intent and process of divorce in Islam.

Thawban reported God's Messenger as saying, "If any woman asks her husband to divorce her without some very good reason, the odor of Paradise will be forbidden her."

Ibn Umar reported the Prophet as saying, "The lawful thing which God hates most is divorce."

Abu Hurayra reported God's Messenger as saying, "There are three things which, whether undertaken seriously or lightly, are treated seriously: marriage, divorce, and taking back a wife before a divorce is final."

And on the triple repetition of the divorce formula, which was obviously not intended to be done on a single occasion.

Mahmud ibn Labib told that when God's Messenger was informed about a man who divorced his wife by declaring it three times without any interval between them, he arose in anger and said, "Is sport being made of the Book of God Who is great and glorious even while I am among you?" At that a man got up and said, "Messenger of God, shall I kill him?" (Baghawi, *Mishkat al-Masabih* 12.12.3)

23. Controversial Questions

Though there might be general agreement on the basic principles of the law, there was certainly a great deal of room for debating some of its specifics, and indeed this area of "controversial questions" discussed among the four classical schools of Islamic law constituted an entire subspecies of the discipline of jurisprudence. It is once again Ibn Khaldun who is writing.

It should be known that the jurisprudence just described, which is based upon religious evidence, involves many differences of opinion among scholars of independent judgment. Differences of opinion result from the different sources they use and their different outlooks, and they are unavoidable, as we have stated before.

These differences occupied a very large space in Islam. Originally people could adhere to any juridical authority they wished. Later on the matter was in the hands of the four leading authorities in the Muslim cities. They enjoyed a very high prestige. Adherence was restricted to them, and people were thus prevented from adhering to anyone else. This situation was the result of the disappearance of independent initiative (in the Law), because this was too difficult a matter and because, in the course of time, the scholarly disciplines constituting material for independent judgments had multiplied. Also, there existed nobody who might have organized a school in addition to the existing four. Thus, they were set up as the basic schools of Islam.

Differences of opinion among the adherents of these schools and the followers of their laws received equal status with differences of opinion concerning religious texts and legal principles in general. The adherents of the four schools held disputations in order to prove the correctness of their respective founders. These disputations took place according to sound principles and fast rules. Everybody argued in favor of the correctness of the school to which he adhered and which he followed. The disputations concerned all the problems of religious law and every subject of jurisprudence. . . . These disputations clarified the sources of the authorities as well as the motives of their differences and the occasions when they exercised independent judgment. (Ibn Khaldun, *Muqaddima* 6.13) [IBN KHALDUN 1967: 3:30–31]

24. "O Believers, Fasting Is Enjoined on You"

Ibn Khaldun's discussion of legal principles is highly abstract and was intended to be so. How the principles he describes were actually applied and controverted may be seen in the instance of the fast during the month of Ramadan, a duty prescribed by the Quran itself for all believers. Here we trace the practice from the chief Quranic text, through the Prophetic traditions, to the commentators.

O believers, fasting is enjoined on you, even as it was on those before you, so that you might become righteous.

Fast a certain number of days, but if someone is ill or travelling, the same number of other days (he had missed), and those who find it difficult should (as compensation) feed a poor person. For the good they do with a little hardship is better for men. And if you fast, it is good for you, if you knew.

. . . When you see a new moon you should fast for the whole month; but a person who is ill or travelling should fast on other days, as God wishes ease and not hardship for you, so that you complete the (fixed) number and give glory to God for the guidance and be grateful. . . .

You are allowed to sleep with your wives on the nights of the fast: they are your dress as you are theirs. God is aware you were cheating yourselves so He turned to you and pardoned you. So now you may have intercourse with them. Eat and drink until the white thread of dawn appears clear from the dark line, then fast until night falls; and abstain from your wives to stay in the mosques for assiduous devotion. These are the bounds fixed by God, so keep well within them. (Quran 2:183–187)

We begin with some of the Prophetic traditions on the subject of the Ramadan fast.

Ibn Umar, may God be pleased with both of them (father and son), reported God's Messenger, may peace be upon him, as saying in connection with Ramadan: "Do not fast till you see the new moon and do

not break fast until you see it; but if the weather is cloudy, calculate it."
(Muslim, *Sahih* 6.406.2363)

Sahl ibn Saʿd said that when this verse was revealed: "Eat and drink until the white thread becomes distinct to you from the black thread," a person would take hold of a white thread and a black thread and keep eating until he could find them distinct (in the light of the dawn). It was then that God, the Majestic and Great, revealed (the rest of the phrase) "of the dawn," and then it became clear that "thread" refers to the streak of light in the dawn. (Muslim, *Sahih* 6.412.2397)

Ibn Umar reported that the Messenger of God, may peace be upon him, observed fasts uninterruptedly [that is, night and day] in Ramadan, and the people did this (in imitation of him). But he forbade them to do so. It was said to him: "You yourself observe the fasts uninterruptedly (but you forbid us to do so)." Upon this he said: "I am not like you: I am fed and supplied drink (by God)." (Muslim, *Sahih* 6.415.2427)

Abu Hurayra, may God be pleased with him, reported that a person came to the Messenger of God, may peace be upon him, and said: "Messenger of God, I am undone." He (Muhammad) said: "What brought about your ruin?" The man said: "I have had intercourse with my wife (during the day) in Ramadan." Upon this Muhammad said: "Can you find a slave to set free (by way of atonement)?" The man said: "No." Muhammad said: "Can you fast for two consecutive months?" The man said: "No." Muhammad said: "Can you provide food for sixty poor people?" The man said no. The man then sat down and there was brought to the Messenger of God, may peace be upon him, a basket which contained dates. Muhammad said: "Give these dates as an alms." The man said: "Am I to give to one who is poorer than I? There is no family poorer than mine between the two lava plains of Medina." The Messenger of God laughed so broadly that his back teeth showed and said: "Go and give it to your family to eat." (Muslim, *Sahih* 6.418.2457)

Aisha, may God be pleased with her, reported that Hamza ibn Amr al-Aslami thus asked the Messenger of God, may peace be upon him: "Messenger of God, I am a person devoted much to fasting. Should I fast during the journey?" He said: "Fast if you like and break it if you like." (Muslim, *Sahih* 6.421.2488)

Ibn Abbas, may God be pleased with both of them (father and son) reported that when God's Messenger, may peace be upon him, came to Medina, he found the Jews observing the fast on the day of Ashura [that is, the 10th of Muharram; see chapter 6 below]. The Jews were asked

about it and they said: It is the day on which God granted victory to
Moses and the Banu Isra'il over the Pharaoh and we observe fast out of
gratitude to Him. Upon this the Messenger of God, may peace be upon
him, said: "We have closer connection with Moses than you have, and
he commanded (Muslims) to observe fast on this day." (Muslim, *Sahih*
6.423.2518)

Aisha, may God be pleased with her, reported that the Quraysh
used to fast on the day of Ashura in the pre-Islamic days and the Messenger of God, may peace be upon him, also observed it. When he migrated to Medina he himself observed the fast and commanded (others)
to observe it. But when fasting during the month of Ramadan was made
obligatory, he said: "He who wishes to observe the fast (of Ashura) may
do so and he who wishes to abandon it may do so." (Muslim, *Sahih*
6.423.2499)

The following two traditions, reported from the same authority, show
one verse of the Quran abrogating another.

Salama ibn Akwa, may God be pleased with him, reported that
when this verse was revealed: "And for those who can afford it there is
a ransom, the feeding of a man in need" (2:184), he who liked to fast
fasted and he who liked not to observe it ate and expiated till the
(following part of the) verse was revealed which abrogated it.

Salama ibn Akwa reported: During the lifetime of the Messenger
of God, may peace be upon him, in one month of Ramadan he who
wished to fast fasted and he who wished to break it broke it and fed a
needy person as an expiation, till this (following) verse was revealed:
"But whoever does good of his own accord, it is better for him." (Muslim, *Sahih* 6.428.2547–2548)

The reference to fasting as an obligation imposed upon others before
Islam (2:183) elicited these remarks from the exegete Tabari (d. 923 C.E.)
on the origins of the Christians' Lenten fast during the fifty days preceding
Easter.

As for those who were before us, they were the Christians. The
month of Ramadan was prescribed, as it was also prescribed for them
neither to eat nor to drink if they woke up after they had gone to sleep.
Nor were they allowed to go in to their wives during the entire month
of Ramadan. The Christians found the fast of Ramadan hard to endure.
Ramadan rotated from winter to summer. As they realized this, they
agreed to have the fast between winter and summer. They said: "We

shall add twenty days as expiation for what we have done." Thus they made their fast fifty days. Muslims continued to observe the fast in emulation of Christians until the incidents of Abu Qays ibn Sirmah al-Ansari and Umar ibn al-Khattab, when God made lawful for them [that is, the Muslims] eating, drinking and sexual intercourse until the appearance of the dawn. (Tabari, *Commentary* 3.411) [AYOUB 1984: 189]

The "incidents" in question are described by Wahidi (d. 1076 C.E.), on the authority of al-Bara, in his Occasions of Quranic Revelation.

At first the Muslims used to eat, drink and go in to their wives (after sunset in Ramadan) so long as they had not gone to sleep. Once they slept they did not do any of these things until the following evening. It happened that Qays ibn Sirmah al-Ansari was fasting, so he came to his wife at the time of the breaking of the fast (in the evening), but she had nothing for him to eat. While she went to fetch food for him, he fell asleep. Around noon of the next day he fainted. Likewise, Umar ibn al-Khattab came in to his wife after she had slept. All this was reported to the Prophet. Then this verse (2:187) was sent down and the Muslims were pleased with it. (Wahidi 45) [AYOUB 1984: 197]

And on the question of substituting another good work, to wit, feeding a needy person, for the fast during Ramadan:

In sum, abrogation is stipulated only in the case of one in sound health and not on a journey. This is based on God's saying, "Therefore whosoever among you witnesses the moon, let him fast (the month)." The aged one who is near death, however, is allowed not to observe the fast; nor is he obliged to make up fasting by other days. This is because his condition would not change in such a way so as to make up for the days he missed. But if he does break the fast, he should feed a poor man for every day if he has the means to do so. (Ibn Kathir 1.378–379) [AYOUB 1984: 190–191]

And finally, this is Ghazali's prescription for converting a ritual obligation into a genuinely spiritual act.

When you fast, do not imagine that fasting is merely abstaining from food, drink and marital intercourse. Muhammad, God bless and preserve him, has said: "Many a one who fasts has nothing from his fasting save hunger and thirst." Rather, perfect fasting consists in restraining all the members from what God Most High disapproves. You must keep the eye from looking at things disapproved, the tongue from uttering what does not concern you, and the ear from listening to what

God has forbidden—for the hearer shares the guilt of the speaker in cases of backbiting. Exercise the same restraint over all the members as over the stomach and the genitals. A Prophetic tradition runs: "Five things make a man break his fast: lying, backbiting, malicious gossip, the lustful glance and the false oath." Muhammad, God bless and preserve him, said: "Fasting is a protection; if one of you is fasting, let him avoid obscene speech, loose living and folly; and if anyone attacks him or insults him, let him say, 'I am fasting.'"

Then endeavor to break your fast with lawful food, and not to take an excessive amount, eating more than you normally eat at night because you are fasting by day; if you take the whole amount you usually take, there is no difference between eating it at one meal at night and eating it at two meals (one by day and one by night, as when one is not fasting). The aim of fasting is to oppose your appetites, and to double your capacity for works of piety. (Ghazali, *The Beginning of Guidance* 27) [GHAZALI 1953: 129–130]

CHAPTER 6

The Worship of God

At base islam is submission to the will of God and the recognition of the rights of the Creator over His creation. For one who had so submitted, the muslim, the internal spiritual consequences were indeed revolutionary, but they were matched by few external, cultic obligations. From the initial profession of faith ("There is no god but The God and Muhammad is His Messenger") flowed the obligation of prayer five times daily, with the noon prayer on Friday said in common; of almsgiving in the form of a tithe; of fasting and other abstentions in the month of Ramadan; and, if practical, of making a pilgrimage (hajj) to the "House of God" at Mecca.

These are mere bones, the ritual obligations of the Muslim, and though they became the point of departure for a vast body of prescriptions regulating Islamic behavior, they reflect neither the tone nor the urgency of Muhammad's message, and particularly of the earliest revelations. As we shall see in chapter 8 below, the Meccan suras of the Quran have a dramatic eschatological emphasis, expressed now in commercial terms and now in the vivid images of Jewish and Christian apocalyptic. God who created the world will also be its judge, and when the Day of Judgment comes, accompanied by chaos and confusion, the Lord of the World will open the accounts of all men and reckon each at his worth. For those who have gravely sinned or hoarded their goods out of meanness of spirit, there awaits a fiery Gehenna of extreme suffering. But the magnanimous man who has submitted his will to God and committed his goods to the needy and the downtrodden will be rewarded in a garden Paradise of luxurious ease and splendor. Indeed, this is why the Prophet was sent, to be a "warner" to mankind that the reckoning was close at hand.

1. How Paganism and Idol Worship
Came to Mecca

The Quran was first proclaimed amid the cult and rituals of late sixth-century Meccan paganism. The Quran does not accept pagan ritual as such, of course. What was occurring at Mecca in the name of religion was in part the work of a debased paganism, but it also bore some traces of what the Holy Book calls the "religion of Abraham" (2:130), the practices that God had earlier commanded should be instituted in connection with His House in that city. The Quran says nothing about the remote origins of a holy place at Mecca; it speaks only of the era of Abraham and of Ishmael there, and of the providential construction of the Kaᶜba, this "sacred House" (5:100), this "ancient House" (22:29). The Islamic tradition did not rest on that scriptural testimony alone, however. As we have seen, somewhat later generations of Muslims—who had access, through Jewish and Christian converts to Islam, to a vast body of stories and legends about the earliest times of God's dispensation—were able to trace the history of the Kaᶜba and its sanctuary back to the very beginning of Creation, and even before. So too there is in the Muslim Scripture no mention of Hagar or Sarah, nor of the Bible's elaborate story of the births of Ishmael and Isaac, but we have also seen in chapter 1 above how the Muslim tradition fleshed out in elaborate detail how Abraham and Ishmael got from the land of Palestine to Mecca, how Abraham and Ishmael built the Kaᶜba—or perhaps "rebuilt" it, since there had been one standing there before the Flood—and how finally the two patriarchs instituted the set of rituals known collectively as the hajj *or Pilgrimage.*

All those events were in the remote "biblical" past of Arabia; the reality of the sixth century C.E.*, however, was that Mecca was a pagan cult center and that the Arabs were engaged in worshiping divine beings and even more mundane objects despised by the later Muslims. One aspect of the worship of the pre-Islamic Arabs attracted the attention not only of Greek and Latin authors who had come in contact with Arab society but of the later Muslim authorities on the "Era of Ignorance"; this was a widespread cult of stones. For both sets of observers it seemed an odd practice to venerate stones, whether they were totally unshaped or fashioned into some kind of very rudimentary idol. Later Muslims had some idea of these practices, and they traced them back to the earliest history of Mecca, when the sons of Ishmael had lapsed into paganism. Ibn al-Kalbi (d. 821* C.E.*), who made* *a special study of the pre-Islamic past of Arabia in his* Book of Idols, *connected it directly to the degeneracy of the Banu Ishmael.*

The reason that led them [that is, the descendants of Ishmael] to the worship of images and stones was the following. No one left Mecca without carrying away with him a stone from the stones of the Sacred House as a token of reverence to it, and as a sign of deep affection to Mecca. Wherever he settled he would erect that stone and circumambulate it in the same manner he used to circumambulate the Kaʿba (before his departure from Mecca), seeking thereby its blessing and affirming his deep affection for the Holy House. In fact, the Arabs still venerate the Kaʿba and Mecca and journey to them in order to perform the pilgrimage and the visitation, conforming thereby to the time-honored custom which they inherited from Abraham and Ishmael.

In time this led them to the worship of whatever took their fancy, and caused them to forget their former worship. They exchanged the religion of Abraham and Ishmael for another. Consequently they took to the worship of images, becoming like nations before them.

It was important, however, in the light of Muhammad's own adoption of certain of the cult practices in the Mecca of his day, to maintain some kind of continuous link with this ostentatious paganism and the authentic Abrahamic past.

Among these devotional practices were some which had come down from the time of Abraham and Ishmael, such as the veneration of the House and its circumambulation, the *hajj*, the ʿ*umra* [or lesser pilgrimage], the "standing" on Arafat and Muzdalifa, sacrificing she-camels, and raising the voice (*tahlil*) (in acclamation of God) at the *hajj* and ʿ*umra*, but they introduced into the latter things that did not belong to it.

Ibn al-Kalbi then supplies an example of just such an "unorthodox" pre-Islamic "acclamation" (talbiyya).

Here we are, O Lord! Here we are! Here we are! You have no partner save the one who is yours; you have dominion over him and whatever he possesses.

Ibn al-Kalbi continues his own remarks:

Thus they declared His unity through the "acclamation" and at the same time associated their gods with Him, placing their [that is, their gods'] affairs in His hands. (Ibn al-Kalbi, *Book of Idols* 6–7) [IBN AL-KALBI 1952: 4–5]

Later Ibn al-Kalbi turns his attention to the cult of the idols.

Every family in Mecca had at home an idol which they worshiped. Whenever one of them purposed to set out on a journey, his last act before leaving the house would be to touch the idol in hope of an auspicious journey; on his return, the first thing he would do was to touch it again in gratitude for a propitious return. . . .

The Arabs were passionately fond of worshiping idols. Some of them had a temple around which they centered their worship, while others adopted an idol to which they offered their adoration. The person who was unable to build himself a temple or adopt an idol would erect a stone in front of the Sacred House [that is, the Ka°ba at Mecca] or in front of any other temple they might prefer, and then circumambulate it in the same manner in which they would circumambulate the Sacred House. The Arabs called these stones "betyls" (*ansab*), but whenever these stones resembled a living form they called them "idols" (*asnam*) and "images" (*awthan*). The act of circumambulating them they called "circumrotation" (*dawar*).

Whenever a traveler stopped at a place or station (to spend the night), he would select for himself four stones, pick out the finest of them and adopt it as his god, and then use the remaining three as supports for his cooking pot. On his departure he would leave them behind, and would do the same at the other stops.

And, like many other Muslims, Ibn al-Kalbi was convinced that Arab paganism was simply a degenerate form of rituals of the Ka°ba.

The Arabs were accustomed to offer sacrifices before all these idols, betyls and stones. Nevertheless, they were aware of the excellence and superiority of the Ka°ba, to which they went on pilgrimage and visitation. What they did on their travels was merely a perpetuation of what they did at the Ka°ba, because of their devotion to it. (Ibn al-Kalbi, *Book of Idols* 32–33) [IBN AL-KALBI 1952: 28–29]

2. Islam and the Graven Image

The preaching of the Quran meant the end of the old paganism. Muhammad was forced to leave his native city in 622 C.E., as we have seen, but when he returned in triumph in 630 C.E., he left no doubt about his intentions.

The Messenger, after arriving in Mecca, once the populace had settled down, came to the shrine and went round it seven times on his camel, touching the black stone with a stick which he had in his hand. This done, he summoned Uthman ibn Talha and took the keys of the Ka'ba from him, and when the door was opened for him, he went in. There he found a dove made of wood. He broke it in his hands and threw it away. . . . (According to another account) the Messenger entered Mecca on the day of the conquest and it contained 360 idols which Iblis (or Satan) had strengthened with lead. The Messenger was standing by them with a stick in his hand saying, "The truth has come and falsehood has passed away" (Quran 17:81). Then he pointed at them with his stick and they collapsed on their backs one after another.

When the Messenger had prayed the noon prayer on the day of the conquest (of Mecca) he ordered that all the idols which were around the Ka'ba should be collected and burned with fire and broken up. . . . The Quraysh had put pictures in the Ka'ba including two of Jesus son of Mary and of Mary, on both of whom be peace. Ibn Shihab said: Asma the daughter of Shaqr said that a woman of the Banu Ghassan had joined in the pilgrimage of the Arabs and when she saw a picture of Mary in the Ka'ba she said: "My father and my mother be your ransom! (Mary), you are surely an Arab woman!" The Messenger ordered that the pictures be erased, except those of Jesus and Mary. (*Life* 821) [IBN ISHAQ 1955: 552]

We know little of what to make of that last curious event. What we can say is that, for all Muhammad's opposition to idolatry, there is no sign in the Quran of any preoccupation—no open approval or disapproval even—of pictures or images. But conditions must soon have changed, since by the time we come to read the collections of Prophetic traditions, they are filled with condemnations of images and image making.

Abu Talha reported the Prophet as saying, "The angels do not enter a house which contains dogs or pictures." Bukhari and Muslim transmit this tradition.

Aisha told that she had screened a storeroom of hers with a curtain on which there were figures and the Prophet tore it down; so she made two cushions out of it and had them in the house for sitting on. Bukhari and Muslim transmit this.

She also reported the Prophet as saying, "Those who will receive the severest punishment on the Day of Resurrection will be those who imitate what God has created."

Sa'id ibn Abi Hasan said: When I was with Ibn Abbas a man came to him and said, "Ibn Abbas, I am a man whose livelihood comes only

from the work of my hands, and I make these representations of things."
Ibn Abbas replied that he would tell him only what he had heard from
God's Messenger. He had heard him say, "If anyone makes a representa-
tion of anything, God will punish him until he blows a spirit into it, and
he will never be able to do that." Then when the man gasped and
became pale, he said to him, "Out upon you! If you must do so, make
representations of these trees or of anything which does not possess a
soul." Bukhari transmitted this tradition.

Ibn Abbas reported God's Messenger as saying, "The one who receives the severest punishment on the Day of Resurrection will be he
who kills a prophet, or who is killed by a prophet, or kills one of his
parents, or who makes representations of things, and a learned man
who derives no benefit from his learning." (Baghawi, *Mishkat al-masabih*
21.5.1–3)

*We do not know when those traditions were put into circulation. If
they are authentic, we are faced with the same kind of dilemma that the
figuratively decorated synagogues of Palestine posed to a supposedly ani-
conic Jewish tradition. Muslim coinage bore representations of the Caliph
down to the reign of Abd al-Malik (685–705 c.e.), and even after that
date Muslim sovereigns continued to build Syrian steppe palaces decorated
in a style that was not merely figurative but even aggressively and sugges-
tively secular. It is perhaps safer to conclude that Islam came to its icono-
phobia gradually, and that the Prophetic traditions reflect a later and not
a primary stage in that evolution.*

*The later official Islamic sentiment on images is clear enough, how-
ever. This is how it is expressed in one of the standard Islamic law books,
that written by the Syrian jurist al-Nawawi (d. 1377 c.e.). Now all fear
of idolatry is gone, and the reasons for the prohibition are overtly theological.*

The learned authorities of our (Shafi'ite) school and others hold
that painting a picture of any living thing is strictly forbidden, because
it is threatened with grievous punishment as mentioned in the Prophetic
traditions, whether it is intended for common domestic use or not. So
the making of it is forbidden under every circumstance, because it implies a likeness to the creative activity of God. . . . On the other hand,
the painting of a tree or of camel saddles and other things that have no
life is not forbidden. Such is the decision on the actual making of a
picture.

Similarly, it is forbidden to make use of any object on which a
living thing is pictured, whether it is to be hung on a wall or worn as a

dress or a turban or on any other object of common domestic use. But if it is on a carpet trampled underfoot, or on a pillow or cushion . . . then it is not forbidden. Whether such an object will prevent the angels of God from entering the house in which it is found is quite another matter.

In all this there is no difference between what casts a shadow and what does not cast a shadow. This is the decision of our school on the question, and the majority of the Companions of the Prophet and their immediate followers and the learned of succeeding generations accepted it. . . . Some later authorities make the prohibition refer only to objects that cast a shadow, and see no harm in objects that have no shadow. But this view is quite wrong, for the curtain to which the Prophet objected was certainly condemned, as everyone admits, yet the picture on it cast no shadow; and the other traditions make no distinction between one picture and another. Al-Zuhri holds that the prohibition refers to pictures in general, and similarly to the use of them and to entrance into a house in which they are found, whether it is a case of design on a dress or any other design, whether the picture hangs on a wall or is on a robe or a carpet, whether in common domestic use or not, as is the clear meaning of the Prophetic traditions. (Nawawi, *Guide to an Understanding of Muslim* 8.398)

3. The Muslims' Prayer

Muslims understood from the Quran's own words that performance of the liturgical prayers was obligatory upon all Muslims, male and female, who had attained the use of reason. They had to be performed facing the direction of Mecca five times daily and at prescribed times. According to the classic Treatise on the Roots of Jurisprudence *of al-Shafiᶜi, the Egyptian legal scholar who died ca. 820 C.E., the obligations imposed by God on men can be derived (1) explicitly from the Quran, though with progressive abrogations; (2) in general terms from the Quran and explicitly regarding its modalities from the Prophet; (3) from the Prophet's teachings alone, which are also binding; and, finally, deductively from the Quran or the teachings of the Prophet, the famous "personal initiative" of Islamic jurisprudence. How the first two operated in the question of liturgical prayer is made clear in the following passage from the same* Treatise.

Shafiᶜi said: I have heard some scholars who related that God had imposed a certain duty for prayer before He laid down that for the five prayers. For He said:

> O you wrapped in your mantle,
> Stay up the night, except a little,
> Half of it, or a little less
> Or a little more,
> And chant the Quran distinctly.
> (Quran 73:1–4)

God abrogated this duty by another, which may be found in the same Sura, and it reads as follows:

> "The Lord knows that you stay up nearly two-thirds of the night, or half of it, or a third of it, and a party of those with you likewise, and God determines the night and the day. He knows that you will never count it up, so He has turned toward you in mercy. So recite what may be convenient for you of the Quran; He knows that some of you will be sick and others journeying about in the land, seeking the bounty of God, and others fighting in the path of God. So recite what is convenient of it, and observe the prayer and pay the alms." (Quran 73:20)

Even these latter modifications are not entirely clear, Shafiᶜi argues, and so it is necessary to turn to the Prophetic tradition for clarification.

Shafiᶜi said: In such a case it is obligatory to seek the evidence of the Prophetic tradition for determining which of the meanings is valid. Thus the Prophetic tradition has indicated that no duty other than that of the five prayers is obligatory and that any earlier prayers have been abrogated by that tradition. (Shafiᶜi, *Treatise*) [SHAFIᶜI 1961: 128–129]

Shafiᶜi resumes the standard teaching.

God, Blessed and Most High, said: "Truly prayer has become for the believers a thing prescribed at stipulated times" (Quran 4:103). And He said, "Observe the prayer and pay the alms tax" (Quran 2:43 etc.). And He said to His Prophet, "Take of their wealth an alms tax to cleanse and purify them thereby and pray for them" (Quran 9:103). And He said: "Pilgrimage to the House [that is, the Kaᶜba] is a duty to God from the people, whoever is able to make his way there" (Quran 3:97).

Thus God has laid down in the Quran the duties of prayer, alms tax and pilgrimage and specified the modes of their performance through His Prophet's tongue.

So the Messenger specified that (each day) prayers shall number five, that the number of the cycles in the noon, afternoon and evening prayers shall number four repeated twice in the towns, and the cycles at the sunset prayer shall number three and at the dawn prayer two.

He decreed that in all (the prayers) there should be recitals (from the Quran), audible at the sunset, evening and dawn prayers, and silent recitals at the noon and afternoon prayers.

He specified that at the beginning of each prayer there shall be the declaration "God is great" and at the ending salutations on the Prophet and his house, and that each prayer consists of the "God is great," the recital (from the Quran), the bowing and two prostrations after each inclination, but that beyond these nothing is obligatory.

He decreed that prayer while one is on a journey can be shorter, if the traveler so desires, in the three occasions that have four cycles, but he made no change in the sunset and dawn prayers when those prayers are performed in town. However, all prayers must be (performed) in the direction of Mecca, whether one is in town or on a journey. (Shafiʿi, *Treatise*) [SHAFIʿI 1961: 158–159]

4. Prophetic Traditions on Prayer

When Shafiʿi speaks of Muhammad "decreeing" the specifics of the obligation to prayer set down in general terms in the Quran, he is referring to the "traditions" or reports originally transmitted by Muhammad's contemporaries and professing to recount the Prophet's teachings or conduct. Even in Shafiʿi's own lifetime these were beginning to be collected for legal purposes, as we have seen, and in the end they provided, together with the Quran, the chief foundation stone of Islamic law. The following are some typical and widely circulated Prophetic traditions on the subject of prayer. First, as to its times.

Burayda told of a man asking the Messenger of God about the time of prayer, to which he (Muhammad) replied: "Pray with us these two," meaning two days. When the sun passed the meridian he summoned Bilal, who uttered the call to prayer; then he commanded him and he made the announcement declaring that the time to begin the afternoon prayer had come when the sun was high, white, and clear. Then he gave him command and he made the announcement declaring that the time to begin the sunset prayer had come when the sun had set. Then he gave command and he made the announcement declaring that the time to begin the night prayer had come when the twilight had ended. Then he gave command and he made the announcement declaring that the time to begin the dawn prayer had come when the dawn appeared.

The next day he commanded him to delay the (summons to the) noon prayer until the extreme heat had passed and he did so, and he allowed it to be delayed until the extreme heat had passed. He observed the afternoon prayer when the sun was high, delaying it beyond the time when he had previously observed it. He observed the sunset prayer before the twilight had ended; he observed the night prayer when a third of the night had passed; and he observed the dawn prayer when there was clear daylight. Then asking where the man was who had inquired about the time of prayer and receiving from him a reply that he was present, he said, "The time for your prayer is within the limits of what you have seen." Muslim has transmitted this report. (Baghawi, *Mishkat al-Masabih* 4.2.1)

Ibn Mas῾ud said that the extent of the shadow when the Messenger of God prayed the noon prayer was three to five feet in summer and five to seven feet in winter. Abu Dawud and Nasaʾi have both transmitted this report. (Baghawi, *Mishkat al-Masabih* 4.2.3)

Abu Hurayra reported the Messenger of God as saying, "No prayer is more burdensome to the hypocrites than the dawn and the evening prayer; but if they knew what blessings lie in them, they would come to them even if they had to crawl to do so." Muslim transmits this report. (Baghawi, *Mishkat al-Masabih* 4.4.1)

Amr ibn Shu῾ayb on his father's authority reported his grandfather as saying that God's messenger prohibited the recitation of poems in a mosque, buying and selling in it, and sitting in a circle in a mosque on Friday before the prayer. Abu Dawud and Tirmidhi transmitted this report.

Ibn Umar said that there were seven places where the Messenger of God forbade men to pray: a dunghill, a slaughterhouse, a graveyard, the middle of the road, a bath, places where camels kneel to drink, and the roof of God's House. Tirmidhi and al-Maja have transmitted this report. (Baghawi, *Mishkat al-Masabih* 4.8.2)

Anas ibn Malik reported the Messenger of God as saying, "A man's prayer in his house is equivalent to a single observance of prayer, his prayer in a tribal mosque is worth twenty-five, his prayer in a Friday mosque is equivalent to five hundred, his prayer in the Aqsa mosque (in Jerusalem) is equivalent to fifty thousand, his prayer in my mosque (in Medina) is (also) equivalent to fifty thousand, and his prayer in the Sacred Mosque [that is, the Haram at Mecca] is equivalent to a hundred thousand." Ibn Maja has transmitted this report. (Baghawi, *Mishkat al-Masabih* 4.8.3)

Ibn Umar reported the Messenger of God as saying, "Do not prevent your women from coming into mosques, but their houses are better for them." Abu Dawud transmitted this report.

Ibn Mas᷾ud reported the Prophet as saying, "It is more excellent for a woman to pray in her house than in her courtyard, and more excellent for her to pray in her own room than (elsewhere) in the house." Abu Dawud transmitted this report. (Baghawi, *Mishkat al-Masabih* 4.24.2)

Jabir ibn Samura said: the Messenger of God came out to us . . . and said, "Why do you not draw yourselves up in rows (for prayer) as the angels do in the presence of the Lord?" We asked, "Messenger of God, how do the angels draw themselves up in rows in the presence of the Lord?" He replied, "They make the first rows complete and keep close together in the row." Muslim transmitted this report.

Anas reported the Messenger of God as saying, "Complete the front row, then the one that comes next, and if there is any incompleteness, let it be in the last row." Abu Dawud transmitted this report.

Abu Hurayra reported the Messenger of God as saying, "The best of the men's rows (in prayer) is the first and the worst is the last, but the best of the women's rows is the last and the worst is the first." Muslim transmitted this report. (Baghawi, *Mishkat al-Masabih* 4.25.1–2)

Abu Sa᷾id reported the Messenger of God as saying, "When there are three people (praying together), one of them should lead them. The one among them most worthy to act as prayer-leader (*imam*) is the one most versed in the Quran." Muslim transmitted this report. (Baghawi, *Mishkat al-Masabih* 4.27.1)

Abu Hurayra reported the Messenger of God as saying, "When one of you leads the people in prayer, he should be brief, for among them are the sick, the weak, and the aged. But when one of you prays by himself, he may be as long as he likes." This report has been transmitted by Bukhari and Muslim. (Baghawi, *Mishkat al-Masabih* 4.28.1)

Tariq ibn Shihab reported the Messenger of God as saying, "The Friday prayer in congregation is a necessary duty for every Muslim, with four exceptions: a slave, a woman, a minor, and an invalid." Abu Dawud transmitted this report. (Baghawi, *Mishkat al-Masabih* 4.44.2)

Salman reported the Messenger of God as saying, "If any man bathes on Friday, purifies himself as much as he can with ablution, anoints himself with oil or puts on a touch of perfume which he has in his house, then goes out and, without squeezing between two men, prays what is prescribed for him, then remains silent when the prayer-leader preaches, his sins between that time and the next Friday will be forgiven him." Bukhari has transmitted this tradition. (Baghawi, *Mishkat al-Masabih* 4.45.1)

5. The Direction of Prayer

The Muslim must pray facing toward Mecca, the qibla or the prayer-direction in Islam. While still at Mecca, and even after his arrival at Medina, Muhammad was said to have prayed "toward Syria." "Toward Syria," as a good many Muslims understood it, meant toward Jerusalem, a custom that would have unmistakably aligned the Prophet with the practice of the Jews who faced toward the Temple when they prayed (1 Kings 8:44). Muhammad may have done so as well, but his own developed sense that his religion was—and perhaps had always been, some would add—Abrahamic rather than Jewish gave birth to a number of traditions that Muhammad prayed toward the Ka'ba even at Mecca and that he switched briefly to Jerusalem after his arrival at Medina in order to conciliate the Jews. By the time Ibn Ishaq came to write his Life of the Prophet, *a least one version of story had become "harmonized": Muhammad prayed facing both Jerusalem and the Ka'ba!*

While he [that is, Muhammad] was in Mecca he faced Syria in prayer; and when he prayed, he prayed between the southern corner and the black stone, putting the Ka'ba between himself and Syria. (*Life* 190) [IBN ISHAQ 1955: 135]

But a little later what is probably the more authentic version appears.

And when the prayer-direction was changed from Syria to the Ka'ba—it was changed in (the month of) Rajab at the beginning of the seventeenth month after the Messenger's arrival in Medina—Rifa'a ibn Qays (and a number of others from among the Jews of Medina) . . . came to the Messenger asking why he had turned his back on the *qibla* he used to face when he alleged that he followed the religion of Abraham. If he would return to the *qibla* in Jerusalem they would follow him and declare him to be true. (*Life* 381) [IBN ISHAQ 1955: 258–259]

The Jews' sole intention, Ibn Ishaq or some other editorial hand adds, "was to seduce him from his religion." This, according to the same editor, was the occasion that prompted the revelation of those Quranic verses which do not so much announce as defend the decision to change his prayer-direction.

The foolish among the people will say, "What has turned them away from the direction of prayer toward which they formerly prayed?" Say: "To God belongs the East and the West, and He guides whom He wills in the straight way."

Thus We have made you a community of the middle path in order that you may be witnesses over humankind and that the Messenger be a witness over you. We appointed the prayer-direction to which you formerly prayed only to make known those who follow the Messenger and those who would turn back on their heels. It (that is, the change in the direction of prayer) is indeed a grave matter, except for those whom God has guided aright. As for you, God would never count your faith for naught. Truly God is Gracious and Compassionate toward mankind.

We have seen you turning your face about toward heaven. We shall therefore direct you toward a prayer-direction which would please you. Turn your face toward the Sacred House of Worship; wherever you may be, turn your faces toward it. As for those who were given the Scriptures, they know well that it is the truth from their Lord, nor is God unaware of what they do.

Even if you were to bring those who were given the Scriptures every manifest sign, still they would not follow your prayer-direction, nor will you follow theirs, nor yet will they follow each other's. If therefore you were to follow their desires after the knowledge that has come to you, you would surely be one of the wrongdoers. (Quran 2:142–145)

The uncertainty of later Muslims regarding these verses, or the circumstances that promoted them, is illustrated by the traditions preserved in Tabari's classic tenth-century commentary.

On the authority of Ikrima and Hasan al-Basri: The first injunction which was abrogated in the Quran was that concerning the direction of prayer. This is because the Prophet used to prefer the Rock of the Holy House of Jerusalem, which was the prayer-direction of the Jews. The Prophet faced it for seventeen months [after his arrival in Medina] in the hope that they would believe in him and follow him. Then God said: "Say, To God belong the east and the west. . . ."

Al-Rabiᶜ ibn Anas relates on the authority of Abu al-Aliya: The Prophet of God was given his choice of turning his face in whatever direction he wished. He chose the Holy House in Jerusalem in order that the People of the Book would be conciliated. This was his prayer-direction for sixteen months (after his arrival in Medina); all the while, however, he was turning his face toward the heavens until God turned him toward the House [that is, the Ka'ba].

It is related, on the other hand, on the authority of Ibn Abbas: When the Messenger of God migrated to Medina, most of whose inhabitants were Jews, God commanded him to face Jerusalem, and the Jews were glad. The Prophet faced it for some time beyond ten months, but he loved the prayer-direction of Abraham [that is, the Ka'ba]. Thus he used to pray to God and gaze into the heavens until God sent down (the verse) "We have seen you turning your face toward heaven" (2:144). The Jews became suspicious and said, "What has turned them away from the direction of prayer toward which they formerly prayed?" Thus God sent down (the verse) "Say, To God belongs the east and the west." (Tabari, *Tafsir ad loc.*)

As a result of this momentous change a basic adjustment had to be made in the prayer-direction in the only oratory Islam knew, the mosque built by Muhammad at his residence in Medina. We do not know how that direction was marked—the prayer-niche (mihrab) was introduced somewhat later as an architectural feature in the mosque—but the direction was determined as absolutely as possible.

6. The Prophet Builds His Mosque

Muhammad's small community of converts could not openly pray to their God in Mecca, but once settled in Medina the Prophet directed the construction, in the courtyard of his own residence, of a place for ritual prayer, and particularly for the Friday congregational prayer. It was the first mosque. The historian Tabari writing in the tenth century is simple and to the point.

We shall now mention the other noteworthy events of this year, the first year of the Hijra. Among these is his holding the Friday prayer with his [that is, Muhammad's] companions on the day on which he left Quba for Medina. This was on a Friday, and the time for prayer—the Friday prayer—overtook him in the territory of the Banu Salim ibn Awf in the bed of a wadi belonging to them, and this was used as a mosque that day. This was the first Friday prayer which the Messenger of God held in Islam. (Tabari, *Annals* 1.1256) [TABARI 1987: 1–2]

Muhammad chose his dwelling place in Medina in much the same way as he had in the suburb of Quba five days previously: he gave his camel her head, and where she stopped, there he would live. By one account the site was a drying-floor for dates, but Tabari preferred a different version.

The site of the mosque (and living quarters) of the Prophet belonged to the Banu al-Najjar and contained palm trees, cultivated land
and pre-Islamic graves. The Messenger of God said to them, "Ask me a
price for it," but they said, "We do not want a price for it, but only the
reward we shall receive from God." The Messenger of God then gave
orders concerning the site; the palm trees were cut down, the cultivated
land levelled, and the graves dug up. Before this mosque was completed
the Messenger of God used to pray in sheep enclosures or wherever the
time of prayer overtook him. (Tabari, *Annals* 1.1259–1260) [TABARI
1987: 5]

*The fourteenth-century traveler Ibn Battuta has a somewhat different
version of the tradition.*

The site of the mosque was an enclosure used for drying dates. The
Messenger of God—God bless him and give him peace—bought this
drying ground . . . then built the mosque, himself working on it with his
Companions, and put a wall around it, but gave it neither roofing nor
pillars. He made it square in shape, its length being a hundred cubits and
its breadth the same, though some say that its breadth was a little less,
and fixed the height of the wall at the stature of a man.

Later on, when the heat grew intense, his Companions spoke of
roofing it, so he set up for this purpose a number of columns formed of
trunks of palms, and made its roof of their branches. Then when it
rained the mosque dripped, so the Companions of the Messenger of
God—God bless him and give him peace—spoke to him about making
it with clay, but he said "On no account! A booth like the booth of
Moses," or "A shelter like the shelter of Moses, and man's estate is even
less enduring than that." On being asked, "What is the shelter of Moses
like?" he replied: "When he stood up, the roof struck his head." He
made three gateways in the mosque, but the southern gateway was
blocked up when the prayer-direction was changed [from Jerusalem on
the north side of the mosque to Mecca on the south]. [IBN BATTUTA
1959–1962: 168]

7. The Institution of the Call to Prayer

Ibn Ishaq's Life of Muhammad *provides the setting for the institution of
many of the practices that became standard in the devotional life of the
Muslim community, among them the public call to prayer.*

When the Messenger was firmly settled in Medina and his brethren
the "Emigrants" were gathered to him and the affairs of the "Helpers"

were arranged, Islam became firmly established. Prayer was instituted, the alms tax and fasting were prescribed, legal punishments
fixed, the forbidden and the permitted prescribed, and Islam took up its
abode with them. . . . When the Messenger first came (to Medina), the
people gathered about him for prayer at the appointed times without
being summoned. At first the Messenger thought of using a trumpet like
that of the Jews who used it to summon to prayer. Afterwards he disliked the idea and ordered a clapper to be made [like the Christians'],
so that it was duly fashioned to be beaten when the Muslims should
pray.

 Meanwhile Abdullah ibn Zayd ibn Thaʿlaba . . . heard a voice in a
dream and came to the Messenger saying: "A phantom visited me at
night. There passed by me a man wearing two green garments carrying a clapper in his hand, and I asked him to sell it to me. When he asked
me what I wanted it for I told him that it was to summon people to
prayer, whereupon he offered to show me a better way: it was to say
thrice: 'God is great. I bear witness that there is no god but the God.
I bear witness that Muhammad is the Messenger of God. Come to
prayer. Come to prayer. Come to success. Come to success. God is
great. God is great. There is no god but the God.'" When the Messenger of God was told of this he said that it was a true vision if God so
willed it, and that he should go to Bilal and communicate it to him so
that he might call to prayer thus, for he had a more penetrating voice.
When Bilal acted as muezzin Umar heard him in his house and came to
the Messenger dragging his cloak on the ground and saying he had seen
precisely the same vision. The Messenger said, "God be praised for
that!" (*Life* 346–347) [IBN ISHAQ 1955: 235–236]

8. On the Manner and Intent of Prayer

*One of the greatest Muslim reformers of the Islamic Middle Ages was the
lawyer and theologian Ghazali (d. 1111 C.E.). In many of his works, and
most notably in his* Revivification of the Sciences of Religion, *Ghazali
attempted to breathe a deeper spirituality into the practice of ordinary
Muslims by heightening their awareness in the performance of ritually prescribed actions. It was necessary to prepare the soul for ritual acts, Ghazali
insisted, and to perform them with proper and explicit intention. Here, for
example, is the appropriate way to fulfill the obligation of washing before
prayer, with all the lawyer's attention to detail but accompanied by the
spiritual awareness of the saint.*

Make the intention of removing the filth or of fulfilling the ceremonial preparation for worship. The making of the intention must not be omitted before the washing of the face, for otherwise the ablution is invalid. Then take a handful of water for your mouth and rinse your mouth three times, making sure that the water reaches the back of it—unless you are fasting, in which case, act gently—and say: "O God, I am purposing to read Your Book and to have Your name many times on my lips; through the steadfast word make me steadfast in this life and the world to come." Then take a handful of water for your nose, draw it in three times and blow out the moisture in your nose; while drawing it in say: "O God, make me breathe in the fragrance of Paradise, and may I be pleasing to You," and while blowing it out, "O God, I take refuge with You from the odors of Hell and from the evil abode." Then take a handful for your face, and with it wash from the beginning of the flattening of the forehead to the end of the protuberance of the chin, up and down and from ear to ear across. . . . Make the water reach the four places where hair grows: the eyebrows, the moustache, the eyelashes and the cheeks. . . . As you wash your face say, "O God, make my face white through Your light on the day when You whiten the faces of Your elect, and do not blacken my face with darkness on the day when You blacken the face of your enemies." Do not omit wetting the thick part of the beard.

Then wash your right hand, and after that the left, together with the elbow and half the upper arm; for the adornment in Paradise reaches to the places touched in ablution. As you wash your right hand say, "O God, give me my book (of accounting) in my right hand and grant me an easy reckoning." As you wash your left say, "O God, I take refuge with You from being given my book in my left hand or behind my back." Then, moistening the fingers, rub all over your head, keeping the finger tips of right and left hands close together, placing them on the fore part of the head and moving them back to the nape of the neck and forward again. Do this three times—and similarly with the other parts of the body—"O God, cover me with Your mercy, send down Your blessing upon me, shelter me beneath the shadow of Your Throne on the day when there is no shadow save Yours; O God, make my hair and my flesh forbidden things to the Fire."

Then run your ears outside and inside with clean water; place your fingers in your earholes and rub the outside of your ears with the ball of your thumbs and say, "O God, make me one of those who hear the word and follow the good in it; O God, make me hear the crier of Paradise along with the righteous in Paradise." Then rub your neck and say, "O God, deliver my neck from the Fire; O God, I take refuge with You from the chains and fetters."

Then wash your right foot and after that the left, together with the ankles. With the little finger of your left hand wash between your toes, beginning with the little toe on the right foot and finishing with the little toe on the left. Approach the toes from below and say, "O God, establish my feet on the straight path along with the feet of Your righteous servants." Similarly, when you wash the left, say, "O God, I take refuge with You that You may not cause my feet to slip from the path into the Fire on the day when You cause the feet of the hypocrites and idolaters to slip."

If a man says all these prayers during his ablution, his sins will have departed from all parts of his body, a seal has been set upon his ablution, it has been raised to beneath the Throne of God and unceasingly praises and hallows God, while the reward of that ablution is recorded for him to the Day of Resurrection. (Ghazali, *The Beginning of Guidance* 8–9) [GHAZALI 1953: 95–97]

9. The Friday Service

The noon prayer on Friday, "when the sun passes over the meridian," was the congregational prayer obligatory on all Muslims. As might be expected, a number of Prophetic traditions are reported on the subject.

Abu Hurayra reported the Messenger of God, may peace be upon him, as saying: "The best day on which the sun has risen is Friday: on it Adam was created, on it he was made to enter Paradise, on it he was expelled from it. And the Last Hour will take place on no other day but Friday."

Abu Hurayra reported God's Messenger, may peace be upon him, as saying: "We are the last (religious community) but we would be the first on the day of Resurrection and we would be the first to enter Paradise except that they [that is, the Jews and Christians] were given the Book before us and we were given it after them. They disagreed regarding the truth. And it was this day of theirs about which they disagreed, but God guided us to it, and that is Friday for us; the next day is for the Jews and the day following for the Christians." (Muslim, *Sahih* 4.302.1857, 1860)

Ghazali, as we have just seen, took as his goal the revivification of religious practices in Islam, which he hoped to accomplish by emphasizing both their spiritual content and the intent of the worshiper. This, for example, is his treatment of the Friday prayer.

Friday is the festival of the believers. It is an excellent day, ordained specially for this community by God, may He be magnified and exalted. In the course of it there is a period, the exact time of which is unknown; and if any Muslim, making request to God most high for what he needs, chances to do so in this period, God grants his request. Prepare then for it (Friday) on Thursday by cleansing of the clothes, by many acts of praise and by asking forgiveness on Thursday evening, for that is an hour equal in merit to the (unknown) hour of the Friday. Make the intention of fasting on Friday, but do so on Saturday or Thursday as well, since there is no prohibition on fasting on Friday alone.

When the morning breaks, wash, since Friday washing is obligatory on every adult, that is, it is "established" and "confirmed." Then array yourself in white clothes, for these are the most pleasing to God. Use the best perfume you have. Cleanse your body thoroughly by shaving, cutting your hair and nails, using the tooth-pick and practicing other forms of cleanliness, as well as by employing fragrant perfumes. Then go early to the mosque, walking quietly and calmly. . . . It is said that, in respect to nearness to the beholding of the face of God, people come in the order of their early arrival for the Friday observance.

When you have entered the mosque, make you the first [that is, the nearest] row. If the congregation has assembled, do not step between their necks and do not pass in front of them while they are praying. Place yourself near a wall or pillar so that the people do not pass in front of you. Before sitting say the prayer of "greeting." Best of all, however, is to perform four prostrations, in each of which you recite the Sura of Purity (Sura 112). There is a tradition to the effect that whoever does that will not die until he has seen, or, in a variant reading, has been shown, his place in Paradise. . . .

When the leader had come out to commence the worship, break off your private worship and conversation and occupy yourself with responding to the muezzin, and then by listening to the sermon and taking it to heart. Do not speak at all during the sermon. It is related in a prophetic tradition that "whoever says 'Hush!' to his neighbor while the leader is giving the sermon, has spoken idly, and whoever speaks idly has no Friday observance (credited to him)." The point is that in saying "Hush" he was speaking, whereas he ought to have checked the other man by a sign, not by a word. . . .

After the Friday observance perform two prostrations, or else four or six in pairs. All this is traditionally related of the Messenger of God, God bless him and preserve him, in various circumstances. Then remain in the mosque until the sunset worship, or at least until the late afternoon service. Watch carefully for the "excellent hour," for it may occur in any part of the day, and perhaps you will light upon it while making humble supplication to God. In the mosque do not go to the circle of people or the circle of story-tellers, but to the circle of profitable knowledge, that is, the knowledge that increases your fear of God most high and decreases your desire for this world; ignorance is better for you than all the knowledge which does not draw you away from this world towards the next. Take refuge with God from unprofitable knowledge. Pray much at the rising, declining and setting of the sun (on Fridays), at the formal institution of worship, at the preacher's ascending the pulpit, and the rising of the congregation for worship; the likelihood is that the "excellent hour" will be at one of those times. Endeavor on this day to give such alms as you can manage, even if it is little. Divide your time between the worship, fasting, almsgiving, reciting the Quran, recollection of God, solitary devotions, and "waiting for prayer." Let this one day of the week be devoted to what pertains to the future life, and perhaps it will be an atonement for the rest of the week. (Ghazali, *The Beginning of Guidance* 26) [GHAZALI 1953: 127–128]

10. The Two Liturgical Festival Days

In addition to Friday, other days liturgically commemorated by Muslims are the Feast of the Immolation or Great Festival celebrated during the pilgrimage month in honor of Abraham's sacrifice of Isaac—an event re-enacted on the pilgrimage itself—and the Lesser Festival or the "Feast of Breaking the Fast" at the end of Ramadan. Both have their social and popular aspects in Muslim societies, as they do in the following traditions, but liturgically they resemble the Friday service with sermon.

Jabir ibn Abdullah reported: The Messenger of God, may peace be upon him, stood up on the day of the Breaking of the Fast and observed prayer. And he began the prayer before the sermon. He then delivered the sermon. When the Messenger of God, may peace be upon him, had finished the sermon, he came down from the pulpit and made his way to the women and exhorted them (to do good acts), and he was leaning on the arm of (his muezzin) Bilal. Bilal had stretched out his cloth into which women were throwing alms. (Muslim, *Sahih* 4.313.1925)

And another tradition specifies:

He then walked on till he came to the women (in the mosque) and preached to them and admonished them and asked them to give alms, for most of them are the fuel for Hell. A woman having a dark spot on her cheek stood up and said: Why is it so, O Messenger of God? He said: For you grumble often and show ingratitude to your spouses. And then they began to give alms out of their ornaments such as their earrings and rings which they threw onto the cloth of Bilal. (Muslim, *Sahih* 4.313.1926)

Umm Atiya reported: We were commanded to bring out on the feast days sequestered women and those unmarried. Menstruating women (also) came out but remained behind people and pronounced the "God is Great!" along with them. (Muslim, *Sahih* 4.314.1933)

Aisha reported: Abu Bakr came to see me (at the Prophet's house) and I had two girls with me from among the girls of the Helpers; they were singing what the Helpers recited to one another at the Battle of Bu'ath. They were not, however, (professional) singing girls. Abu Bakr said: What, the playing of this wind instrument of Satan in the house of the Messenger of God, may peace be upon him, and this too on the Festival Day? Upon this the Messenger of God, may peace be upon him, said: Abu Bakr, every people have a festival and this is ours. (Muslim, *Sahih* 4.317.1938)

11. A Muslim Holy Day: The Tenth of Muharram

Like the religious calendars of the Jews and the Christians, the Muslims' was filled with days commemorating some past event of special significance to the community. One of the most important, on a scale similar to Passover for the Jews or Easter for the Christians, was the tenth day of the lunar month of Muharram. Biruni (d. 1048 C.E.) explains its significance in his Traces of the Past.

The 10th (of Muharram) is called Ashura, a most distinguished day. The Prophet is reported to have said: "O men, hasten to do good works on this day for it is a grand and blessed day, on which God had mercy on Adam."

The day was, and is, of special significance to Shiʿite Muslims, however, since it marked (as we have seen in chapter 3 above) the martyrdom of Husayn, the son of Ali and the grandson of the Prophet, at Karbala in Iraq in 680 C.E.

People marked this day with celebration until the murder of Husayn ibn Ali ibn Abi Talib occurred on it, when he and his adherents were treated in such a way as never in the whole world the worst criminals have been treated. They were killed by hunger and thirst, through the sword; they were burned and their heads roasted, and horses were made to trample over their bodies. Therefore people came to consider this day as an unlucky one.

On the contrary, the Umayyads [that is, the Muslim dynasty in power that engineered the slaughter] dressed themselves on this day in new garments, with various kinds of ornaments, and painted their eyes with kohl; they celebrated a feast, and gave banquets and parties, eating sweetmeats and pastries. Such was the custom in the nation during the rule of the Umayyads, and so it remained also after the downfall of the dynasty (in 750 C.E.).

The Shiʿite people, however, lament and weep on this day, mourning over the protomartyr Husayn in public, in Baghdad, for example, and in other cities and villages; and they make a pilgrimage to the blessed soil [that is, the tomb of Husayn] in Karbala. As this is a mourning day, their common people have an aversion to renewing the vessels and utensils of the household on this day.

And as with most of the other sacred days in the three religions, there was an attempt to connect Ashura back to biblical prototypes, and here with Gospel ones as well.

People say that on this day God took compassion on Adam, that the Ark of Noah stood still on the mountain, that Jesus was born, that Moses was saved (from the Pharaoh). . . . Further, on this day Jacob regained his eyesight, Joseph was drawn out of the well, Solomon was invested with the royal power, the punishment was taken away from the people of Jonah, Job was freed from his plague, the prayer of Zachariah was granted and John (the Baptist) was given to him. . . .

Though it is possible that all these events should have occurred on this day, we must state that all this rests on the authority of popular story-tellers, who do not draw upon learned sources nor upon the consensus among the Peoples of the Book.

Some people say that Ashura is an Arabicized Hebrew word, to wit, Ashur, that is, the tenth of the Jewish month of Tishri, in which falls the fasting of (Yom) Kippur; that the date of this fasting was compared with the months of the Arabs, and that it was fixed on the tenth day of the Arabs' first month, as it falls with the Jews on the tenth day of their first month.

The Prophet gave order to fast on this day in the first year of the Hijra, but afterwards this fast was abrogated by the other law, to fast during the month of Ramadan, which falls later in the year. People relate that the Prophet of God, on arriving in Medina, saw the Jews fasting on Ashura. On inquiring of them, he was told that this was the day on which God had drowned Pharaoh and his people and had saved Moses and the Israelites. Then the Prophet said, "We have a nearer claim on Moses than they." In consequence he fasted on that day and ordered his followers to do the same. But when he afterwards issued the law regarding the fasting of Ramadan, he no longer ordered them to fast on Ashura, but neither did he forbid them.

This tradition is not correct, however, since scientific examination proves against it. . . . You could not maintain that the Prophet fasted on Ashura on account of its coincidence with the 10th of Tishri in this year, unless you transfer it from the first of the Jewish months to the first of the Arab months so as to make them fall together. Also in the second year of the Hijra the Jewish Ashura and the day of Muhammad's arrival cannot have coincided. (Biruni, *Traces of the Past*) [BIRUNI 1879: 326–328]

12. The Pilgrimage of Islam

The Muslims' mix of local and biblical traditions surrounding the boxlike building called "the Kaʿba" in Muhammad's Mecca was the result of an attempt to link what was patently a very old, and in Muhammad's day a pagan, religious tradition in Mecca with the past age of the "religion of Abraham." The process begins, as we have just seen, in the Quran, where first Abraham and then, as a post-Quranic reflex, Adam are identified as the builders of the Kaʿba. The linkage goes further, however, and the chief pilgrimage rituals of both Mecca and its immediate environs are confirmed as Muslim *rituals.*

When We chose the site of the House for Abraham (We said): Associate no one with Me and clean My House for those who will circumambulate it, stand (in reverence), and bow in homage.

Announce the Pilgrimage to the people. They will come to you on foot and riding along distant roads on lean and slender beasts, in order to reach the place of advantage for them, and to pronounce the name of God on appointed days over cattle He has given them as food; then eat the food and feed the needy and the poor.

Let them attend to their persons and complete the rites of Pilgrimage, fulfill their vows and circuit around the ancient House. . . .

There are advantages for you in these (animals to be sacrificed) up to a time, then their place is in the ancient House for sacrifice.

For every community We have ordained certain rites that they may commemorate the name of God by reciting it over the cattle We have given them for sacrifice. Your God is One God, so be obedient to Him. (Quran 22:26–34)

Known are the months of Pilgrimage. If one resolves to perform the Pilgrimage in these months, let him not indulge in concupiscence, sin or quarrel. And the good you do shall be known to God. Provide for the journey, and the best of provisions is piety. O men of understanding, obey Me.

It is no sin to seek the favors of your Lord (by trading). When you start from Arafat in a concourse, remember God at the monument that is sacred, and remember Him as He has shown you the way, for in the olden days you were a people astray. Then move with the crowd impetuously, and pray God to forgive you your sins. God is surely forgiving and kind.

When you have finished the rites and ceremonies, remember God as you do your fathers, in fact with greater devotion. (Quran 2:197–200)

13. Muhammad's Farewell Pilgrimage

The Quran had simply commanded that the hajj be made, "during the well-known months"; that it was "a duty men owe to God"—everyone, that is, "who is able to afford the journey" (3:97). The command was, then, a plain and direct one, doubtless on the correct assumption that the parties addressed were well acquainted with this pre-Islamic ritual. But as we have seen, the rite was complex even at the beginning, and its complexities assured that a later generation of Muslims would have a host of questions on the subject. The Quran had already addressed some of them, the case of an interrupted Pilgrimage, for example.

Complete the *hajj* or *ʿumra* in the service of God, but if you are prevented, send a sacrificial offering from what is available; do not,

however, shave your heads [that is, signal the completion of the obliga-
tion] until the offering reaches the place of sacrifice. But if any of you
becomes ill (after formally beginning the rites) or has a scalp ailment
(requiring shaving), he should compensate by either fasting or feeding
the poor. (Quran 2:196)

As the citation itself reveals, the ritual complexities of the hajj might
be considerable—later they spawned an entire guild of guides to assist the
pilgrim through them—and, as on other issues, the answers were sought
among the hadith, the reported utterances of the Prophet himself, and more
particularly those that clustered around the so-called Farewell Pilgrimage
in 632 C.E.

We know little of Muhammad's connection with Meccan rituals, including the hajj, either before or after his call to prophethood, though it
seems safe to assume that he took part in the rites of his native city. Once
removed to Medina, however, he was obviously in no position to participate
in any of the cultic observances in Mecca and its vicinity—not, at any rate,
until the month of Dhu al-Qaʿda (February) 629 C.E., when, as we have
seen, he was permitted to perform the umra as part of a general political
settlement concluded at Hudaybiyya. Mecca fell in January of 630 C.E.,
and though Muhammad performed the ʿumra in March of that year, he did
not participate in the hajj. In March of 631 C.E. the hajj was led by Abu
Bakr, and Muhammad was once again absent. Thus it was not until Dhu
al-Hijja (March) in 632 C.E., the year of his death, that Muhammad went
on what was to be his first and final hajj as a Muslim.

Since the Pilgrimage was a known and ongoing rite in Muhammad's
day, the Quran has no need of prescribing its rituals in inclusive detail:
what was done before will continue to be done, though now under Islamic
auspices. But another, later generation of Muslims needed somewhat more
guidance, and they could find it in the circumstantial account of the
Prophet's Farewell Pilgrimage in the year of his death. Not unnaturally it
became the model for the performance of this obligation incumbent on all
competent Muslims: at least once in their lifetime to go to Mecca and perform the ceremonies described here.

Jaʿfar ibn Muhammad [the sixth Shiʿite Imam, d. 765 C.E.] reported on the authority of his father [Muhammad al-Baqir, the fifth
Imam, d. 732 C.E.]: We went to Jabir ibn Abdullah [one of the last
surviving Companions of the Prophet, d. 693 C.E., aged ninety-four]
and he had begun inquiring about the people till it was my turn. I said:
I am Muhammad ibn Ali ibn Husayn [that is, the grandson of Husayn,

Muhammad's own grandson]. Jabir placed his hand upon my head and opened my upper button and then my lower one and then placed his palm on my chest (to bless me), and I was, during those days a young boy, and he said: You are welcome, my nephew. Ask whatever you want to ask. . . .

I said to him: Tell me about the Pilgrimage of God's Messenger, may peace be upon him. He held up nine fingers and then stated: The Messenger of God, may peace be upon him, stayed at Medina for nine years but did not perform the Pilgrimage; then he made public announcement in the tenth year to the effect that God's Messenger, may peace be upon him, was about to perform the Pilgrimage. A large number of persons came to Medina, and all of them were anxious to follow the Messenger of God, may peace be upon him, and do according to his doing. We set out till we reached Dhu al-Hulayfa [in the vicinity of Mecca]. Asma daughter of Umays gave birth (there) to Muhammad ibn Abi Bakr. She sent a message to the Messenger of God, may peace be upon him, asking him: What should I do (in my present state of ritual impurity)? He said: Take a bath, wrap up your private parts and put on the (pilgrim's) garment of purification. The Messenger of God, may peace be upon him, then prayed in the mosque (there) and after that mounted al-Qaswa (his she-camel) and it stood up with him on its back at al-Bayda.

And I saw as far as I could see in front of me nothing but riders and pedestrians, and also on my right and my left and behind me. And the Messenger of God, may peace be upon him, was prominent among us, and the (revelation) of the Quran was descending upon him, and it is he who knows its (true) significance. And whatever he did, we also did that. He pronounced the Oneness of God, saying: "At Your service, O Lord, at Your service, at Your service. You have no partner. Praise and Grace is Yours, and Sovereignty too. You have no partner." And the people also pronounced this invocation, which they (still) pronounce today. . . .

We had no intention but that of the (formal) Pilgrimage, being unaware of the Lesser Pilgrimage, but when we came with him to the House [of God; that is, the Ka'ba], he touched the pillar [that is, the black stone] and made (seven) circuits, running three of them and walking four. And then going to the Place of Abraham (in the Haram), he recited: "And adopt the Place of Abraham as a place of prayer" (Quran 2:125). And this place was between him and the House. . . . He recited in two prostrations "Say: He is God, One" (Sura 112) and "Say: O

unbelievers . . ." (Sura 109). He then returned to the pillar and kissed
it. He then went out the gate to al-Safa [a place adjoining the Haram],
and as he reached it he said: "Al-Safa and al-Marwa are among the signs
appointed by God" (Quran 2:158), (adding) I begin with what God has
commanded me to begin. He first mounted al-Safa until he saw the
House, and facing in the direction of the Ka'ba, he declared the Oneness of God and glorified Him, and said: "There is no god but the God,
One; there is no partner with Him. His is the Sovereignty, to Him
praise is due, and He is Powerful over everything. There is no god but
the God alone, who fulfilled His promise, helped His servant and routed
the confederates alone." He then made supplication in the course of
that, saying such words three times. He then descended and walked
toward al-Marwa, and when his feet came down in the bottom of the
valley, he ran, and when he began to ascend he walked until he reached
al-Marwa. There he did as he had done at al-Safa.

And when it was his last running at al-Marwa, he said: If I had
known beforehand what I have come to know afterwards, I would not
have brought sacrificial animals and would have performed a Lesser
Pilgrimage. So he who among you has not the sacrificial animals with
him should put off the (pilgrim's) garment of purification and treat it as
a Lesser Pilgrimage. Suraqa ibn Malik ibn Ju'sham got up and said:
Messenger of God, does it apply to the present year or does it apply
forever? Thereupon the Messenger of God, may peace be upon him,
intertwined his fingers and said twice: The Lesser Pilgrimage has become incorporated in the (formal) Pilgrimage, adding: "No, but forever
and ever." . . . Then all the people, except the Messenger, may peace
be upon him, and those who had with them sacrificial animals, put off
the garment of purification and got their hair clipped.

When it was the eighth day of the Pilgrimage Month they went to
Mina and put on the garment of purification for the Pilgrimage, and the
Messenger of God, may peace be upon him, rode forth and led the
noon, afternoon, sunset, evening and dawn prayers. He then waited a
little till the sun rose, and commanded that a tent should be pitched at
Namira [at the limits of the territory of Mecca]. The Messenger of God,
may peace be upon him, then set out, and the Quraysh did not doubt
that he would halt at the (hillock called) "the sacred site" as they used
to do in the pre-Islamic period. The Messenger of God, may peace be
upon him, passed on, however, until he reached (the hill of) Arafat and
he found that the tent had been pitched for him at Namira. There he
halted until the sun had passed the meridian; he commanded that his

camel be brought and saddled for him. Then he came to the bottom of the valley (there) and addressed the people.

There follows Muhammad's farewell discourse to the Muslims (see chapter 2 above), after which the narrative continues.

The Messenger of God, may peace be upon him, then mounted his camel and came to the halting place, making his camel turn toward the side where there were rocks, with the path taken by those on foot in front of him, and faced toward the Kaʿba. He kept standing there (from the time of the noonday prayer) till the sun set, and the yellow light had somewhat gone and the disk of the sun had disappeared. He made Usama sit behind him, and he pulled the nosestring of the camel so forcefully that its head touched the saddle, and he pointed out to the people on his right hand to be moderate (in their pace) . . . and this is how he reached al-Muzdalifa.

There he led the evening and sunset prayers. . . . The Messenger of God, may peace be upon him, then lay down till dawn and then offered the dawn prayer . . . when the morning light was clear. He again mounted his camel, and when he came to "the holy site" he faced toward the Kaʿba, supplicated God, glorified Him, and pronounced His Uniqueness and Oneness, and kept standing until the daylight was very clear. He then went quickly before the sun rose . . . till he came to the bottom of Muhassir [between Muzdalifa and Mina]. He urged his camel a little, and following the middle road, which comes out at the greatest pile of stones, he came to the pile near the tree. At this he threw seven small pebbles, saying "God is Great" while throwing each one of them in the manner in which small pebbles are thrown (with the fingers), and this he did at the bottom of the valley.

He then went to the place of sacrifice, and sacrificed sixty-three camels with his own hand. Then he gave the remaining ones to Ali, who sacrificed them, and he made him share in his sacrifice. He then commanded that a piece of flesh from each animal sacrificed should be put in a pot, and when it was cooked, both of them [that is, Muhammad and Ali] took some meat of it and drank its broth. The Messenger of God, may peace be upon him, again rode and came to the House (of God) and offered the sunset prayer at Mecca. He came to the tribe of Abd al-Muttalib, who were supplying (pilgrims) the water of the (sacred spring) Zamzam, and said: Draw water, O tribesmen of Abd al-Muttalib; were it not that people would usurp this right of supplying themselves with water from you (if I did so), I would have drawn it along with you. So they handed him a container and he drank from it. (Muslim, *Sahih* 7.462.2803)

Though they cannot be dated with precision, the Quran too has verses that seem to be offering clarification on ritual points of the Pilgrimage. Sura 22, for example, offers extensive and detailed instruction on the sacrifices performed during the hajj. *Specifically it addresses the question—which remains, as often, unasked in the body of the Quran but unmistakably underlies the answer—as to whether it is permissible to eat the flesh of the animals offered for sacrifice.*

You are permitted (to eat) the sacrificial animals, except those specified (as prohibited), but shun the abomination of idols and shun the word that is false.

In them [that is, the sacrificial animals] you have benefits for a term appointed; in the end their place of sacrifice is near the Ancient House. [At the time of this verse the place of sacrifice was apparently still near the Ka'ba, as it had been throughout pre-Islamic times.] To every people did We appoint a place of sacrifice, that they might celebrate the name of God over the sustenance He gave them from animals. (Quran 22:33–34)

For your benefit we have made the sacrificial camels one of the signs from God; there is good for you in them. So pronounce the name of God over them as they line up (for sacrifice), and afterwards as they lie slain, eat thereof and feed such as already have food and such as beg in humility; thus have We made animals subject to you, that you might be grateful.

It is not their meat or their blood that reaches God; it is your piety that reaches Him. He has thus made them subject to you, that you may glorify God for the Guidance He has given you. (Quran 22:36–37)

14. Islamicizing the Hajj

The Medinese suras of the Quran are filled with instruction and remarks linking Abraham and Ishmael not merely with the Ka'ba but with the rituals of the hajj *as well. Attention has already been drawn to the following verses of the twenty-second sura, which appear in the form of a command to Abraham after he had finished building the Ka'ba.*

Announce to the people the Pilgrimage. They will come to you on foot and on every lean camel, coming from every deep and distant highway that they may witness the benefits and recollect the name of

God in the well known days over the sacrificial animals he has provided for them. Eat thereof and feed the poor in want. Then let them complete their rituals and perform their vows and circumambulate the Ancient House.

Such is it [that is, the Pilgrimage]. Whoever honors the sacred rites of God, for him is it good in the sight of his Lord. (Quran 22:27–30)

The Quran merely suggests; as we have seen, the later Muslim tradition hastened to fill in the details explaining how Abraham, and indeed Adam before him, had initiated the hajj, *and that whatever modifications Muhammad was undertaking represented a restoration of the original form of the* hajj.

The third verse of Sura 9 of the Quran, which has already been cited in connection with the hajj *of the year 9 (630 C.E.) contains what it itself announces is a formal proclamation* (adhan).

And a proclamation from God and His Messenger on the Day of the Great Pilgrimage—that God and His Messenger dissolve treaty obligations with the pagans. If you repent, it is better for you. But if you turn our backs, then know that you cannot frustrate God. Inform those wh disbelieve of a painful punishment.

While the surrounding verses might plausibly be assigned to the Abu Bakr–led Pilgrimage of 631 C.E., this verse appears to be the fulfillment of that prior warning that thereafter *the pagans would be excluded from the* hajj. *Here they are themselves informed of the ban. The presence of pagans at a* hajj *in which Muhammad himself led the Muslim contingent doubtless troubled many of the ancient authorities who preferred to keep Muhammad remote from all forms and manifestations of paganism. More disturbingly for the traditional assignment of this verse to the pilgrimage of the previous year, there is no very convincing reason for calling the Abu Bakr* hajj *the "Great Pilgrimage." The ancient commentators sensed the difficulty as well.*

It was more certainly on the occasion of this Pilgrimage that the Quran abolished the Arab practice of intercalation, the insertion of an interval into a time-reckoning system in order to reconcile the solar year of 364¼ days and the lunar year of 360 days. The way the Arabs accomplished it was by periodically inserting an extra month (nasi) *into the lunar year, and it was to that practice that the Quran adverted.*

In the sight of God the number of months is twelve, and so it was decreed on the day He created the heavens and the earth. Of them four are sacred: that is the correct religious practice, so do not wrong yourselves in them and fight the pagans altogether, as they fight you altogether. And know that God is with those who restrain themselves.

Know that intercalation (*nasi*) is an addition to disbelief. Those who disbelieve are led to error thereby, making it lawful in one year and forbidden in another in order to adjust the number of (the months) made sacred by God and make the sacred ones permissible. The evil of their course appears pleasing to them. But God gives no guidance to those who disbelieve. (Quran 9:36–37)

The passage draws our attention to a confusion with the sacred months as the reason for the prescribed calendar reform: the "pagans" are accused of using the complex practice of intercalation to manipulate for their own advantage the sacred months in which shrines were visited, fighting was interdicted, and trade and commerce encouraged. Though we are not certain exactly how it was accomplished, it is easy to understand how the arbitrary juggling of the sacred months under the guise of intercalation might give an advantage to the Quraysh or any others who controlled a major shrine or market fair.

It may not have been the only reason Muhammad had in mind. The hajj fell on 10 March in the intercalated year 632 C.E., the vernal equinox in the Julian calendar then in use, and if the traditionists were correct, in that year it coincided with the Passover and Easter tides. With intercalation, which annually tied the hajj to the spring season, that must not have been a rare occurrence, but Muhammad's abolition of the practice insured that that coincidence would not soon happen again: henceforward the hajj would occur according to the lunar cycle and thus annually retrogress, along with all other Muslim festivals, eleven days against the solar calendar. Both the umra and the hajj forever lost their seasonal associations.

The abolition of intercalation, and so the cutting free of the Muslims from either the Christians' solar or the Jews' lunisolar calendar, had another effect that must have begun to be felt only somewhat later. In 637 C.E., during the Caliphate of Umar (r. 634–644 C.E.), a calendar commission proposed and Umar decreed that the Muslim era began with Muhammad's migration to Medina, an event that took place in September of 622 C.E. The initial date of the new era was, however, pushed back for calendrical purposes to the first day of the first month of that year, 1 Muharram or 16 July 622 C.E. The intent was to introduce order and a degree of self-identity into the affairs of the new Islamic commonwealth; one perhaps unanticipated side effect was to introduce a degree of anarchy into the Muslims' recollection of the date of events during the intercalation era at Medina. As a result, one modern Muslim author has remarked, "there is more calendrical confusion connected with these ten years of Muhammad's mission in Medina than with any other decade of human history either before or after this period."

Though the Quran was reassuring on the point that the "greater" and the "lesser" Pilgrimages were both part of God's original revelation to Abraham, there was a common sense at Mecca that the associated rituals were remnants of a pagan past. We can read the source of the concern between the lines of Quran 2:158 and even more clearly in the anecdotes prompted by clarifications of that verse.

Surely Safa and Marwa are among the signs of God. Whoever goes on Pilgrimage to the House (of God), or performs the Lesser Pilgrimage, is not guilty if he walks around [or "circumambulates"] them; and he who does good of his own accord will find appreciation with God who knows every thing. (Quran 2:158)

Thus, as appears from the texts themselves—"is not guilty . . . "— there were some misgivings about these Pilgrimage rituals among Muhammad's Muslim contemporaries, and the Quranic commentators scanned the Prophetic traditions for evidence of it.

Wahidi (d. 1076 C.E.) relates that when asked about al-Safa and al-Marwa, Anas ibn Malik said: "We were of the opinion that they belonged to the era of heathenism. Thus when Islam came we ceased running between them. God therefore sent down this verse" [2:158, just cited].

Qurtubi the jurist (d. 1273 C.E.) relates that Urwah ibn al-Zubayr said to (Muhammad's wife) Aisha: "I see nothing against anyone who does not run between al-Safa and al-Marwa, nor would I be concerned if I myself did not run between them." She answered: "Ill is that which you speak, O son of my sister! The Messenger of God ran between them and so did the Muslims. It was rather those who sacrificed to Manat, the idol that was in the Mushlal who did not run between them. Thus God sent down (2:158). Had it been as you say, the verse would have read 'in him there is no blame if he does not run between them.' "

Al-Shaʿbi said: "During the Era of Ignorance there was an idol on al-Safa called Isaf and another on al-Marwa called Naʾilah. People used to touch them when they ran (between the two hills). The Muslims did not wish to run between them on that account; hence God sent down this verse." [AYOUB 1984: 177]

And somewhat in the same vein is this tradition concerning the kissing of the black stone embedded in the corner of the Kaʿba.

Abdullah ibn Sarjis reported: I saw the bald one, that is, Umar ibn al-Khattab, may God be pleased with him, kissing the stone and saying: By God, I am kissing with the full knowledge that you are a stone and that you can do neither harm nor good; if I had not seen the Messenger of God, upon whom be peace, kissing you, I would not have kissed you. (Muslim, *Sahih* 7.434.2914)

15. The Twelfth-Century Haram

Ibn Jubayr was born at Valencia or Xativa on 1 September 1145, left Granada on 1 February 1183, and did not return until 25 April 1185. In the interval he had visited Alexandria and Cairo, had gone up the Nile to Qus, had crossed the desert to Aydhab, had sailed over the Red Sea to Jidda, and had spent more than eight months at Mecca where he completed the hajj *and* ʿumra *in 1184. Ibn Jubayr left Mecca on 5 April 1184 in the pilgrim caravan to Iraq, spent five days visiting Medina, and then followed the classical route to Baghdad and thence on to the rest of his extensive travels. His description of the Holy Places of Mecca is one of the most careful and detailed that we possess from before the nineteenth century.*

We begin with his account of the haram.

The Sacred Mosque is surrounded by three galleries resting on three (series of) columns, joined in such a way that they form but a single gallery which would be 400 cubits long and 300 wide. . . . The space enclosed by the galleries is a vast place, which was, however, quite small at the time of the Prophet; the domed shrine of the Zamzam was then on the outside (of the *haram*). Opposite the Syrian corner (of the Kaʿba) there survives the base of a column fixed in the ground; this column, which was the boundary of the original enclosure of the sanctuary, is 24 paces from the Syrian corner. The Kaʿba is in the middle of this space, equidistant from all four sides, east, south, north and west. . . .

The Assembly Hall was added to the sanctuary and incorporated into the gallery that runs from west to north and facing which is found the "Station of Abraham" as well as the Iraqi corner (of the Kaʿba). The Assembly Hall has a large court which one enters from the gallery. The wall of this gallery is throughout provided with stone benches under the loges of the arcades, and there have their place the copyists, the teachers of the Quran and certain artisans. The sanctuary is so to speak enclosed by circles of teachers and men of learning. Along the wall of the gallery facing this there are likewise benches under similar arcades; this is the gallery that runs from south to east. The other galleries have benches at the base of their walls but without arcades above them. These constructions are presently in a perfect state of preservation.

The sanctuary has seven minarets: four are distributed on the four sides; a fifth is on the Dar al-Nadwa; a sixth on the Safa Gate—it is the smallest . . . and too narrow for anyone to mount it; and a seventh, finally, over the Gate of Abraham. [IBN JUBAYR 1949–1951: 107–108/ Ar. 90–91]

*Ibn Jubayr then approaches the Ka*c*ba, the cube-shaped "House of God" set in the midst of the Haram.*

The venerated House has four corners; it is almost square. I learned from the head of the Banu Shayba, who are the guardians of the House, Muhammad ibn Isma c il ibn Abd al-Rahman, descended from Uthman ibn Talha ibn Abd al-Dar, Companion of the Prophet and charged with the preservation of the House, that its elevation on the side that faces the Safa Gate and extends from the Black Stone to the Yemeni corner is 29 cubits, while the elevation is 28 cubits on the other sides because of the drop in the surface toward the rainspout. The first corner is that of the Black Stone, and it is there that the faithful begin their circumambulation. . . . The next corner one comes to is the Iraqi corner, which looks toward the north; then the Syrian corner, looking toward the west; finally the Yemeni corner looking toward the south. Then you return to the corner of the Black Stone which faces the east and thus the circuit is completed.

The door of the venerable House is on the side between the Iraqi corner and that of the Black Stone. It is near the Black Stone, ten spans from it, a personally verified measure. Between these two [i.e., the door and the Stone] there is a space called al-Multazam, where prayers are uttered. The venerable door is eleven and a half spans from the ground. It is of gilded silver, perfect in its art and magnificent in its form. . . . When you enter the door, the first thing you see on your left is the corner on the outside of which is the Black Stone. There are two boxes which contain Qurans and which have above them, in the corner, two small silver window-like doors which span the corner. This was also the case in the adjoining corner, the Yemeni one, but they have been removed and only the wooden frames remain. The same is to be found in the Syrian and Iraqi corners, where they are preserved.

On the right (as he enters), the visitor sees the Iraqi corner with a door called "the Door of Mercy," through which one goes up to the roof. There is there an opening which reaches to the roof of the venerable House and inside of which is a stairway. Below is a room which contains the noble Station of Abraham. By reason of this opening you would think that the Ancient House has five corners. . . . The opening encloses the Iraqi corner into two equal parts, on each of the faces of the Ka'ba. [IBN JUBAYR 1949–1951: 94–97/Ar. 81–84]

Even before the preaching of Islam and the conversion of Mecca from a pagan to a Muslim sanctuary, the charge of the various holy places and activities associated with the cult there were hereditary offices passed down within a family from generation to generation. And no one of them per-sisted longer than the control of the Ka'ba—and, more appositely, access to it—by the clan called the Shayba. They were there before Muhammad, and they were there in 1050 C.E. when the pilgrim and traveler Nasir-i Khusraw visited the city.

An Arab clan called the Banu Shayba holds the key to the Ka'ba. They function as servants of the House and receive a stipend and robes of honor from the Sultan of Egypt. Their chief keeps possession of the key, and when he comes to the mosque, five or six persons accompany him. As they approach the building, ten or so pilgrims bring the stairs . . . and place them at the door. The old man mounts and stands at the threshold, and to open the door a man on either side of him holds back the brocade covering as though holding a great robe with which he has been vested. He opens the lock and removes it from the rings. A great number of pilgrims will have assembled at the door, and when it is opened, they raise their hands and shout in prayer. Since the voices of the pilgrims can be heard throughout Mecca, all know that the Ka'ba door has been opened, and all at once shout in prayer so that a great tumult fills the city.

Then the old man goes inside, with the other two men holding back the covering, and prays a prayer of two prostrations. Both wings of the door are then opened and the chief, standing on the threshold, delivers a sermon in a loud voice and invokes blessings upon the Mes-senger of God and his family. Then the old man and his assistants stand aside at the door, and the pilgrims begin to pour in. . . . When praying inside the Ka'ba, you turn your face toward the door, though any other direction is licit. I counted the number of people inside when the build-ing was filled to capacity and reckoned 720. . . .

During the months of Sha'ban, Ramadan and Shawwal, the door of the Ka'ba is opened on Mondays, Thursdays and Fridays. When Dhu al-Qa'da comes, it is not opened again. [NASIR-I KHUSRAW 1986: 79–80]

So it was too in Ibn Jubayr's day.

The door of the Kaʿba is opened every Monday and Friday, except in the month of Rajab, when it is opened every day. For its opening at daybreak there arrive the guardians of the House, the Banu Shayba. Some of them undertake to bring a stepladder similar to a large chair which had nine rungs along its length. It is set on legs which are equipped with iron-shod wheels to facilitate its contact with the ground. The stepladder is rolled on those wheels up to the venerable House just so its top rung reaches the level of the blessed sill of the doorway. The chief of the Shaybites climbs up. He is a man of mature age, of a perfect bearing and manner. He has in his hand the key of the blessed lock; he is accompanied by one of the guardians who holds a black veil which he extends in his hands in front of the door at the moment the chief of the Shaybites opens it. When he has opened the door this latter kisses the sill, then goes alone into the House, closing the door behind him. He remains there for the space of two *rakʿas*. Then the Banu Shayba enter, also closing the door behind them, and perform their *rakʿas*. While they are awaiting the opening of the venerable door, the people stand, turning their humble regards toward it, their hands extended in humble supplications to God. When the door is opened they cry "God is great" and their shout goes up to heaven; their mouths call out and beg: "Lord, open to us the gates of your mercy and of your paradise, O most merciful of the merciful." Then they enter "in peace, secure" (Quran 15:46). [IBN JUBAYR 1949–1951: 110–111/Ar. 93]

Ibn Jubayr next turns his attention to the "Station of Abraham," the place and the stone.

The venerated "station" (*maqam*) which is inside this opening is the "station" of Abraham. . . . It is a stone covered with silver, about three spans high and two spans wide and the upper part is bigger than the lower. One might say—may God raise it above a comparison which ought to be more noble—a great pottery "oven" whose middle is narrower than its top and bottom. We have seen it with our own eyes, and we have received the blessing of touching and kissing it. They poured out for us water from Zamzam onto the two footprints (of Abraham when he was building the Kaʿba) and we drank of it—may God make us profit by it! Their mark is clearly visible, likewise those of his venerable, blessed toes—praise be to Him who rendered it soft for the feet that marked it in such a way as they left their traces, while his feet left no mark in the impressionable sand. [IBN JUBAYR 1949–1951: 97/Ar. 84–85]

As Ibn Jubayr testified, in his day the stone associated with Abraham's construction of the Ka'ba was normally kept in a niche inside that building. But it was also brought out on occasion for the veneration of the faithful. At first it was a rather makeshift arrangement: during the Pilgrimage season the covered stone was placed on a platform in the haram to protect it from the recurrent danger of flooding. At prayer times the stone was lifted out of its box and shown to the people. Afterwards stone and box were returned to the Ka'ba. In 778 C.E. the stone was dropped and cracked during this ceremony; it was quickly repaired with golden straps. The pedestal was then made more permanent, first in 855 C.E. and then in 870 C.E., and it was on this latter occasion that the Meccan historian al-Fakihi had occasion to describe the stone and copy an inscription on it.

This, then, was the state of affairs when Ibn Jubayr saw the stone, and its outside dome-shrine, in 1183 C.E.

The actual placement of the noble Stone, that behind which one makes prayer, faces the side of the Ka'ba which is between the noble door and the Iraqi corner, but visibly closer to the door. It is surmounted by a wooden cupola, about a man's height or less, with sharp corners, magnificently decorated, and four spans wide from corner to corner. . . . The Stone is installed where we have described it, inside the venerable House, to protect it. . . . In addition the emplacement of the Stone also has an iron cupola, located next to the dome-shrine of the Zamzam. During the months of Pilgrimage, when visitors are numerous and the Iraqis and Khurasanis arrive, they take off the wooden cupola and put on the iron one since it is better able to resist the pressure of the crowd. [IBN JUBAYR 1949–1951: 97/Ar. 85]

At the side of the venerable "station" (of Abraham) . . .

—here apparently it is the domed shrine of the maqam outside the Ka'ba that is being referred to—

. . . is the pulpit of the Friday preacher, which is likewise mounted on four wheels. On Fridays, when the moment of prayer approaches, they push it against the side of the Ka'ba facing the "station" and which runs from the corner of the Black Stone to the Iraqi corner. [IBN JUBAYR 1949–1951: 113/Ar. 95]

Next is the celebrated well called Zamzam.

The dome-shrine of the well of Zamzam faces the corner of the Black Stone, from which it is 24 paces distant, and the "station" (of Abraham), behind which the ritual prayer is made, is to the right of this

domed shrine and ten paces from its corner. The interior is covered
with white marble of a very pure whiteness. The opening of the well is
in the middle, with a slight inclination to the side facing the venerable
House. Its depth is eleven heights of a man, according to our own measurements, and a height of seven, according to reports. The door of the
dome-shrine is turned toward the east, while the two doors of the
dome-shrine of al-Abbas and the dome-shrine of the Jewish woman face
toward the north. . . . The dome-shrine of the Zamzam well is contigu-
ous at its rear with the "Dome-Shrine of the Water Supply" or "Dome-
Shrine of al-Abbas," and this latter is joined obliquely to another called
"the Dome-Shrine of the Jewish Woman." These two dome-shrines
serve as storage for the endowed furniture of the noble House: copies
of the Quran, various manuscripts, candle-holders, etc. The dome-
shrine of al-Abbas continues to earn the name of "The Drinking Place";
it was there that pilgrims were given to drink. [IBN JUBAYR 1949–1951:
103/Ar. 88]

16. Ghazali on the Proper Performance
of the Hajj

*The medieval Muslim most responsible for spiritualizing the ritual obliga-
tions of Islam was undoubtedly al-Ghazali (d. 1111 C.E.), onetime professor at the prestigious Nizamiyya Madrasa in Baghdad. In his influential*
Revivification of the Sciences of Religion *dating from the end of the
eleventh century, he took up the* hajj *along with the other "Pillars of Islam"
and attempted to put it in its appropriate, and most spiritually beneficial,
context.*

*When the incoming pilgrim arrives at the formal boundary-points of
the Mecca* haram, *he performs the first of the ritual acts of the* hajj: *he dons
the pilgrim garment and utters the famous cry called the* talbiyya, "At Your
service, O Lord; at Your service." *Ghazali resumes:*

As for *donning the ihram* and *uttering the talbiyya* from the haram
boundaries onward, let him understand that it signifies answering the
summons of God. Thus you must hope that you will be acceptable and
take a care that your *talbiyya* be not answered with a rejection. You
must stand there hesitating between hope and fear and repent with all
your might on power, relying on God's grace and generosity, for the
moment of the *talbiyya* is the beginning of something momentous. . . .

While raising his voice in the *talbiyya* at the boundary-point, let him who is doing so remember how he answered God's call, "And proclaim among men the Pilgrimage" (Quran 22:27), and remember as well the trumpet's summons to all humans, how they will be gathered together from their graves; how they will assemble in crowds in the courtyard on Judgment Day to answer God's call; how they will be divided into those who will be made new (to God) and those who are hated, those who are accepted and those who are rejected. . . .

As for *entering Mecca*, at that point let him remember that he has arrived safely at God's *haram*, and let him hope that in entering the Haram he might be safe from God's punishments, and let him be fearful that he might not be found suitable for that closeness, and thus by entering the *haram* be disappointed and worthy of (God's) hate. But let his hope ever overcome, for (God's) generosity everywhere prevails and God is merciful. The honor of the House is great: what is due the guest is always observed and the obligation to whoever seeks refuge and shelter is not denied. . . .

As for the *circumambulation*, you must know that circumambulation is a prayer, so your heart should be filled with veneration, fear, hope, and love, as we have explained in the "Book of Prayer." You must also know that in circumambulation you resemble the angels who are near to God and who circle round about the throne, circumambulating it. And do not think that what is (primarily) intended is the circumambulation of your body around the House, but rather the circumambulation of your heart through recollection (*dhikr*) of the Lord of the House, so that you do not begin your recollection except with Him, just as you begin your circumambulation at the House and end with the House as well. You should know that the most sublime circumambulation is the circumambulation of the heart in the presence of the Divinity, and that the House is an outward manifestation in the world of kingship of that presence that cannot be seen by eyes and is in the realm of the Kingdom of Heaven, much in the same way that the body is an external manifestation in the visible world of the heart which cannot be seen by sight and is in the hidden world. The world of kingship and visibility is a route to the unseen world and the Kingdom of Heaven for those to whom God has chosen to open. Likewise in accordance with this same comparison is the suggestion that the Well-Peopled House in heaven [see chapter 1 above] is opposite the Ka'ba, and that the circumambulation of the angels around it is like the circumambulation of mortals around the Ka'ba. And since most humans fell short of achieving that (angelic) circumambulation, they were bidden to imitation to the closest degree possible. They were promised that "whoever imitates a folk, he is one of them." Whoever is capable of such a circumambulation is the one of whom it is said that the Ka'ba visits him and circumambulates around him, as has been seen by some of God's friends who have had mystical revelations.

As for *touching and kissing the Black Stone*, you must reflect at that point you are pledging your allegiance to the obedience of God. You must determine to be obedient to your pledge, for whoever breaks faith deserves (God's) hatred. Ibn Abbas related from the Messenger of God—upon him be peace—that he said: "The Black Stone is God's right hand of earth; with it He shakes hands with people as a man shakes hands with his brother."

As for *clinging to the veil of the Ka'ba and the holding-place* [al-mul-tazam, the place between the Black Stone and the door of the Ka'ba; prayers uttered there had a particular efficacy], let your intention in the holding-place be to seek closeness to the House and the Lord of the House in love and eagerness, getting blessed through contact and hoping to be shielded from hellfire in every part of your body. Let your intention in clinging to the veil of the Ka'ba be to implore forgiveness and seek clemency like a wrongdoer clinging to the clothes of someone he has wronged, begging his forgiveness. . . .

As for the *running between Safa and Marwa* in the outer courtyard of the House, it is like a slave's frequent coming and going in the outer courtyard of a king's palace to show the sincerity of his service. It is similar to a person who came into the presence of a king and then left without knowing what the king had decided about him; thus he keeps going in and out of the courtyard hoping that if not on the first occasion, he will receive (the king's) mercy.

When running between Safa and Marwa let him remember his own (future) wavering on the Scales (of Judgment) in the courtyard of the Resurrection. Let Safa stand for the scale (holding) good deeds and Marwa that (holding) evil deeds and let him think of his own hesitant wavering between them . . . and between punishment and forgiveness.

As for the *standing at Arafat*, see the crowding of the people and din of voice and the different languages, and how each group follows its *imam* in going around the different shrines of the *hajj* . . . and recall the courtyard of Judgment Day and how all nations will gather together with the prophets and the imams and each community will follow its prophet in the hope that he will intercede on its behalf, and how they will waver on that common ground between rejection and acceptance.

As you recall that, continue in your supplication and imploring so that you might be gathered into the company of those who have achieved their objectives and attained the mercy (of God). (Try also to) attain your hope of being accepted, for that is a venerable standing (on Arafat), and mercy comes from His Majesty to all people through the cherished hearts of this world's poles and deputies [see chapter 7 below], as well as a group of pious and good-hearted people. If their endeavors are united, and their hearts devoted to supplication and to prayer, and their hands are raised toward God, and their faces turned toward Him, and their eyes look toward heaven, all uniting in a single effort to request mercy, do not think that they will be disappointed or that their efforts will be wasted. . . . That is why it is said that one of the greatest sins is to stand at Arafat and have doubts that God has granted His forgiveness.

For the next part of the hajj *ritual, the stoning of the three rock pillars in the valley of Mina, Ghazali takes a different tack. This is, as some remarked, an example of a ritual without reason: it is purely commemorative of Abraham's act at that place and its merit consists in its being performed out of blind obedience to God's command.*

As for the *casting of stones,* I mean by it compliance with a ritual as a manifestation of slavery (to God), and an action out of mere obedience, without any opportunity for the intellect or the soul (to apprehend) in it. I also mean by it the imitation of Abraham—upon him be peace—when Iblis [that is, Satan] appeared to him in that place to cast doubts upon his Pilgrimage or to cause him to fall into affliction. God ordered Abraham to stone him in order to drive him away and disappoint him. If it occurs to you that Satan might have appeared to Abraham and that Abraham saw him and so stoned him, but that Satan will not appear to you, then you should know that this notion is from Satan. Iblis has put it in your heart to lessen your determination to cast the stones and to make you think that it is a deed to no avail but rather more like a game not worth busying yourself with. Then you must all the more assiduously drive him away, rallying all your force in casting the stones in defiance of Satan. You must realize that though in appearance you are casting stones at a slope, in fact you are hurling them in Satan's face and dealing him a mortal blow, for acting in despite of Satan comes through observing God's orders out of reverence for him and out of obedience alone, without any opportunity for the soul or the intellect (to operate) in it.

And though he is not so explicit as in the case of the stoning, the next ritual, the sacrifice at Mina, seems to fall for Ghazali into the same category of an act whose merit consists in its mere performance out of obedience to God's command.

As for the *sacrifice of the offerings*, you must know that it is a drawing close to God out of obedience. So make the offering, and hope that with every part of it a part of you will be liberated from Hell, for such is the promise. And the bigger the offering, and the more substantial its parts, the more comprehensive will be your emancipation from hellfire. . . .

This is the duty of the heart in the rites of Pilgrimage. (Ghazali, *The Revivification* 1.7.218–222)

17. The Prophet's Mosque and Tomb at Medina

The ambiguity of the pre-Islamic veneration of the dead rests only in its motive. Was it, as has been suggested, merely the continuation of social obligations beyond the grave? Or were these genuine cult acts, performed in the belief that the dead (or some dead) had power and that their intercession might or should be sought? The comparative evidence seems to incline toward the latter: the pagan Arabs offered to the dead the selfsame ritual acts they performed in honor of gods. Libations were offered, animals slaughtered, and often a taboo area—the hima, *the ritual predecessor of the later* haram*—was cordoned off around the grave.*

The strongest evidence that we are in the presence of a religious rather than merely a social phenomenon is the strength of Muslim opposition to the practices. In one apparently nonjudgmental passage, the Quran alludes to the practice of ancestor veneration, even though it occurs in the unmistakably religious context of the Pilgrimage.

And when you have completed the ceremonies of Pilgrimage, make recollection of Allah just as you make recollection of your forefathers, and more. (Quran 2:200)

It is not clear whether one practice is being replaced by another or simply being compared to it. In any case, the practice in question—as we are told by the classical commentaries on the passage—was the pilgrims' custom in pagan times of pausing in the valley of Mina after the completion of the Pilgrimage and celebrating their ancestors. It is difficult to avoid connecting this celebration with the just completed sacrifices at Mina, particularly since, as the Swiss explorer John Lewis Burckhardt discovered,

*there persisted even among nineteenth-century bedouin the practice of sacri-
ficing in the name of their deceased relatives on that very same day.*

On the day of *qurban*, the great sacrifice on Mount Arafat [that is,
at Mina during the course of the annual Pilgrimage], each Arab family
kills as many camels as there have been deaths of adult persons during
the last year in that family, whether the deceased were males or females.
Though a dead person should have bequeathed but one camel to his heir,
that camel is sacrificed; and if he did not leave one, his relations kill one
of their own camels. Seven sheep may be substituted for a camel; and
if the whole number cannot be procured for the *qurban* of the death-
year, the deficiency may be supplied by killing some on the next or
subsequent year. [BURCKHARDT 1831: 1:100]

*The most eminent of the Muslims died in 632 C.E. and was buried
at Medina. Muhammad was interred in the apartment he had lived in, with
the apartments of his wives on one side and the mosque he had established
adjoining it on the other. It was the first mosque in Islam, as we have
already seen, and according to the tenth-century geographer Muqaddasi,
the mosque appears to have undergone enlargement but little alteration
under the earliest of the Prophet's successors.*

The mosque . . . is at the side of the cemetery of al-Gharqad, made
like the mosque in Damascus, and not very large. It and the Damascus
mosque were constructed by al-Walid ibn Abd al-Malik, and the Abbasids enlarged it. . . . The first Umar enlarged it from the pillars to which
the latticework grille is today attached as far as the south wall. Then
Uthman enlarged it toward the south as far as it now reaches. (Muqaddasi 3.80)

*In the four-hundred-odd years that separate Muqaddasi from the
fourteenth-century traveler Ibn Battuta, the tradition about the early
changes in the mosque had grown substantially, and Ibn Battuta copied
them all.*

The mosque remained in this condition [that is, the way Muhammad had ordered it built] during the lifetime . . . of Abu Bakr, may God
be pleased with him. Umar ibn al-Khattab—may God be pleased with
him—during his government enlarged the Mosque of the Messenger of
God—God bless him and give him peace—saying, "Had I not heard the
Messenger of God say 'We shall have to enlarge the mosque,' I should
not have enlarged it." He took down the wooden columns and set up in
their place columns of brick, made it lower courses of stone up to the
height of a man, and raised the number of gateways to six, of which

there were two on each side except the southern (or *qibla*) side. Of one of these gateways, he said, "It is requisite to leave this one for the women." . . . He said also, "If we were to enlarge this mosque until it extended to the burial ground, it would still be the mosque of the Messenger of God—God bless him and give him peace." [IBN BATTUTA 1959–1962: 168]

But according to the Medinese historian Samhudi, Umar did make some changes in the tomb.

He [that is, Umar] first carried a wall around the chamber, or place where the body of Muhammad had been deposited at his death, and which was at first enclosed only with palm branches. (Samhudi, *Khulasat*) [Cited by BURCKHARDT 1829: 350]

Ibn Battuta's account continues:

It was enlarged next by Uthman [r. 644–656 C.E.]—may God be pleased with him—who built with vigor and himself labored on it, and who used to spend the whole day in it. He whitened it, gave solidity to its location by hewn stones and widened it on all sides except the eastern (where the huts of the Prophet's wives still stood). He had pillars set up in it, made of stones firmly fixed by pegs of iron and lead, and roofed it with teak. He also constructed a prayer-niche (*mihrab*) in it, though others say that Marwan was the first to build the prayer-niche, and others again say it was Umar ibn Abd al-Aziz, during the Caliphate of al-Walid. [IBN BATTUTA 1959–1962: 170]

Al-Walid (r. 705–715 C.E.) was, like his Caliph father, an ambitious builder, and he had ambitious plans for the Prophet's mosque in Medina, as reported in Tabari's more circumstantial account of his work under the year 707 C.E.

This year al-Walid ibn Abd al-Malik ordered the demolition of the mosque of the Prophet and the demolition of the apartments of the wives of the Prophet and their incorporation into the mosque. Muhammad ibn Umar reported that Muhammad ibn Ja‘far ibn Wirdan, the builder, had said: "I saw the messenger sent by Abd al-Malik. He arrived in First Rabi‘ of 88 [February–March 707 C.E.], his face covered, and people wanted to know why he had come. He went and gave to Umar ibn Abd al-Aziz [that is, the future Caliph Umar II (r. 715–717 C.E.] the letter bidding him incorporate the apartments of the wives of the Prophet into the mosque of the Prophet and acquire (the buildings) behind and around the mosque so that it would measure two hundred by two hundred cubits. He said to him: Push back the south wall if you can—and you can—back to the place where your maternal uncles live, since they will not oppose you. If any of them resists, order the local people to calculate a fair price (for the property), tear it down, and pay the owner its value. You have the authentic precedent of Umar and Uthman to guide you."

The local property owners offered no resistance, however. They took their payments and surrendered their houses to the mosque renewal project.

Muhammad ibn Umar said . . . on the authority of Salih ibn Kaysan: When the letter of al-Walid arrived from Damascus after a trip of fifteen days, Umar ibn Abd al-Aziz took the work in hand. Salih also said: "He put me in charge of the demolition and reconstruction of the mosque. . . . We set about demolishing it with laborers from Medina, beginning with the apartments of the wives of the Prophet. Then there arrived the workers sent by al-Walid. . . . We began the demolition of the mosque of the Prophet in Safar of 88 [that is, January 707 C.E.]. Al-Walid had sent and informed the Byzantine ruler that he had given orders for the demolition of the mosque of the Prophet and that he should assist in this enterprise. The latter sent him one hundred thousand *mithqals* of gold, a hundred artisans and forty loads of *tesserae* for the mosaics. He had given orders that the *tesserae* should be recovered from ruined towns and sent them to Walid, who sent them on to Umar ibn Abd al-Aziz." (Tabari, *Annals* 2.1192–1194)

As we have seen, the Spanish traveler and pilgrim Ibn Jubayr was in Medina in 1184 C.E., and he inspected the mosque mosaics done more than four hundred years earlier. They were on the upper registers—the lower sections were covered with decorative marble panels described in detail by Ibn Abd Rabbihi—of the southern, eastern, and western walls of the mosque's main hall.

The upper section of this wall is decorated in its entirety with golden cubes that are called mosaics, and those who made them have produced a marvel of art. They are comprised of representations of trees, all different looking and with their branches weighed down with fruit. The entire prayer-hall is decorated in this fashion, except that the workmanship on the southern wall is somewhat more careful (than on the others). The wall facing the courtyard is done in like manner on its northern and southern faces. [IBN JUBAYR 1949–1951: 194]

Samhudi supplies an important additional detail.

Some of those who produced the mosaics said: "We have reproduced here the images we have found of the trees and villas of Paradise."

When the artist finished the finely done great mosaic tree (in the composition), Umar (ibn Abd al-Aziz) gave him a bonus of thirty dirhams. (Samhudi, *Khulasat* 139)

Umar ibn Abd al-Aziz's work at Medina had included a new treatment of the Prophet's tomb. It had been surrounded, as we have seen, only by a low wall, roughly of a man's height, installed by command of the Caliph Umar. Now, however, on the testimony of Samhudi's informants, the tomb proper disappeared from sight behind an enclosure.

Ibn Shabba has said, according to Abu Ghassan, that the apartment of the Prophet, in which he had been buried, remained visible until Umar ibn Abd al-Aziz had constructed around it an enclosure of irregular shape when he rebuilt the mosque under the Caliphate of al-Walid. He made it irregular out of fear that, if it were in the same square shape as the Ka'ba, it would be taken as a *qibla* and people would make their ritual prayers in its direction. (Samhudi, *Khulasat* 114)

The thickness of the screen surrounding (the tomb) is somewhat more than a cubit and its height above the surrounding floor of the mosque is thirteen and one-third cubits, or a little higher in some places. It was built of stone. . . . As for the statement of Ibn al-Najjar [A historian whose history of Medina, still preserved in manuscript, was completed in 1196 C.E.] and those who follow him that it measured twenty-three cubits in height, that comes from their inclusion in the measurement of the height of the grille which (today) exists from the top of this wall to the ceiling of the mosque. Umar ibn Abd al-Aziz did not, however, raise his surrounding wall to the roof of the mosque. . . . Ibn Najjar reports that above the apartment, forming its roof, is a kind of oilcloth-like tent fabric, above which is the ceiling of the mosque. (Samhudi, *Khulasat* 147–149)

18. A Visit to Medina

A trip to Medina was not part of the formal hajj *but a* ziyara, *a pious visit. Most pilgrims chose to make the journey, however, on their way to or from Mecca, and visited the places sacralized by their association with the Prophet. Ghazali included in his* Revivification *a meditation on the spiritual value of such a visit.*

When your sight falls on its walls, recall that this is the town which God chose for His Prophet—upon him be peace—and to which He caused him to emigrate. It was the Prophet's residence from which he made manifest the obligatory rules of his God and his own tradition. From there he conducted a Holy War against his enemies and there his religion triumphed until his death. In it are his tomb and the tombs of his two ministers [that is, Abu Bakr and Umar] who ruled with justice after him.

Within yourself imagine the place of the Prophet's footsteps as he walked about the city. Every footstep you take is on a place where his dear feet stepped, so do not step there except peacefully and carefully. Remember his walking and striding along its roads, and imagine his humility and tranquillity as he walked, and how much and how great knowledge God put in his heart, and how He exalted his name to His own till He coupled both names together. . . . Remember God's grace on those who accompanied him and had the pleasure of seeing him and listening to his words. Your regret at missing his company and that of his Companions must be great. . . .

When you reach the mosque, recall that this is the courtyard which God chose for His Prophet and for the first, and best, Muslims. Remember that God's (ritual) laws were first observed in this courtyard, which embraced God's best creature in both life and death. . . . As for visiting the Messenger of God—upon him be peace— . . . visit him in death as if you were visiting him in life. Approach his tomb in the same manner as you would approach him alive. And as you would consider it a matter of reverence not to touch him or kiss him, but rather to stand at a distance before him in audience, do the same here, because the touching and kissing of shrines is a Christian and Jewish practice.

You must know that he is aware of your arrival, presence, and visit, and that he is informed of your prayer and salutation to him. So imagine him in his tomb just before you, and recall his great rank in your heart. It is recounted that he said that God had assigned an angel to his tomb to tell him of the salutation of whoever of his community salutes him. . . .

Then go to the pulpit of the Messenger of God and imagine him ascending the pulpit. Reenact in your heart the scene of him on the pulpit surrounded by the Emigrants and the Helpers and urging them in his sermon to obey God. Then ask God not to separate you from him in the world to come. (Ghazali, *The Revivification* 1.7.222)

One who made such a visit was Ibn Jubayr who arrived in Medina on 16 April 1184 C.E. in the company of the Iraqi caravan coming up from Mecca.

The evening of that same day we went into the sacred mosque to visit the pure and venerated tomb. We delivered our greeting standing before it, piously touching the dust of its sacred walls. We prayed in the "Garden," the space that extends between the holy tomb and the pulpit; we touched the wood of the venerable pulpit trod by the foot of the Prophet and touched the surviving fragment of the palm tree which whimpered for him. This latter is enclosed in a pillar which is in front of the "Garden" between the tomb and the pulpit, on your right when you face the pulpit. We then joined the assembly in making the late afternoon prayer. Fortunately we had on this occasion a certain freedom in our movements since people were mostly engaged in seeing to their baggage and setting up their tents. Thus we were able to achieve the object of our desire and go right into this venerated monument and offer our due greetings to the two Companions of the Prophet who lie there, "The Just One" [that is, Abu Bakr] and "The Discerner" [that is, Umar]. [IBN JUBAYR 1949–1951: 218–219/Ar. 189]

Ibn Jubayr then describes the Prophet's mosque tomb as it appeared in the late twelfth century.

The blessed mosque is rectangular in shape and surrounded on all four of its sides by galleries which enclose it. The center is entirely filled by a courtyard, where the soil is covered with sand and pebbles. The *qibla* [that is, the south] side has five aisles running from west to east, and the north side the same; the eastern side has a gallery of three aisles and that on the west four.

The venerated mosque is 196 paces long and 126 wide; there are 290 columns on which the ceiling rests immediately, without benefit of any arches to support it. . . . They are made of stones dressed piece by piece, put together and cut with the hollow joint within; molten lead is poured in the joints to insure the stones' being joined into a single, compact pillar. They are covered with a coating of whitewash which renders them bright and smooth and gives them the appearance of marble. [IBN JUBAYR 1949–1951: 219/Ar. 190]

The word Rawda *or "Garden," is used, as we can already discern, in two senses: first, as the entire area running across the southern gallery, from the Gate of Peace on the west to the Prophet's tomb on the east; and second, as here, of the tomb, or rather, the tomb building, proper. At a later period the term "Rawda" was used exclusively for the first and the tomb building was designated as "The Chamber" (al-Hujra).*

The sacred "Garden" is on the extreme south side (of the mosque), toward the east. It occupies, in the (northerly) direction toward the courtyard, two entire galleries and a little more than four spans of the third. It has five corners and five faces; its shape is unusual and difficult to express. Its four (accessible) faces are exactly different from the prayer-direction so that no one can take any one of them for his prayer direction since he would thus deviate from the (true) prayer-direction. I was told by the shaykh . . . Abu Ibrahim Ishaq ibn Ibrahim al-Tunsi that this construction notion was Umar ibn Abd al-Aziz's, for fear lest the faithful might make the tomb building a mosque for the ritual prayer.

From west to east the tomb building has the width of two galleries, and the interior of this space is divided into six aisles. The length of its southern face is 24 spans and the eastern face 30 spans; between the eastern and the northern corner is a face of 39 spans; between the western and the southern corner 24 spans. On this latter side an ebony coffer, worked with geometric designs in sandalwood, and plated with silver so that it shines like a star, is placed to the right of the head of the Prophet; it measures five spans in length, by three wide, by four high. On the side which connects the northern and the western corner there is an opening covered with a veil; it is said that this is the place where the Angel Gabriel descended.

All (five) of the sides of this venerated tomb building extend to a total of 272 spans. They are covered with marble marvelously dressed and well arranged. This marble facing covers a little less than a third of the walls' height. Above it, and covering another third, is a coating of musk and perfume that is blackened and cracked with age. The upper part of the walls is a wooden wainscotting that goes up to the ceiling, since the ceiling of the blessed "Garden" is connected with that of the mosque. Hangings end at the border of the marble. They are blue-green in color with eight- and four-sided geometric designs. Within these polygons are traced white circles and dots. . . .

On the wall facing toward Mecca there is a silver nail opposite the face of the Prophet to mark his venerated visage, and people stand in front of it to say their greetings. At his feet is the head of Abu Bakr the Just, and the head of Umar touches the shoulders of Abu Bakr the Just. For the greeting you stand with your back to the direction of prayer and facing toward Muhammad. The greeting made, you turn toward your right toward Abu Bakr and then toward Umar.

In front of this (southern) wall about twenty silver lamps are hung,

and two golden ones. To the north of the holy "Garden" is a small de-
pression in marble with a prayer-niche on its prayer-direction side. It is
said that this was the chamber of Fatima, and indeed her grave as well.
God alone knows the truth. [IBN JUBAYR 1949–1951: 219–221/Ar.
190]

*The doubt is occasioned, of course, by the fact that Fatima's tomb was
also shown in the nearby Baqiyya* cemetery.*

*Ibn Jubayr next describes the Prophet's pulpit. Here he adverts to the
other meaning of "Garden" (rawda), here called the "little Garden," as an
area—the space between the pulpit and the tomb—rather than the tomb
building itself.*

To the right of the venerated "Garden," at a distance of forty-two
paces, is the venerated pulpit. . . . There are eight paces between this
place and the "little Garden" which is between the tomb and the pulpit
and which is the object of a Prophetic tradition according to which it is
"one of the gardens of Paradise." The faithful come to this "little Garden"
to perform their prayers, and with good reason. Opposite it, on the
Mecca side, is a pillar which is said to cover the remains of the palm-tree
trunk which whimpered for the Prophet, and a piece of it is still visible
in the middle of the pillar; people kiss it and seek out the blessing they
would obtain by touching it and rubbing their cheeks against it. . . .

The venerated pulpit is somewhat less than the height of a man,
five spans wide and five deep; it has eight steps. It has a door in the form
of a wooden lattice which is kept closed and opened (for the sermon)
on Fridays; it measures four and a half spans. The pulpit is covered with
ebony. At its top you can see the place where the Prophet sat; it is
covered with an ebony plank which is not fixed to it but merely prevents
anyone's sitting there. People put their hands in to touch it and then pass
their fingers over their own clothes to get the blessing that comes from
touching this venerated seat. [IBN JUBAYR 1949–1951: 221–222/Ar.
191–192]

CHAPTER 7

Saints and Mystics

1. This World and the Next: The Islamic Preaching

Much in the manner of developed Christianity, the preaching of Islam drew a sharp distinction between this world and its values and that other world that is both the Hereafter and the abode of God.

Know that the life of this world is only a frolic and a mummery, an ornamentation, boasting and bragging among yourselves, and lust for multiplying wealth and children. It is like rain so pleasing to the cultivator for his vegetation which sprouts and swells, and then begins to wither, and you see it turn to yellow and reduced to chaff. There is severe punishment in the Hereafter, but also forgiveness from God and acceptance. As for the life of this world, it is no more than the merchandise of vanity. (Quran 57:20)

Al-Mustawrid ibn Shaddad told that he heard God's Messenger say, "I swear by God that this world in comparison to the world to come is just like one of you putting his finger in the sea. Let him consider what he brings out on it." (Baghawi, *Mishkat al-Masabih* 25.1.1)

Abu Hurayra reported God's Messenger as saying, "The world is the believer's prison and the infidel's Paradise." (Baghawi, *Mishkat al-Masabih* 25.1.1)

Abu Hurayra reported God's Messenger as saying, "The world is accursed and what it contains is accursed, except remembrance of God and what He likes, a learned man or a learner." (Baghawi, *Mishkat al-Masabih* 25.1.1)

Ibn Mas°ud told that God's Messenger slept on a reed mat and got up with the marks of it on his body, so Ibn Mas°ud said, "Messenger of

God, I wish you would order us to spread something out for you and make something (on which you might rest)." He replied, "What do I have to do with the world? In relation to the world I am just like a rider who shades himself under a tree, and then goes off and leaves it." (Baghawi, *Mishkat al-Masabih* 25.1.2)

Ibn Umar told that God's Messenger caught hold of him and said, "Be in the world as though you were a stranger and a wayfarer, and reckon yourself to be among the inhabitants of the grave." (Baghawi, *Mishkat al-Masabih* 25.2.1)

There are echoes too of "Blessed are the poor . . ."

Usama ibn Zayd reported God's Messenger as saying, "I stood at the gate of Paradise, and the majority of those who entered it were poor, the rich being held back, except that those who were to go to Hell were ordered to be sent there. I stood at the gate of Hell, and the majority of those who entered it were women." This tradition is reported by Bukhari and Muslim. (Baghawi, *Mishkat al-Masabih* 25.2.1)

Anas told that the Prophet said: "O God, grant me life as a poor man, cause me to die as a poor man and resurrect me in the company of the poor." Aisha asked him why he said this, and he replied, "Because they will enter Paradise forty years before the rich. Do not turn away a poor man, Aisha, even if all you can give him is half a date. If you love the poor and bring them near you, Aisha, God will bring you near Him on the day of resurrection." (Baghawi, *Mishkat al-Masabih* 25.2.2)

Amr ibn al-Awf reported God's Messenger as saying, "I swear by God that it is not poverty I fear for you, but I fear that worldly goods may be given to you as lavishly as they were to your (pagan) ancestors, that you may vie with one another in desiring them as they did, and that they may destroy you as they destroyed them." (Baghawi, *Mishkat al-Masabih* 25.1.1)

A belief in this Other World of God meant of course embracing its values. The classical collections of Prophetic traditions are filled with reported sayings of the Prophet on the virtues of prayer and fasting, not merely the canonically prescribed prayers and the equally obligatory fast of Ramadan, but the supererogatory performance of these spiritual exercises, though with cautious awareness that any practice attributed to the Prophet might be construed as a precedent for an additional obligation upon all Muslims.

Abu Hurayra and Abu Sa'id reported God's Messenger as saying, "People will not sit remembering God without angels surrounding them, mercy covering them, peace descending upon them, and God mentioning them among those who are with Him." (Baghawi, *Mishkat al-Masibih* 9.2.1)

Abu al-Darda reported God's Messenger as saying, "Would you like me to tell you the best and purest of your deeds in the estimation of your King, those which raise your degrees highest, those which are better for you than spending gold and silver, and better for you than that you should meet your enemy and cut off one another's head?" On receiving a reply in the affirmative, he said, "It is remembering God." (Baghawi, *Mishkat al-Masabih* 9.2.2)

Abdullah ibn Busr told of a desert Arab coming to the Prophet and asking who was the best among men, to which he replied, "Happy is he whose life is long and whose deeds are good." He asked God's Messenger what deed was most excellent, and he replied, "That you should leave the world with the mention of God fresh on your tongue." (Baghawi, *Mishkat al-Masabih* 9.2.2)

Abu Saʿid said God's Messenger was asked who would be the most excellent and most exalted in degree in God's estimation on the day of resurrection, and he replied, "The men and women who make frequent mention of God." He was asked if they would be superior even to the man who had fought in the path of God, and he replied, "Even though he plied his sword among infidels and polytheists till it was broken and smeared with blood, the one who made mention of God would have a more excellent degree than he." (Baghawi, *Mishkat al-Masabih* 9.2.3)

Muʿadh ibn Jabal said, "A man does nothing more calculated to rescue him from God's punishment than making mention of God." (Baghawi, *Mishkat al-Masabih* 9.2.3)

Abu Hurayra reported God's Messenger as stating that God says, "I am with My servant when he remembers Me and his lips move making mention of Me."

Abdullah ibn Shaqiq said that when he asked Aisha whether the Prophet used to fast the whole month of Ramadan, she replied, "I never knew him to fast a whole month except Ramadan, nor to refrain from fasting some part of every month until he died." (Baghawi, *Mishkat al-Masabih* 7.7.1)

Aisha said that God's Messenger used to fast on Mondays and Thursdays. Abu Hurayra reported God's Messenger as saying, "Men's deeds are presented to God on Mondays and Thursdays, and I like mine to be presented when I am fasting." (Baghawi, *Mishkat al-Masabih* 7.7.2)

Abu Hurayra reported God's Messenger as saying, "There is an almsgiving that is applicable to everything, and the almsgiving of the body is fasting. (Baghawi, *Mishkat al-Masabih* 7.7.3)

2. The Historical Origins of the Sufi Movement

Many of the early names to which the title of "Sufi" is attached in Muslim hagiography are little more than that, names alone. Hasan al-Basri is a firmly historical witness, however, and he stands close to the top of the page in every attempt, medieval and modern, to get back to the beginnings of the spiritual discipline that the Muslims call Sufism. He is an important authority for the Spanish philosopher-historian Ibn Khaldun (d. 1406 C.E.), who, as he did with Islamic jurisprudence (chapter 4 above), provides in his Prolegomenon to History a schematic view of the origins of Sufism.

The Science of Sufism. This science belongs to the sciences of religious law that originated in Islam. Sufism is based on the assumption that the method of those people (who later came to be called Sufis) had always been considered by the important early Muslims, the men around Muhammad and the men of the second generation, as well as those who came after them, as the path of true and right guidance. Their approach is based upon constant application to divine worship, complete devotion to God, aversion to the false splendor of the world, abstinence from pleasure, property and position to which the great mass aspires, and retirement from the world into solitude for divine worship. These things were general among the men around Muhammad and the early Muslims. (Ibn Khaldun, *Muqaddima* 6.10) [IBN KHALDUN 1967: 3:76]

The habit of a simple and unworldly life, if not actually the practice of what a later generation understood as asceticism, was traced back, then, to the earliest generation of Muslims, and even to the most eminent and powerful of them, as this account by the early Sufi author al-Kharraz (d. 890 C.E.) illustrates.

When Abu Bakr [Caliph, 632–634 C.E.] succeeded to the leadership, and the world in its entirety came to him in abasement, he did not lift up his head on that account, or make any pretensions; he wore a single garment, which he used to pin together, so that he was known as "the man of the two pins." Umar ibn al-Khattab [Caliph, 634–644 C.E.], who also ruled the world in its entirety, lived on bread and olive-oil; his clothes were patched in a dozen places, some of the patches being of leather; yet there were opened to him the treasures of Khusraw and Caesar. As for Uthman [Caliph, 644–656 C.E.], he was like one of his slaves in appearance; of him it is related that he was seen coming out of one of the gardens with a faggot of firewood on his shoulders, and when questioned on the matter, he said, "I wanted to see whether my soul would refuse." Ali [Caliph, 656–661 C.E.] bought a waistband for four dirhams and a shirt for five dirhams; finding the sleeve of his garment too long, he went to a cobbler and taking his knife, he cut off the sleeve level with the tips of his fingers; yet this same man divided the world right and left. (Kharraz) [Cited by ARBERRY 1950: 32]

It was at that point, at the death of Ali and the accession of the dynasty called the Umayyads, that there occurred a turning in the spiritual direction of Islam, according to what later became a commonly held view of the community's history. Ibn Khaldun resumes:

Then worldly aspirations increased in the second century [= eighth century C.E.] and after. People now inclined towards worldly affairs. At that time, the special name of "Sufis" was given to those who aspired to divine worship. . . . The most obvious etymology (of the term Sufi), if one uses one, is that which connects the word with *al-suf*, because Sufis as a rule were characterized by the fact that they wore woolen garments. They were opposed to people wearing gorgeous garments, and, therefore, they chose to wear wool.

Ibn Khaldun then passes to the transition within the still young Sufi movement from asceticism to mysticism, the latter here characterized by its possession of a "particular kind of perception."

The Sufis came to represent asceticism, retirement from the world and devotion to divine worship. Then, they developed a particular kind of perception which comes about through ecstatic experience. This comes about as follows. Man, as man, is distinguished from all the other animals by his ability to perceive. His perception is of two kinds. He can perceive sciences and matters of knowledge, and these may be certain, hypothetical, doubtful or imaginary. Also, he can perceive "states" persisting in himself, such as joy and grief, anxiety and relaxation, satisfaction, anger, patience, gratefulness and similar things. (Ibn Khaldun, *Muqaddima* 6.16) [IBN KHALDUN 1967: 3:76–78]

These "states" of self-awareness referred to by Ibn Khaldun represent stages in the Sufi's training, as we shall see, and lead eventually to the mystical experience. All of this had been worked out in great detail by Ibn

Khaldun's day. But the road to that point was a long one; the Sufi had to make a place for himself in the Islamic experience, a process that was accompanied by opposition, rejection, suffering, and even on occasion death.

3. Conversions and Affirmations

By all accounts the earliest Muslims to bear the name "Sufi" were ascetics, Muslims whose rejection of "this world" bore all the signs of a religious conversion. Such was certainly the case for the early and much celebrated holy man Ibrahim ibn Adham, a prince of Balkh in eastern Iran who died sometime about 777 C.E.

My father was of Balkh, Ibrahim ibn Adham is reported to have said, and he was one of the kings of Khurasan. He was a man of wealth and taught me to love hunting. One day I was out riding with my dog, when a hare or a fox started. I spurred on my horse; then I heard a voice behind me saying, "It was not for this that you were created. It was not this you were charged to do." I stopped and looked right and left, but I saw no one; and I said, "God curse the devil!" Then I spurred on my horse again; and I heard a voice clearer than before, "O Ibrahim! It was not for this that you were created; it was not this you were charged to do." I stopped once more and looked right and left, but still I saw no one. And I repeated, "God curse the devil!" Then I spurred on my horse once again; and I heard a voice from the bow of my saddle, "O Ibrahim, it was not for this that you were created. It was not this that you were charged to do." I stopped and said, "I have been roused! I have been roused! A warning has come to me from the Lord of the Worlds. Truly, I will not disobey God from this day on, so long as the Lord shall preserve me." Then I returned to my people, and abandoned my horse. I came to one of my father's shepherds, and took his robe and cloak, and put my raiment upon him. Then I went towards Iraq, wandering from land to land. (Abu Nuʿaym, *The Ornaments of the Saints* 7.368) [Cited by ARBERRY 1950: 36]

Or, in the manner of the holy in every religion, the saint is marked as such from birth. The following is told, with an interesting prologue, of Rabiʿa, a famous holy woman of Basra in Iraq who died in 752 or 801 C.E.

If anyone asks, "Why have you included Rabiʿa in the rank of men?" my answer is that the Prophet himself said, "God does not regard your outward forms." The root of the matter is not form, but intention,

as the Prophet said, "Mankind will be raised up according to their intentions." Moreover, if it is proper to derive two-thirds of our religion
from Aisha [referring to the great bulk of Prophetic traditions reported
on the authority of the Prophet's wife Aisha], surely it is permissible to
take religious instruction from a handmaiden of Aisha. When a woman
becomes a "man" in the path of God, she is a man and one cannot any
more call her a woman.

The night when Rabiᶜa came to earth, there was nothing whatsoever in her father's house; for her father lived in very poor circumstances. He did not possess even one drop of oil to anoint her navel;
there was no lamp, and not a rag to swaddle her in. He already had three
daughters, and Rabiᶜa was his fourth, which is why she was called
Rabiᶜa, "the fourth."

"Go to our neighbor So and So and beg him for a drop of oil so I
can light the lamp," his wife said to him. Now the man had entered into
a covenant that he would never ask any mortal for anything. . . . The
poor woman wept bitterly. In that anxious state the man placed his head
on his knees and went to sleep. He dreamed that he saw the Prophet.

"Be not sorrowful," the Prophet bade him. "The girl child who has
just come to earth is a queen among women, who shall be the intercessor for seventy thousand of my community. . . ."

When Rabiᶜa had become a little older, and her mother and father
were dead, a famine came upon Basra, and her sisters were scattered.
Rabiᶜa ventured out and was seen by a wicked man who seized her and
sold her for six dirhams. Her purchaser put her to hard labor.

One day when she was passing along the road a stranger approached her. She fled and, as she ran, she fell headlong and her hand
was dislocated. "Lord God," she cried, bowing her face to the ground,
"I am a stranger, orphaned of mother and father, a helpless prisoner
fallen into captivity, my hand broken. Yet for all this I do not grieve; all
I need is Your good pleasure, to know whether You are well pleased or
not." "Do not grieve," she heard a voice say, "Tomorrow a station will
be yours such that the cherubim in heaven will envy you."

So Rabiᶜa returned to her master's house. By day she continually
fasted and by night she worshiped standing until day.

Her owner one night sees Rabiᶜa at her prayers, a lantern suspended without chain above her head, and whose light fills the house.
He is moved and chastened and gives her her freedom.

She left the house and went into the desert. From the desert she
proceeded to a hermitage where she served God for a while. Then she

determined to perform the pilgrimage and set her face toward the desert (road from Basra to Mecca). She bound her bundle of possessions
on a donkey. In the middle of the desert her donkey died. . . . "O God,"
she cried, lifting her head, "do kings so treat the powerless? You have
invited me to Your House, then in the midst of the way, You have suffered my donkey to die, leaving me alone in the desert."

Hardly had she completed her prayer when her donkey stirred and
rose up. Rabiᶜa placed her load on its back and continued on her way.
. . . She travelled on through the desert for some days, then she halted.
"O God," she cried, "my heart is weary. Where am I going? I am a lump
of clay and Your house is a stone! I need You here."

God spoke unmediated in her heart. "Rabiᶜa, you are travelling in
the life-blood of eighteen thousand worlds. Have you not seen how
Moses prayed for the vision of Me? And I cast a few motes of revelation
upon the mountain, and the mountain shivered into forty pieces. Be
content here in My name!" (Attar, *Recollections of the Saints* 1.73) [ATTAR
1966: 40–43]

*The long process of experience and meditation upon that experience
that constituted the beginnings of the Sufi path in Islam is largely concealed from our eyes. But as occurred in Christianity, the "path" eventually
became a broad and well-posted highway whose every turning had been
charted by those who had gone before. By the time the philosopher-historian Ibn Khaldun came to write his* Prolegomenon *in 1377* C.E., *there
was already an extensive body of Sufi literature, much of it highly theoretical in nature. Indeed, Sufism constituted a well-defined discipline with its
own somewhat ambivalent place in the hierarchy of Muslim religious disciplines, as Ibn Khaldun explains.*

Thus the Sufis had their special discipline, which is not discussed
by other representatives of the religious law. As a consequence, the
science of the religious law came to consist of two kinds. One is the
special field of jurists and muftis. It is concerned with the general laws
governing the acts of divine worship, customary action and mutual deal-
ings. The other is the special field of the "people" [that is, the Sufis]. It
is concerned with pious exertion, self-scrutiny with regard to it, discussion of the different kinds of mystical and ecstatic experience occurring
in the course of it, the mode of ascent from one mystical experience to
another, and the interpretation of the technical terminology of mysticism in use among them.

When the sciences were written down systematically, and when
the jurisprudents wrote works on jurisprudence and the principles of

jurisprudence, on speculative theology, Quran interpretation and other subjects, the Sufis too wrote on their subject. Some Sufis wrote on the laws governing asceticism and self-scrutiny, how to act and not act in imitation of model (saints). That was done by Muhasibi [ca. 781–825 C.E.] in his *Consideration of the Truths of God*. Other Sufi authors wrote on the behavior of Sufis and their different kinds of mystical and ecstatic experiences in the "states." Al-Qushayri [986–1072 C.E.] in his *Letter* and Suhrawardi [1145–1234 C.E.] in his *Connoisseurs of Wisdom*, as well as others did this. Al-Ghazali combined the two matters in his book called *The Revivification*. In it he dealt systematically with the laws governing asceticism and the imitation of models. Then he explained the behavior and customs of the Sufis and commented on their technical vocabulary. (Ibn Khaldun, *Muqaddima* 6.16) [IBN KHALDUN 1967: 3:79–80]

4. Two Sufi Autobiographies: Ibn Abi al-Khayr and al-Ghazali

All these authors regarded by Ibn Khaldun as critical in the formulation of the canons of Sufism are known to us, and one could easily compose a history of Sufism, particularly of its more moderate type, from their theoretical writings on the subject. Let us turn instead to personal statements by two very different men who experienced the Sufi life and left us their recollections: Abu Saʿid ibn Abi al-Khayr (967–1049 C.E.) and al-Ghazali (d. 1111 C.E.).

Whatever else it might eventually become, Sufism began, and to some extent always remained, an exercise in the same kind of self-restraint and even self-chastisement that was present in the early Christian tradition. The annals of Christianity, particularly as that faith was understood and practiced in Syria, are filled with tales of the most extraordinarily severe asceticism, and while Islamic piety rarely indulged in such extremes of self-abasement, physical and psychological severity were not entirely alien to it, as witnessed by this account of the early days of Abu Saʿid ibn Abi al-Khayr. The narrator at the outset is his father, who was curious about the doings of his son and one night followed him.

My son walked on till he reached the Old Cloister. He entered it and shut the gate behind him, while I went up on the roof. I saw him go into a chapel which was in the convent and close the door. Looking through the chapel window, I waited to see what would happen. There was a stick lying on the floor, and it had a rope fastened to it. He took up the stick and tied the end of the rope to his foot. Then, laying the stick across the top of a pit that was in a corner of the chapel, he slung himself head downwards, and began to recite the Quran. He remained in that posture until daybreak, when, having recited the whole Quran, he raised himself from the pit, replaced the stick where he found it, opened the door, came out from the chapel, and commenced to perform his ablution in the middle of the convent. I descended from the roof, hastened home and slept till he came in. (Abu Saʿid, *The Secrets of Oneness* 32.4) [Cited by NICHOLSON 1921: 13–14]

Here it is Abu Saʿid himself who explains his manner of life in those earliest days of his career as a Sufi, and incidentally provides an explanation of why he recited the Quran hanging upside down.

When I was a novice, I bound myself to do eighteen things: I fasted continually; I abstained from unlawful food; I practiced recollection of the name of God uninterruptedly; I kept awake at night; I never reclined on the ground; I never slept but in a sitting posture; I always sat facing the Kaʿba; I never leaned against anything; I never looked at a handsome youth or a woman whom it would have been unlawful for me to see unveiled; I did not beg; I was content and resigned to God's will; I always sat in the mosque and did not go into the market because the Prophet said that the market is the filthiest of places and the mosque the cleanest. In all my acts I was a follower of the Prophet. Every twenty-four hours I completed a recitation of the Quran.

In my seeing I was blind, in my hearing deaf, in my speaking dumb. For a whole year I conversed with no one. People called me a lunatic, and I allowed them to give me that name, relying on the Tradition that a man's faith is not made perfect until he is supposed to be mad. I performed everything I had read or heard of as having been done or commended by the Prophet. Having read that when he was wounded in the foot at the battle of Uhud, he stood on his toes in order to perform his devotions—for he could not set the sole of his foot on the ground—I resolved to imitate him, and standing on tiptoe I performed a prayer of forty genuflections. I modeled my actions, outward and inward, upon the Custom of the Prophet, so that habit at last became nature.

Whatever I had heard or found in books concerning the acts of worship performed by the angels, I performed the same. I had heard and seen in writing that some angels worship God on their heads. Therefore I placed my head on the ground and bade the blessed mother of Abu Tahir tie my toe with a cord and fasten the cord to a peg and then shut the door behind her. Being left alone, I said "O Lord! I do not want myself; let me escape from myself!" and I began a recitation of the entire Quran. When I came to the verse, "God shall suffice you against them, for He hears and knows all" (Quran 2:131), blood poured from my eyes and I was no longer conscious of myself.

At that point began Abu Saʿid's conversion from mere asceticism to the life of a mystic saint. As he himself tells us, what had previously been simply his efforts were now transformed into God's spiritual gifts, the "graces" and "blessings" with which Sufi literature is filled.

Then things changed. Ascetic experiences passed over me of a kind that cannot be described in words, and God strengthened and aided me therein, but I had fancied that all these acts were done by me. The grace of God became manifest and showed me this was not so, and that these acts were acts of divine favor and grace. I repented of my belief and realized that it was mere self-conceit. Now if you say that you will not tread this path because it is self-conceit, I reply that your refusal to tread it is likewise self-conceit, and until you undergo all this, its self-conceit will not be revealed to you. Self-conceit appears only when you fulfill the Law, for self-conceit lies in religion and religion is of the Law. To refrain from religious acts is unbelief, but to perform such acts self consciously is dualism, because if "you" exists and "He" exists, then two exist, and that is dualism. You must put your self away altogether.

I had a cell in which I sat, and sitting there I was enamored of passing-away from myself. A light flashed upon me, which utterly destroyed the darkness of my being. God Almighty revealed to me that I was neither that nor this: that this was His grace even as that was His gift.

Abu Saʿid was well aware of the sudden adulation that accompanied Sufi "celebrity" in medieval Islam, and the equally swift reversal to which all such celebrity is subject.

Then the people began to regard me with great approval. Disciples gathered round me and converted to Sufism. My neighbors too showed their respect for me by ceasing to drink wine. This proceeded so far that a melon-skin I had thrown away was bought for twenty pieces of gold. One day when I was riding on horseback, my horse dropped dung. Eager to gain a blessing, the people came and picked up the dung and smeared their heads and faces with it.

After a time it was revealed to me that I was not the real object of their veneration. A voice cried from the corner of the mosque, "Is not your Lord enough for you?" (Quran 41:53). A light gleamed in my breast and most veils were removed. The people who had honored me now rejected me, and even went before the judge to bear witness that I was an infidel. The inhabitants of every place that I entered declared that their crops would not grow on account of my wickedness. Once, while I was seated in a mosque, a woman went up on to the roof and bespattered me with filth; and still I heard a voice saying, "Is not your Lord enough for you?" The congregation desisted from their prayers, saying, "We will not pray together so long as this madman is in the mosque. . . ."

This joyous transport was followed by a painful contraction of spirit. I opened the Quran and my eye fell on the verse, "We will prove you with evil and with good, to try you; and to Us shall you return" (Quran 21:36), as though God said to me, "All this which I put in your way is a trial. If it is good, it is a trial, and if it is evil, it is a trial. Do not stoop to good or to evil but swell in Me!" Once more my self vanished and His grace was all in all. (Abu Saʿid, *The Secrets of Oneness* 37.8) [Cited by NICHOLSON 1921: 15–17]

What affected people's attitude toward Ibn Abi al-Khayr were changes in his own external behavior. From a severe asceticism he turned to what appeared to be a profligate life-style, luxurious feasts and splendid entertainments filled with song and dance. This caused another ambitious but somewhat naive Sufi to think that perhaps the famous Abu Saʿid had been overrated, a serious miscalculation. He approached the Master.

O Shaykh (he said), I have come in order to challenge you to a forty days' fast. The poor man was ignorant of the Shaykh's novitiate and of his forty years of austerities: he fancied that the Shaykh had always lived in this same manner. He thought to himself, "I will chasten him with hunger and put him to shame in the eyes of the people, and I shall be the object of their regard." On hearing this challenge, the Shaykh said, "May it be blessed!" and spread his prayer rug. His adversary did the like, and they both sat down side by side.

While the ascetic, in accordance with the practice of those who keep a fast of forty days, was eating a certain amount of food, the Shaykh Abu Saʿid ate nothing; and though he never once broke his fast, every morning he was stronger and fatter and his complexion grew more and more ruddy. All the time, by his orders and under his eyes, his dervishes feasted luxuriously and indulged in spiritual concerts, and he himself danced with them. His state was not changed for the worse in any respect. The ascetic, on the other hand, was daily becoming feebler and thinner and paler, and the sight of the delicious viands which were served to the Sufis in his presence worked more and more upon him. At length he grew so weak that he could scarcely rise to perform the obligatory prayers. He repented of his presumption and confessed his ignorance.

When the forty days were finished the Shaykh Abu Saʿid said, "I have complied with your request: now you must do as I say." The ascetic acknowledged this and said, "It is for the Shaykh to command." Abu Saʿid said, "We have sat for forty days and eaten nothing and gone to the privy; now let us sit another forty and eat nothing but never go to the privy." His adversary had no choice but to accept the challenge, though he thought to himself that it was impossible for any human to do such a thing. (Abu Saʿid, *The Secrets of Oneness* 160.18) [Cited by NICHOLSON 1921: 71–72]

The man ended, of course, by becoming the disciple of Abu Saʿid ibn Abi al-Khayr.

Ghazali (d. 1111 C.E.), whose distinguished intellectual career spanned philosophy, theology, and law, was a Sufi as well, and it was chiefly his moderate and sympathetic writing on the subject of Sufism that made the Islamic world a safer place for the sometimes extravagant likes of Ibn Abi al-Khayr. There is an extended treatment of Sufism in his Re-vivification of the Sciences of Religion. *Ghazali gives a personal but still highly schematic and intellectualized sketch of his own search for certitude in the autobiographical* Deliverer from Error. *After experimenting with the other disciplines, Ghazali tells us, he came at length to Sufism.*

When I had finished with those sciences, I next turned with set purpose to the method of Sufism. I knew the complete mystic "way" includes both intellectual belief and practical activity; the latter consists of getting rid of obstacles in the self and stripping off its base characteristics and vicious morals, so that the heart may attain to freedom from what is not God and to constant recollection of Him.

Ghazali, ever the intellectual, begins by reading the Sufi classics.

. . . I thus comprehended their fundamental teachings on the intellectual side, and progressed, as far as is possible by study and oral instruction, in the knowledge of Sufism. It became clear to me, however, that what is most distinctive of Sufism is something which cannot be apprehended by study, but only by tasting, by ecstasy and by moral change. . . . From the sciences I had labored at and the paths I had traversed in my investigation of the revelational and revealed sciences, there had come to me a sure faith in God Most High, in prophethood and the Last Day. These three credal principles were firmly rooted in my being, not through any carefully argued proofs, but by reason of various causes, coincidences and experiences which are not capable of being stated in detail.

It has already become clear to me that I had no hope of the bliss of the world to come save through a God-fearing life and the withdrawal of myself from vain desire. It was clear to me too that the key to all this was to sever the attachment of the heart to worldly things by leaving the mansion of deception and returning to that of eternity.

Next Ghazali, the distinguished professor on the faculty of Islamic law at the university of Baghdad, takes stock of his life.

I considered the circumstances of my life, and realized that I was caught in a veritable thicket of attachments. I also considered my activities, of which the best was my teaching and lecturing, and realized that in them I was dealing with sciences that were unimportant and contributed nothing to the attainment of eternal life. After that I examined my motive in my work of teaching, and realized that it was not a pure desire for the things of God, but that the impulse moving me was the desire for an influential position and public recognition. I saw for certain that I was on the brink of a crumbling bank of sand and in imminent danger of hell-fire unless I set about to mend my ways. . . .

For nearly six months beginning in July 1095 I was continuously tossed about between the attractions of worldly desires and the impulses towards eternal life. In that month the matter ceased to be one of choice and became one of compulsion. God caused my tongue to dry up so that I was prevented from lecturing. One particular day I would make an effort to lecture to gratify the hearts of my following, but my tongue would not utter a single word nor could I accomplish anything at all.

Now in the full grip of spiritual impotence, Ghazali quits Baghdad, his family, and his post there and disappears into a ten-year seclusion, some of it spent in Jerusalem, some on pilgrimage to Mecca, and two years on spiritual retreat in Damascus.

In due course I entered Damascus and there I remained for nearly two years with no other occupation than the cultivation of retirement and solitude, together with religious and ascetic exercises, as I busied myself purifying my soul, improving my character and cleansing my heart for the constant recollection of God Most High, as I had learnt from my study of Sufism. I used to go into retreat for a period in the mosque of Damascus, going up the minaret of the mosque for the whole day and shutting myself in so as to be alone. . . .

I continued at this stage for the space of ten years, and during these periods of solitude there were revealed to me things innumerable and unfathomable. This much I shall say about that in order that others may be helped: I learnt with certainty that it is above all the Sufis who walk on the road of God; their life is the best life, their method the soundest method, their character the purest character; indeed, were the intellect of the intellectuals and the learning of the learned and the scholarship of the scholars, who are versed in the profundity of revealed truth, brought together in the attempt to improve the life and character of the Sufis, they would find no way of doing so; for to the Sufis all movement and all rest, whether external or internal, brings illumination from the lamp of prophetic revelation; and behind the light of prophetic revelation there is no other light on the face of the earth from which illumination may be received. (Ghazali, *Deliverer* 122–132) [GHAZALI 1953: 54–60]

5. "No Monasticism in Islam"

Christian monks in the Near East were to some extent characterized by their association with a woolen cloak—their version of the "religious habit" of Western Christendom—an association that at least suggests that "Sufism" owed more than a passing resemblance to Christian monastic practices on the Syrian steppe. Monks and monasticism are in fact mentioned in the Quran. In two of the citations it is not so much a question of the institution of monasticism as of praise for monks who "are not proud" (5:82) or the condemnation of those Christian monks "who devour the wealth of mankind wantonly" or "hoard up gold and silver and spend it not in the way of God" (9:34). If this were the end of it, one would assume that Muhammad neither admired nor condemned Christian monasticism as such. But there is another, somewhat longer passage on the subject that is far more problematic. It occurs in the midst of the now familiar history of God's revelation.

We sent Noah and Abraham, and We gave prophethood to their progeny and the Book, and some of them were well-directed, but many of them were disobedient. Then in their train we sent Our apostles, and succeeding them Jesus, son of Mary, and gave him the Gospel, and put into the hearts of his followers and caused Our messengers, God declares, to follow in their [that is, Noah and Abraham and their seed] footsteps; and We caused Jesus, son of Mary, to follow, and gave him the Gospel, and in the hearts of those who followed him we placed compassion and kindness. And monasticism, they created it, which had not been prescribed for them by Us except for seeking the pleasure of God; yet they did not observe it as it should have been rightly observed. (Quran 57:27)

And monasticism . . . : The meaning, and so the translation, of this bit of the verse is by no means certain. Is "monasticism" in parallel with "compassion and kindness," a virtuous practice begun by the Christians of their own volition, or is "monasticism" contrasted with what immediately precedes, a blameworthy human innovation? In Arabic the verse yields both meanings, and its inherent ambiguity is reflected in early Muslim comments upon it, as in this example from Muhasibi (d. 837 C.E.).

God blamed those among the Israelites [that is, the Christians] who, having instituted the monastic life to which He had not previously obliged them, did not observe it in an exact fashion. And He said "this monastic life which they instituted; We ordained it not for them. . . ."

There is disagreement on this verse. Mujahid interprets it as "We have not ordained it for them only to make them desire to conform themselves to the divine pleasure," that is to say, "We have prescribed it. . . . God placed in them, for their own good, the seeds of the monastic life, and then reprimanded them for abandoning it." But Abu Imama al-Bahili and others comment upon it as follows: "We have not prescribed, that is to say, it was not We who ordained this. They instituted it only to please God and even so God blamed them for abandoning it." This latter opinion is the more probable and one which embraces most of the scholars of the community. [MASSIGNON 1968: 149]

We cannot say which in fact is the more probable interpretation, but Muhasibi is certainly correct in maintaining that the reading of the verse in a pejorative sense—namely, that monasticism is a Christian innovation, unrequired, even undesired, by God—became the common interpretation of this verse among Muslims. It is no surprise then that there soon began to circulate a tradition on the subject attributed to Muhammad himself. "No monasticism in Islam," the Prophet is reported to have said.

6. Monks and Sufis

There was in fact no monasticism in Islam, not in the Christian sense of individuals or groups removing themselves from the world and society and living under perpetual vows of poverty, chastity, and obedience. But the spirituality of Muslims and Christians often took parallel and very similar paths, and both the similarities and the differences appear in this advice given to the aspiring Sufi novice by one of the great masters, Ibn al-Arabi (1164–1240 C.E.) of Murcia.

Among the things you must possess, my brother, is (the grace) not to live at the expense of other people, to be a burden to no one, to accept no support from man either for yourself or anyone else, but to practice your own trade and be abstemious in the matter of your living expenses. (Exercise restraint) also in your words and glances on all occasions, whether you are moving about or are stationary. Be not extravagant in matters of housing or dress or food, for what is lawful (therein) is but little and leaves no room for lavishness. . . .

Among the things you must possess, my friend, is (the grace of doing with but) little food, for (abstinence) in this and cheerfulness in obedience drives away laziness. You must be careful to apportion out your time by day and by night. As for the hours when the religious law summons you to stand before God, they are the five prayer periods for the canonical prayers. But beyond them are the other times consecrated by the custom of the Prophet. So if you are a craftsman, labor diligently to make enough in one day to provide your needs for several days. If you are a business man, do not hasten away from your place of prayer after the dawn prayer until the sun has risen, nor after the afternoon prayer until the sun has set. . . . Do not sleep until you are quite overcome by slumber. Do not eat save what is needful, nor dress save as is necessary to guard against heat and cold, with the intention of covering the genitals and removing a peremptory impediment to the worship of God. . . .

Among the things you must possess is (the grace of) having an accounting with yourself, a seasonable examination of your innermost thoughts, putting a shamefacedness before God as the raiment on your heart, for if you possess a true feeling of shame before God you will prevent your heart from harboring fancies which God would find blameworthy, or from being moved by emotions with which God Most High would not be pleased. We ourselves used formerly to have a master who was accustomed to record his emotional states during the day in a book that he had, and when night came he would set the pages in front of him and have an accounting with himself for what was written therein. . . .

Take care to be continent. That is, avoid everything that would leave an impression on your soul. . . . If you live in that state of continence which is the foundation of religion and the path to God, your works will thrive and your undertakings be successful, your condition in life will prosper, supernatural blessings will hasten toward you, and you will be guided by divine care in all your affairs. We have no doubt about it. But whenever you turn aside from the path of continence and go straying in every valley (of desire), God departs from you and leaves you to yourself, so that Satan gets the mastery of you. (Ibn al-Arabi, *A Treatise on What the Novice Must Possess*) [JEFFERY 1962: 643–645, 653]

At times even the externals of the two types of spiritual endeavor, that of the monk and that of the Sufi, bore remarkable similarities, as one Muslim had occasion to observe. The era is the eleventh century, the Latin Crusader century in Palestine, and it is a community of Christian monks that first attracts the attention of Usama.

I visited the tomb of John [the Baptist], the son of Zachariah—God's blessing on both of them—in the village of Sebaste in the province of Nablus [that is, the biblical Samaria]. After I said my prayers, I went into the square that was bounded on one side by the holy precinct (where the tomb was located). I found a half-closed gate, opened it and entered a church. Inside were about ten old men, their bare heads as white as combed cotton. They were facing eastward, and wore [embroidered?] on their breasts staffs ending in crossbars turned up like the rear of a saddle [that is, some form of a cross, as Usama likely knew very well]. They swore their oaths on this sign, and gave hospitality to those who needed it. The sight of their piety touched my heart, but at the same time it displeased and saddened me, for I had never seen such zeal and devotion among the Muslims.

I brooded on this experience for some time, until one day, as Muᶜin al-Din and I were passing the Peacock House, he said to me. "I want to dismount here and visit the shaykhs." "Certainly," I said, and so we dismounted and went into a long building set at an angle to the road. At first I thought that there was no one there. Then I saw about a hundred prayer-mats and on each one of them a Sufi, his face expressing a peaceful serenity, and his body humble devotion. This was a reassuring sight, and I gave thanks to Almighty God that there were among Muslims men of even more zealous devotion than those Christian priests. Before this I had never seen Sufis in their convent and so was ignorant of the way they lived. (Usama, *Book of the Staff* 528–529)

A century later, in 1183 C.E., the Muslim traveler Ibn Jubayr likewise had occasion to note communities of ascetics, now in Damascus, and he too was impressed and edified.

Ribats for Sufis, which are here called *khanaqas*, are numerous. They are adorned residences; water flows through all of them and they present the most delicious prospect imaginable. The members of this type of Sufi organization live like kings here since God had provided for them even beyond the necessities and so freed their minds from any concern for earning a living, and thus they can devote themselves entirely to His service. He has lodged them in halls which give them a foretaste of those of Paradise. So these fortunate men, the most favored of the Sufis, enjoy by God's favor the blessings of both this world and the next. They follow a praiseworthy vocation and their life in common is conducted in an admirable fashion.

Ibn Jubayr observed, and obviously approved of, something else new and unusual about the Sufi life, their manner of prayer.

Their manner of worship is peculiar to them. Their custom of assembling for highly charged musical recitals is most pleasant. Sometimes, so carried away are some of these rapt ascetics when they are under the influence of this condition, that they can scarcely be thought of as belonging to this world at all. (Ibn Jubayr, *Travels* 284)

7. Sufi Communities

Ibn Jubayr has a name for the Sufis' common lodging, ribat, *a familiar term to him, though in Damascus, he explains, they are called by the less familiar* khanaqa. *This latter, a Sufi cloister or convent, was the third, and in the end the most common, of a trio of institutions that served the needs and ends of ascetics and mystics in Islam.*

The oldest of the three was, as Ibn Jubayr intimates, the ribat. *By tradition this was originally a fortified keep to protect the lands and coasts of Islam, but in the course of time it had evolved into a kind of cloistered hospice for Muslims who for reasons of need—widows were often housed in them—or by preference chose to separate themselves from the world. In the end the* ribat *became totally identified with Sufism, though it had neither the personal stamp of the shrine-tomb (zawiya) nor the official character and internal organization of what seems very akin to a Christian monastery—the text of Usama already suggests the comparison—the* khanaqa.

If the Sufi convent had some of the features of the Christian monastery, the shrine-tomb corresponded to another development in Christian spirituality. The earliest Christian holy men attracted others to themselves and provided both a model and an ideal for those admirers to follow. The shaykh of the Islamic tradition had much the same effect: his sanctity drew others to himself and so his quarters, perhaps enlarged to permit others to lodge there as well became a very loosely organized school, a "way" (tariqa), as the Muslims called it.

Most Sufis passed across the terrain of asceticism and spiritual exercises in the company of an accomplished master (murshid, pir). At first that elder may have been simply a skilled and experienced director of souls, but eventually that ideal was replaced, as it was in Christianity, by the notion of a charismatic guide, a "spiritual father" who possessed the gift of divine grace (baraka). It was the murshid, *in any event, who introduced the novice into two of the most common practices of Sufism, the "recollection" (dhikr) and the "hearing" (sama˶). The* dhikr *has its spiritual, internal sense of recollecting God's blessings, but its more visible form in Sufism is the repetition of set formulas, notably the Muslim profession of faith or the ninety-nine names of Allah. The repetition was rhythmical and often accompanied, as was the "Jesus-prayer" used to the same end in Christianity, by controlled breathing. The ecstatic state of "annihilation" (fana), which was for the Sufi a natural antecedent of union with the Divine, was often accompanied by an elaborate ritual of singing and dancing within which the* dhikr *might be commingled. This latter,* sama˶ *or "spiritual concert," as it has been called, though highly characteristic of certain Sufi associations such as the whirling dervishes, was not everywhere approved or accepted in Islam. Why some more sober Muslims might be scandalized becomes apparent in Edward Lane's account of* dhikrs *of the more extravagant type that he witnessed in Cairo in 1825 and described in chapter 24 of his* Account of the Manners and Customs of the Modern Egyptians.

At the shaykh's death he was often buried in the place where he had lived, and so in the final stage of its evolution the zawiya *was both a shrine and a tomb, and not always on a modest scale. Ibn Battuta describes a tomb-shrine he visited near Wasit in Iraq in 1327 C.E.*

This gave me the opportunity of visiting the grave of the saint Abu al-Abbas Ahmad al-Rifa˶i [d. 1182 C.E.], which is set at a village called Umm Ubayda, one day's journey from Wasit. . . . It is a vast convent in which there are thousands of poor brethren. . . . When the afternoon prayers have been said, drums and kettle drums were beaten and the poor brethren began to dance. After this they prayed the sunset prayer and brought in the repast, consisting of rice-bread, fish, milk and dates.

After the meal there begins the community "recollection" (dhikr), the widespread form of Sufi devotion already noted by Ibn Jubayr; it is performed in this instance under the direction of the master of the tomb-shrine together with his adepts. Shaykh Ahmad, it is noted, was a lineal descendant of the saint buried there. Finally, the "Rifaᶜi" version of a "spiritual concert" was considered notorious even in its own day.

When all had eaten and prayed the first night prayer, they began to recite their "recollection," with the shaykh Ahmad sitting on the prayer-carpet of his ancestor above mentioned, when they began the musical recital. They had prepared loads of fire-wood which they kindled into a flame, and went dancing into the midst of it; some of them rolled in the fire, and others ate it in their mouths, until finally they extinguished it entirely. This is their regular custom, and it is the peculiar characteristic of this corporation of Ahmadi brethren. Some of them will take a large snake and bite its head with their teeth until they bite it clean through. [IBN BATTUTA 1959–1962: 273–274]

The community resident within one of these convents or tomb-shrines might be formal or informal, loosely or tightly structured, made up of permanent members or with transient "sojourners." Where the life and the community was more formal, it was associated with a "way," practices and blessings modeled on and derived from a saintly master.

Spiritual attraction and spiritual authority came together to form the Sufi "orders," also called tariqas *or "ways." These "orders," which were generally neither monastic nor enclosed, and so somewhat different from the Christian religious orders, had an immense popular appeal in Islam—not least because they were a social and spiritual reaction to the increasingly clerical and legal character of what had come to be official Islam, which was dominated by a rabbinate with powerful economic, social, and political connections. More, the Islamic* tariqa *was far more charismatic and had a greater orientation toward a master-novice relationship than its Christian, and particularly its Western Christian, counterpart. In the Sufi reception and training of postulants, for example, we can observe both the similarities to and differences from Christian practice. Ibn Battuta describes the arrival of a postulant, who has already had some training, at the gates of a Cairo convent.*

When a new arrival makes his appearance, he has to take up his stand at the gateway of the convent, girded about the middle, with a prayer-rug slung over his back, his staff in his right hand, and his ablution-jug in his left. The gatekeeper informs the steward who goes out and ascertains from what country he has come, what convents he has resided in during his journey (or earlier training), and who was his initiator. If he is satisfied with the truth of his replies, he brings him into the convent, arranges a suitable place for him to spread out his prayer-mat, and shows him the washroom. The postulant then restores himself to a state of ritual cleanliness, goes to his mat, ungirds himself, and prays two prostrations. After this he clasps the hands of the shaykh [that is, the *murshid* or spiritual master] and of those who are present and takes his seat among them. (Ibn Battuta, *Travels* 1.20)

The postulant has become a novice and is set upon the course of his spiritual training.

The Sufi masters observe the following rule. When a novice joins them with the purpose of renouncing the world, they subject him to a spiritual training for the space of three years. If he fulfills the requirements of this discipline, well and good; otherwise they declare that he cannot be admitted to the Path. The first year is devoted to the service of the people, the second year to service of God, and the third year to watching over his own heart.

At the end of his three-year training and probation, the novice is ready for investiture with the patched Sufi cloak, the "religious habit" of this way of life.

The adept, then, who has attained the perfection of saintship takes the right course when he invests the novice with the Sufi cloak after a period of three years during which he has educated him in the necessary discipline. In respect of the qualifications which it demands, the Sufi cloak is comparable to a winding sheet: the wearer must resign all his hopes of the pleasures of life, and purge his heart of all sensual delights, and devote his life entirely to the service of God. (Hujwiri, *The Unveiling*) [HUJWIRI 1911: 54–55]

8. Convent Life in Islam

Sufi convent life evolved over a long period of time in Islam, from the most informal, almost anarchical arrangements, to institutions that rivaled Christendom's orderly monasteries. The first example here is from Muqaddasi, a professional traveler roaming the "Abode of Islam" sometime before 980 C.E., when Sufi congregations were still grasping for a sense of themselves.

When I entered Sus [a town in southwestern Iran] I went to the main mosque to seek out a shaykh whom I might question concerning certain points of Prophetic tradition. It happened that I was wearing a cloak of Cypriot wool and a Basran waist-wrapper and so I was directed to a congregation of Sufis. As I approached they assumed that I too was a Sufi and welcomed me with open arms. They settled me among them and began questioning me. Then they sent a man with food. I felt uneasy about taking the food since I had had nothing to do with such (Sufi) congregations before this. They expressed surprise at my reluctance and my not joining in their rituals. But I felt drawn to associate myself with this congregation and find out about their method, and learn the true nature of Sufism. I said to myself, "This is your chance, here where nobody knows you."

I cast off all restraint in their regard. . . . At one time I joined in their antiphonal singing, on another occasion I shouted with them, and on another recited poems with them. I went with them to visit hospices and to engage in religious recitals, with the result that I won a remarkably high place in the affections of both the Sufis and the people there. I gained a great reputation; I was visited for my virtue and was sent presents of clothes and money, which I accepted but straightway handed over untouched to the Sufis, since I was well off. I spent every day in my considerable devotions, and they imagined that I did it out of piety. People began touching me and spreading reports of my fame, saying that they had never seen a more excellent ascetic. So it continued until, when the time came that I had penetrated into their secrets and learned all that I wished, I just ran away from them in the middle of the night and by the morning I was well away. (Muqaddasi 415)

Three and a half centuries later, when Ibn Battuta is describing the convents of Cairo ca. 1355 C.E., the institutional landscape looks very different.

Each convent in Cairo is affected to the use of a separate congregation of ascetics [here in Arabic, a *fakir*; the Persian equivalent is a dervish] most of whom are Persians, men of good education and adepts in the "way" of Sufism. Each has a shaykh and a warden, and the organization of their affairs is admirable. It is one of their customs in the matter of their food that the steward of the house comes in the morning to the dervishes, each of whom then specifies what food he desires. When they assemble for meals, each person is given his bread and soup in a separate dish, none sharing with another. They eat twice a day. They receive winter clothing and summer clothing and a monthly allowance varying from 20 to 30 *dirhams* each. Every Thursday evening they are given sugar cakes, soap to wash their clothes, the price of admission to the bath house and oil to feed their lamps. These men are celibate; the married men have separate convents. Among the stipulations required of them are attendance at the five daily prayers, spending the night in the *khanaqa* and assembly in mass in a chapel within the convent. [IBN BATTUTA 1959–1962: 44]

Or here, in even broader strokes, of Damascus of the same era:

The people of Damascus vie with one another in the building and endowment of mosques, religious houses, colleges and shrines. . . . Every man who comes to the end of his resources in any district of Damascus finds without exception some means of livelihood opened to him, either as a prayer-leader in a mosque, or as a reciter in a law school or by occupation [of a cell] in a mosque, where his daily requirements are supplied to him, or by recitation of the Quran, or employment as a keeper at one of the blessed sanctuaries, or else he may be included in the company of Sufis who live in the convent, in receipt of a regular allowance for upkeep money and clothing. Anyone who is a stranger there living on charity is always protected from [having to earn it at] the expense of his self-respect and dignity. Those who are manual workers or in domestic service find other means of livelihood, for example as guardian of an orchard or intendant of a mill or in charge of children, going with them in the morning to their lessons and coming back with them in the evening, and anyone who wishes to pursue a course of studies or devote himself to the religious life receives every aid to the execution of his purpose. [IBN BATTUTA 1959–1962: 149–150]

9. The Lamp in the Niche

Asceticism is a life-style, a process, and though in both Christianity and Islam the way of life it characterized was understood to have its own merits and its own rewards, eventually in both traditions it came to be regarded as the preparatory means to an even higher, and far rarer, state, the experience of the divine: the devout Sufi might also aspire to be a mystic.

The scriptural accounts of Moses on Sinai and Jesus on Tabor served, when and where needed, as Jewish and Christian paradigms of the vision of God. The Muslim had no such straightforward narrative text in the Quran to certify Muhammad for the same purpose, and so the mystics of Islam turned instead for their inspiration to the famous "Light Verse."

God is the Light of the heavens and the earth.
The semblance of His Light is that of the niche in which is a
    lamp, the flame within the glass, the glass as it were a
    glittering star, lit with the oil of a blessed tree, the

olive, neither of the East nor of the West, whose oil
appears to light up even though fire touches it not—
light upon light.
God guides to His Light whom He will.
So does God advance precepts [or "allegories"] for men,
For God has knowledge of every thing.
(Quran 24:35)

The last sentence in the verse reads like an open invitation to allegorical exegesis, and so it was generally interpreted, here from the work entitled The Pure in the Interpretation of the Quran *by the Shi͑ite scholar al-Kashi (d. 1505 C.E.). His interpretation, which is overtly Shi͑ite in intent, goes back, as he tells us, to another, much earlier eminence in that tradition, Ibn Babuya al-Qummi (d. 939 C.E.). And Qummi's authorities are no less than the fifth and sixth Shi͑ite Imams, Muhammad al-Baqir (d. 731 C.E.) and Ja͑far al-Sadiq (d. 756 C.E.).*

In *The Oneness* (of al-Qummi) it is reported, on the authority of al-Sadiq: What is at question here is a simile that God has fashioned for us.

God is the Light of the Heavens and the Earth: Just so, said al-Sadiq.

His Light: al-Sadiq said: This refers to Muhammad.

That of a niche: al-Sadiq said that what is meant here is Muhammad's breast.

In which is a lamp: al-Sadiq said: In which is the light of knowledge, that is, of prophecy.

The flame within the glass: al-Sadiq said: The knowledge of the Messenger of God went forth from the latter into the heart of Ali.

. . . neither of the East nor the West: According to al-Sadiq these words refer to the Commander of the Believers, Ali ibn Abi Talib, who was neither a Jew nor a Christian.

Whose oil appears to light up even though fire touches it not: al-Sadiq said: The knowledge would issue forth from the mouth of the knowing one of the family of Muhammad [that is, Ali] even if Muhammad had not spoken it.

Light upon light: al-Sadiq said that this means from one Imam to the next.

Then Kashi turns to another Shi͑ite commentator, al-Tabarsi (d. 1153 C.E.) for a somewhat more general interpretation of the same verse.

It is said . . . (by Tabarsi) from the Imam al-Baqir in a Tradition that the verse "God is the Light of the heavens and the earth" means: "I [that is, God] am the rightly guided director of the heavens and the earth. The knowledge that I have given, namely, My light through which the guidance results, 'is like a niche wherein is a lamp.' The niche is the heart of Muhammad, and the lamp is his light, wherein lies knowledge." Further, God's words "the flame in a glass" mean: "I [that is, God] want to lay hold of you and what is with you so that I might manifest the Executor [a standard Shi'ite designation for Ali] like the flame in the glass, 'as it were a glittering star.' Then will I give men news of the excellence of the Executor."

Lit with the oil of a blessed tree: The root of that blessed tree is Abraham. This is referred to in God's words: "The mercy of God and His blessings be upon you, O people of the House. Surely he [that is, Abraham] is worthy of praise and glory" (Quran 11:76). . . .

That is neither of the East nor the West means: You are neither Jews, so that you would perform the prayer facing toward the west [that is, Jerusalem] nor Christians, so that you would face toward the east. Rather you follow the creed of Abraham, of whom God has said: "No, in truth Abraham was neither a Jew nor a Christian, but a *hanif* who had submitted to God. Certainly he was never one of the idolaters" (Quran 3:60). (Kashi *ad. loc.*)

10. What Is the Mystic Way?

In section 4 of this chapter we followed the jurist and theologian Ghazali (d. 1111 C.E.) on his voyage of discovery of Sufism as he described it in his Deliverer from Error. *At the end of his quest he attempts to define what he has found, beginning with a comparison with the ablution that purifies a Muslim for prayer.*

In general, then, how is the mystic way described? The purifying which is the first condition of it is the purification of the heart completely from what is other than God Most High; the key to it, which corresponds to the opening act of adoration in prayer, is the sinking of the heart completely in the recollection of God; and the end of it is complete annihilation in God. At least this is its end relative to those first steps which almost come within the sphere of choice and personal responsibility; but in reality in the actual "way" it is the first step, what comes before it being, as it were, the antechamber for those who are journeying towards it.

With this first stage of the "way" there begin the revelations and visions. The mystics in their waking state now behold angels and the

spirits of the prophets; they hear these speaking to them and are instructed by them. Later, a higher stage is reached; instead of beholding
forms and figures, they come to stages in the "way" which it is hard to
describe in language; if a man attempts to express these, his words
inevitably contain what is clearly erroneous.

In general what the mystics manage to attain is nearness to God;
some, however, would conceive of this as "infusion," some as "union,"
and some as "identity" (with God). All that is erroneous. He who has
attained the mystic state need do no more than say that "Of the things
I do not remember, what was, was; think it good; do not ask an account
of it." . . .

In general, the man to whom He has granted no immediate experience at all, apprehends no more of what prophetic revelation really is
than the name alone. The miraculous graces given to the saints are in
truth the beginnings of the prophecy, and that was the first "state" of the
Messenger of God (peace be upon him) when he went out to Mount
Hira, and was given up entirely to his Lord, and worshiped Him so that
the bedouin said, "He loves his Lord passionately."

Now this is a mystical "state" which is realized in immediate experience by those who walk in the way leading to it. Those to whom it is
not granted to have the immediate experience can become assured of it
by trial [that is, observation of Sufis] and by hearsay, if they have sufficiently numerous opportunities of associating with mystics to understand that [that is, the mystical experience] with certainty by means of
what accompanies the states. Whoever sits in their company derives
from them this faith; and no one who sits in their company is pained.
(Ghazali, *Deliverer* 132–135) [GHAZALI 1953: 60–62]

*Ibn Khaldun too attempts to explain the Sufi experience, though now
not through the sensibilities of one who had himself traveled the path but
from the perspective of the cultural historian.*

Mystical exertion, retirement, and the recollection exercise are as
a rule followed by the removal of the veil of sensual perception. The Sufi
beholds divine worlds which a person subject to the senses cannot. The
spirit belongs to those worlds. The reason for the removal of the veil is
the following. When the spirit turns from external sense perception to
inner perception, the senses weaken and the spirit grows strong. It gains
predominance and a new growth. The recollection exercise helps to
bring that about. It is like food to make the spirit grow. The spirit continues to grow. It had been knowledge; now it becomes vision. The veil
of sensual perception is removed, and the soul realizes its essential exis-

tence. This is identical with perception. The spirit now is ready for the holy gifts, for the sciences of divine presence, and for the outpouring of the Deity. Its essence realizes its own true character and draws close to the highest sphere, the sphere of the angels.

The removal of the veil often happens to people who exert themselves in mystical exercise. They perceive the realities of existence as no one else does. They also perceive many future happenings in advance. With the help of their minds and psychic powers they are active among the lower existents, which thus become obedient to their will. The great Sufis do not think much of the removal of the veil and of activity among the lower existents. They give no information about the reality of anything they have not been ordered to discuss. They consider it a tribulation when things of that sort occur to them, and try to escape them whenever they afflict them.

By the "great Sufis" Ibn Khaldun means the earliest generation of Muslims, beginning with the men of Muhammad's own generation. Though they received abundant visitations of the divine grace, they paid little attention to such manifestations. The self-conscious pursuit of such experiences set in only at a later date, among more recent mystics.

Recent mystics have turned their attention to the removal of the veil and the discussion of perceptions beyond sensual perception. Their ways of mystical exercise in this respect differ. They have taught different methods of mortifying the sensual perception and nourishing the reasoning spirit with recollection exercises, so that the soul might fully grow and attain its own essential perception. When this happens they believe that the whole of existence is encompassed by the perceptions of the soul, that the essences of existence are revealed to them, and that they perceive the reality of all the essences from the divine throne to light rain. This was said by al-Ghazali in the *Revivification*, after he had mentioned the forms of spiritual exercises. . . .

The recent Sufis who have occupied themselves with this kind of removal of the veil talk about the real character of the higher and lower existents and about the real character of the kingdom, the spirit, the throne, the seat, and similar things. Those who did not share their approach were not able to understand their mystical and ecstatic experiences in this respect. The muftis partly approve of these Sufis and partly accept them. Arguments and proofs are of no use in deciding whether the Sufi approach should be rejected or accepted, since it belongs to intuitive experience. (Ibn Khaldun, *Muqaddima* 6.16) [IBN KHALDUN 1967: 3:81–83]

11. Junayd on Oneness of and with God

It is not always easy to understand where Ibn Khaldun is drawing his systematic line between the "earlier" and "later Sufis," but the Sufi Junayd (d. 910 C.E.) certainly falls in the very heart of the earlier category. A Baghdad master, he stands midway between the Sufi pioneer Muhasibi (d. 837 C.E.) and his erstwhile disciple, the far more extreme Hallaj, executed at Baghdad in 922 C.E.

Like Muhasibi and most of the other "sober" Sufis, Junayd was a skilled director of souls, as this brief analysis indicates.

There are three types of people: the man who seeks and searches, the man who reaches the door and stays there, and the man who enters and remains.

As for the man who seeks God, he goes toward Him guided by a knowledge of the religious precepts and duties (of Islam), concentrating on the performance of all external observances toward God. Regarding the man who reaches the doorway and stays there, he finds his way there by means of his internal purity, from which he derives his strength. He acts toward God with internal concentration. Finally, as for the man who enters into God's presence with his whole heart and remains before Him, he excludes the vision of anything other than God, noting God's every sign to him, and ready for whatever his Lord may command. This readiness is characteristic of the man who recognizes the Oneness of God. [JUNAYD 1962: 176]

This last perception of the "Oneness of God," an expression that in Arabic also does service as "Oneness with God," was for Junayd and his ninth-century Baghdad contemporaries both the touchstone and the climax of the mystical experience. It was not an easy notion either to grasp or to describe. Although Junayd defined the "Oneness of/with God" in typically aphoristic fashion as "the separation of the Eternal from the contingent"— a phrase not uncommonly offered by his successors as a definition of Sufism, or rather of mysticism purely and simply—he also addressed the central concept of Oneness in a somewhat fuller fashion.

Know that the first condition of the worship of God—may He be exalted and magnified—is the knowledge of God, and the basis of the knowledge of God is the recognition of His being One, and that His Oneness precludes the possibility of describing God in terms of responses to the questions "How?" or "Where?" or "When?" . . .

God's Oneness connotes belief in Him. From belief follows confirmation which in turn leads to knowledge of Him. Knowledge of Him
implies obedience to His commands, obedience carries with it the ascent towards Him, which leads ultimately to reaching Him.

*This apparent success in the mystical quest leads only to a further
paradox, however.*

When God is attained His manifestation can be expounded, but
from His manifestation there also follows bewilderment which is so
overwhelming that it inhibits the possibility of the exposition of God,
and as a result of losing this manifestation of God the elected worshiper
is unable to describe God. And there, when the worshiper is unable to
describe God, he finds the true nature of his existing for God. And from
this comes the vision of God, together with the loss of his individuality.
And with the loss of his individuality he achieves absolute purity . . . he
has lost his personal attributes: . . . he is wholly present in God . . .
wholly lost to self.

*But then there is an inevitable return to a more normal condition,
though not without permanent alterations in spiritual temperament.*

He is existent in both himself and in God after having been existent in God and non-existent in himself. This is because he has left the
drunkenness of God's overwhelming and come to the clarity of sobriety. Contemplation is once again restored to him, so that he can put
everything in its right place and assess it correctly. Once more he assumes his individual attributes, after the "obliteration" his personal qualities persist in him and in his actions in this world, when he has reached
the height of spiritual perfection granted by God, he becomes a pattern
for his fellow men. [JUNAYD 1962: 171–172]

Know that this sense of the Oneness of God exists in people in four
different ways. The first is the sense of Oneness possessed by ordinary
people. Then there is the sense shared by those well versed in formal
religious knowledge. The other two types are experienced by the elect
who have esoteric knowledge. [JUNAYD 1962: 176]

*God's Oneness is in fact the cornerstone of Islam—every Muslim's
profession of faith begins with the statement that "There is no god by the
God . . ."—and Junayd bases his analysis on its simple assertion.*

As for the sense of Oneness possessed by ordinary people, it consists in the assertion of God's Oneness, in the disappearance of any notion of gods, opposites, equals or likenesses to God, but with the persis-

tence of hopes and fears in forces other than God. This level of Oneness has a certain degree of efficacy since the simple assertion of God's Oneness does in fact persist.

As for the conception of Oneness shared by those who are well versed in religious knowledge, it consists not only in the assertion of God's Oneness, in the disappearance of any conception of gods, opposites, equals or likenesses to God, but also in the performance of the positive commands (of religion) and the avoidance of that which is forbidden, so far as external action is concerned, all of this being the result of their hopes, fears and desires. This level of Oneness likewise possesses a degree of efficacy since there is a public demonstration of the Oneness of God.

As for the first type of esoteric Oneness, it consists in the assertion of the Oneness of God, the disappearance of the conception of things referred to, combined with the performance of God's command externally and internally, and the removal of hopes and fears in forces other than God, all of this the result of ideas that conform with the adept's awareness of God's presence with him, with God's call to him and his answer to God.

A second type of esoteric Oneness consists in existing without individuality before God with no intermediary between, becoming a figure over which His decrees pass in accordance with His omnipotence, a soul sunk in the flooding sea of His Oneness, all sense lost of himself, God's call to him and his response to God. It is a stage wherein the devotee has achieved a true realization of the Oneness of God in true nearness to Him. He is lost to both sense and action because God fulfills in him what He has willed of him. . . . His existence now is like it was before he had existence. This, then, is the highest stage of the true realization of the Oneness of God in which the worshiper who sustains this Oneness loses his own individuality. [JUNAYD 1962: 176–178]

12. Self-Obliteration

Obliteration, the loss of one's personal or individual characteristics before God, is also the key to attaining that same state. It is both the method and the goal of the mystic's pursuit, as Ghazali (d. 1111 C.E.) explains in his great work of spiritual renewal, The Revivification of the Sciences of Religion.

Whoever looks upon the world only because it is God's work, and knows it because it is God's work, and loves it because it is God's work, does not look except to God and knows nothing except God, and loves naught except God—he is the true One-maker who does not see anything but God, indeed, he does not regard even himself for his own sake but because he is God's servant, and of such a person it is said that he is annihilated in Oneness and he is annihilated from himself. (Ghazali, *Revivification* 4.276)

According to Junayd, the first step on the path to self-annihilation consists in training the will.

The obliteration of attributes, characteristics and natural inclinations in your motives when you carry out your religious duties, making great efforts and doing the opposite of what you may desire, and compelling yourself to do the things which you do not wish to do.

Nor must asceticism be neglected.

The obliteration of your pursuit of pleasure and even the sensation of pleasure in obedience to God's commands; so that you are exclusively His, without intermediary means of contact.

Finally, the mystic achieves true obliteration, a complete loss of self-awareness, and with it, a higher level of existence.

The obliteration of the consciousness of having attained the vision of God at the final stage of ecstasy when God's victory over you is complete. At this stage you are obliterated and have eternal life with God, and you exist only in the existence of God because you have been obliterated. Your physical being continues but your individuality has departed. [JUNAYD 1962: 81]

13. Oneness with God Is Not Identity with God

Sufi theoreticians on the one hand cut their definitions of annihilation of self and Oneness with God exceedingly fine, while ecstatics on the other, the "drunken Sufis" who did not share Junayd's measured sobriety, followed whither their fevered experience and expressions led them. The result was, not unpredictably, a conservative reaction, or at least a degree of caution, and in the first instance on the part of certain Sufi masters themselves. One such was al-Sarraj (d. 988 c.e.), whose great systematic treatise on Sufism ends with a kind of syllabus of errors directed at Sufi theory and practice.

Some mystics of Baghdad have erred in their doctrine that, when they pass away from their qualities, they enter into the qualities of God.

This involves infusion (*hulul*) or leads to the Christian belief concerning Jesus. The doctrine in question has been attributed to some of the earlier (Muslim) mystics, but its true understanding is this: when a man goes forth from his own qualities and enters into the qualities of God, he goes forth from his own will, which is a gift to him from God, and enters into the Will of God, knowing that his will has been given to him by God, and that by virtue of this gift he can stop regarding himself and become entirely devoted to God. This is one of the stages of those who seek after Oneness. Those who have erred in this teaching are the ones who have failed to note that the qualities of God are not the same as God. To make God identical with His qualities is to be guilty of infidelity, because God does not descend into the heart but what does descend into the heart is faith in God and belief in His Oneness and reverence for the thought of him. (Sarraj, *The Splendor of Sufism* 432) [Cited in JUNAYD 1962: 84]

Some have abstained from food and drink because they fancy that, when a man's body is weakened, it is possible that he may lose his humanity and be invested with the attributes of divinity. The ignorant persons who hold this doctrine cannot distinguish between humanity and the innate qualities of humanity. Humanity does not depart from a man any more than blackness departs from that which is black or whiteness from that which is white, but the innate qualities of humanity are changed and transmuted by the all-powerful radiance that is shed upon them from the Divine Realities. The attributes of humanity are not the essence of humanity. Those who speak of the doctrine of obliteration mean the cessation of our regarding our own actions and works of devotion through continuously regarding God as the doer of those acts on behalf of His servants. (Sarraj, *The Splendor of Sufism* 426) [Cited in JUNAYD 1962: 84–85]

14. The Life and Death of a Mystic: Al-Hallaj

Sarraj was willing to exonerate Junayd from his charges, but far more culpable was the tenth century's—and all of Sufism's—best-known example of extravagant utterance, al-Hallaj.

We have already seen Ghazali's reflections on his spiritual career. But these are thoughts recollected and reshaped in tranquillity. Indeed, some Sufi lives may have been tranquil, but certainly not that of Islam's most

notorious seeker after God, the Baghdad saint and mystic Husayn ibn
Mansur, surnamed al-Hallaj, "the carder," who was put to death, a martyr
of esoteric Sufism, in the capital of the Islamic empire in 922 C.E. Hallaj
had earlier studied with Junayd, then broke with his master and eventually
installed himself, his family, and a number of disciples in Baghdad. But he
did not rest there for long. His life was full of restless wandering, and on
this occasion he set out for the "land of idolatry," India and Turkestan.
And, his son adds in a memoir, "the gossip about him increased after this
journey."

He departed again after that and made a third pilgrimage, including a two year spiritual retreat in Mecca. He returned this time very
changed from what he had been before. He purchased property in
Baghdad and built a house. He began to preach in public a doctrine only
half of which I understood. In the end (the lawyer) Muhammad Dawud
rose against him, together with a whole group of *ulama*; and they took
their accusations against his views to (the Caliph) al-Mu'tadid. . . .
Some people said: he is a sorcerer. Others: he is a madman. Still others:
he performs miracles and his prayer is granted (by God). And tongues
wrangled over his case up to the moment when the government arrested
and imprisoned him.

At that time (the Grand Chamberlain) Nasr Qushuri went to the
Caliph, who authorized him to build my father a separate cell in prison.
Then a little house was constructed for him adjoining the prison; the
outside door to the building was walled up, the building itself was
surrounded by a wall, and a door was made opening into the interior of
the prison. For about a year he received visits from people there. Then
that was forbidden him, and he went for five months without anyone
being able to see him. . . . At that time I was spending my night with my
maternal family outside, and staying during the day near my father.
Then they imprisoned me with him for a period of two months. At that
time I was eighteen years old.

And when the night came in which my father was to be taken, at
dawn, from his cell (for execution), he stood up for the prayer, of which
he performed one of two prostrations. Then, with this prayer completed, he continued repeating over and over again the word "illusion
. . . illusion," until the night was almost over. Then for a long time he
was silent, when suddenly he cried out "truth . . . truth." He stood up
again, put on his head cloak and wrapped himself in his coat, extended
his hands, turned toward the prayer-direction and went into ecstatic
prayer. . . .

When the morning came, they led him from the prison, and I saw him walking proudly in his chains. . . . They led him then (to the esplanade) where they cut off his hands and feet, after having flogged him with 500 lashes of the whip. Then he was hoisted up onto the cross, and I heard him on the gibbet talking ecstatically with God: "O my God, here I am in the dwelling place of my desires, where I contemplate Your marvels. O my God, since You witness friendship even to whoever does You wrong, how is it You do not witness it to this one to whom wrong is done because of You?" . . .

At the time of the evening prayer, the authorization by the Caliph to decapitate Hallaj came. But it was declared: "It is too late; we shall put it off until tomorrow." When morning came, they took him down from the gibbet and dragged him forth to behead him. I heard him cry out then, saying in a very high voice: "All that matters for the ecstatic is that his Only One bring him to his Oneness." Then he recited this verse: "Those who do not believe in the Final Hour call for its coming; but those who believe in it await it with loving shyness, knowing that this will be (the coming of) God" (Quran 42:17). These were his last words.

His head was cut off, then his trunk was rolled up in a straw mat, doused with fuel and burned. Later his ashes were carried to Lighthouse Point (on the Tigris) to disperse them to the wind. [MASSIGNON 1982: 10–18]

15. "I Am the Truth"

Hallaj's son's account of his father's life and death makes no mention of his trial, which had to do with the examination of Hallaj's views on the pilgrimage. This apparent attack on Islamic ritual may indeed have merited Hallaj the death sentence in 922 C.E., but it was by no means his only, or perhaps even his most scandalous, departure from Islamic religious teaching. What attracted even more attention in later generations was another remark let he drop, in what appears to be utter simplicity, to Junayd.

It is related that Hallaj met Junayd one day, and said to him, "I am the Truth." "No," Junayd answered him, "it is by means of the Truth that you are! What gibbet will you stain with your blood!" [MASSIGNON 1982: 127]

That appears to be the full extent of the incident and the exchange. But there is little doubt as to how Hallaj intended the expression "I am the

Truth" (or, as it has been translated, "My 'I' is God") or how Junayd understood it: "the Truth" is a title of God and Hallaj was arrogating it to himself; and not, it is noted, in a state of ecstatic "intoxication," but in its aftermath, the believer's normal state of "sobriety," a distinction that meant little to Hallaj but was of crucial importance to Junayd. Our source is the Persian Sufi Hujwiri (fl. 1057 C.E.).

I have read . . . that when Husayn ibn Mansur, in a sort of trance, broke with Amr al-Makki and came over to Junayd, the latter said: "Why did you come?"

"To live in community with you as a master."

"I do not live in community with madmen; community life requires balance, otherwise what happened to you with Sahl Tustari and Amr occurs."

"O master, sobriety and intoxication are only the two human aspects of the mystic, who remains separated from his Lord as long as these two aspects are not both annihilated."

"O Ibn Mansur, you are wrong in your definition of those states, sobriety and intoxication; the first means the state of normal equilibrium of the faithful before God; it is not a qualification of the faithful that he may get it through his own effort as a creature; likewise the second, which signifies extremes of desire and love. O Ibn Mansur, I see in your language an indiscreet curiosity and some expressions that are useless." (Hujwiri, *The Unveiling* 235) [Cited by MASSIGNON 1982: 125–126]

16. Ecstatic Utterances

What Junayd tactfully characterized as "some expressions that are useless" many other Muslims called "ecstatic utterances," cries like Hallaj's "I am the Truth" or Bistami's "Glory be to Me," uttered in a moment of mystical transport—valid for the Muslim "Gnostics" or "knowers," as they are called here, no doubt, but the cause of some disturbance, and even scandal, to the ordinary believer. Both Ghazali and Ibn Khaldun tried to put the best face upon what was admittedly a difficult subject.

Those Gnostics, when they return from their ascent into the heaven of Reality, confess with one voice that they saw no existent there save the One Real Being. Some of them arrived at this scientifically, others experimentally and subjectively. For these last the plurality of things entirely fell away; they were drowned in the absolute Oneness, and their intelligences were lost in Its abyss. . . . They became like persons struck dumb, and they had no power within them except to recall God, not even the power to recall themselves. So there remained with them nothing save God. They became drunk with a drunkenness wherein the sense of their own intelligence disappeared, so that one cried out "I am the Truth," and another "Glory be to Me! How great is My Glory!" and still another "Within this robe is nothing but God!" . . . But the words of lovers passionate in their intoxication and ecstasy must be hidden away and not spoken of. (Ghazali, *Niche for Lights*)

There are the suspect expressions which the Sufis call "ecstatic utterances" and which provoke the censure of orthodox Muslims. As to them, it should be known that the attitude that would be fair to the Sufis is that they are people who are removed from sense perception. Inspiration grips them. Eventually, they say things about their inspiration that they do not intend to say. A person who is removed from sense perception cannot be spoken to. More, he who is forced to act is excused. Sufis who are known for their excellence and exemplary character are considered to act in good faith in this and similar respects. It is difficult to express ecstatic experiences, because there are no conventional ways of expressing them. This was the experience of Abu Yazid al-Bistami and others like him. However, Sufis whose excellence is not known and famous deserve censure for utterances of this kind, since the (data) that might cause us to interpret their statements (so as to remove any suspicion attached to them) are not clear to us. Furthermore, any Sufis who are not removed from sense perception and are not in the grip of a (mystical) state when they make such utterances, also deserve censure. Therefore the jurists and the great Sufis decided that al-Hallaj was to be killed, because he spoke (ecstatically) while not removed from sense perception but in control of his state. And God knows better. (Ibn Khaldun, *Muqaddima* 6.16) [IBN KHALDUN 1967: 3:102]

17. The Face in the Mirror

Ghazali's moderating influence won for Sufism a respected if always somewhat suspect place in the Sunni household. But as the Sufi movement continued to develop, instances of what Juyawni would doubtless have considered "indiscreet curiosity" and "useless expressions" continued to occur in Sufi circles, and even the fate of Hallaj did nothing to dampen the adventuresome thought of some Sufi masters. When accompanied by continuing

vigil on the part of the Sunni authorities, however, awareness of Hal-
laj's end may have counseled some mystics to resort to the somewhat safer
ground of allegory or inference.

One of the more prolonged and celebrated of the Sufi allegories is a
long poem in Persian, The Conference of the Birds, *written by Farid*
al-Din Attar in 1177 C.E. *Its premise is that the birds of the world collect*
to go in search of an ideal king. In the end they discover him, but not before
they tell and have told to them a great number of stories illustrative of the
Sufi life, whose path they are themselves in fact allegorically tracing.

Attar's allegorical birds finally reach their goal, the abode of a
mythical king called Simorgh, whose Persian name derives etymologically
from si = *"thirty" and* morgh = *birds.*

> A world of birds set out, and there remained
> But thirty when the promised goal was gained,
> Thirty exhausted, wretched, broken things,
> With hopeless hearts and tattered, trailing wings. . . .
>
> The king's herald counsels them to turn back:
> The herald said: "The blaze of Majesty
> Reduces souls to unreality,
> And if your souls are burnt, then all the pain
> That you have suffered will have been in vain."
> They answered: "How can a moth flee fire
> When fire contains its ultimate desire?
> And if we do not join Him, yet we'll burn,
> And it is for this that our spirits yearn—
> It is not union for which we hope;
> We know that goal remains beyond our scope." . . .
>
> Though grief engulfed the ragged group, love made
> The birds impetuous and unafraid;
> The herald's self-possession was unmoved,
> But their resilience was not reproved—
> Now gently he unlocked the guarded door;
> A hundred doors drew back, and there before
> The birds' incredulous, bewildered sight
> Shone the unveiled, the inmost Light of Light.
> He led them to a noble throne, a place
> Of intimacy, dignity and grace,
> Then gave them all a written page and said
> That when its contents had been duly read

The meaning that their journey had concealed,
And of the stage they'd reached, would be revealed. . . .

The thirty birds read through the fateful page
And there discovered, stage by detailed stage,
Their lives, their actions, set out one by one—
All their souls had ever been or done. . . .

The chastened spirits of these birds became
Like crumbled powder, and they shrank with shame.
Then, as by shame their spirits were refined
Of all the world's weight, they began to find
A new life flow toward them from that bright
Celestial and ever-living Light—
Their souls rose free of all they'd been before;
The past and all its actions were no more.
Their life came from that close and insistent sun
And in its vivid rays they shone as one.
There in the Simorgh's radiant face they saw
Themselves, the Simorgh of the world—with awe
They gazed, and dared at last to comprehend
They were the Simorgh and the journey's end.
They see the Simorgh—at themselves they stare,
And see a second Simorgh standing there;
They look at both and see the two are one,
That this is that, that this, the goal is won.
They ask (but inwardly; they make no sound)
The meanings of these mysteries that confound
Their puzzled ignorance—how is it true
That "we" are not distinguished here from "You"?
And silently their shining Lord replies:
"I am a mirror set before your eyes,
And all who come before my splendor see
Themselves, their own unique reality."
(Attar, *Parliament of Birds*) [ATTAR 1984: 214–219]

*The image of the face in the mirror was not original with Attar. It
had appeared in one of its most striking forms in the writings of the
dominant figure in all of Islamic mysticism, the Spaniard Muhyi al-Din
ibn al-Arabi (1165–1240 C.E.). It is introduced at the very beginning of
his* Bezels of Wisdom, *in the expression of one of his fundamental themes:
the ultimate and primordial unity of Reality or Being, polarized into the*

God and the Cosmos only after and because of the Reality's desire to ex-
perience itself in another.

The Reality wanted to see the essences of His Most Beautiful
Names, or, to put it another way, to see His own Essence in an all-
inclusive object encompassing the whole (divine) Command, which,
qualified by existence, would reveal to Him His own mystery. For the
seeing of a thing, itself by itself, is not the same as its seeing itself in
another, as it were in a mirror; for it appears to itself in a form that is
invested by the location of the vision by that which would only appear
to it given the existence of the location and its [that is, the location's]
self-disclosure to it.

The reality gave existence to the whole Cosmos (at first) as an
undifferentiated thing without anything of the spirit in it, so that it was
like an unpolished mirror. It is in the nature of the divine determination
that He does not set out a location except to receive a divine spirit,
which is also called "the breathing into him" (Quran 21:91). The latter
is nothing other than the coming into operation of the undifferentiated
form's (innate) disposition to receive the inexhaustible overflowing of
Self-Revelation, which has always been and will ever be. . . .

Thus the (divine) Command required (by its very nature) the re-
flective characteristic of the mirror of the Cosmos, and Adam was the
very principle of reflection for that mirror and the spirit of that form.
(Ibn al-Arabi, *Bezels of Wisdom*, "Adam") [IBN AL-ARABI 1980: 50–51]

Here the image is turned around, and it is God who is the mirror.

If you are a believer, you will know that God will manifest Himself
on the Day of Resurrection, initially in a recognizable form, then in a
form unacceptable (to ordinary belief), He alone being the Self-mani-
festing One in every form, although it is obvious that one form is not the
same as another.

It is as if the single Essence were a mirror, so that when the observer sees in it the form of his belief about God, he recognizes and
confirms it, but if he should see it in the doctrinal formulation of someone of another creed, he will reject it, as if he were seeing in the mirror
His form and then that of another. The mirror is single, while the forms
(it reveals) are various in the eye of the observer.

None of the forms are in the mirror wholly, although a mirror has
an effect on the forms in one way and not in another. For instance, it
may make the form look smaller, larger, taller or broader. Thus it has
an effect on their proportions, which is attributable to it, although such

changes occur only due to the different proportions of the mirrors themselves. Look, then, into just one mirror, without considering mirrors in
general, for it is the same as your beholding (Him) as being one Essence,
albeit that He is beyond all need of the worlds. Insofar as He is Divine
Names, on the other hand, He is like (many) mirrors. In which Divine
Name have you beheld yourself, or who is the one who beholds? It is
only the reality of the Name that is manifest in the beholder. Thus it is,
if you will but understand. (Ibn al-Arabi, *The Bezels of Wisdom*, "Elias")
[IBN AL-ARABI 1980: 232–233]

Ibn al-Arabi returns to the relationship of the Reality and the Cos-
mos, now in terms of light and shadow.

Know that what is "other than the Reality," which is called the
Cosmos, is, in relation to the Reality, as a shadow is to what casts the
shadow, for it is the shadow of God, this being the same as the relationship between Being and the Cosmos, since the shadow is, without
doubt, something sensible. What is provided there is something on
which the shadow may appear, since if it were that that whereon it
appears should cease to be, the shadow would be an intelligible and not
something sensible, and would exist potentially in the very thing that
casts the shadow.

The thing on which this divine shadow, called the Cosmos, appears
is the (eternally latent) essences of contingent beings. The shadow is
spread out over them, and the (identity of the) shadow is known to the
extent that the Being of the (original) Essence is extended upon it. It is
by His Name, the Light, that it is perceived. This shadow extends over
the essences of contingent being in the form of the unknown Unseen.
Have you not observed that shadows tend to be black, which indicates
their imperceptibility (as regards content) by reason of the remote relationship between them and their origins? If the source of the shadow is
white, the shadow itself is still so [that is, black].

This is how the universe exists; Ibn al-Arabi then begins to move from
its existence to our way of knowing both this world of ours called the Cosmos
and its source.

No more is known of the Cosmos than is known from a shadow,
and no more is known of the Reality than one knows of the origin of a
shadow. Insofar as He has a shadow, He is known, but insofar as the
form of the one casting the shadow is not perceived in the shadow, the
Reality is not known. For this reason we say that the Reality is known
to us in one sense and unknown in another.

We are, then, seriously misled about the "real existence" of the sensible universe.

If what we say is true, the Cosmos is but a fantasy without any real existence, which is another meaning of the Imagination. That is to say, you imagine that it [that is, the universe] is something separate and self-sufficient, outside the Reality, while the truth is that it is not so. Have you not observed (in the case of the shadow) that it is connected to the one who casts it, and would not its becoming unconnected be absurd, since nothing can be disconnected from itself?

It is, Ibn al-Arabi immediately continues, in the mirror we should look.

Therefore know truly your own self [that is, your own essence], who you are, what is your identity and what your relationship with the Reality. Consider well in what way you are real and in what way (part of) the Cosmos, as being separate, other, and so on.

Thus God is seen in many different modes: in one way—"green"—by the ordinary believer relying on the givens of Scripture, in another— "colorless"—by the theologian with his refined deductive portrait. And they are both correct, and, of course, both wildly wrong.

The Reality is, in relation to a particular shadow, small or large, pure or purer, as light in relationship to the glass that separates it from the beholder to whom the light has the color of the glass, while the light itself has no particular color. This is the relationship between your reality and your Lord; for, if you were to say that the light is green because of the green glass, you would be right as viewing the situation through your senses, and if you were to say it is not green, indeed it is colorless, by deduction, you would also be right as viewing the situation through sound intellectual reasoning. That which is seen may be said to be a light projected from a shadow, which is the glass, or a luminous shadow, according to its purity. Thus, he of us who has realized in himself the Reality manifests the form of the Reality to a greater extent than he who has not. . . .

God created shadows lying prostrate to right and left only as clues for yourself in knowing yourself and Him, that you might know who you are, your relationship with Him, and His with you, and so you might understand how or according to which divine truth all that is other than God is described as being completely dependent on Him, as being (also) mutually independent. Also that you might know how and by what truth God is described as utterly independent of men and all worlds, and how the Cosmos is described as both mutually independent with respect to its parts and mutually dependent. (Ibn al-Arabi, *The Bezels of Wisdom*, "Joseph") [IBN AL-ARABI 1980: 123–126]

18. Al-Jili and the Perfect Man

Sufism from Ibn al-Arabi onward developed a repertory of esoteric learning that was as vast and at times as impenetrable as the Kabbala. This was theosophy pure and simple, an arcane and transcendental way of looking at this world in terms of a higher reality, a blend of knowing and doing, of gnosis and theurgy, with strong derivative roots in the late Platonic tradition of the fifth and sixth centuries C.E. One of the central themes of this world view was the theory of the "Perfect Man," a figure who simultaneously embraces the Holy Spirit, the Word, Adam, Muhammad, and the fully enlightened mystic himself. Ibn al-Arabi was one of the pioneers in the development of this motif, but it found its classic expression in the treatise called The Perfect Man *by Abd al-Karim al-Jili (d. ca. 1410 C.E.).*

God created the angel called Spirit from His own light, and from him He created the world and made him His organ of vision in the world. One of his names is the Word of God. He is the noblest and most exalted of all existent beings. The Spirit exercises a Divine guardianship, created in him by God, over the whole universe. He manifests himself in his perfection in the Ideal Muhammad: therefore the Prophet is the most excellent of all mankind. While God manifests Himself in His attributes to all other created beings, He manifests Himself in His essence to this angel [that is, the Spirit] alone. Accordingly, the Spirit is the Pole of the present world and the world to come. He does not make himself known to any creature of God but to the Perfect Man. When the saint knows him [that is, the Perfect Man] and truly understands the things which the Spirit teaches him, then he too becomes a Pole around which the entire universe revolves. But Poleship belongs fundamentally to the Spirit, and if others hold it, they are only his delegates. (Jili, *The Perfect Man* 2.12) [Cited by NICHOLSON 1921: 110–111]

The Perfect Man is the Pole on which the spheres of existence revolve from first to last, and since things came into being he is one for ever and ever. He has various guises and appears in diverse bodily tabernacles: in respect of some of these his name is given to him, while in respect to others it is not given to him. His original name is Muhammad, his name of honor is Abu al-Qasim [that is, "father of Qasim," the latter the name of Muhammad's first son], his description Abdullah [that is, "servant of God"], and his title is Shams al-Din [that is, "the sun of religion"]. In every age he bears a name suitable to his guide in that age. I once met him [that is, the Perfect Man, Muhammad] in the form of my Shaykh, Sharaf al-Din Isma'il al-Jabarti, but I did not know that he [that is, the Shaykh] was the Prophet, though I knew the Prophet was the Shaykh. . . . The real meaning of this matter is that the Prophet has the power of assuming every form. When the adept sees him in the form of Muhammad which he wore during his life, he names him by that name, but when he sees him in another form but knows him to be Muhammad, he names him by the name of the form in which he appears. The name Muhammad is not applied except to the Real Muhammad. . . . If you perceive mystically that the Reality of Muhammad is displayed in any human form, you must bestow upon the Reality of Muhammad the name of that form and regard its owner with no less reverence than you would show our Lord Muhammad, and after having seen him therein you may not behave towards it in the same manner as before.

This appearance of the Real Muhammad in the form of another could be misconstrued as the condemned doctrine of the transmigration of souls, and so al-Jili hastens to disassociate the two.

Do not imagine that my words contain any tincture of the doctrine of metempsychosis. God forbid! I mean that the Prophet is able to assume whatever form he wishes, and the Tradition declares that in every age he assumes the form of the most perfect men (of that age) in order to exalt their dignity and correct their deviation: they are his caliphs externally and he is their reality inwardly.

The Perfect Man in himself is identified with all the individualizations of existence. With his spirituality he stands with the higher individualizations, in his corporeality with the lower. His heart is identified with the Throne of God, his mind with the Pen, his soul with the Well Guarded Tablet, his nature with the elements, his capability of receiving form with matter. . . . He stands with the angels with his good thoughts, with the demons and the devils with the doubts that beset him, with the beasts in his animality. . . .

You must know that the Perfect Man is a copy of God, according to the saying of the Prophet, "God created Adam in the image of the Merciful," and in another tradition, "God created Adam in His own image." . . . Further, you must know that the Essential names and the

Divine attributes belong to the Perfect Man by fundamental and sovereign right in virtue of a necessity inherent in his essence, for it is he whose "reality" is signified by these expressions and whose spirituality is indicated by these symbols: they have no other subject in existence (to which they might be attached) except the Perfect Man.

Once again the figure of the mirror is adduced, and in a manner familiar from Ibn al-Arabi: man, and in particular the Perfect Man, is the mirror in which God sees and recognizes and admires Himself, as does man.

As a mirror in which a person sees the form of himself, and cannot see it without the mirror, such is the relation of God to the Perfect Man, who cannot possibly see his own form but in the mirror of the name "God." And he is also a mirror to God, for God laid upon Himself the necessity that His names and attributes should not be seen save in the Perfect Man. (Jili, *The Perfect Man* 2.58) [Cited by NICHOLSON 1921: 105–107]

19. Ibn Khaldun:
An Evaluation of the Sufi Tradition

Ibn Khaldun had all these developments before him, from the earliest Muslim ascetics, through the "ecstatic utterances" of Bistami and Hallaj, to the daring "existential monism" of Ibn al-Arabi and the theosophical speculation of his successors, when he composed his thoughts on Sufism for the Prolegomenon to History. He was well aware of the strong current of disapproval, or at least of reservation, that many in the Islamic legal establishment had expressed on the subject of Sufis and Sufism. For his part, however, Ibn Khaldun attempts to isolate the dubious areas in Sufi speculation, in the first instance by laying out the topics with which Sufis generally concerned themselves.

Many jurists and muftis have undertaken to refute these . . . recent Sufis. They summarily disapproved of everything they came across in the Sufi "path." The truth is that discussion with the Sufis requires making a distinction. The Sufis discuss four topics. (1) Firstly, they discuss pious exertions, the resulting mystical and ecstatic experiences, and self-scrutiny concerning one's actions. They discuss these things in order to obtain mystical experience, which then becomes a station from which one progresses to the next higher one. . . . (2) Secondly, they discuss the removal of the veil and the perceivable supernatural realities, such as the divine attributes, the throne, the seat, the angels, revelation, prophecy, the spirit, and the realities of everything in existence, be it supernatural or visible; furthermore, they discuss the order of created things, how they issue from the Creator Who brings them into being. . . . (3) The third topic is concerned with activities in the various worlds and among the various created things connected with the different kinds of divine grace. (4) The fourth topic is concerned with expressions which are suspect if understood in their plain meaning. Such expressions have been uttered by most Sufi leaders. In Sufi technical terminology they are called "ecstatic utterances." Their plain meaning is difficult to understand. They may be something that is disapproved of, or something that can be approved, or something that requires interpretation.

Now that the territory has been charted, Ibn Khaldun can proceed to his critique. First, on the matter that by all accounts constituted the mainstream of Sufism and which had won, at least since the time of Ghazali, a recognized place among acceptable Islamic practices and experiences:

As for their discussion of pious exertions and stations, of the mystical and ecstatic experiences that result, and of self-scrutiny with regard to shortcomings in the things that cause these experiences, this is something that nobody ought to reject. These mystical experiences are sound ones. Their realization is the very essence of happiness.

Ibn Khaldun then reverses the second and third points he had established above, treating first the Sufis' perceptions about the operation of divine grace, which he is inclined to accept, and their description, after the "removal of the veil," of that other, higher world where God and His angels and the other higher realities have their being, about which he is much less certain.

As for their discussion of the acts of divine grace experienced by the Sufis, the information they give about supernatural things, and their activity among created things, these are sound and cannot be disapproved of, even though some religious scholars tend to disapprove . . . since they might be confused with prophetic miracles.

There is no problem here. The scholastic apparatus of theology had its distinctions well in order.

Competent orthodox scholars have made a distinction between (miracles and acts of divine grace) by referring to "the challenge (in advance)," that is, the claim made (by the prophet in advance) that the miracle would occur in agreement with the prophetic revelation. It is not possible, they said, that a miracle could happen in agreement with the claim of a liar. Logic requires that a miracle indicate truthfulness. By definition a miracle is something that can be verified. If it were performed by a liar it could not be verified and thus would have changed its character, which is absurd. In addition, the world of existence attests the occurrence of many such acts of divine grace. Disapproval of them would be a kind of negative approach. Many such acts of divine grace were experienced by the men around Muhammad and the great early Muslims. This is a well-known and famous fact.

The Sufis' charting of the higher realities, on the other hand, might appear to constitute a kind of private, intuitive and so unverifiable revelation. In this case Ibn Khaldun recommends a kind of circumspect neglect.

Most of the Sufi discussion about the removal of the veil of the reception of the realities of the higher things, and of the order in which the created things issue, falls, in a way, under the category of ambiguous statements. It is based upon the intuitive experience of the Sufis, and those who lack such intuitive experience cannot have the mystical experience that the Sufis receive from it. No language can express what the Sufis want to say in this connection, because languages have been invented only for the expression of commonly accepted concepts, most of which apply to sensible reality. Therefore, we must not bother with the Sufi discussion of those matters. We ought merely to leave it alone, just as we leave alone the ambiguous statements in the Quran and the Prophetic custom. Those to whom God grants some understanding of these mystical utterances in a way that agrees with the plain meaning of the religious law do, indeed, enjoy happiness. (Ibn Khaldun, *Muqaddima* 6.16) [IBN KHALDUN 1967: 3:99–101]

20. Sufis and Shiʿites

Ibn Khaldun then turns his attention to trends that began to develop in Sufism after its heroic period. In his reading of Sufi history it was the Shiʿites who led Islamic mysticism astray.

The ancient Sufis did not go into anything concerning the Mahdi [that is, the expected Muslim Messiah]. All they discussed was their mystic activity and exertion and the resulting ecstatic experiences and states. It was the Imamite and extremist Shiʿa who discussed the preferred status of Ali, the matter of his Imamate, the claim made on his behalf to have received the Imamate through the last will of the Prophet, and the rejection of the two Shaykhs [that is, Abu Bakr and Umar]. . . .

Among the later Sufis, the removal of the veil and matters beyond the veil of sense perception came to be discussed. A great many Sufis came to speak of incarnation and oneness. This gave them something in common with the Imamites and the extremist Shiʿa who believed in the divinity of the Imams and the incarnation of the deity in them. The Sufis also came to believe in the "Pole" and in "saints." This belief looked like an imitation of the opinions of the extremist Shiʿa concerning the Imam and the Alid "chiefs."

Ibn Khaldun will return to the Shiʿa-Sufi theory of "Poles" and "saints." He continues:

The Sufis thus became saturated with Shiʿa theories. Shiʿa theories entered so deeply into their religious ideas that they based their practice of using a cloak on the fact that Ali clothed al-Hasan al-Basri in such a cloak and caused him to agree solemnly that he would adhere to the mystic path. This tradition (begun by Ali) was continued, according to the Sufis, through al-Junayd, one of the Sufi shaykhs.

However, it is not known for a certainty whether Ali did any such thing. The mystic path was not reserved to Ali, but all men around Muhammad were models of the various paths of religion. The fact that the Sufis restrict precedence in mysticism to Ali smells strongly of pro-Shiʿa sentiments. This and other afore-mentioned Sufi ideas show that the Sufis have adopted pro-Shiʿa sentiments and have become enmeshed in them. (Ibn Khaldun, *Muqaddima* 3.51) [IBN KHALDUN 1967: 2:186–187]

And so, on Ibn Khaldun's view as a Sunni historian, the chief tenets of the "recent Sufis" that show the influence of Shiʿism are their discussions of the Godhead's becoming incarnate in certain chosen souls and their insistence on the Divine Oneness to the extent that it became in effect pantheism.

Tradition scholars and jurists who discuss the articles of faith often mention that God is separate from His creatures. The speculative theologians say that He is neither separate nor connected. The philosophers say that He is neither in the world nor outside it. The recent Sufis say that He is one with the creatures in the sense that He is incarnate in them or in the sense that He is identical with them and there exists nothing but Himself either in the whole or in any part of it. . . .

A number of recent Sufis who consider intuitive perceptions to be scientific and logical hold the opinion that the Creator is one with His creatures in His identity, His existence and His attributes. They often assume that this was the position of philosophers before Aristotle, such as Plato and Socrates. . . . The Oneness assumed by the Sufis is identical with the incarnation the Christians claim for the Messiah. It is even stranger, in that it is the incarnation of something primeval in something created and the Oneness of the former with the latter.

The Oneness assumed by the Sufis is also identical with the stated opinion of the Imamite Shiʿa concerning their Imams. In their discussions, the Shiʿa consider the ways in which the oneness of the Deity with the Imams is achieved. (1) The essence of the primeval Deity is hidden in all created things, both sensible and intelligible, and is one with them in both kinds of perception. All of them are manifestations of it, and it has control over them—that is, it controls their existence in the sense that, without it, they would not exist. Such is the opinion of the people who believe in incarnation.

(2) There is the approach of those who believe in absolute Oneness. It seems as if in the exposition of those who believe in incarnation, they have sensed the existence of an (implicit) differentiation contradicting the concept of Oneness. Therefore, they disavowed the (existence of any differentiation) between the primeval Deity and the creatures in essence, existence, and attributes. In order to explain the difference in manifestations perceived by the senses and the intellect, they used the specious argument that those things were human perceptions that are imaginary. By imaginary . . . they mean that all those things do not exist in reality and exist only in human perception. Only the primeval Deity has real existence and nothing else, either inwardly or outwardly. (Ibn Khaldun, *Muqaddima* 6.16) [IBN KHALDUN 1967: 3:83–86]

Ibn Khaldun has no doubts about whence these notions derived, or about their essential falsehood.

The recent Sufis who speak about the removal of the veil and supersensory perception have delved deeply into these subjects. Many of them have turned to the theory of incarnation and oneness, as we have indicated. They have filled many pages with it. That was done, for instance, by al-Harawi [ca. 1010–1089 C.E.] in the *Book of Stations* and by others. They were followed by Ibn al-Arabi [1165–1240 C.E.] and Ibn Sabʿin [1226–1271 C.E.] and their pupils, and then by Ibn Afif [ca. 1260–1289], Ibn al-Farid [d. 1235 C.E.] and Najm al-Din al-Israʾili [1206–1278 C.E.] in the poems they composed.

The early Sufis had had contact with the Neo-Isma'ili Shi'ite extremists who also believed in incarnation and in the divinity of the
Imams, a theory not known to the early Isma'ilis. Each group came to
be imbued with the dogmatics of the other. Their theories and beliefs
merged and were assimilated. In Sufi discussion there appeared the theory of the "Pole," meaning the chief gnostic. The Sufis assumed that no
one can reach his station in gnosis until God takes him to Himself and
gives his station to another gnostic. . . .

The theory of successive "Poles" is not, however, confirmed by
logical arguments or evidence from the religious law. It is a sort of rhetorical figure of speech. It is identical with the theory of the extremist
Shi'a about the succession of the Imams through inheritance. Clearly,
mysticism has plagiarized this idea from the extremist Shi'a and come
to believe in it.

The Sufis furthermore speak about the order of existence of the
"saints" who come after the "Pole," exactly as the Shi'a speak of their
"representatives." They go so far (in the identification of their own concepts with those of the Shi'a) that when they construed a chain of transmitters for the wearing of the Sufi cloak as a basic requirement of the
mystic way and practice, they made it go back to Ali. This points in the
same direction. Among the men around Muhammad, Ali was not distinguished by any particular practice or way of dressing or by any special
condition. Abu Bakr and Umar were the most ascetic and pious people
after the Messenger of God. Yet, none of these men was distinguished
by the possession of any particular religious practice peculiar to him. In
fact, all the men around Muhammad were models of religion, austerity,
asceticism, and pious exertion. This is attested by their way of life and
history. Indeed, with the help of these stories, the Shi'a try to suggest
that Ali is distinguished from the other men around Muhammad by
being in possession of certain virtues, in conformity with well-known
Shi'a beliefs. (Ibn Khaldun, *Muqaddima* 6.16) [IBN KHALDUN 1967:
3:92–93]

*There are clear parallels between the Gnostic current in Islamic
Sufism and the developing ideology of Sufism. Though the wedding of the
two strains was not officially consummated until the creation of the Safavid
state in Iran in the sixteenth century, the liaison was being prepared much
earlier. It is not certain when the affinities between Shi'ism and Sufism first
developed, but they were already present when Shi'ism elaborated its theory
of the Imam as a charismatic figure who possessed an authoritative spiritual*

knowledge and imparted it to adepts. The distance between the Shi͏ᶜite Imam and the Sufi saint, particularly the archetypical saint, the "Pole" around whom the saints of each generation revolved, was not great. From the twelfth century onward the distance grew even smaller with the evolution of what has been called "theosophical Sufism" or "Illuminationism." The wisdom (hikma) of the Shi͏ᶜites was quite simply the mystics' gnosis (maᶜrifa).

CHAPTER 8

Islamic Theology

1. The Origins of Theology in Islam

Ibn Khaldun in his Prolegomenon to History *gives a rapid survey of what he calls the "traditioned sciences" (see chapter 5 above), and in it he takes up the question of theology, first offering his rather general definition of its nature and function.*

The duties of the Muslim may concern either the body or the heart. The duties of the heart are concerned with faith and the distinction between what is to be believed and what is not to be believed. This concerns the articles of faith which deal with the essence and the attributes of God, the events of the Resurrection, Paradise, punishment and predestination, and entails discussion and defense of these subjects with the help of intellectual arguments. (Ibn Khaldun, *Muqaddima* 6.9) [IBN KHALDUN 1967: 2:438]

Islam in fact knew two theologies. The first was the Greeks' science about God, often called metaphysics after the Aristotelian work that was the Muslims' chief source of instruction in it. The second was what was called in Arabic by Jews, Muslims, and Christians kalam and has been translated throughout as "dialectical theology." Unlike metaphysics, which began with the premises of pure reason, dialectical theology in Islam resembled the Christians' "sacred theology," which took the givens of revelation as its starting point and attempted to demonstrate dialectically the conclusions that flowed from them. These two aspects of dialectical theology are clearly present in Ibn Khaldun's description of it, which includes both the Quranic menu of its subject matter and its method, "intellectual arguments."

Ibn Khaldun returns to the earliest days of Islam and undertakes to provide his own sketch of the conditions that brought this discipline into being, though with a notable, and understandable, reluctance to trace it to Christian origins, as some others had. Ibn Khaldun begins by summing up what might be called the "articles of faith," the propositions that every Muslim must believe in order to be saved (see chapter 5 above). He then continues:

These main articles of faith are proven by the logical evidence that exists for them. Evidence for them from the Quran and the Prophetic traditions also is ample. The scholars showed the way to them and the religious leaders verified them. However, later on, there occurred differences of opinion concerning the details of these articles of faith. Most of the difference concerned the "ambiguous verses" of the Quran [see chapter 4 above]. This led to hostility and disputation. Logical argumentation was used in addition to the traditional material. In this way, the science of dialectical theology originated.

We shall now explain this summary statement in detail. In many verses of the Quran the worshiped Master is described as being absolutely devoid (of human attributes), and this in absolute terms requiring no interpretation. All these verses are negative (in their statements). They are clear on the subject. It is necessary to believe them, and statements of the Lawgiver (Muhammad) and the men around him and the men of the second generation have explained them in accordance with their plain meaning.

Then there are a few verses in the Quran suggesting anthropomorphism, with reference to either the essence or the attributes of God. The early Muslims gave preference to the evidence for God's freedom from human attributes because it was simple and clear. They knew that anthropomorphism is absurd, but they decided that those (anthropomorphic) verses were the word of God and therefore believed them, without trying to investigate or interpret their meaning. . . . But there were a few innovators in their time who occupied themselves with those "ambiguous verses" and delved into anthropomorphism. One group operated with the plain [that is, literal] meaning of the relevant verses. They assumed anthropomorphism for God's essence, in that they believed that He had hands, feet and a face. Thus they adopted a clear-cut anthropomorphism and were in opposition to the verses stating God is devoid of human attributes. . . . The people who gave consideration to the anthropomorphic verses then tried to escape from the anthropomorphic abomination by stating that God has "a body unlike (ordinary human) bodies." . . . Another group turned to anthropomorphism with regard to the attributes of God. They assumed direction, sitting, descending, voice, letter (sound) and similar things on the part of God. Their stated opinions imply anthropomorphism, and like the former group they took refuge in statements like "a voice unlike voices," "a direction unlike directions," "descending unlike descending." . . .

Later on the sciences and the crafts increased. People were eager to write systematic works and to do research in all fields. The speculative theologians wrote on God's freedom from human attributes. At that juncture the Muᶜtazila innovation came into being. The Muᶜtazila extended the subject (of God's freedom from human physical attributes) to the negative verses and decided to deny God's possession of the ideational attributes of knowledge, power . . . and life, in addition to denying their consequences. . . . The Muᶜtazila further decided to deny God's possession of volition. This forced them to deny predestination, because predestination requires the existence of a volition prior to the created things. They also decided to deny God's hearing and vision, because both hearing and vision are corporeal accidents. . . . They further decided to deny God speech for reasons similar to those they used in connection with hearing and vision. . . . Thus the Muᶜtazila decided that the Quran was created [see chapter 3 above]. This was an innovation; the early Muslims had clearly expressed the contrary view. The damage done by this innovation was great. Certain leading Muᶜtazilites indoctrinated certain Caliphs with it, and the people were forced to adopt it [see chapter 3 above]. The Muslim religious leaders opposed them. Because of their opposition, it was permissible to flog and kill many of them. This caused orthodox people to rise in defense of the articles of faith with logical evidence and to push back the innovations.

The leader of the speculative theologians, Abu al-Hasan al-Ashᶜari [d. 935 C.E.] took care of that. He mediated between the different approaches. He disavowed anthropomorphism and recognized the (existence of the) ideational attributes. He restricted God's freedom from human attributes to the extent to which it had been recognized by early Muslims, and which had been recognized by the proofs stating the general applicability (of the principle) to special cases. He recognized the four ideational attributes [that is, of knowledge, power, volition, and life], as well as hearing, vision and speech, as an essential function of God, and this with the help of both logical and traditional methods. He refuted the innovators in all these respects. He discussed with them their stated opinions with regard to (God's concern for) human welfare and what is best for man, and their definition of good and evil, which they had invented on the basis of their innovation. He perfected the dogmas concerning the rising of the dead, the circumstances of the Resurrection, Paradise and Hell, and reward and punishment. Ash'ari added a discussion of the Imamate [see chapter 3 above], because the Imamite Shi'ites at that time suggested the novel idea that the Imamate was one of the articles of faith and that it was the duty of the Prophet as well as of the Muslim nation to fix (the succession to) the Imamate and to free the person who would become the Imam from any responsibility in this respect. However, the Imamate is at best a matter of public interest and social organization; it is not an article of faith. But it was added to the problems of this discipline. The whole was called "the science of dialectical theology." (Ibn Khaldun, *Muqaddima* 6.14) [IBN KHALDUN 1967: 3:45–50]

2. The Intrusion of Philosophy into Dialectical Theology

Even as this was happening, during the roughly century and a half span between the Mu'tazilite beginnings about 800 C.E. and the death of Ash'ari in 935, a great many Greek philosophical works were translated into Arabic, many of them done, in fact, under the patronage of the very Caliph Ma'mun (813–833 C.E.) who had given ear to the Mu'tazilites. The effects were not long in being felt on the nascent discipline of dialectical theology, not directly from the translations but from the adaptation of the analytical method into their own work by certain Muslim thinkers, as Ibn Khaldun continues.

Thus Ash'ari's approach was perfected and became one of the best speculative disciplines and religious sciences. However, the forms of its arguments are, at times, not technical [that is, not scientifically rigorous] because the scholars (of Ash'ari's time) were simple and the science of logic which probes arguments and examines syllogisms had not yet made its appearance in Islam. Even if some of it had existed, the theologians would not have used it because it was so closely related to the philosophical sciences, which are altogether different from the beliefs of the religious law and were, therefore, avoided by them. . . . After that the science of logic spread in Islam; people studied it. And they made a distinction between it and the philosophical sciences in that logic was merely a norm and yardstick for arguments and served to probe the arguments of the philosophical sciences as well as those of other disciplines.

Then, (once they had accepted the legitimacy of logic) scholars studied the premises the earlier theologians had established. They refuted most of them with the help of arguments leading them to a different opinion. Many of these (earlier) arguments were derived from philosophical discussions of physics and metaphysics, and when the scholars now probed them with the yardstick of logic, it showed that the earlier arguments (like those used by Ash°ari) were applicable only to those other (philosophical) disciplines and not to dialectical theology. But they did not believe that if the arguments were wrong, the conclusion was also wrong. . . . This approach differed in its technical terminology from the earlier one; it was called "the school of recent scholars" [or, "the modern school"], and their approach often included a refutation of the philosophers as well, where the opinions of the latter differed from the articles of faith. They considered the philosophers the enemies of the articles of faith because in most respects there is a relationship between the opinions of the innovators and the opinions of the philosophers.

The first scholar to write in accordance with the (new) theological approach was al-Ghazali (d. 1111 C.E.). He was followed by the imam Ibn al-Khatib [Fakhr al-Din al-Razi; d. 1209 C.E.]. A large number of scholars followed in their steps and adhered to their tradition. (Ibn Khaldun, *Muqaddima* 6.14) [IBN KHALDUN 1967: 3:50–52]

Ibn Khaldun follows the evolution of dialectical theology down closer to his own time.

If one considers how this discipline (of dialectical theology) originated and how scholarly discussion was incorporated in it step by step, and how, during this process, scholars always assumed the correctness of the articles of faith and paraded proofs and arguments in their defense, one will realize that the character of this discipline is as we have established it, and that the discipline cannot go beyond those limits. However, the two approaches have been mixed up by recent scholars: the problems of theology have been confused with those of philosophy. This has gone so far that one discipline is no longer distinguishable from the other. The student cannot learn theology from the books of the recent scholars, and the same situation confronts the student of philosophy. Such mixing was done by Baydawi (d. 1286 C.E.) . . . , and by later, non-Arab scholars in all their works. . . .

The approach of the early Muslims can be reconciled with the beliefs of the science of dialectical theology only if one follows the old approach of the theologians (and not the mixed approach of more recent scholars). The basic work here is the *Right Guidance* of al-Juwayni (d. 1083 C.E.), as well as works that follow its example. Those who want to inject a refutation of the philosophers into their dogmatic beliefs must use the books of Ghazali and Fakhr al-Din Razi. These latter do show some divergencies from the old technique, but do not make such a confusion of problems and subjects as is found in the approach of the recent scholars who have come after them.

Ibn Khaldun then sums up with his own reflections on speculative or dialectical theology. The year, it will be recalled, is 1377 C.E.

In general, it must be known that this science, the science of dialectical theology, is not something that is necessary to the contemporary student. Heretics and innovators have been destroyed. The orthodox religious leaders have given us protection against heretics and innovators in their systematic works and treatments. Logical arguments were needed only when they defended and supported (their views with them). Now, all that remains of those arguments is a certain amount of discussion, from most of whose ambiguities and inferences the Creator can be considered to be free. (Ibn Khaldun, *Muqaddima* 6.14) [IBN KHALDUN 1967: 3:53–54]

3. The Limited Role of Dialectical Theology

It was not, then, an entirely successful enterprise in Islam, this dialectical theology. The fundamentalists regarded its use of intellectual arguments as unnecessarily rationalistic, while more philosophically sophisticated Muslims criticized its lack of scientific rigor. Ghazali—for Ibn Khaldun the first of the "modernists" in theology—a scholar who had studied the methods of discursive reasoning used by Greek and Muslim philosophers, understood both the usefulness and the limits of dialectical theology, and like Ibn Khaldun, he emphasizes its essentially defensive function.

God sent to His servants by the mouth of His Messenger, in the Quran and the prophetic traditions, a creed which is the truth and whose contents are the basis of man's welfare in both religious and secular affairs. But Satan too sent, in the suggestions of heretics, things contrary to orthodoxy; men tended to accept his suggestions and almost corrupted the true creed for its adherents. So God brought into being the class of (dialectical) theologians, and moved them to support traditional orthodoxy with the weapon of systematic theology by laying bare the confused doctrines invented by the heretics at variance with traditional orthodoxy. This is the origin of (dialectical) theology and theologians.

In due course a group of theologians performed the task to which God invited them; they successfully preserved orthodoxy, defended the creed received from the prophetic source and rectified heretical innovations. Nevertheless in so doing they based their arguments on premises which they took from their opponents and which they were compelled to admit by naive belief or the consensus of the community or bare acceptance of the Quran and the prophetic traditions. For the most part their efforts were devoted to making explicit the contradictions of their opponents and criticizing them in respect of the logical consequences of what they admitted.

This might serve with Muslims who were willing to start at the same shared premises, but it would hardly do with those other philosophers and theologians trained in the Hellenic mode and committed to beginning with the first principles of reason.

This was of little use in the case of one who admitted nothing at all save logically necessary truths. . . . It is true that, when theology appeared as a recognized discipline and much effort had been expended in it over a considerable period of time, the theologians, becoming very earnest in their endeavors to defend orthodoxy by the study of what things really are, embarked on the study of substances and accidents with their natures and properties. But since that was not the (principal) aim of their science, they did not deal with the question thoroughly in their thinking and consequently did not arrive at results sufficient to dispel universally the darkness of confusion due to the different views of men. I do not exclude the possibility that for others than myself these results have been sufficient; indeed, I do not doubt that this has been so for quite a number. But these results were mingled with naive beliefs in certain matters which are not included among first principles. (Ghazali, *Deliverer from Error* 81–83) [GHAZALI 1953: 27–29]

4. The Fundamentalist Position: "Without Howing" versus Dialectical Theology

One of the areas in which the early Muslim proponents of dialectical theology used their newly discovered skills was in explaining the various attributes attached to God in the Quran, "merciful," "compassionate," "powerful," "seeing," "knowing," "hearing," and the like. Some raise an immediate problem: how indeed can God see without eyes, or shall we credit Him with eyes as well? The problem is anthropomorphism, a problem that, upon closer inspection, all the attributes raise in one way or another. The early dialectical theologians attempted to address the problem in the same time-honored fashion invoked by Jewish and Christian theologians, the prudent use of allegorical exegesis (see chapter 4 above).

The allegorizing of the divine attributes is an issue that never quite disappeared in Islam, and it was one of the grounds of choice for Muslim conservatives—the overwhelming number of them lawyers—to confront the theologians. Among the lawyers it was the followers of Ahmad Ibn Hanbal (d. 855 c.e.) who took the most conservative positions of all. A Hanbalite spokesman in late twelfth-century Damascus was Ibn Qudama (d. 1223 c.e.), whose works include one pointedly entitled The Prohibition of the Study of the Works of the Dialectical Theologians. *He is here concluding.*

We have already clearly shown by what has preceded, the evilness of the science of dialectical theology by virtue of its very source, the censure of it by our religious leaders, the universal agreement of the learned men that its advocates are partisans of heretical innovations and error, that they are not considered to belong to the ranks of learned men, that whoever occupies himself with it becomes a heretic and will not prosper. (Ibn Qudama, *Prohibition* 90) [IBN QUDAMA 1962: 36–37]

The issue is a familiar one, and it serves to clarify what precisely constitutes heresy in Islam.

Allegorical interpretation is a novelty in religion. Now a novelty is any doctrine in religion with regard to which the Companions [that is, the generation of Muhammad's "contemporaries," the latter term construed broadly] had died without ceasing to keep their silence. Novelty in religion is the heretical innovation against which our Prophet has cautioned us, and of which he informed us that it is the most evil of things. He has said (in a tradition): "The most evil things are the innovated ones." He has also said (likewise in a tradition): "Keep to my course of conduct and the course of conduct of the (first four) rightly guided Caliphs after me; hold fast thereto." "Beware of innovated things; for every innovation is a heretical innovation, and every heretical innovation is an error." Now, the allegorical interpreter has deserted the course of conduct of the Apostle of God and that of the rightly guided Caliphs; he is an inventor of heretical novelties, gone astray by virtue of the tradition mentioned. (Ibn Qudama, *Prohibition* 56) [IBN QUDAMA 1962: 21–22]

How then is one to deal with all the apparent anthropomorphisms used to characterize God in the Quran and the Prophetic traditions? Simply by accepting them, Ibn Qudama asserts, and offers a clear exposition of the conservative position in theology, the doctrine known in shorthand fashion as "Without Howing." The authority is no less than the eponym of the school himself.

An (earlier) Hanbalite has said: I asked Abu Abdullah Ahmad ibn Muhammad ibn Hanbal about those traditions which relate that God will be seen, and that He sets His foot down, and other relations similar to these. Whereupon Abu Abdullah answered: We believe in them, and accept them as true, without rejecting any part of them, when their chains of transmitters are sound; nor do we refuse the statements of the Apostle, for we know that what he has brought to us is true.

God should not be described in excess of His own description of Himself, boundless and immeasurable: "There is nothing like Him! He is the Hearing, the Seeing" (Quran 42:11). Therefore we say exactly what He has said, and describe Him as He has described Himself, without going beyond His description, nor removing from Him any of His attributes merely for fear of some possible slander which might be leveled against us. We believe in these traditions, we acknowledge them, and we allow them to pass intact as they have come down to us, *without being able to understand the how of them*, nor fathom their intended sense, except in accordance with his own description of Himself; and He is, according to His own description, the Hearing, the Seeing, boundless, immeasurable. His attributes proceed from Him and are His own. We do not go beyond the Quran or the traditions of the Prophet and his Companions; *nor do we know the how of these*, save by the acknowledgement of the Apostle and the confirmation of the Quran. (Ibn Qudama, *Prohibition* 19) [IBN QUDAMA 1962: 8–9; emphasis added]

5. Ash'ari on the Charge of Heretical Innovation

Ibn Qudama's view that dialectical theology constituted a reprehensible innovation in Islam was hardly novel. The charge had been leveled against theologians almost from the beginning; indeed, Ash'ari himself (d. 935 C.E.), one of the fathers of the discipline, had taken up arms against this allegation in a tract called On Thinking Well of Engaging in the Science of Theology. *The Prophet, it was said by the opponents of theology, knew nothing about such newfangled notions as "motion and rest, body and accident, accidental modes and states." Wrong, says Ash'ari.*

The Apostle of God did know these questions about which they have asked, and he was not ignorant of any detail involved in them. However, they did not occur in his time in such specific form that he should have, or should not have, discussed them—even though their basic principles were present in the Quran and the tradition of the Prophet. But whenever a question arose which was related to religion from the standpoint of the Law, men discussed it, and inquired into it, and disputed about it, and debated and argued. . . . Such questions, too numerous to mention, arose in their days, and in the case of each one there had come no explicit determination from the Prophet. For if he had given explicit instructions concerning all that, they would not have differed over those questions, and the differences would not have lasted till now.

The mere fact of these differences of opinion shows that men investigated, and will continue to investigate, matters of importance on which neither the Quran nor the tradition gives guidance. More, Ash'ari continues, the analogical method so typical of theology was the same one used in these investigations.

But even though there was no explicit instruction of the Apostle of God regarding each one of these questions, they referred and likened each to something which had been determined explicitly in the Book of God, and the Tradition, and their own independent judgment. Such questions, then, which involved judgments on unprecedented secondary causes, they referred to those determinations of the Law which are derivative, and which are to be sought only along the line of revelation and the Prophetic tradition. But when new and specific questions pertaining to basic dogmas arise, every intelligent Muslim ought to refer judgment on them to the sum of principles accepted on the grounds of reason, sense experience, intuition, etc.

Judgment on legal questions which belong to the category of what is passed down by tradition is to be based on reference to legal principles which likewise belong to the category of the traditioned, and judgment on questions involving the data of reason and the senses should be a matter of referring every such instance to (something within) its own category, without confounding the rational with the traditioned or the traditioned with the rational. So if dialectical theology on the creation of the Quran and on the atom . . . had originated in those precise terms in the Prophet's time, he would have discussed and explained it, just as he explained and discussed all the specific questions which did originate in his time. (Ash°ari, *The Science of Dialectical Theology* 21–22) [ASH°ARI 1953: 130–131]

6. Rationalist Theology

As some thinkers noted, there was, however, a fatal flaw in the dialectical theology of the medieval Muslims and their Jewish imitators, namely, that it was mostly dialectic and very little theology. But there were also those few determined rationalists who, as Ghazali described them, "admitted nothing at all save logically necessary truths," to wit, the partisans of metaphysics or rationalistic theology on the Greek model. In his autobiographical Deliverer from Error Ghazali offers a capsule history of this kind of theology from its point of origin among the Hellenes.

The study of philosophy began, Ghazali explains, with the "Materialists," who simply denied a Creator and posited an eternal cycle of everlasting generation, "animals from seed and seed from animals." The second group, the "Naturalists," were constrained by the order and excellence of nature to admit the existence of a Creator God, but they deny any spiritual existence and so the immortality of the soul and an afterlife. Finally there are the "more modern" philosophers called "Theists," who include Socrates, Plato, and Aristotle, the last of whom "systematized logic for them and organized the sciences, securing a higher degree of accuracy and bringing them to maturity."

The Theists in general attacked the two previous groups, the Materialists and the Naturalists, and exposed their defects so effectively that others were relieved of the task. . . . Aristotle, moreover, attacked his predecessors among the Theistic philosophers, especially Plato and Socrates, and went so far in his criticisms that he separated himself from them. Yet he too retained a residue of their unbelief and heresy from which he did not manage to free himself. We must therefore reckon as unbelievers both those philosophers themselves and their followers among the Islamic philosophers, such as Ibn Sina (or Avicenna), al-Farabi and others; in transmitting the philosophy of Aristotle, however, none of the Islamic philosophers has accomplished anything comparable to the two men named. . . . (Ghazali, *Deliverer from Error* 87–88) [GHAZALI 1953: 31–32]

The principal area of unbelief lay, according to Ghazali, in the science called theology or metaphysics.

Here occur most of the errors of the philosophers. They are unable to satisfy the conditions of proof they lay down in logic and consequently differ much from one another here. The views of Aristotle, as expounded by Farabi and Avicenna, are close to those of the Islamic writers. All their errors are comprised under twenty heads, on three of which they must be reckoned infidels and on seventeen heretical innovators. . . . The three points in which they differ from all Muslims are as follows:

(1) [On the physical reality of Paradise and Hell], they say that for bodies there is no Resurrection: it is bare spirits which are rewarded or punished; and the rewards and punishments are spiritual, not bodily. They certainly speak true in affirming the spiritual ones, since these do exist as well; but they speak falsely in denying the bodily ones and in their pronouncements disbelieve the revelation.

(2) [On divine providence], they say that God knows universals, but not particulars. This too is plain unbelief. The truth is that "there does not escape Him the weight of an atom in the heavens or in the earth" (Quran 34:3).

(3) [On the eternity of the world], they say that the world is everlasting, without beginning. But no Muslim has adopted any such view on this question. (Ghazali, *Deliverer from Error* 96–97) [GHAZALI 1953: 35–36]

7. Farabi on God's Providence

We shall shortly note the issue between theology and Islam on the subject of the afterlife; here we see one of Islam's premier philosophers, al-Farabi, attempting to pick his careful way through the thorny and dangerous subject of divine providence.

Many people hold divergent beliefs concerning the Lord's care of His creation. It is held by some that He cares for His creation in the same manner that a king cares for his subjects and their well-being, though without personally conducting the affairs of any of them, and without connection between Himself and any partner or wife; rather He appoints to the task someone who will undertake it and perform it, and in its performance do whatever right and justice demand.

Farabi makes no comment on that view, so it may be his own, though we cannot be certain. The second is distinctly not his opinion, however.

Others are of the opinion that His care is not sufficient short of His undertaking the personal management of each one of His creatures in each one of his actions, and directing him aright, and leaving none of His creatures to (the care of) others. It would then follow that He would be responsible for many actions which are defective, ignoble, and ugly, errors and abominable words and deeds, and when any of His creatures aims at attacking one of His clients—a reversal of truth merely for the sake of argument—He is his helper and responsible for leading him and guiding him. . . . And if they deny that He directs and helps such for some things, they must likewise deny the whole doctrine. Such principles give rise to wrong ideas and are the source of vicious and abominable ways of acting. (Farabi, *Aphorisms of the Statesman* 82)

8. Ghazali on Theology and Muslim Belief

Ghazali remained unconvinced by such explanations.

Among the most extreme and extravagant of men are a group of scholastic theologians who dismiss the Muslim common people as unbelievers and claim that whoever does not know scholastic theology in the form they recognize and does not know the prescriptions of the Holy Law according to the proofs which they have adduced is an unbeliever.

These people have constricted the vast mercy of God to His servants and made Paradise the preserve of a small clique of theologians. They have disregarded what is handed down by the Prophetic traditions, for it is clear that in the time of the Prophet, may God bless and save him, and in the time of the Companions of the Prophet, may God be pleased with them, the Islam of whole groups of rude Arabs was recognized, though they were busy worshiping idols. They did not concern themselves with the science of analogical proof and would have understood nothing of it if they had.

Whoever claims that theology, abstract proofs, and systematic classification are the foundations of belief is an innovator. Rather is belief a light which God bestows on the hearts of His creatures as a gift and a bounty from Him, sometimes through an explainable conviction from within, sometimes because of a dream in sleep, sometimes by seeing the state of bliss of a pious man and the transmission of his light through association and conversation with him, sometimes through one's own state of bliss. (Ghazali, *The Basis of Distinction* 202)

9. The Truth of Philosophy

And yet Ghazali was by no means a fundamentalist in the mold of Ibn Qudama. He understood both the attractions and the dangers of philosophy and science, but he was unwilling to permit the dangers to be used as a reason for dismissing the truth and the certitude that philosophy brought. Mathematics provides an almost classic instance.

None of its results are connected with religious matters, either to deny or affirm them. They are matters of demonstration which it is impossible to deny once they have been understood and apprehended. Nevertheless there are two drawbacks which arise from mathematics. The first is that every student of mathematics admires its precision and the clarity of its demonstrations. This leads him to believe in the philosophers (and scientists generally) and to think that all their sciences resemble this one in clarity and cogency. Further, he has already heard the accounts on everyone's lips of their unbelief, their denial of God's attributes and their contempt for revealed truth; he becomes an unbeliever merely by accepting them as authorities, and says to himself, "If (revealed) religion were true, it would not have escaped the notice of these men since they are so precise in this science."

That is one extreme, seduction by mathematics; the other is no more attractive.

The second drawback arises from the man who is loyal to Islam but ignorant. He thinks that religion must be defended by rejecting every science connected with the philosophers, and so rejects all their sciences and accuses them of ignorance therein. He even rejects their theory of the eclipse of the sun and the moon, considering that what they say is contrary to religion. . . . A grievous crime indeed against religion has been committed by the man who imagines that Islam is defended by the denial of the mathematical sciences, seeing that there is nothing in revealed truth opposed to these sciences by way of either negation or affirmation, and nothing in these sciences opposed to the truths of revelation. (Ghazali, *Deliverer from Error* 90–91) [GHAZALI 1953: 33–34]

10. Rationalist Ethics and Revealed Morality

Ghazali had no brief for or interest in mathematics; it simply provided him, by the clarity and cogency of its demonstrations, with a casebook model for the truth of science, even the foreign and often heretical science of the Greeks and their Muslim followers. Ethics, on the other hand, with its judgments about conduct and morality, is a rival of revealed religion, and so a more interesting and complicated case. There are, for example, instances in which the teachings of philosophical ethics, a well-defined branch of the Hellenic philosophical tradition, are identical with those of the Muslim moral theologians working with the data of revelation, as Ghazali saw himself doing. Two explanations are possible: that the former borrowed from the latter—an argument already familiar from Philo—or that the truth of God is essentially one and so there should be little wonder that different groups can reach it by different means. "Ethics," Ghazali begins, "consists in defining the characteristics and moral constitution of the soul and enumerating the various types of soul and the method of moderating and controlling them." He continues:

This they (that is, the philosophers) borrow from the teaching of the mystics, those men of piety whose chief occupation is to meditate upon God, to oppose the passions, and to walk in the way leading to God by withdrawing from worldly pleasure. In their spiritual warfare they have learnt about the virtues and vices of the soul and the defects in its actions, and what they have learned they have clearly expressed. The philosophers have taken over this teaching and mingled it with their own disquisitions, furtively using this embellishment to sell their rubbishy wares more readily. . . .

From this practice of the philosophers of incorporating in their books conceptions drawn from the prophets and the mystics, there arise two evil tendencies, one in their partisans and one in their opponents.

The evil tendency in the case of the opponent is serious. A crowd of men of slight intellect imagines that, since these ethical conceptions occur in the books of the philosophers mixed with their own rubbish, all reference to them must be avoided, and indeed any person mentioning them must be considered a liar. They imagine this because they heard of the conceptions in the first place only from the philosophers, and their weak intellects have concluded that, since their author is a falsifier, they must be false.

We have heard the argument before from Ghazali, in the case of those who wished to throw out all of mathematics, baby, bathwater, and eclipses of the sun and moon. Here, however, the instance is different.

This is like a man who hears a Christian assert, "There is no god but the God, and Jesus is the Messenger of God." The man rejects this, saying, "This is a Christian conception," and does not pause to ask himself whether the Christian is an infidel only in respect of his denial of the prophethood of Muhammad, peace be upon him. If he is an infidel only in respect of his denial of the prophethood of Muhammad, then he need not be contradicted in other assertions, true in themselves and not connected with his unbelief, even though these are also true in his eyes (like the Christian statement cited above).

Ghazali then passes onto far more personal terrain than a defense of the Christians' right to be correct on certain religious matters.

To some of the statements made in our published works on the principles of the religious sciences an objection has been raised by a group of men whose understanding has not fully grasped the sciences and whose insight has not penetrated to the fundamentals of the systems. They think that these statements are taken from the works of the ancient philosophers, whereas the fact is that some of them are the product of reflections which occurred to me independently—it is not improbable that one foot should fall on another footprint—while others come from the revealed Scriptures, and in the case of the majority the sense, though perhaps not the actual words, is found in the works of the mystics.

After this not entirely spirited defense of his own originality, Ghazali comes to the difficult heart of the matter, the spoliatio Aegyptorum *or, to use Ghazali's own figure, honey in a cupping glass.*

Suppose, however, that the statements (that is, certain moral teachings) are found only in the philosophers' books. If they are reasonable in themselves and supported by proof, and if they do not contradict the Book and the Custom of the Prophet, then it is not necessary to abstain from using them. If we open this door, if we adopt the attitude of abstaining from every truth that the mind of a heretic has apprehended before us, we should be obliged to abstain from much that is true. We should be obliged to leave aside a great number of verses of the Quran and the traditions of the Messenger and the accounts of the early Muslims, and all the sayings of the philosophers and the mystics. . . . The lowest degree of education is to distinguish oneself from the ignorant ordinary man. The educated man does not loathe honey even if he finds it in the surgeon's cupping-glass; he realizes that the cupping-glass does not essentially alter the honey. The natural aversion from it in such a case rests on popular ignorance, arising from the fact that the cupping-glass is made only for impure blood. Men imagine that the blood is impure because it is in the cupping-glass, and are not aware that the impurity is due to a property of the blood itself. (Ghazali, *Deliverer from Error* 99–105) [GHAZALI 1953: 38–42]

11. Ibn Rushd:
The Law Commands the Study of Philosophy

There were few in Islam who were willing to dispute Ghazali on this point; indeed, as is clear from Ibn Qudama's position, many Muslims found Ghazali's stance far too liberal when it came to the use of reason in thinking about God. The one voice raised against Ghazali in the name of philosophy was that of the Spanish scholar Ibn Rushd (d. 1198 C.E.), demonstrably the greatest student of the Hellenic philosophical tradition ever produced in Islam. Ghazali's Incoherence of the Philosophers *was countered point by point in Ibn Rushd's* Incoherence of the Incoherence. *Here, however, we hear the man the West knew as Averroes speaking to the issue of philosophy in Islam in more general, and very Muslim, terms. We are now at the opposite pole from Ibn Qudama: not only is intellectual investigation not heresy; it is commanded by the Islamic law.*

Praise be to God with all due praise, and a prayer for Muhammad, His chosen servant and Messenger. The purpose of this treatise is to examine, from the standpoint of the study of the (Islamic) Law, whether the study of philosophy and logic is allowed by the Law, or prohibited, or commanded, either by way of recommendation or as obligatory.

We say: If the activity of philosophy is no more than the study of existing beings and the reflection on them as indications of the Artisan (or Creator), that is, inasmuch as they are products of art, for beings also indicate the Artisan through our knowledge of the art in them, and the more perfect this knowledge is, the more perfect the knowledge of the Artisan becomes, and if the Law has encouraged and urged reflection on beings, then it is clear that what this name (of philosophy) signifies is either obligatory or recommended by the Law.

That the Law summons us to reflection on beings, and the pursuit of knowledge about them by the intellect, is clear from the several verses of the Book of God, blessed be He and exalted, such as the saying of the Exalted, "Reflect, you have vision" (Quran 59:2); this is textual authority for the obligation to use intellectual reasoning, or a combination of intellectual and legal reasoning. Another example is His saying, "Have you not studied the kingdom of the heavens and the earth, and whatever things God has created?" (Quran 8:185); this is a text urging the study of the totality of beings. Again, God the Exalted has taught that one of those whom He singularly honored by this knowledge was Abraham, peace be upon him, for the Exalted said, "So we made Abraham see the kingdom of the heavens and the earth, that he might be etc." (Quran 2:5–6). The Exalted also said, "Do they not observe the camels, how they have been created, and the sky, how it has been raised up?" (Quran 2:6–7); and He said, "and they gave thought to the creation of the heavens and the earth" (Quran 2:7), and so in countless other verses.

Since it has now been established that the Law has rendered obligatory the study of beings by the intellect, and reflection on them, and since reflection is nothing more than inference and drawing out of the unknown from the known, and since this is reasoning or at any rate done by reasoning, therefore we are under an obligation to carry on our study of beings by intellectual reasoning. It is further evident that this manner of study, to which the Law summons and urges, is the most perfect kind of study using the most perfect kind of reasoning; and this is the kind called "demonstration."

The Law, then, has urged us to have demonstrative knowledge of God the Exalted and all the beings of His creation. But it is preferable and even necessary for anyone who wants to understand God the Exalted and the other beings demonstratively to have first understood the kinds of demonstration and their conditions (of validity), and in what respects demonstrative reasoning differs from dialectical, rhetorical and fallacious reasoning. But this is not possible unless he has previously learned what reasoning as such is, and how many kinds it has, and which of them are valid and which invalid. This in turn is not possible unless he has previously learned the parts of reasoning, of which it is composed, that is, the premises and their kinds. Therefore he who believes in the Law and obeys its commands to study beings, ought prior to his study to gain a knowledge of these things, which have the same place in theoretical studies as instruments have in practical activities. (Ibn Rushd, *The Decisive Treatise* 1–2) [AVERROES 1961: 44–46]

One objection can be easily dispensed with.

It cannot be objected: "This kind of study of intellectual reasoning is a heretical innovation since it did not exist among the first believers." For the study of legal reasoning and its kinds is also something which has been discovered since the (time of) the first believers, yet it is not considered a heretical innovation. So the objector should believe the same about the study of intellectual reasoning. For this there is a reason, which is not the place to answer here. But most (masters) of this religion (that is, Islam) support intellectual reasoning, except a small group of gross literalists, who can be refuted by (sacred) texts. (Ibn Rushd, *The Decisive Treatise* 3) [AVERROES 1961: 46]

Ibn Rushd was not, however, naive; he was well aware of the dangers to the faith, real or alleged, that are associated with the study of Greek philosophy.

From (all) this it is evident that the study of the books of the ancients is obligatory by (Islamic) Law, since their aim and purpose in their books is just the purpose to which the Law has urged us, and that whoever forbids the study of them to anyone who is fit to study them, that is, anyone who unites the two qualities of natural intelligence and religious integrity, is blocking people from the door by which the Law summons them to knowledge of God, the door of theoretical study which leads to the truest knowledge of Him; and such an act is the extreme of ignorance and estrangement from God the Exalted.

And if someone errs or stumbles in the study of these books owing to a deficiency in his natural capacity, or bad organization of his study of them, or being dominated by his passions, or not finding a teacher to guide him to an understanding of their contents, or a combination of all or more than one of these causes, it does not follow that one should forbid them to anyone who is qualified to study them. For this manner of harm which arises owing to them is attached to them by accident, not by essence; and when a thing is beneficial by its nature and essence, it ought not to be shunned because of something harmful contained in it by accident. This was the thought of the Prophet, peace be upon him, on the occasion when he ordered a man to give his brother honey to drink for his diarrhea, and the diarrhea increased after he had given him the honey; when the man complained to him about it, he said, "God spoke the truth; it was your brother's stomach that lied." We can even say that a man who prevents a qualified person from studying books of philosophy, because some of the most vicious people may be thought to have gone astray through their study of them, is like a man who prevents a thirsty person from drinking cool, fresh water until he dies from thirst because some people have choked to death on it. For death from water by choking is an accidental matter, but death by thirst is essential and elementary. (Ibn Rushd, *The Decisive Treatise* 5–6) [AVERROES 1961: 48–49]

12. The Mystic's Gnosis and the Theologian's Science

The philosopher and the theologian both claimed a privileged access to a knowledge of God, claims resting essentially on the primacy and autonomy of reason. But there was another such claim in Islam, as there had been in the two Abrahamic faiths that preceded it: the mystic too claimed the benefit of a privileged knowledge of God, primary, authentic and immediate, visionary, intuitive—a genuine gnosis.

Ghazali, who was in the unique position of being both a theologian and a mystic, has left us a comparative evaluation of the mystic's inspired gnosis and the theologian's discursively developed understanding in his Revivification of the Sciences of Religion. *Both ways of knowing do indeed open a way to God, but there are fundamental and crucial differences between them, as he pedagogically explains in a chapter subtitled "Wherein there is set forth the difference between inspiration and study, between the way of the Sufis in discovering the truth and the way of those given over to speculative knowledge."*

Be aware that the types of knowledge which are not necessarily possessed by everyone come into the heart in different ways and the mode by which they arrive varies. At times they appear unexpectedly in the heart as if they had been thrown in from the heart knows not what source. At other times they are acquired by the method of intellectual elaboration and study. The knowledge which arises neither by way of acquisition nor by the operation of a deductive chain is called inspiration; that which comes about from intellectual elaboration is called examination or reflection.

The knowledge which presents itself in the heart of a sudden and without striving, study, or work on the part of the subject is of two types: the first of the kind that a man is unaware how it came to him or whence; the second carries with it an understanding of the means whereby it came, that is, the vision of the angel who cast it into the heart. The first type is called inspiration and breathes in the depths of the heart; the second is called revelation and properly belongs to the prophets. As for the first, it is characteristic of the saints and the pure of heart, while the previously mentioned type of knowledge, the kind acquired by means of intellectual elaboration, is proper to the learned.

After this somewhat scholastic introduction, Ghazali turns to more Quranic—and more mystic—images and language.

What can be truly said of the subject (of such inspired knowledge) is that his heart is ready to receive the irradiation of the Truth of Truths which is in all things. Nothing in effect can interpose itself between the heart and things . . . a kind of veil which puts itself between the mirror of the heart and the Well-Guarded tablet upon which is inscribed all that God had decreed until the Day of Resurrection. The truths of knowledge radiate from the mirror of the tablet onto the mirror of the heart, as an image produced on a mirror will imprint itself on another place in front of it.

The veil which is between the two mirrors is sometimes drawn aside by the hand, sometimes by the breaths of air that move it. Thus there blow at times the breaths of grace; the veils are then lifted from before the eyes of the heart and certain of the things inscribed on the Well-Guarded Tablet are reflected in him. That occurs from time to time in sleep and by this means one knows what will happen in the future. As for the complete removal of the veil, that will occur at the point of death when there will be removed that which conceals. But it also happens that the veil is drawn aside during the waking state to the extent of being lifted by a hidden grace of God Most High, and then something of the marvels of knowledge gleam in hearts from behind the veil of the Mystery. At times it is like a quick lightning flash; at other times a whole series of them, but limited, and it is extremely rare that this condition is much prolonged.

Just as it is only the mode of its acquisition that distinguishes the mystic's grace-inspired knowledge from the scholar's—whether he is one of the philosophers or one of the ulama class—sweat-equity knowledge, the same distinction prevails between inspiration, God's gift to the saint, and revelation, God's gift to the prophet.

Inspired knowledge differs from acquired knowledge neither by its nature nor its locus nor its cause but only with respect to the removal of the veil: that is not within the power of man. And revelation in turn does not differ from inspiration with respect to any of these but only by the vision of the angel who brings the knowledge, which comes into our hearts only through the agency of angels. God Most high alludes to it in His words "It is not given to man that God should speak to him, except by a revelation, or from behind a veil, or by sending an apostle in order that this latter, by God's permission, reveals to man what God wishes" (Quran 42:50–51).

With these preliminaries out of the way, the mystics' most influential and respected spokesman in Islam comes to the parting of the paths and follows the one that leads to his real subject, the Sufi way to God.

With this introduction, know that Sufis prefer the knowledge that comes by inspiration, to the exclusion of that acquired by study. Again, they desire neither to study such learning nor to learn anything of what authors have written on the subject: to inspect neither their teachings nor their arguments. They maintain on the contrary that the "way" consists in preferring spiritual combat, in getting rid of one's faults, in breaking one's ties and approaching God Most High through a single-minded spiritual effort. And every time those conditions are fulfilled, God for His part turns toward the heart of His servant and guarantees him an illumination by the lights of understanding.

Since God Most High has reserved to Himself the power of governing the heart, when the Mercy of God is extended upon this latter, light shines there, his breast expands, the secret of the Kingdom is revealed to him, the veil which blinded him disappears from before his face by the grace of the Mercy and the Truths shine out before him. The only thing in the power of the believer is that he prepare by the purification that strips him clean and that he arouse in himself a care for such things, as well as a sincere will, a consuming thirst and an attentive observation in the constant expectation of what God most High will reveal to him of His Mercy.

As for the prophets and the saints, this object was never revealed to them and the light was never expanded in their breasts either by dint of study or intellectual labors or by things written in books, but they arrived at it by renouncing the world to lead an ascetic life, by freeing themselves of their attachments, by emptying their hearts of their earthly occupations, and by approaching God Most High by a single-minded spiritual effort. And he who is God's, God is his.

The Sufis say that the way that leads to such an end consists first of all in cutting off all one's attachments to the world, to cease preoccupying oneself with family, wealth, children, one's homeland, as well as with learning, with authority, with honor; and more, to bring the heart to a state where the existence or nonexistence of everything is a matter of indifference. Then the Sufi retires into his own company, into a cell, obliging himself to fulfill the obligatory religious precepts and obligations. He remains thus, his heart empty, concentrating on a single objective. He does not dissipate his thoughts either by reading the Quran or meditating on one of its commentaries, or on the books of Prophetic traditions or any other. He attempts to achieve just the opposite, that nothing should enter his spirit save God Most High.

When he is seated in solitude, he does not cease to say "God, God," continuously and with a recollected heart. And he carries on until he comes to a state where he abandons the movement of his tongue and imagines the word [that is, the name of God] rolling off his tongue. Then he arrives at the point of obliterating any trace of the word from his tongue and he finds his heart continuously applied to (the exercise of) recollection. And he perseveres in it with determination until he reaches the point where he effaces the image of this word from his heart, the letters and the form of the word, and only the sense of the word remains in his heart, present within him, as if joined to him and never leaving him.

It is within his power to arrive at this point and to make this stage endure while resisting temptations. He cannot, however, draw upon himself the Mercy of God Most High. Rather, by his efforts he makes himself ready to receive the breaths of the divine Mercy and there remains nothing else for him to do but to await what God will reveal to him of His Mercy, as He revealed it, by this same way, to the prophets and the saints.

Then, if the will (of the Sufi) has been sincere, his spiritual effort a pure one, and his perseverance perfect; if he has not been carried in the opposite direction by his passions nor preoccupied by an unrest arising from his attachments to the world, then the rays of the Truth will shine in his heart. At the outset this will be like a sudden lightning that does not last, then returns, but slowly. If it does return, sometimes it remains and sometimes it is only passing. If it remains, sometimes its presence is extended and sometimes not. And at times illuminations like the first appear, one following the other; at other times they are reduced to a single experience. The saints "resting" in that state are without number, just as their natures and characters are innumerable.

In sum: this way leads solely, insofar as it concerns you, to a complete purity, purification and clarity, and then to being ready, expectant.

Finally Ghazali returns to the opening theme, the difference between the inspired knowledge of the Sufi and the discursive knowledge of the theologian.

As for those who practice speculation and discursive examination, they do not deny the existence of this way (of the Sufi), nor its possibility, nor that it can arrive at such an end on rare occasions: it is, after all, the state often achieved by the prophets and the saints. But they have looked upon it as an arduous way, slow to yield its fruits, requiring a complex of conditions rarely achieved. They have maintained that at this point it is almost impossible to break one's attachments to the world and that to arrive at a "state" and remain there is more difficult still. . . . As a consequence of this kind of spiritual struggle (they say), the temperament is spoiled, the reason disordered and the body made ill. If the soul has not been exercised (by the practices of piety) and formed by the realities of the sciences to begin with, the heart is monopolized by corrupt imaginings in which the soul takes its rest over an extended period of time, to the point that one's life is past and over without success having been achieved. How many Sufis who have followed this route have remained for twenty years in the grip of some imaginary fantasy, while someone who had previously been solidly grounded in learning would have immediately recognized the dubious quality of this product of the imagination. To devote oneself to following a course of study is the surest way of proceeding and accomplishing the end.

(The dialectical theologians) say that this attitude of the Sufis is like that of a man who neglects the study of the religious law by maintaining that the Prophet, may the peace and blessing of God be upon him, did not study but became expert in this discipline by revelation and inspiration, without studying texts or writing commentaries on them, and so will I, perhaps, by the practice of asceticism and sheer perseverance. Whoever thinks that way, they maintain, does ill to himself and is squandering his life. Indeed, he is like a man who leaves off trying to earn a living and cultivating the soil in the hope of chancing upon some buried treasure or other, something that is possible but highly improbable. (Ghazali, *Revivification of the Sciences of Religion* 3.16–17)

13. The Illumination of the Intellect

The chief Muslim agent of the turning of both philosophy and mysticism in the direction of theosophy was the philosopher Ibn Sina or Avicenna (d. 1038 C.E.). His contribution to the development and refinement of Islamic philosophy in its then current blend of Plato and Aristotle was enormous, but there are hints throughout his work that Avicenna had, behind and beyond his public and scholastic treatments of philosophical themes, a more esoteric "oriental philosophy" whose contents could only be hinted at. The obliqueness of Avicenna's own allusions make its identification somewhat problematic, but a great many Muslims who came after him understood Avicenna's esoteric philosophy as some form of mysticism, and identified its author as a Sufi.

Whether or not he was a Sufi in any formal sense, Avicenna laid heavy emphasis upon some form of divine illumination (ishraq) as the means whereby the philosopher received the knowledge that was the object of his quest. Avicenna's "illumination" probably owed a great deal more to Neoplatonism than his many commentators and imitators were prepared to admit. It was, at any rate, an individual effort and an individual achievement, this pursuit of union with God, and there is nothing in Avicenna suggesting the classic Sufi theme of the passage of a spiritual baraka from master to novice, no charismatic "chain" upon which to mount on high.

One of Avicenna's most influential interpreters read him somewhat differently, however. Suhrawardi (d. 1191 C.E.) took up and completed Avicenna's "visionary recitals" and interpreted the philosopher's "oriental philosophy" as a genuine renaissance of Eastern, that is, Persian wisdom. For those ancient sages the First Being was Xvarneh, "the light of glory" of Zoroastrianism, and that opened for Suhrawardi the opportunity of converting what had been for Avicenna and Ghazali an epistemological metaphor into a true metaphysic: existence and light are identical; the Necessary Being is Absolute Light.

Though the Sunni lawyer and theologian was probably a less congenial figure to him than the Shi\`ite philosopher, Suhrawardi learned as much from Ghazali as he did from Avicenna. Ghazali (d. 1111 C.E.) had already anticipated, as we shall see, a new task for that perennial handmaiden, philosophy, and Suhrawardi developed it with enthusiasm. Specu-

lative knowledge, the wisdom that comes from research and investigation, was simply a preparation for the "wisdom that savors," the experimental knowledge of God. Philosophy thus received its justification and at the same time was assigned an appropriate place as a preparation for the final stages of the search for the Absolute. Suhrawardi likewise followed Ghazali in his elaboration of the rich possibilities of allegorical exegesis in the service of mysticism.

Suhrawardi's work, with its assertion of Persia's place in the history of Wisdom, its attractive metaphysic of light, its developed theory of allegorical exegesis, and its valorization of experience over theoretical knowledge, provided a program for both the philosophers and the mystics of Iran, and a convenient bridge upon which they might thereafter meet. That the meetings were frequent and rewarding is attested by the twin traditions of mystical poetry in Persian and the ill-charted but impressive course of theosophical and philosophical speculation during the reign of the Safavids in Iran.

A distinction has been drawn between the "Mysticism of Infinity" and the "Mysticism of Personality," and it has been argued that later Sufism is unmistakably in the former category, which acknowledges God as the Ultimate and Unique Reality whereas the world possesses only the "limited reality" of a distant emanation from the One Being. In the latter view all Reality is in fact One. This position was not very congenial to Muslim revelation, which stresses the gulf between the Creator and His creation, and which preached, in its mystical mode, an approach to God through moral activity and not identity with Him. Union or identity (ittihad) *with God was already a troublesome Sufi concept for the traditionists, but even more scandalous was the message broadcast by the influential philosopher and poet Ibn Arabi (d. 1204 C.E.), that of the "unity of Being."*

The Muslim scholastics' reverence for Ghazali and Ghazali's own moderating influence may have prevented a full-scale reaction to the rationalist strain in theology. But there are responses other than reaction, and the more radical mystical thinkers in Islam, more radical than al-Ghazali at any rate, illustrate another view of rationalism. For example, Ibn al-Arabi (1165–1240 C.E.) speaks from a supremely confident position—the text of his book The Bezels of Wisdom, *he informs the reader at the outset, was handed to him by none other than Muhammad himself in Damascus in the month of Muharram, 1230 C.E. Ibn al-Arabi simply dismisses the rationalizing and rationalist ways of trying to understand God as at worst ignorant and at best irrelevant. He tells this highly revealing anecdote about a meeting in Cordova between himself, the still very young patron saint of Islamic theosophy, and Ibn Rushd, the "second Aristotle" of Islam, in his* Meccan Revelations.

I spent a good day in Cordova at the house of Abu al-Walid ibn Rushd. He had expressed a desire to meet with me in person, since he had heard of certain revelations I had received while in retreat, and had shown considerable astonishment concerning them. In consequence, my father, who was one of his close friends, took me with him on the pretext of business, in order to give Ibn Rushd the opportunity of making my acquaintance. I was at the time a beardless youth.

As I entered the house the philosopher rose to greet me with all the signs of friendliness and affection, and embraced me. Then he said to me, "Yes!" and showed pleasure on seeing that I had understood him. I, on the other hand, when I became aware of the motive of his pleasure, replied "No!" At this Ibn Rushd drew back from me, his color changed and he seemed to doubt what he had thought of me. He then put to me the following question: "What solution have you found as a result of mystical illumination and divine inspiration?" I replied, "Yes and No. Between the Yea and the Nay the spirits take their flight beyond matter, and the necks detach themselves from their bodies." At this Ibn Rushd became pale, and I saw him tremble as he muttered the formula "There is no power save from God." This was because he had understood my allusion. (Ibn al-Arabi, *Meccan Revelations* 1.153) [IBN AL-ARABI 1980: 2]

We are somewhat less certain than Ibn Rushd about the meaning of the allusion, but there is no mistaking Ibn al-Arabi's views on what and how we know about God—or better, the Reality. He begins with an attack on the very foundation of the rationalist enterprise, the principle of causality.

An indication of the weakness of intellectual speculation is the notion that a cause cannot be (also) the effect of that to which it is a cause. Such is the judgment of the intellect, while in the science of divine Self-revelation it is known that a cause may be the effect of that for which it is a cause. . . . The most that the intellectual will admit to on this matter, when he sees that it contradicts speculative evidence, is that the essence, after it is established that it is one among many causes, in some form or other, of a (given) effect, cannot be an effect to its effect, so that that effect should become its cause, while the first still remains a cause, but that if its determination becomes changed by its transformation in forms, then it may thus become an effect to its own effect, which might then become its cause. This then is as far as he will go, when he perceives that the matter does not agree with his rational speculation.

There have been none more intelligent than the Messengers, God's blessing be on them, and what they brought us derives from the divine Majesty. They indeed confirmed what the intellect confirms, but added more that the intellect is not capable of grasping, things the intellect declares to be absurd, except in the case of one who has had an immediate experience of divine manifestation; afterwards, left to himself, he is confused as to what he has seen. If he is a servant of the Lord, he refers his intelligence to Him (to respond to his perplexities), but if he is a servant of reason, he reduces God to its yardstick. This happens only so long as he is in this worldly state, being veiled from his otherworldly state in this world. (Ibn al-Arabi, *The Bezels of Wisdom*, "Elias") [IBN AL-ARABI 1980: 234]

The "servant of the Lord" and the "servant of reason" are thus neatly distinguished. Other similar distinctions, all to the same point, appear often in his work.

For the believers and men of spiritual vision it is the creation that is surmised and the Reality that is seen and perceived, while in the case of those not in these two categories, it is the Reality Who is surmised and the creation that is seen and perceived by the senses. . . .

Men are divided into two groups. The first travel a way they know and whose destination they know, which is their Straight Path (Quran 11:56). The second group travel a way they do not know and of whose destination they are unaware, which is equally the Straight Path. The gnostic calls on God with spiritual perception, while he who is not a gnostic calls on Him in ignorance and bound by a tradition.

Such a knowledge is a special one stemming from "the lowest of the low" (Quran 95:5), since the feet are the lowest part of the person, what is lower than that being the way beneath them. He who knows that the Reality is the way knows the truth, for it is none other than He that you progress and travel, since there is naught to be known save Him, since He is Being Itself and therefore also the traveller himself. Further, there is no Knower save Him; so who are you? Therefore, know your true reality and your way, for the truth has been made known to you on the tongue of the Interpreter [that is, Muhammad], if you will only understand. He is a true word that none understands, save that his understanding be true; the Reality has many relations and many aspects. . . .

. . . You may say of Being what you will; either that it is the creation or that it is the Reality, or that it is at once both the creation and the Reality. It might also be said that there is neither creation nor the Reality, as one might admit to perplexity in the matter, since by assigning degrees the difficulties appear. But for the limitation (that arises in defining the Reality), the Messengers would not have taught that the Reality transforms Himself in cosmic forms nor would they have described Him (at the same time) as abstracting Himself from all forms. . . .

Because of this (inevitable limitation by definition), He is both denied and known, called incomparable and compared. He who sees the Reality from His standpoint, in Him and by Him, is a gnostic. He who sees the Reality from His standpoint, in Him, but with himself as the seer, is not a gnostic. He who does not see the Reality in this way, but expects to see Him by himself, he is ignorant.

In general most men have perforce an individual concept of their Lord, which they ascribe to Him and in which they seek Him. So long as the Reality is presented to them according to it, they recognize Him and affirm Him, whereas if it is presented in any other form, they deny Him, flee from Him and treat Him improperly, while at the same time imagining that they are acting toward Him fittingly. One who believes (in the ordinary way) believes only in a deity he has created in himself, since a deity in "beliefs" is a (mental) construction. They see (in this deity) only themselves and their own constructions within themselves. (Ibn al-Arabi, *The Bezels of Wisdom*, "Hud") [IBN AL-ARABI 1980: 132–133]

Sufism took eagerly to Ibn Arabi's version of a pantheistic universe and its supporting apparatus of Gnostic esoterics. Such traditionists as Ibn Taymiyya (d. 1328 C.E.) were equally quick to discover the dangers of the Sufi metaphysic and its freewheeling exegesis to what had by then been shaped into a consensual version of Sunni Islam. But the Sufis were by no means the only proponents of Gnosticism in the Islamic lands. There are Gnostic premises at the base of most of the occult sciences that flourished in the ancient and medieval world—alchemy for one—and the ease with which so many of them passed from one to another of the very different religious climates of ancient Greco-Roman paganism, Near Eastern Islam, and both Eastern and Western Christianity and Judaism underscores both the appeal and the adaptability of Gnosticism. And in Islam Gnosticism demonstrated that it could adapt itself as readily to political as to scientific ends.

The Isma ͨilis were a subdivision of the Shi ͨite movement who, unlike the main body of the Shi ͨa in the Middle Ages, had a political program for overthrowing the Sunni Caliph and replacing him with a revolutionary Mahdi-Imam (see below). They were not successful, but they had access to and put to effective use the entire Gnostic apparatus of cosmic history, in which the Shi ͨite Imams became the Gnostic Aeons: a secret revelation of the "realities" that lay hidden in the concealed (batin) rather than the evident sense of Scripture; an imamic guide who possessed an infallible and authoritative magisterium (ta ͨlim); and an initiated elite that formed, in the Isma ͨili case, the core of an elaborate political underground. At their headquarters in Cairo, a city that the Isma ͨili Fatimids founded in 969 C.E., agents were instructed in the Isma ͨili gnosis and program, and were sent forth with the "call" of the Mahdi-Imam to cells and cadres that had been set up in the caliphal lands in Iraq and Iran.

Sunni and Isma ͨili Islam shared a common foundation of reliance on authority and tradition. For the Sunni, that tradition was embodied in the elaborate structure of Muslim law which in turn rested upon hadith reports that went back to the Prophet's own words and deeds, and so constituted a second revelation with an authority equal to the Quran's own. The Quran and the "sunna of the Prophet" prescribed a certain order in the religious sphere. However, that order was impossible to achieve without the establishment of a parallel political order that could guarantee the performance of religious duties by securing for each believer the security of his life and property, and was capable at the same time of maintaining the unity of the community in the face of civil disorders. From this was derived the political authority of the Caliph and his delegates.

For the Isma ͨilis, the Imam was not a political corollary of a religious system but an integral part of the religious system itself. In a famous Shi ͨite hadith, already described in chapter 3 above, the Prophet Muhammad, upon his return from his "ascension" to the highest heavens where the truths of creation were revealed to him, cast his mantle over his daughter Fatima and his grandsons Hasan and Husayn and so signified the transmission of those same truths to his Fatimid-Alid descendants. Thus it was the Imam and he alone who held, at least in theory—every Sufi and philosopher from the twelfth century onward claimed the same privilege—the key to ta᾽wil, the allegorical exegesis of Scripture that penetrated the surface meaning to the Truths beneath.

The intellectual defense of Sunnism against this claim was undertaken by al-Ghazali in a series of tracts that mounted a frontal attack on what he called "the Partisans of the Concealed" (al-batiniyya)." But the

issue appears in all its complexity in a more personal statement, his Deliv-
erer from Error, which describes his own investigation of the competing
claims upon the faith of the Muslim. Faith tied to simple acceptance on the
authority of others was insufficient for Ghazali; it could be shaken by the
conflicting claims put forward by different parties and sects within Islam
and by the equally strong adherence to their own faith by the Christians
and Jews. Unless he was prepared to lapse into an agnostic skepticism, as
Ghazali was not, there had to be some other way for the seeker after truth.
Four possibilities presented themselves: the way of speculative theology,
kalam, which professed to support its religious beliefs with rational argu-
ment; the way of the philosophers, who laid claim to true scientific demon-
*stration; the Isma*c*ili way, which promised religious certitude by reliance*
upon the teaching of an infallible Imam; and finally the way of the Sufis
or mystics, who offered intuitive understanding and a certitude born of
standing in the presence of God.

*The attraction of ta*c*lim was undeniable, and Ghazali could reply*
that if such were the answer, then it was far preferable to accept the in-
fallible teaching of the Prophet than of some derivative Imam, whose teach-
ings in any event turned out to be a debased form of Greek philosophy. But
neither can really cure the malady: it is part of the human condition to
doubt and to disagree, and on the rational level the only solution is not to
throw oneself on the authority of another but to work out an answer with
patience and intelligence, an answer based equally on the Quran and the
principles of right reason. The solution is, in short, Ghazali's own rigorous
version of dialectical theology.

14. The Life after Death

All religions agree on the fact that souls experience states of happiness and misery after death, but they disagree in the manner of symbol-
izing these states and explaining their existence to men. (Ibn Rushd,
Unveiling of the Programs of Proof 122) [AVERROES 1961: 76]

So Ibn Rushd at the beginning of a chapter on the "Future Life." His
mood in writing it was more defensive, perhaps, than philosophical, as
we shall see, but he knew whereof he spoke. Again, referring to the future
life, Ibn Rushd remarks that this was not a question that confronted the
"ancients."

This is a problem which is not found in the older philosophers,
although resurrection has been mentioned in different religions for at

least a thousand years, and the philosophers whose theories have come to us are of more recent date. The first to mention bodily resurrection were the prophets of Israel after Moses, as is evident from the Psalms and many books attributed to the Israelites. Bodily resurrection is also affirmed in the New Testament and attributed by tradition to Jesus. (Ibn Rushd, *Incoherence of the Incoherence* 580) [AVERROES 1954: 359]

And, the Muslim Ibn Rushd had no need of adding, resurrection sounds like a trumpet throughout the Quran.

15. The Second Coming: The Muslim Tradition

As we have already seen in chapter 1 above, the Muslim view was that Jesus did not die on the cross, as the Christians alleged, but had been taken up alive by God to heaven. He would, then, have to return to earth and suffer the death that is the common fate of all mankind. But his return had for the Muslims as much eschatological significance as it did for the Christians, and it was closely connected with the events of the End Time, as appears in this summary statement of Muslim messianism by Ibn Khaldun (d. 1406 C.E.).

It has been well known by all Muslims in every epoch, that at the end of time a man from the family of the Prophet will without fail make his appearance, one who will strengthen the religion and make justice triumph. The Muslims will follow him, and he will gain domination over the Muslim realm. He will be called the Mahdi [that is, the "Guided One"]. Following him, the Antichrist will appear, together with all the subsequent signs of the Hour (of the Last Judgment), as established in the sound tradition. After the Mahdi Jesus will descend and kill the Antichrist. Or, Jesus will descend with the Mahdi, and help him kill the Antichrist, and have him as the leader in his prayers. (Ibn Khaldun, *Muqaddima* 3.51) [IBN KHALDUN 1967: 2:156]

The matter did not rest there, of course; the Muslim tradition had filled in many of the details regarding Jesus' return.

Abu Salih Shuʿayb ibn Muhammad al-Bayhaqi has informed us with a chain of authorities back to Abu Hurayra how this latter related that the Messenger of God, upon whom be God's blessing and peace, said: "The Prophets are brethren, though of different mothers, and their religion is one and the same. I am the nearest of mankind to Jesus son of Mary, on both of whom be peace, because there has been no Prophet between him and me. It will come to pass that the son of Mary will descend among you as a just ruler. He will descend to my community and be my deputy (or Caliph) over them, so when you see him, give him recognition. He will be a man symmetrical in stature, of reddish-white (complexion), lank-haired, as though his hair were dripping perfume though it had not been moistened. He will come down in a greenish-yellow garment, will break crosses and kill swine, will put an end to the poll-tax (paid by non-Muslims under Islam), will raise the welcoming cry from al-Rawha when he comes for the Greater and the Lesser Pilgrimage, undertaking them both with zeal. He will make war on behalf of Islam, until in his time he destroys all religions save that of Islam, and there will thenceforward be but one single prostration of obeisance, namely that to God, Lord of the Worlds. Also in his time God will destroy the Antichrist, the lying al-Dajjal. Then there will be such security on earth that lions will pasture freely with camels, tigers with cattle, wolves with sheep, children will play with serpents and no one will do harm to anyone. Then he will die, and the Muslims will pray over him and bury him at Medina beside the grave of Umar. Read, if you will, the words 'There are none of the People of the Book but will believe in him before his death, and on the Day of Resurrection he will be a witness against them.'(Quran 4:159)." (Tha'alibi, *Stories of the Prophets*) [JEFFERY 1962: 596–597]

Additional specifics are given in a series of traditions cited by Ibn Khaldun.

The final descent of Jesus will be at the time of the afternoon prayer, when three-fourths of the Muslim day have passed. . . . It has been stated in the tradition that Jesus will descend at the white minaret east of Damascus. He will descend between two yellowish colored ones, that is, two light saffron-yellow colored garments. He will place his hands upon the wings of two angels. His hair is as long as though he had just been released from a dungeon. When he lowers his head, it rains, and when he lifts it up, jewels resembling pearls pour down from him. He has many moles on his face. Another tradition has: "Square built and reddish white." Still another has: "He will marry in the *gharb*," *gharb* meaning a bucket as used by the Bedouins. Thus the meaning is that he will take a woman from among the Bedouins as his wife. She will bear his children. The tradition also mentions that Jesus will die after forty years. It is also said that Jesus will die in Medina and be buried at the side of Umar ibn al-Khattab. And it is said that Abu Bakr and Umar

The April Dead

ALSO BY ALAN PARKS
FROM CLIPPER LARGE PRINT

Bloody January
February's Son
Bobby March Will Live Forever